A life on the ocean waves

This one is the finished story!

Frustrated by yet another recession, the move to the Caribbean would be our only hope of redeeming something from the mess this lot had put us in.

Published by New Generation Publishing in 2013

Copyright © D R Hamber 2013

First Edition

The author asserts the moral right under the Copyright, Designs and Patents Act 1988 to be identified as the author of this work.

All Rights reserved. No part of this publication may be reproduced, stored in a retrieval system or transmitted, in any form or by any means without the prior consent of the author, nor be otherwise circulated in any form of binding or cover other than that which it is published and without a similar condition being imposed on the subsequent purchaser.

www.newgeneration-publishing.com

 New Generation Publishing

Contents

Chapter 1: Sydney 1
Chapter 2: A Simple Matter 5
Chapter 3: Recession 1974 10
Chapter 4: The Caribbean 11
Chapter 5: Soufriere 13
Chapter 6: Settling In 18
Chapter 7: Bill Curry 23
Chapter 8: Peton Climbing 27
Chapter 9: On Official Business 38
Chapter 10: Dia Neale 42
Chapter 11: Bruce Johnson 45
Chapter 12: Arthur Bradley 46
Chapter 13: I'm in! 49
Chapter 14: Mike Atkinson 52
Chapter 15: Off to Martinique 54
Chapter 16: Panama and M.A.P.P. 56
Chapter 17: Coco Solo 61
Chapter 18: Portobelo at last 68
Chapter 19: To be or not to be? 84
Chapter 20: The Experts 91
Chapter 21: Drake's Coffin? 95
Chapter 22: What the eye don't see! 101
Chapter 23: To be or not to be - I've forgotten! 156
Chapter 24: It's the leaving that matters 169
Chapter 25: Panama to St Lucia 174
Chapter 26: Just a run across the Caribbean 193
Chapter 27: Hispaniola 205
Chapter 28: Dominican Republic 212
Chapter 29: Onwards to Puerto Rico 225
Chapter 30: St Croix 232
Chapter 31: St Lucia at last 236
Chapter 32: Picking up the pieces 239
Chapter 33: Nassau 263

Chapter 34: Lifesaving 286
Chapter 35: The Flaglers Inn 290
Chapter 36: Oh Well 293
Chapter 37: Jylland April '77 294
Chapter 38: Homeward Bound 307
Chapter 39: July '77 308
Chapter 40: September 22nd '77 - 318
Chapter 41: Boatyard Emsworth '77 321
Chapter 42: January to February '78 334
Chapter 43: April 16th '78 342
Chapter 44: June too soon 352
Chapter 45: June 12th '78 356
Chapter 46: A Good Catch 359
Chapter 47: July stand by 362
Chapter 48: August get ready 365
Chapter 49: September Remember 367
Chapter 50: September, I said, Remember 370
Chapter 51: Shylah Body 371
Chapter 52: Saba 373
Chapter 53: October all over 374
Chapter 54: To the rescue 381
Chapter 55: A bit of trouble 383
Chapter 56: January 1st 1979 386
Chapter 57: The Hustle 389
Chapter 58: More challenges 391
Chapter 59: April '79 395
Chapter 60: April/May '79 401
Chapter 61: May '79 406
Chapter 62: July '79 418
Chapter 63: Dry-dock Martinique 422
Chapter 64: September -79 435
Chapter 65: Bill the Badger 438
Chapter 66: At Last 440
Chapter 67: The Aftermath 445
Chapter 68: Has any one seen a Ghost around? 454
Chapter 69: Waiting – Waiting –Waiting!! 457
Epilogue 491

Chapter 1: Sydney

"Just shoot some bastard for me will you" said the man handing my brother the 38 Smith and Wesson. To have carried out the request would have been quite easy - just a simple matter of pointing it at the head of the man giving up his weapon, and pulling the trigger!

In that sweaty jungle of Central America there was no bigger, nor more deserving bastard than the one stood before Howard. Many would have been happy to see this genius of seduction get his just rewards. What stood before my brother then was the figure of a broken man - broken by the failure of his scheming ways which had brought all his promises and planning to a miserable end. It was a tragic frame now, one pleading forgiveness and mercy from someone he'd done his best to exploit, exclude and, if by taking his final words as to his character, would surely have shot what he thought was one himself, given the chance!

20 years later, and the hand that had taken that gun, passed on to me an extract from its owner's latest book, printed in the Weekend Telegraph dated April 20th 1996. The paragraph at the top read "He rammed in the magazine, cocked the gun and placed it against the side of my head; I knew what was coming next". "Panama" I thought.

It would not be for the first time such predictions for the future would fail him, for this was referring to another 20 years in his past, 20 years before we had the honor of meeting him. Beneath this sentence of a wild imagination was a drawing, one of a man being held fast by the neck, an arm under the chin, while the left fingers of the other hand gripped his hair. The face I didn't recognize, but the eyes seemed not to look at the glistening barrel of the rifle, as was intended, but in terror towards me - or was it *of* me I thought???

The central figure of this group of seven 'nasties' was holding a piece of paper, as if to say "Own up boy! Was it you that wrote this pack of lies?" It was not the Chinese Red Guards I saw but a bunch of fellows, each one waiting his turn to extract the truth from him in the only way they knew how. Even his name - Sydney Wignall - makes people who have not heard of him ask, "Who?" as if it's hard to believe someone exists with such a name. But he does, and there it was before me, above the large heading which claimed yet another 'Great Adventure'

The article went on to make the statement, "In 1955 a Welsh mountaineer agreed to spy on the Chinese in Tibet while climbing the Himalayas. He promised his contacts in Indian intelligence that the remarkable story of his torture and daring walk out through the mountains in winter would remain a secret for decades. Now, in this exclusive extract from his forth coming book, he tells it for the first time."

Anyone that has seen Syd's legs would find it terribly difficult to believe they were, at any time, capable of transporting a body 25,000ft up anything vertical - horizontal yes, vertical never. Even Sherpa Tensing and Edmund Hillary, with large amounts of backup would not have attempted to climb in that area during October (even with their legs!) Never mind promise to keep this 'remarkable' story a secret for decades and only to tell it now for the first time.

I feel I must therefore tell my story before I'm as cold as the hills around 'Taklakot', just in case Syd outlives any of those associated with Panama and the expedition to search for Drakes coffin in 1995. Yet again, another remarkable story might surface for the 'first time' after those who can say 'liar' are dead, like his so called Indian contact and Harrop, who carried (as Harrop explained once) "Syd's whinging frame on his back for far too long!"

"I hope my book will flush him out," says Syd. I would say (knowing my pernicious, well-informed friend) he knows John Harrop's usual Spartan use with words has reached a place where the laconic feel at home!! As for a SPY? Certainly Syd was not cast in the Ian Fleming 007 mould, more one of John Le Carre 'Smilies People'. Like one of them, Syd would not have told his companions the perilous position he was putting them in and, we might add, that if he went in to Tibet as one, he was the kind very likely to double his money coming out!

The grinding of axes in the academic world just doesn't happen - the sparks created might start a fire, so all band together, buckets of water at the ready to douse the 'Whinger'.

Protecting a colleague's name is the duty of all belonging to this band of brothers, so it leaves me free to speak with honesty about someone, who not only climbed on the back of Harrop, but rode rough shod over many to feed his rapacious desires.

It's as easy to get the adventurous involved in some excitement as it is to get the greedy to invest in a sure bet. Having 'had enough of mountains', as Syd puts it rather penuriously about a once love affair with Snowdonia, and the rebuke suffered in that Harem of un-mounted virgins, the Himalayas sees the 'lucky-to-get-away-with-it' Syd fall not in to a depression, but a soft landing – water!!

Making a name for yourself in this new field, the footage to fame is downwards, some 24,900ft less too. It would happen upon the world of archaeology that Syd would move and, at the time of his baptism to the wet stuff, donned in the rubber and breathing apparatus, the marine side of this academic world didn't exist.

Archaeology till then was depicted by little old men with little old beards whose heads went no deeper under water than at hair washing time. For those who took the first plunge, like the earthbound digger who claimed he was an Archaeologist, for a marine one, certain things must change.

This auspicious society who are able to move the goal posts of the line between historical value and that of grave robber, would have in their midst someone who could work undisturbed by the spotlight of the media, and claim a seat on which to sit in judgment of others in this up and coming field.

It was the luck of the Irish coast that the 'Santa Maria Del Rosa' ran against when returning from that ill-fated Armada. Syd may have won a Gold Medal for his excavations of the wreck but, as I would experience by the tongue that promised much and gave little, an invitation to return to the scene of his only triumph might well result in some Irish violence from the brothers McCormack - for reasons known well to Syd! But at home the medal and the photo of him accepting it from the Duke of Edinburgh counts for a lot.

Theories of his very own reason why the Armada failed were explained on a television programme. Inferior iron to shoot, was his claim, one of which he managed to get the army to fire out of a sawn-off Centurion tank gun. Aimed at a heap of sleepers, the shot disintegrated before reaching its mark - a point proven to the ignorant viewer, aided by the slickest tongue to come out of Wales since Lloyd George.

It is the one thing you remember most about Syd upon meeting him, he has the rapid fire of sweet words to soften you up. Just the slightest change to the name of his house and - 'Taklakot' becomes 'Talkalot' and it fits him to perfection. A man that talks a lot can't listen, and later extracts from his pen proves that fact.

It is not a conversation. just a one-sided barrage of dates, name's and figures that, before a challenge might be made by the 'amateur ' historian, he has moved on at such a speed that to backtrack over any point, might suggest the listener be a little 'slow', not to mention distrusting!

To say he was very intelligent, one must be able to judge from the basis of questioning their intellect first. Charming he could certainly be, and will be to all till he figures out who it's wasted on. Listening to him, for that's all you can do, the impression given was one of a man that could confirm historical events that had all others dithering in the world of supposition, that maybe here was the original 'Wandering Jew' telling of how it was at first hand. It was the performance that Syd gave, as good as any great actor to an audience who wished to listen - and a greater one - if in that crowd stood someone Syd thought had the money to pay for it. This was Syd's

'Begging Bowl' - a performance as worthy of William Fitz-Osborne and full of as many false promises. By the end of such, like the greatest of thespians, he was 'spent', needing time to return to the real world for the fear of madness that might take hold if he didn't. Manners, and a lack of knowledge of his chosen subject, you must leave him be. To ask "What do you think of John McEnroe?" to lighten the subject, might deem you a moron!

Chapter 2: A Simple Matter

It had been the fault of Mike Atkinson that got Syd all fired up and driving to Essex. Mike, the Sheffield lad that had gone with him to the Azores in search for Grenvilles 'Revenge', was the son of rich store owners in that city. It made Mike acceptable in the very fact that North Country people are careful with their 'brass', so it was more than likely he, Mike, would inherit a goodly sum one day, a little of which might come Syd's way!

What had, when the phone rang, was not news of his parent's sudden death, but something just as exciting. Mike had met a fool! Been made captain of his ship, and the owner is going to let him loose with it in the Caribbean. It all comes to those who wait, and Syd had certainly been patient in the waiting of the recognition that had so far eluded him. Nearly as patient as his poor wife Jean had been for some time, awaiting the promised gold to come her way!

The medal and fame both stood on the mantelpiece now, and both not enough alone to buy bread. Who could tell without checking that the gold was gold, not some worthless base metal just covered in leaf and encased in resin by some stingy civil servant with a strange sense of humour? To find out the truth was tempting enough, but not worth the risk either way.

Together, they stood as a symbol for what men have craved after - murdered, lied and died for. Fame and fortune, united like some cynical gesture to the frustrated failures in both fields. This phone call might just change things so, picking up whatever the Duke had handed him, he decided to bring it along as proof to whom we were talking to!

It was where the schooner was bound for that had rung in this man's ears. The Caribbean! That sea of intrigues, of Hispaniola, the Spanish Main. The gold and fame wrapped up together that had Columbus, Morgan, and Hawkins and of course DRAKE! To the man who found him, Drake, the world of archaeology would be at his feet. All he needed to do was convince those who held the key to his success. "A simple matter of going over the side of a boat with a 150' of rope!" we were told! Hoping such a statement would not bring the response, "Well what do you want us for?" but more, "Lucky us!" So was the trap intended?

Saltpetre, Sulphur, and Charcoal alone are harmless. Mixed together they can go off with a big hang - as Gunpowder. The salt I would say was my brother Dennis, the Charcoal Syd and as for the third ingredient needed to make the substance lethal? It would come in a form of someone used to the spotlight and, in his way, hurting more than Syd.

Fame in his own country had eluded him. Syd, blinded by the impression of great wealth from Graham's appearance, lost sight of a very important point! That to climb on the shoulders of others to reach another already perched on high; make sure those you're treading on are stupid! The perfect match in the field of treachery had been made, and the venue that saw the end of Hawkins and Drake, awaited the pair of them in a daggers drawn fight!

Graham Ernest Arthur George Bradley would be as faithful to a promise as a bitch on heat in a doghouse. A promise made in writing, with his signature as proof to be loyal, would not be worth the paper it's written on - except to a firm of solicitors maybe. I say *maybe* here, for when dealing with 'our' Graham, even those that took on the work defending that promise would find, in the end, another promise not forthcoming from him. One which contained the words, 'I promise to pay the bearer' on it! Failure is the safe bet when promises are needed in a written pledge and, for those that want it all 'Legally' tied up at the beginning, caution should be taken. It shows from the very outset distrust, and worse, a lack of judgment when choosing your man. Had Bradley been Harrop back in 1955, the only way Syd was likely to get a piggy-back ride home from Nepal was if the Chinaman 'Schickelgruber' was open to a bribe and had the strength in his legs to carry two, Graham and Syd. How Graham become involved in this 'Pie in the sky' idea, or better, Seeing our business flourish did not go un-noticed by Graham. Always the opportunist, the idea of moving closer to success was how he was made - their shoulders being used to launch himself from. Living at the time in Ealing with his wife Annette, might have seen him close to Heathrow and an easy exit from the country to his other home, Germany, but it was a little far from the action involving us! A move to Danbury in Essex was eventually chosen, 'Elm House' in White Elms Road the location. It had a riding stables and Bungalow on offer. Stretching himself financially to purchase these, an introduction to our bank manager John Rich, came up with the answer.

This small town manager had never seen a 'Star' inside his doors before, and Graham's fur coat and promises, made a big impression, not to mention the odd concert ticket and free albums of John's favourite music.

Syd in the meantime had pursued us relentlessly with the idea of an expedition to Panama. All manner of persuasions used to extract the needed cash and promises brought forth a collection of guns (weapons being something he has a fascination about) which one was lead to believe could be yours but for some commitment!

This collection of antiques were, even to a novice, beautifully made and looked perfect in every way. Flintlock pistols that looked as if they'd never been fired, let alone be over 200 years old. Closer inspection from an expert might just well prove they may have been made to order while in India where such men lived, capable of the perfect copy! But to us then, they were real, told so by the man who does not lie. A promise of such a 'valuable' piece to Howard was made by Syd - but even that carrot could not persuade us to venture upon such a risky affair.

Asked to put figures together for the cost of such a venture kept Syd busy and quiet for a time. Returning with a nice round one of £100,000 he was met with a, "How much???" A response that had him back to Wales going over his sums yet again!

It had been made plain to Syd that, though the idea to search for Drakes coffin was a wonderful venture, such vast sums he envisaged were beyond us. To supply the 'Jylland' as a base to work from was a possibility, but the funds to maintain her on station could not come from we brothers, even though Dennis might have given him the impression we could by paying Syd's way to Panama to meet with those whose permission was needed before an expedition could be mounted.

It was at a meeting to listen in on his latest proposals and the outcome of his visit that Syd first met Graham. It was 'love' at first sight, for both saw what they wished in the other, a nice back to climb upon, but what both failed to notice was the width of the other man's shoulders!!

The air fare to Panama, paid by us to Syd, was considered by Graham an indication of our determination to proceed with this project, and the thought of being left out of a photo call of us and that old sea-dog together, would put all his achievements to shame. "It can't happen - it won't happen without me" were his thoughts when considering the possible returns. "No bloody 'Graham who' then! - if I find Drake, England will remember my name!"

So from the outside he decided to move in closer to Syd, and from his appearance of wealth, Syd thought "Eu-bloody-reka!! I just had this feeling in my bones today was going to be my day"

How easy life would be if lived in retrospect, but bloody boring too I guess. If Syd had taken the hint from us, that regards funding this project was impossible, he wouldn't have met his Waterloo in the game of treachery and Graham wouldn't have made a fool of himself when claiming on T.V. (as he did that day) "Yes, I have found CHARLIE Drake!" and for us, the experience of a fiasco just wouldn't have happened!

Instead, what giving Syd the airfare to go to Panama did, was not to return with him bearing a coffin at the 'Something to declare' desk at Heathrow, but a more determined man to return to that scene of historic events. To do so would mean cost cutting in the extreme, more promises to others unknown to us for gifts - loans and donations - and all, as leader of the assault on Portobello, the means and promises for getting such.

Sydney Wignall had started spinning that 'wicked web' of deception from the start, a bunch of little secrets wrapped up in lies. As surely as that one in 1559, this expedition was to be as ill-fated by mistrust from the outset - and Syd's determination not to let the right hand know what the left was up to, trying to cover his tracks, would meet with the same disaster.

Casting that web in Panama to catch the fly - Syd would find he'd thrown it over one angry bunch of Hornets - ones that not only don't play by the rules, but don't give a damn for them! Strange to us then, but obvious now, was how the costs which had first been submitted came down with as many times as his visits to Essex. Had we known the reasons from the start, the suspicions of a rapacious mind would not have been suspected. But as it was a £100,000 turned to £80,000 – £80,000 to £60,000 – then like some antique dealer his best price of £40,000 smackeroos seemed still a lot to pay for 150ft of rope!! A lot of money back in 1974 – and still is today - promised to a stranger.

Chapter 3: Recession 1974

What can change events, plans and lives even, was recession. It hangs like a dark cloud on, or just over the horizon. Everyday life brings an uncertainty of what the weather will be like the next day, to sow or not to sow? When confidence returns and a clear forecast is predicted, watch out! You'll wake up one morning in fog, a curtain descending while all slept soundly in peace counting their fortunes. The dark ages on progress have had the blinds pulled shut! The sinister hand that rifles the wallet and strips the frugal of their asset has begun.

Such a time came in the early 70's, the same time gold was making daily gains, bank managers coming to work in a different hat saying "What are you going to do about your overdraft'?" Stupid question from he that allowed it in the first place. There certainly wasn't time to think about expeditions for us – even after the meeting at Graham's house sometime before, with John Rich telling Syd "Graham is a very wealthy man!" and accountants in attendance nodding over figures. None could hide the fact that, as far as we were concerned, the idea had to be shelved.

With what was about to hit the fan, and because the self-employed catch most of the shit first, we could soon he looking ruin in the face, scratching around for work. A time had come when decisions had to be made while time was still on our side and, wise or not, they were made. It was time to move with what you could carry, or get plastered trying to protect what was left after 'Bleak House' had been snatched from us. Could you trust the man now who had you in the palm of his hand with that gone - not likely!

Since Will had been in charge of 'Jylland', money had ceased to flow across the Atlantic. What came back was a picture, that if a move by me didn't happen soon, I could very likely never get to see it. So much pressure could be brought to bear on those with the most to lose back in England that she ('Jylland') in St Lucia might have to go! Go, I thought, before I'd sailed in her, go before I'd seen where she was now, and go before the navigation course I'd spent so much time over could be used.

The times I'd spent listening to the night wind, wondering just how she'd move in that free air, the blocks and rigging I'd helped Bill Percy place taking the strain in those trades - wondering if I was capable of taking her from A to B safely – snatched from my grasp? Not if I could help it!

All such thoughts drove the common, responsible sense of the father, husband, provider of a home, to a small corner of my mind. Even the birth of Helen, just weeks old, stood not in the way. If we didn't make a move, then it was very likely we never would. So decided and planned - it was executed in a mad rush to be gone!

Chapter 4: The Caribbean

The trade winds are the first thing you notice when you arrive, it hits you like a warm blast from a furnace. The speed of transport now doesn't allow for the change of climate.

From the window of the plane and now that of the taxi, the Caribbean was all as I imagined it to be. Under every red corrugated roof sat small wooden homes of the people of this country freed by an act of Parliament in 1834. The vast sum of money paid to the slave owners made no allowances to those that had contributed to the Planters wealth. Though I guess for the slave, freedom then was more than enough. Once forced to work, they could now put their feet up, the climate and the soil of Barbados gave them all they really needed – food.

This was a sugar island, where owners of great Plantations took all comers, black and white, as slaves - Irish, Scot and English caught up in history's turmoil, sent here for one reason – cut and plant the Cane! Throughout the whole Caribbean I would see in the coming years small communities hanging on to their past, their only defiance now seeming to be in retaining their identity. Those that have not mixed their blood live under the same small roof as their poor black neighbour. The price for holding ranks shows worse in areas where the mind has long forgotten what that stance was for!

I ended up spending the first night with a black lady who owned a small guesthouse some miles from the airport. He that delivered me to "A place to put my head down for the night" was probably a relative, or on a bonus, but he would be back in the morning in time for me to catch our flight on to St Lucia. Waking up for the first time in these climates is another experience. The morning sun reflects off the white walls where lizards are seen taking a break after an evening of chasing their prey. Scurrying to the wooden rafters, its position is taken by a bigger brother – one very likely to eat the other than argue who gets the best chair. Outside the trade winds slap a banana palm, as strange birds whistle stranger songs. But it's that warmth that hits you, all night you slept under just one sheet. Getting used to sleeping in such conditions will take time you think, for the sleep last night did little to comfort you!

It is only 150 miles from Barbados to St Lucia, about an hour's flight. Landing at Vigie airport, close to the islands capital Castries, would also be close to where 'Jylland' was based, at Vigie Cove. Each country has its 'Ellis Island' attitude – those who believe the world is full of vagrants who have come to steal their crown jewels. Stick a uniform on a person and watch the change in his or her attitude. All the questions they asked I could not have answered and, as I had come to join a boat, superfluous.

Will was there to meet me, looking healthy and happy. Was it worth the effort and the sacrifice that had to be made? All now hinged on 'Jylland'. She would have to provide for us now, and the 'us' would increase when Howard came, and both our families.

Chapter 5: Soufriere

It had been just over two years since I last saw our old girl and, although she had been mistreated by those who knew no better, she still looked good.

Tied up to the small wooden jetty at Ganters wharf, 'Jylland's' hull took up every inch of its eastern side - and more. Shallow drafted, she could nose herself close under the trees where, behind, lay the 'Wicky Up' - a small restaurant run by Marie Cross, an English woman once married to an islander. Not a jetty to spring one's self from, nor had it the strength to stop you - you just lent on it, lines ashore to the trees just in case the still waters of the cove moved in the surge of some passing depression.

Ganters was run by two youngish Americans, Doug and Phil – Doug, taking the dock master role, the dishing out of fuel, and orders in some panic of "Watch my Duck!'" as we returned each day from the cruise. If we hadn't, 'Doug's Duck' would have been a raft. It was, and had to be, a very slow ahead affair, checking and slipping of lines to mooring bits ashore, any strain would have torn something designed for ten tonners from their fastenings.

Will had got contracts to carry passengers from hotels and the weekly Cunard cruise ship that came each Thursday, on a stopover on their weekly cruise out of Miami or San Juan. Day trips down the coast under sail to Soufriere was the offer, rum punch and food all in at $25 U.S each.

The island's second town that sat under the shadow of the Pitons was then pretty well isolated by bad roads. It was reached quicker by sea, if not much safer too for the tourist wishing to visit the sulphur springs. 'Visitor 4', an old cruiser ran by an American which could take 6 to 8 people on day trips, was nothing like 'Jylland', capable of carrying 130 passengers.

After the stagnation of England's pending fall in to recession, my mind was focused on a bright future, for what Will had got under way was becoming the centre of people's conversation round hotel bars and dinner tables -"You're leaving when you haven't seen the sulphur springs? Wow!" Weekly it was becoming more popular.

Al Hyman who made our 'quiche-la-Rain' as the main part to our lunch offering, rubbed his hands in delight with each larger order, as did the local T-shirt company, for we sold our passengers a little reminder of that day for $5 a time.

10 o'clock was departure time, and buses brought the 'not knowing what to expect' to the dock. Mike, in charge as skipper now, would back her out under engine till clear of the cove, then up all headsails to turn her towards the open sea. Raising the sail was done heading down the channel, and once turned south, bang! Three topsails were broken out on one order. The final act was perfect for me, the shutting down of her engine!

The sudden silence turned many a head, people thinking something was amiss till told it was done on purpose. Boy! What a thrill you saw upon people's faces, people used to the sound of motors for movement and assurance - that sailing ships were only on the screen, not in real life. It is only when you remember that first time under sail, especially for those with some salt in their veins, the thrill of movement in such silence. It was, for our passengers, just a small taste of something rather wonderful, exciting, something that made them feel alive for the first time by some instinct that now stirred through the blood like magic!

It was a tonic like no other, a mixture of salt, water and silence, only broken by the wind upon canvas. It's only for those that leave the rush and noise of city life for the peace of the country who actually have a chance to realize what they preferred, or switch off the radio and say "Lovely – peace and quietness at last!" It is in our genes, embedded there by thousands of years of a once silent past, where nature moved us - sang to us - provided all for us - not just the food. As surely as the genes of another mother are within us, so is that of nature.

It would take about an hour before Soufriere came in to view. It lay back in its bay, an old town of many wooden structures (very French) when balconies were the style with shuttered windows. From the middle of the town was a small concrete jetty, big enough to take the coaster who delivered to this out-of-the-way place, some general cargo.

Will had taxis arranged ready to carry those who wished to go to the springs – and most did. Starting the engine to bring us to this area was necessary, for the wind came directly out of a valley formed by Petite Piton to the south and the high ground to the north. Further south lay Gros Piton, taller but not as steep as its brother. The two together making an impressive sight to the passenger coming from the sea.

The arrival of 'Jylland' with its daily cargo of 'Honkeys' to that rather isolated community, brought something for the youngsters to look forward to, as well as some much desired business to the taxi drivers. Lining the dock were children of all ages. The one striking similarity all the boys had as they stood before us was that they were as naked as the day they were born.

In charge of this happy lot was an older boy, about 16 I would guess, he was paid a small fee to keep some order and take our lines. Once secured alongside, a mass of youngsters, that didn't seem to have a school to go to, plunged in to the sea, shouting for passengers to throw coins for them to dive after. Before this advice from us to do some entertaining for their money, begging had not been so rewarding, nor good for our business. I'd often thrown a handful of small change to watch the fun and laughter as bright, smiling young faces would vanish in a swirl of water, like a school of fish after a handful of maggots - up they would bob coins in their mouths, ready for another handful. Always it was the boys that did the swimming. Either the girls, who were very small, were not good swimmers - or not allowed to share the money. I believe it was the latter.

Now some of these boys' ages ranged from 6 to 14, the only ones in uniform were our dock master and the young girls. I would watch the faces of our passengers as the dock got closer, nudges, pointing and sharing of binoculars went on in some disbelief as to what they were looking at. Some were a little embarrassed, but for some it was a dream come true, an answer to all their prayers - made every 4 years come the Olympics - for standing there in a full frontal was a bunch of Carl Lewis's and Linford Christies all jumping up and down as if preparing for the 100 meters - bollock naked!!

Now some of those lads were more than well hung and, try as we may to get them to wear shorts, or have an operation, it was useless. In fact, in the end, we weren't sure what attracted the passengers most, the Springs or the Springing! I must say I did try on behalf of the men folk for some 'Equal Rights' here. Gathering round me a group of smiling fares, I asked "How many of you have sisters your age?" pointing to a little Stallion in his teens, who by his own manly attributes, if he had to have a sister as well proportioned, it would turn a few heads. "Well next time we arrive, I want you to bring them here all dressed just like you!" Some needed the English to he translated in to the Patois French, but when fully understood, the screams of laughter with the slapping of legs showed not only they knew what they were up to - that they had a sense of humour, but also there was no way that would happen!! The feminist movement hadn't a chance in hell here for a few years in this male 'very' dominant and very 'prominent' society!

I'm sure many a woman (and some men too I guess) left behind some wild imaginations when it was time to leave there. Hubby would never feel quite the same after that, and when it was time for lights out back at the hotel, the condition of the promise was 'Fred would have to speak with a West Indian accent and wear a large Dasheen!' To be quite honest, most of the boys were quite normal, but then, and here's where the fallacy starts, it's the big ones that make the impression -'stick out' if you like - that give 'rise to' the lie that all are so well endowed. Many a mixed marriage has failed due to the 'Black' joke.

We would leave for sea with a few of these boys hanging like black jewels dripping from the rigging and bowsprite, finally dropping off to swim for home when the distance was thought easy for their little arms. Always last to go was our 16 year old - higher and just that bit further than the rest by being out on the jib-boom end! Every departure would see the brave, judging the distance by his last successful swim back - till in the end, if we hadn't ordered them off, some would have to walk home.

Our lunch stop would be a small cove called Anse-Cusone where, before eating, those wishing to swim could do so. "May I have your attention please? Do not dive in the water until the schooner has come to anchor! You will hear the ringing of a bell. One aft - or at the back-end, that's when the skipper wants the hook let go! The other one forward will ring when it has come to rest! Do not get in to the water till after the second bell"

Always told they were, but for many it was a waste of breath. Too many Rum-punches and one hears bells all the time. They also remember the high school gala, and after that young black his wife couldn't keep her eyes off back there – he'd show her!! Some were bent on showing what American virility really meant!

Bang! They were in – arms going like the clappers!

Now a large craft, creeping slowly ahead seems to most, stationary, or, if you're pissed, moving a lot slower than you can swim. Believe me it isn't - and you can't. I've seen, and we've had to rescue many an exhausted lump that, diving in forward of the main mast, sees it pass him as his eyes roll with the head and mouth for air doing an impression of Johnny Weismuller. A thought rushes to him that he is maybe caught by the ankles, caught by some unknown strong current dragging him backwards. So! Faster and faster go the arms to save himself from certain death - his eyes full of panic as the stern slips by, Thank god he would say as a hand grabbed him, for we always had the dinghy ready, a lifebelt and man for such people.

Some had even a greater surprise for the extra effort, for as 'Jylland' went astern on the hook, they found themselves actually overtaking us - at some rate of knots too! Only once did we nearly 'lose' someone. The relief one poor fellow got when at last his feet felt the bottom was a heart attack! There just happened to be a doctor aboard that trip, a mouth to 'rum punch' mouth job, and a slow ride back in the dinghy.

Before motoring home, it would be a little tour round Marigot Bay - for us it was the best Hurricane hole around, for the Americans it was where a movie was made - 'Dr Dolittle' with Rex Harrison etc.! etc! It has a very narrow entrance with a narrower deep channel very close to the southern shore. The clear water soon changes, for once inside the waters are deep and bottom muddy. It is like a pond, a round one some 200 yards across, around which wooded hills isolated the place. We were told, it was the home of a very large Barracuda, but for those who decided upon one last dip before home, we kept the story to ourselves!

Thus satisfied, suntanned and rum-punched out we carried our merry party home to Vigie, T-shirts an' all, arriving around 16.30 hrs. Not once did I hear a complaint as all left for their hotels and a shower – some stopping on the way to buy some 'Dasheen'

For us it was wash plates, wash decks, and on to Marie's and the 'Wicky-up' to wash down a beer before Milly the cook rang the bell calling us to dinner!

Week in week out this went on, and if nothing got in our way, our money worries would be a thing of the past. 'Jylland' was in those later months of '74 paying us back for our faith in her.

Chapter 6: Settling In

St Lucia saw the comings and goings of both British and French soldiers during its seesaw struggles in this area before Trafalgar saw the end to the comings and goings of administrators. Like elsewhere, empire building could be done in a peace that suited the victor. To keep that peace came the soldiers, and to house them were built barracks of a design drawn in England, for that permanent empire upon which the sun would never set.

On Vigie Point were built such that, for a fever stricken fighting man fresh out of India, the very likeness of his surroundings would have made him believe he was still there. The same terraced block built of shipped in brick - their long covered verandas on each floor, were a one off design built to last, and last they did, longer than the empire too, for they were built of better material than those that gave it all away.

When at last I was joined by Sue and the children, it would be in to one of these old army blocks we would move, for they were now apartments. Being December, one would think it would be the best time to settle yourself to the climate. It is - and it isn't'. Though not summer, the sun doesn't go that far south to cool the weather, and you have brought with you some thick blood from England, where it does. When night time comes, and the trade winds stop, a sticky hot bed, surrounded by thick walls awaits you! It is not a place you long for, so you put off the prone position till hopefully sleep comes quickly.

For poor Helen, two months old, the strangeness of not being wrapped up tight for the night, and eyes not seeing a mother but some netting to stop any mosquitoes biting - crying was a constant and endless introduction to the tropics.

Once it was the cries of the regimental sergeant major that carried along the veranda to awake all, now it was the lungs of the disturbed infant that broke the peace of the night. It was a worrying time - have you done the right thing? Does she have a problem? Will she ever settle? And of course - what about the neighbours? There had to be complaints, and there were, but as soon as we moved to a house, she stopped! Maybe she didn't like the army.

For William being 6 years of age, school was essential - and compulsory! With Howard's wife here and with a son Lee two years older than William, for him also would come the time to don the uniform - another thing that was compulsory. Dressed as the majority, if in the minority by race, off they went to learn more about life than just the three R's.

The system of schooling in St Lucia was the way I knew, before it was tampered with by the lovers of change - in fact, by the look of the books they brought home, the now useless stock piles in Britain had been purchased by someone who saw a bargain. Reading and exercise books jogged many a memory of nerves mixed with nostalgia - words I had difficulty with, and sums I was never taught the importance of knowing, came back with them from the little school at Patterson's Gap. What also came back with them was a greater understanding of those books.

It can be a bit of a. blow to the child and parent, especially from the beating heart of the old empire, to find out your child is behind on all subjects compared to another of the same age in a country of 'imagined' inferior standards. Your smugness can soon turn to anger at those that have 'played' with the car engine - changed it even for less horsepower. You only know how much when you race it against the old but well tested model still winning races aboard with the three R's under the bonnet. Muddled in all subjects, clear on none, our boys were taught by teachers well versed in those three most important themes. For they, themselves, were not confused by a greater curriculum.

Some parents would show great concern about having their children taught and raised where they are outnumbered by colour. Some die-hards when faced with the facts before them might even defend the system that is failing their children. Out of some national pride and stubbornness to the truth I guess. Such hard-headed prejudice leads to a 'Jim Crow' attitude, a xenophobia that supports even wrong in your own family. This is, of course, taught outside the gates of 'better' schools as well as states ones and is a subject well versed by those who learnt little while inside.

Attitude is a grain that runs through all our genes. It is raised by the watering of biased opinions - nationalistic pride - right down to the defence of your most precious possession - your child. Whatever went through the minds of our wives during that time of confrontation was difficult to assess, but it was certainly a pill hard to swallow!

There were in St Lucia schools for the 'well heeled' - a place to place the child of island snobbery for a fee. I'm glad we didn't have that fee and sent them to a place where the real people went. Higher in the standards of academics, but lower in what life is really about – people!

Like all places, isolation by land or sea can lead its inhabitants in to believing of superiority by prejudging the intentions of the outsider that enters your area - and it doesn't matter about the colour either. In Cornwall, the person from across the Tamar is an 'Emmit' - an immigrant with lots of money and nothing else between the ears. Tolerated only due to the law that forbids the Cornish kicking him back from whence he came - minus the money of course!

It wasn't just the 'Emit' that met such a welcome, not so long ago, a stranger out of St Austell would be stoned by the children of the 'Higher Quarter' - villages of the China clay area! Falmouth and Penryn men had daggers drawn - Roche and Bugle men have agreed never to agree, while a Redruth man would never go in to Cambourne fur nothin'. Their motto 'One for all' really meant 'All for one" - the one being me and my own!' The superiority such feel is indeed tainted with inferiority - a complex brought on by word of mouth from a breed of people felt hard done by!

As with all empires, Greek – Roman - Nazi nearly - and the British, those that could not trace a direct line to the all-conquering army of hero's - despised them.

In St. Lucia, a strong vein of French blood runs - whites that came from the remnants of a defeated nation, or whites that come from a nation whose history has little to write about but are well educated in the Roman Latin, look down upon the 'English' with a complex so superior it hurts them. If there was any racial prejudice in St Lucia, it was more to come at you from that quarter than from the 'freed slave'

The black West Indian, much to their credit and our envy, was raised to appreciate life in general. Being born was the biggest hurdle to get over, and if they lived, being fed from the abundance that grew around them was pretty simple. They didn't shiver in the cold winters, nor have to dress themselves for half the year in worthless costly clothes - or count the pennies from a hard day's work just to fill the tummy.

You will find most a laughing lot, and laughter means happiness, so how can such people feel inferior? In only one maybe and it is happening as in all the other countries that have been persuaded to join the I.M.F - take out a bank loan for something they can't afford - lend it to the people and charge them over the top in interest rates!

The once old wooden shack left to the family by the dead for the living is deemed now an asset, it can he borrowed on for it sits upon the more important asset – land!   It is now worth something - though far under its true value by the lender. The money doesn't go far in the local bar. The result is the old family heirloom becomes the property of others for the price of a good night out with the boys.

Those same properties can also be - upon the death of a mother or father - now something that has to be divided equally, and only achieved by a bag of money thrown upon the table. There should be some protection against advantage taking of the financially naïve, for it's the un-born that will seek the revenge for the past robbery!

I know there are some out there, then and now, who lack manners, the ignorant - the arrogant - the blights on the country - and we all have them. It was mostly round a majority of good people that in 1974 we had decided to live, but for how long?

Chapter 7: Bill Curry

Two young men came aboard one day, both white, tall, American, and looking like sons of Neptune, delivered on this earth through wooden gun ports. Both had that ground in tan that only long periods in a tropical sun can give, yet it bleaches the hair on your head – Bills curly and Lou's beside him, straight!

Bill, I was to learn, came from Washington State and Seattle on the North West Coast. A lot of salt ran through his veins, and when the calling was strong he upped anchor and made for Miami to try for a job aboard one of the Wind-Jammer craft ran by Mike Burke. Mike Burke and his 'Barefoot Cruises' took in the West Indies, and Bill found a position as deck hand aboard the 'Flying Cloud'. Not the same 'Flying Cloud' built by Donald Mackay some 100 years or so before, but then who could tell, or have the knowledge to know the difference between the beauty and the beast!
These were fun trips for a public born long after the death of sailing vessels that competed in grace along with speed. The only 'speed' likely seen on one of these vessels was in another form.

Passengers were a mixture of lovers of the sea, lovers of some fun and lovers of love. Nothing but floating dorms, where hot sweating bodies were free to practice the art of tying knots with legs and arms. A good looking Captain aboard one of these 'bare body' ships might well get bored by repetition of anchorage, but certainly not of women! There were far more choices as to where he dropped his pants than his anchor - and that went for the crew too - though of course that wasn't in the advert.

I'm sure, if someone had come aboard with some deadly sexual disease in Miami, and it was a real 'snake' with a bite, by the time they had reached St 'John' Thomas, the 'Flying Cloud' would have been another 'Marie Celeste'. To give credit to Burke, he at least kept some of the ships, that would otherwise been destined for the scrap heap, sailing.

For Bill, a good looking fellow of 6'4, but from a distance could have been 5'4" – or 4'4" – 3, 2, or 1'4" being equally proportioned. His frame never gave away his size till standing next to him. Bill was no long streak of piss by any means!

Being 'shagged' to death was not what he had in mind - well not before he'd fulfilled his main ambition he wasn't. Getting off feet first 'unaided' while he could still function was taken when he saw a chance in the shape of 'Jeanine' - a beautiful schooner owned and ran by Captain Boudrouix. 110' long, two-masted, and a racehorse any 'Jockey' would love the chance to be upon. Captain Boudreaux - Born in Nova Scotia with that love of the sea, most Scotian's have - owned and ran many a charter vessel. Two sons and one daughter he had; Lou, Peter and Jeanine – Lou being the eldest, and both boys had that love of the sea the same as their father. Bill was offered a job, so left the 'Flying Cloud' for one on 'Jeanine'. Anchored in Marigot Bay with a house on the hill above, the Boudrouix family took the exclusive class - the Barry Goldwater class of paying passenger to the Grenadines and beyond. Such a customer though, whose fee is enough to keep the hook down most of the year, can leave you, the deckhand, washing down and polishing brass till it hurts. A move to a job aboard a more active schooner, one that frequented Marigot, and one Bill saw most days, would come soon enough.

So one of the two fellows that came aboard that day – as Destiny directed – stayed. Bill and I had much in common, like myself, he had done the navigation theory bit, but had little practice in its art. Sun, stars and moon shots needed practice. Some passenger must have thought it quite odd to see us, Sextants in hand, shouting 'Mark!', then vanishing below while motoring back to Vigie Cove – they sat assured we knew where we were – so what are those two fools up to?

Many's the time Bill and I would jump in the dinghy just before sunset, and make for Vigie Point, stars and an open horizon to fix a better position for the area.

What fun it was, and how good you felt getting it right. The American sight reduction tables and the British, different, but the same results. We never argued, nor boasted whose was the better - and that's all that mattered. One day both would have to do it alone – maybe?

There is a wreck off Vigie Point - it lies in pretty shallow water around the 6-fathom mark. 'The Volga was anchored under Pigeon Island around the turn of the century, her iron hull full of Guano they say. The look at the falling glass had made them anchor in the shelter under the protection of 'The Gorilla' – for from the land, that's what Pigeon Island resembles. The Hurricane would pass them to the north they thought - it didn't. Dragging both her anchors she was blown south wrecking herself off the point.

In the rainy season, when visibility is excellent, looking through a mask you might see her, and the two chains that failed to hold her, still pointing north. You could dive on her, or once you could, and pat the old hull. Silting has filled her up, so you won't find much - maybe an old bottle! Go out of season, as Bill and I once did, and you can't see the bottom let alone the wreck. There is another thing that lies off that point worth remembering, the current! Running southward at a good couple of knots can catch you out, and if panic sets in, kill you!

Another of the things Bill and I had done together was, learning to use some diving gear. One of the many things Dennis had been persuaded as 'essential' for charter work. A 'Braur' compressor was purchased, a top of the range model too. During that 'secret' period under his control, 'Jylland' left Britain with one more piece of 'essential' supplies!

It lay dormant now in the days of charter business, its only user now being Mike Atkinson, acting Captain and water sports enthusiast. Sundays would see Mike load a full tank aboard his speed boat, and off he'd go to meet up with a set of people he believed he had more in common with, the 'jet setters' of whitish St Lucia - all money and no manners.

Bill, having done some diving, rose to the idea of 'teaching' those wanting to have a go! All we needed was a swimming pool, the best place for any beginners. So before any salt water saw us, the art of 'Buddy Breathing' - taking off your tank, weights holding in place, going to the surface, then returning to retrieve your gear. It was all practiced in the 'Vigie Beach Hotel' pool - yet for those who would bother to read Syd Wignall's Autobiography written in 1980, one would well believe it was in Panama where we first learnt to dive. I quote, "I was running short of active divers. The non-diving Hamber brothers filled the gap, as did two members of the crew of their schooner 'Jylland', all of whom learned to scuba dive just to help out. Within a few days of trial Scuba lessons Howard, David and William Hamber were either chipping away at coral with hammer and chisel, or sitting at the foot of the 'air lift' pipe, sucking up coral debris" unquote.

This would, of course, not be the only mistake in his book. If one reads Syd's account as to how we came upon the 'Jylland' and to the true story, it must question the truth to all of his so-called 'Autobiography'. Another quote, whilst I'm at it, "Dennis Hamber knew little about the sea (true of all of us Syd, including you!) He even admitted to me that he did not really care for sailing (true Syd). What took his eye was the fine lines of this jettisoned old Baltic Trader, which he had seen lying on the beach while vacationing in Denmark (total rubbish Syd). Dennis, without more ado, brought the hull, talked to shipwrights and carpenters (all obviously in fluent Danish Syd), went with them into the forest to choose the tall straight trees which would be cut down to provide her masts, and day by day, inch by inch, he and his brothers literally rebuilt the 'Jylland' by themselves,,......" and so it goes on in a mind that makes up the story rather than asks for the real one. Not bad though, eh? But a bit of an insult if I was Henric Knudsen – and if he ever read such nonsense, it didn't come from my lips Henric!

Chapter 8: Peton Climbing

Sunday was a day off, and really the only time to see any of the island, other than its coastline. In those days it was the 'Mini Moke' that provided the wheels for the visiting sightseer, or in our case, illegal worker. Hiring one was pretty simple, but driving it could he rather hazardous. Large holes known by those that make them (buses in particular) can appear before you far too often than for those upon his higher seat. A low load of happy tourists might well hit a hole worthy of being made by a 'Stuker' dive-bomber. Being thrown out of this open sided vehicle can easily happen.

We would hire one of these 'fun' vehicles; its purpose was to drive to Soufriere to climb Petite Piton. For some months we had wondered what the view was like from the top and getting there (so we were told) was to encounter loose rock, and an abundance of the more deadly 'Fer-de-Lance'. This nice introduction to this otherwise 'Snake free' island came during the days of slavery. Plantation owners thought by having a very poisonous one loose, it might stop the slave running off in to the rain forest. So it was brought over from Egypt and, when those days ceased to be, clearing up the mess was left to the Mongoose. What came to our ears was the Mongoose didn't like mountains!

Five of us took off that day - Geoff Terry, Bill Curry, Derek Songhurst, Brother Howard and myself. Two hours was about the time it took to make that drive then, not today, for a new road has been cut, steel being pushed before a most powerful engine. It's half the time now, and half the fun! It was once a bit of a test for man and machine trying to avoid the nasty bits, now you sweep past great scars, the heart of some hillside revealing stones from the pebble size to ones weighing many ton, and all looking perfectly round. Cast in the heart of the earth, they resemble shot, as if fired from some enormous gun at the face of Castle.

It seemed the rain forest was in close combat with the road, and the daily deluge washing away the efforts of man as if trying to defend its territory, now it's held under some control by culverts, and in thousands of small manmade holes on the walls sheer face, shrubs planted whose roots and foliage will help hold this cliff up - if nature gives them time and a mighty downpour doesn't wash them out - along with the road down the valley floor.

The town of Anse-le-Raye is a pretty place, like its big neighbour Soufriere, and strangers in town were few and far between. Gaily painted small wooden buildings housed an isolated people who hung on to how things were with a slow to change attitude. But like any country, where fast transport and the freedom offers the dissatisfied with life, it can destroy the whole community. It allows a return from the restless soul who acts like some Pied Piper on the community, bringing stories of great things just over the hill. Before you can blink an eye, all the young are gone leaving just the old wondering, why?

It was a hot day and sweaty work with Derek Songhurst leading most of the way. Not that he had chosen to be bitten first, just that when it came to climbing try and catch him! Derek had worked with us in the firm back home – erecting scaffolding, laying bricks and running the Hod was his specialty. He'd come out with Will as back–up crew if needed, and stayed and, like the man he was – a good one! Climbing this Piton was no different to shinning up a ladder to Derek, plus his light framework carried no excess baggage.

I can see him now – way ahead, sitting down rolling a fag waiting for us to catch up with him. The decision I'd made to give up smoking had me scratching my head – Bill too. Both sides of the Atlantic the anti-smoking league was gaining ground – 'Breathlessness' as one of the many reasons put down to smoking! If we could catch Derek, we intended on telling him so!

The view from the top was beautiful, the Caribbean stretching out before us being swept to the west by the endless trades. When you have time to sit on a peak after a hard slog and take it all in – the smallness of it all comes home. One can certainly see why Moses was called up one!

Can you imagine today a world leader saying "I'll give my answer when I return from the mountain!" – the fun the media would have with that one. It would be nice though to require all the world's leaders to climb a hill – 'A Summit Meeting' so to speak – and like Moses, stay there till all the chiselling is done! We would leave on Petite Piton, flying from a branch, one of 'Jylland's T-Shirts. Tall enough we believed (and held in place by rocks) to be seen from the schooner on the Mondays cruise – and so we could. To those who might doubt our word we would point - "There - look!" and though it had to be seen through binoculars, a very small stick was seen – and a much smaller T-Shirt set flying! Both gone now – stolen by the wind!

The Old Rogue accepting something he believes is gold, but wouldn't take the chance to find out! The Duke of Edinburgh, Syd Wignall and his dear wife Jean

Syd Wignall with his gold – "Is this thing plated or real gold?"

Vigie cove, Bill and I taking the top mast down to check the rigging

Vigie cove. Haust Doiter, me, Bill Curry, Will and Jeff

Vigie cove. Derek, Bill Curry, me and Mike

Peton Climbing, 1974

Me with Soufriere in the background

Jylland in Dry-Dock, Martinique, before the Panama Expedition – April 1975

Jylland in Dry-Dock, Martinique, before the Panama Expedition –
April 1975

Chapter 9: On Official Business

"Good Morning, is the captain aboard?" I looked up from what I was doing to look at the owner of the voice. It was dressed in the 'tropical ' white of her majesties navy. It was not the usual white uniform that came to the dock on official business - this was a forward foraging party, sent ahead before the arrival of an Onan class submarine to see if there were any freebees on offer that might grab the officer's fancy.

St Lucia had seen the arrival of this 'slug of the sea' for a bit of the old flag waving - to be shown and reminded what keeps them in the way they have become accustomed. It is thus the duty of government departments to lay down the welcoming mat – cucumber sandwiches, neat gin and ladies dressed for the kill at some form of gathering.

Ex-pats that have something unusual to offer are asked if they are willing to contribute to the fun and games. So, jotting down on his pad, the lieutenant put down what we had in mind - which was some free tickets for a day trip. Not really expecting any response, they left.

The white of the navy made a change from the white of immigration officials that frequented the small dock. They came not looking for free-bees but looking for our work permits - our right to stay here and demands we must comply by the rules. Two usually came and in the manner of people of those on official business! Smiles missing from the West Indian face, and minds somewhat confused as to how to handle the situation. They stood, their small 'sticks' of authority tucked beneath arms.

This was not Britain, yet they had a rule book left by the authors regarding immigrants - refugees - political asylum seekers, of which the vast majority that came to dig up the golden streets of London – left it broke! Here before us stood two lovers of cricket, a good carnival, shagging white women, and Rum! It was something that hadn't been foreseen by those who made up the rules - a boat-full of 'Honkies' from the old country - boat people one could say, shouldered out like the red squirrel by the introduction of the grey.

It was grey alright. Very grey, so grey you could say black grey, for it was an issue where the traffic was always assumed to be only one-way. Many a West Indian had no conception of Britain other than it's where the Queen lives. It is rich and powerful so it must he big - so big it can seat the whole of the Empire round the dinner table. The poor, the un-educated, who still use the feet for transport, appreciate what a mile is, but few know how many yards make one.

St. Lucia, being roughly 35 miles - or 61,600 yards to the man on foot if he bothers to count, is a bloody long haul. To explain to some just how big Britain is by an example of how long it would take them to walk from one end of their island to the other, say two days, tell them it would take around 50 for Britain, then to surprise them with 4 times that across the USA. I would, in my years amongst these jovial people, get to know just how misconceived they are - not only about distance, but that not all white people are rich - or educated!

Each time we were due for an official visit, they went away with the situation unresolved but happy to have shown they had done their duty! Of course our argument was a good one. We were not taking work from any locals; in fact we were employing some. From the T-shirt makers to the food suppliers, right through the chain of all employed in the service of entertaining the visitors. We were told we couldn't work - but we did all the same for that very reason - many relied on us for work - and for one other reason - Bob Elliot! The same Bob Elliot who Will had told he thought his percentages insulting to intelligence.

We had learnt that it was pressure from his St. Lucian wife, Sonja, that we were getting these visits. Bob, knowing full well the earning potential, had himself purchased an old Baltic. Re-named and parked outside his restaurant 'The Coal Pot' stood 'The Rum Runner' - a name chosen from the successful Barbados carrier of tourists - and about in the same league in appearance. While 'Jylland' sat across the ways putting his pride in the shade, the choice was obvious as to whom any tourist would wish to sail in. Get rid of the opposition is what they were bent on!

Sonja was an Alice before an Elliot, and with a relation as the labour minister in the St Lucian government, she bent his ears back while sharpening her claws. They must have sat drinking a coffee together while watching the two uniforms board us - smiling no doubt in the satisfaction of knowing people in high places – till! "Well then - you tell me, why are they still working then? - No-no-no! They are just leaving now, full of people. What the hell is going on??"

It was in the early hours when this hunter killer submarine slipped in to the harbour. Its black hull lay against the main docks in Castries looking rather insignificant to the local observer. It was surely hardly anything to shout about as "One of ours Mon!" for those who need a good sized battleship to think once again - 'It's great to be in the Empire'. It's the big drum that beats the loudest, and it is for those that one should be kept in reserve - to fire off a broadside like some firework display so people can go home, eardrums ringing, to sleep in peace knowing all is well!

We picked up our passengers that morning and backed out as usual, getting closer to this sinister looking thing. It was Derek Songhurst that said to one of our local crew - a walker of yards - "See that thing there Jimmy? How long do you think that takes to get to London? Well, it might look slow to you, but when that thing gets under water it goes vooooooomm!!!!" Derek's hand proving to him just how fast in a sweeping dash forward. "Ooooooohhh!" was all Jimmy said, looking again on the sub with a renewed interest and greater admiration. Jimmy was one of two black locals, and one of many we'd employed on 'Jylland' since being here.

He was in his 40's I would guess - or maybe 30's, it's hard to tell with some people. He was a well-tuned man, muscular arms and legs that shone in their blackness when wet. Every morning he'd arrive, his little bag under his arm containing his bits, having walked from his home in the shantytown close in Castries. Changing in to his uniform - white T-shirt and blue shorts - it was washing down the decks time. Scrubbing decks was Jimmy's specialty —"Here, here, here!" he would shout at Felix - holder of the hosepipe and anything 'Up' he had chance to lean against. Felix was a younger black without any purpose in life other than getting out of it more than he put in.

"Here Felix here, here!" screamed our Jimmy, wanting more on a part of the deck he wished to thin by scrubbing hard. Even the easy task of directing water was difficult for Felix, his mind was always far from the body. Get in Jimmy's way and bare feet took a pounding, like dirty teeth after a whisky tasting night. Point Jimmy in a direction and for the hours you paid him, he worked - whereas Felix forgot the direction, but not the hours come payday.

It would be the following morning that the captain and his senior officers turned up to take up our offer - much to our surprise. Any seaman though, seeing her raise sail leaving the harbour, wouldn't forgo such a chance, and for one spending most of the time under it, the offer for a trip above the water in such a craft, was a chance not to be missed.

We had a fair number on board that morning, so the captain mixed unnoticed amongst the paying passengers - probably as he would have wished. The submarine now was decked out in her bunting, and much to the surprise of all, her crew lined the deck of her hull looking our way - smart and white. Passing her, the ancient call from the whistle brought up the inward facing palm of all in perfect timing. "They do that to us every time!" - Again it was the fast wit of Songhurst that made me smile while others looked on very impressed with British manners. "You wouldn't get the U.S navy doing that'" said a North American voice rather ashamed of what he got for paying his taxes. He and many more of his countrymen were drunkardly ashamed when later we returned to see again the spectacle repeated.

Many an able seamen had his photo taken that day by an admiring American who still shows their friends today - British Tars thanking ordinary citizens for their wages!

The car that had been sent to pick up the thankful captain and his officers was told to wait. It did, for untold tales had not yet been exhausted, and long after Jimmy had 'Thinned' a bit more of the deck and rolled up the hose for the night, still the better tales flowed, and happy laughter rattled round Ganters wharf.

"Permission to speak sir! If we don't leave now, we'll be more than late for the Governors reception". It was the patient driver that spoke, and to a man happy to have stayed longer in the casual dress and atmosphere. "Look, why don't you all come over to the sub after the open day tomorrow and let us entertain you all in return!" said the Captain. We did, and they did. The submarines name plaque of metal, painted in bright colours was presented to us as a memento of their appreciation - its name I can't remember now, but the memories I do, and that's what counts.

Memories are of places, situations or people - put all together, and they remain with you forever

Chapter 10: Dia Neale

As I have said, 'The Wicky-up' restaurant sat about the length of 'Jylland', away from where she lay moored at Gangers Wharf. It was the place we gathered and had a beer after the days run and on those days, not very busy. One person, a regular, one could say, was Dia Neale. Dia of course, was a Welshman, and a natural lover of the game of Rugby. It could be said that Dia loved them more when they 'stuffed' the English. The early 70's saw the likes of Phil Bennet, Barry John, J.P-R Williams and Gareth Edwards 'stuffing' us at home, or away on a regular basis, much to the delight of Wales and all that couldn't do it in battle dress.

Dia worked for some construction company (probably English) and when offered the position of 'Roughneck' in St. Lucia grabbed it to 'bully' the job along. Concrete and bridges was, I believe, his part in the new road being pushed south to Hewanorra and the main international airport there. Pushing was what Dia believed in - it got things done, not only in the rugby pack, but also in all things.

He was built for it, certainly for the 'pack'. Shortish and thick set he also had a very loud laugh - a Welsh one, and 'very pr-o-owd he was too of it boyo '

Pushing once too often of those who had a hard job understanding his thick English accent, nearly got Dia stoned to death by some very good throwers of cricket balls. "Bloody fending myself I was with a shovel boyo!! - a hail of bloody rocks - chasing me up the road they were!" Dia not only hated the English, but now "this bunch of bloody black bastards!"

Dia had purchased a small yacht 'Maica' since being there, it became cheaper than living ashore, and much safer too, being anchored a good 'stones' throw from shore. Married, he'd left his wife in Wales, as it would turn out, permanently! The 'other' woman in his life joining him in the 'early bath' was a nice quiet American, an East coast single one that saw in Dia something she assumed he saw in her. Divorced and free to marry Mary, she could now, if she wished, work in England. She certainly wouldn't need a 'Green Card' to do so.

With the Red Dragon flying from her stern 'Miaca' would ease the two of them in to the sea life and north, first, as far as the local Yacht club next to the 'Holiday Inn' for the usual 'piss up' and rugby songs each Sunday, then on to Yacht week in Bequia, and Antigua race week holidays. Both shared clever heads and were quick to learn the art of handling 'Miaca'.

It would be through Dia I'd learn much more than had I been the talker. Dia had another trait inherited from the country of his birth i.e., 'There's only one thing a Welshman can do better than sing, and that's talk! - and in both of these he is better at it than any Fucking Englishman!' As if an Englishman could teach a Welshman anything anyway!! It would be a total insult to his country. To get a word in edgeways, if it was on a subject he had not mastered yet, he would defend his position in the chair with a constant flow of words in that which he believed he knew.

When 'Jylland' first arrived here (So sayeth Dia) all thought it had to belong to some rich fool, for how could anyone but one give his schooner to a bunch of strangers to bring to the Caribbean for no particular reason! Then when the owner did turn up - it seemed he was right after all, for the man didn't live aboard as any owner might - he booked into a hotel! Didn't even go out sailing in her! Most strange and very odd!!

Money too, seemed not a problem to this large, rough looking fellow, and all were in a guessing game as to what was going on next. It was Mike that first introduced the impression that he himself was the owner! Then without warning, news came that the 'real' owner had gone back to England on urgent business, giving the whole show for Bob Elliot to handle - some even believing now Bob as the new owner, certainly seemed like it by the way he was rubbing his hands together.

Time goes by and another fellow turns up with what looks like a 'Minder' - tells Bob to get lost! Something really odd is going on! Now, of all things, two fellows, rough ones, fresh out of jail in Columbia arrive, talk of getting themselves thrown inside on a drugs bust - wow, this is movie type shit! One leaves, one stays, next families arrive, and talk is of Panama. Total confusion now reigns amongst the gossip!

Add to that, talk that one must be prepared for the arrival of a star - two stars in fact, one made in Germany, the other in the USA - one a 'Beach Boy' the other a 'Bleached Boy' Surely now the true owners have definitely been identified!!

It was all good stuff for the quiet observer, and to have interfered with the honesty of the situation one would not only have been disbelieved, but meddling in others wild imaginations, they will convince themselves that you are hiding something. Big has to be bad right? And all villains talk with a Cockney accent right?

It's peoples love for a good story that makes them believe what they wish, and with just a wink and keeping 'Mum' on the subject, you watch the wheels whirl in their minds

Chapter 11: Bruce Johnson

The two stars heading for us were, one Graham Bradley and, on his way home from some music business in England, Bruce Johnson. Graham and this ex-Beach Boy were friends. That means in this business, a 'Provider', and only understood when the day comes that one of them might be in need of it from the other.

In the country where he longed to be recognized in the street as much as he was in Germany, Bruce would 'provide' that, and of course, Grahams face did the same for Bruce in Germany where the group was more famous - but only as a group!

Graham hoped Bruce would provide him with a break in America, for Bruce had his own studios and was in to the producing game as well as the writing mode. "I Write The Songs" - but he didn't and doesn't write the songs that make the whole world cry, though I bet he wished he did, for the flow from his pen would have made him a rich man.

Fame is but a stepping-stone for the ultra-egoist, the word Genius is what he desired. It was the Wilson bros that had given Bruce the taste of what fame was about, but when the genius of their works got blown away by another form of 'dust', Bruce just didn't have the gift to match his songs - not without help from a few 'Providers. The old saying 'Judge a man by the friend he keeps' is the case of Graham and that of Bruce. I would jump to the conclusion that, each time I spoke to my old guitar playing friend, he thought it was the first lines of a song going round in my head - that very soon would became his own!

Whatever Bruce knew of us can only be imagined, but as for Graham's attitude when he saw us in St Lucia, I'm certain Bruce was under the impression that Graham had a vested interest. I was very familiar with the little spoilt boy signs that had now matured in to a jealousy bordering on hatred for not having what I had right then.

So sick was Graham to see us in that winter sunshine of the Caribbean, that he was ready to give up all he had just to be in my shoes. It was odd to me then, not now, that someone making so much money, living in the best hotels, women in every German town ready and willing to be with him, could be so obviously pissed off with his lot! It was as if all I was, by luck and by chance, Graham tried to emulate in misery. If I found falling off a log easy, certainly without the intent of making it seem so, Graham would break his neck trying to match it to perfection - and still trying to show me just how good he was while I had moved on to trees.

Chapter 12: Arthur Bradley

Graham was the type that, when on a fishing trip, and another other than he caught fish, he would move to the side of the boat from which it was hauled aboard. "What bait - what size hook - where exactly did you drop your line???" he would plead as the boat drifted over the sands of Ramsgate - totally illogical but true. West Ham football club, and fishing were his loves. In fishing it was not to talk about what he had caught, more of the size of the one that got away! It was, I guess, the only thing in his life he would allow himself never to want by the very fact of the boast! Even Dolly, his mother, or his poor old Dad Arthur, couldn't provide that one for him, and it was the only thing he'd be willing to forgive them for.

They had given him everything else, much to the many arguments put by Arthur that the boy was far too spoilt. Like all mothers with an only son, the sun shone brightest from her 'perfect' baby's backside. So bright, it blinded her to the faults that belonged only in others. Whilst his elder and only sister Heather watched on, wishing to be born a boy, Graham got it all.

Dolly would find a job, and Arthur would just have to 'Spit' tacks faster at his job in the upholstery trade to provide for the boys wants – that's if the 'wants' Arthur had in mind were ever to be forthcoming.

It was one of those Sunday lunchtime drinking sessions in a pub close to where they lived in Basildon. The ritual (more important to Sunday than church for the ordinary workingman) I happened upon for some forgotten reason. Full to the Pulpits it was of those that use it as a second home, and the only place they can get off their chest what is bothering them.

It was past closing time (yet you wouldn't have guessed by the un-hurried movement of those drinking up) that I had found myself seated next to Arthur round a table that by the many chairs facing it, once held a throng of devout Sunday worshippers. Two places at that table I knew would have sat Dolly's parents, having a health giving stout for longer life – which I must add was the thorn in Arthur's side and the reason he wished to talk!

"David," said the beaten man leaning towards me, "I've had it up to here with it all." The face wasn't smiling, only in the way a person justifies his 'Lot'. "Every man needs to be satisfied, and when you get to be my age, you're never sure when that urge might hit you! Know what I mean?" It was obvious what he was talking about and I looked for Dolly his wife trying to imagine them at it! Dolly was a blond woman that time had been kind to – she was a pretty woman even then. About ten years younger than Arthur I would have guessed, and in her Sunday dress now with make-up on, she looked a lot less than her early 50's. She moved amongst the tables now helping clear away the glasses – for Dolly had a part time job there.

Arthur Bradley must have been a handsome fellow once upon a time, as well as taller. Not a big man by any means for he was slight of frame – work keeping him pretty well in trim. He sat across from me but again leaned forward as if wanting to keep the conversation private – even though we were alone at the table! Arthur had a face that when smiling, his closed mouth nearly reached his ears – open though, would reveal what was left of a once fine set of molars worn away by iron! It was a rather friendly smile upon a face reddened by beer and the English weather.

I knew it was that 'urge' time for Arthur, made worse by all the attention his wife was getting from others. Arthur wasn't too sure which of them was doing the 'getting' rather than him. It would so turn out his concerns about his wife's faithful promise were well founded – but the biggest shock came when he found out who it was!!

Chas had been a 'real pal' – sat at the 'round table' with them every Sunday when home. A Merchant Navy man was our Chas, one with a pocket full of money that made Arthur's seem puny. Drinks were always on 'Chas' – trays full of the stuff arrived at the table round which they all sat – "Keep the change!" said he with the wallet and a hand up Dolly's skirt. 'What a nice man!' said grandma and "What a nice man indeed!" said grandpa - and "Cheer's" said Arthur half pissed to fully understand the man's benevolent motives.

When poor old Arthur was put to bed pissed, he that had been invited home by Dolly and Arthur for a late one was certainly getting a late one alright – and in front of the telly Arthur had purchased from his puny wallet.

'Tell me, what chance have I got," he continued, "if, say, I wanted a little bit in front of the fire this afternoon - none! We'll have Mom and Dad fall asleep watching Telly like every bloody Sunday, and

I'll end up following them – urge an' all!"

Being kind and giving in to his wife's wishes to her parents to live with them 'Temporarily' was, just like his willingness to let Chas buy the rounds, a bad move. While protecting his assets, Dolly got 'pulled' by he that threw his wallet on the table in a move worthy of Casanova for the affect it had – it also 'pulled' her mother on the side of the Seaman.

In the years Arthur had 'lived' with her and her daughter, grandma thought he had become moody, rough with his tongue and nothing but the 'Pig' she thought him to be! She just knew it was he that was farting on purpose around the house – making the fire up when it wasn't needed and watching programs on T.V they didn't like. No! Dolly should have married a proper man – a man like Chas!

Divorce did come, and it was 'Goodbye Dolly' – never again 'Hello Dolly' for Arthur. As for the Merchant seaman Chas, the man she was supposed to spend the rest of her life with doing what poor old Arthur dreamed about - he suddenly found another port, or table to sit round when Dolly moved to a flat in London with a sign up which said 'All yours Chas, come get it!' – The problem was her mom was still with her after her dad died. When Mom eventually died, it was 'All alone Dolly' till she followed Mom.

Graham's sister Heather was .the only support to Arthur, her Dad, and through thick and thin stood by him. She would never forgive her brother for the way he treated his dad, and when I saw the way he didn't wish to even recognize him at those divorce courts, which Graham had duped me in to going to for some support, all that would come upon him in later years, he would totally deserve!!

Chapter 13: I'm in!

"Tell me you're jealous you bastard - please just once" might have said the son of Dolly when surrounded by long legged Aryan blonds in the fatherland. I knew it was the main reasons he had asked me along - to show me just how much better he was than me at falling off a log, He was trying to do a Chas on me, his face rather than the wallet doing the 'pulling', but he knew that I knew what they didn't - that in the motherland the boot was on the other foot, that I and any of my brothers could do much better than Chas, without a wallet!

I see now why he would go out of his way to try and make me feel envious, the harder he tried the less the effect. Graham didn't realize, and had not the faintest idea what I was about, just what impressed me most about people. The reason for wishing to wear the most costly jewels means little to the owner other than why they are worn in the first place - to impress - to make others feel jealous. But also there lies a danger for those un-impressed by grandeur, and it's in the aim of the small minds to bring you down one way or the other

Such was in the mind of Graham when he left St Lucia, it was to be master of that which controlled my brothers and I - 'Jylland'. The only way he could do so was to make promises he wouldn't keep, and sign contracts that meant nothing.

Pulled in to this deception would be Dennis, my brother and believer in the honesty of all - other than that of his brothers! He found himself now the only brother back in England. St Lucia being rather out of bounds in a way, due to the unfortunate display he'd created of being something he wasn't - owner and a wealthy man!

Hardly could one expect him now to join us crewing for just wages. Living ashore, driving down from his hotel to see us off, or go and collect the payments owed the schooner was the only position he'd be willing to accept - maybe, but then he knew that was something totally out of the question with us. Why'? For it wouldn't have matter to me but for one reason.

When my brother used to go to The Ratner Safe Co to collect money owing us, of £1,000 handed him, more than half of it went to pay for his life style. For those that used to wonder why the rest of us didn't drive E Type Jags, Aston Martins or Ferraris - that was the reason!

Two reasons why my brothers wish to grab the reins, certainly not the helm of 'Jylland' was about to happen.

Graham, fresh back and full of enthusiasm for another chat with Syd Wignall was the starter, but there also returned from St Lucia a man Dennis trusted wholeheartedly, a man that sat on his right hand when interviews had been conducted. A person with as much experience as Dennis when it came to telling if the ex-teacher Brian Hoare was good enough to skipper 'Jylland' or, indeed capable of picking a crew that had each paid 125 pounds for the pleasure of adventure - half of which was for return air fares home – and the most damming of all, hidden from us for many years!

Before me was a contract drawn up in 1975 and signed by Syd Wignall. Graham Bradley and Dennis Hamber which states:

(A) Mr Wignall in co-operation with Mr Hamber and with the assistance of Mr Bradley has agreed to produce and market a series of films and to carry out archaeological work in the Republic of Panama and in the Caribbean (known as "The Marine Archaeological Project Panama") and from time to time elsewhere in the world (hereinafter called "the Projects")

(B) Mr Hamber has made available for the Marine Archaeological Project Panama the sole use of the schooner Jylland for a consideration of 40,000 pounds,

(C) Mr Bradley has made available finance for the Projects in the sum of 45,075 pounds.

(D)... Goes on to state all the things Syd undertakes to make available to the Projects, and now matters little to the story. What does matter is what went on behind the backs, and without any consultation with the feelings of those now in charge of the schooner, and more importantly, her joint owners!

There we were, earning good money and for the first time in years capable of paying off the debts Dennis had run up putting her there, and behind the scenes pieces of paper were being signed that would in the end, sign the schooners death warrant.

It is easy now, it always is in retrospect, to say what we should have said when news came the project was on, with the words "Don't worry, it's all been taken care of". Just how many times we would hear those words in the future, and not only fall for, but pay a very heavy price for. 'M.A.P.P' was on, like it or not David - oh yes! and Syd said by the way, the waters along the South American coast are very tricky - we should have on board a very competent navigator!" Cheek!

Chapter 14: Mike Atkinson

"You can tell a Yorkshire man - but not very much!" This little bit of information was dropped over my garden wall one day by an old Cornishman, Garfield Sedgeley.

Mike was very much like that Yorkshire man - and that saying could be used for so many who know it all! It wasn't his fault, for he was bred in a county where he believed only 'The salt of the earth' came from - those with 'grit and determination', the hardy breed and all the rest that goes with the old bollocks that makes 'em proud and, in the same breath, prejudice!

Witty? Intelligent? Mike certainly was. He was also over six feet tall, fair hair and a good-looking chap. For Dennis, he had been the perfect choice as Captain before it was found he hadn't got a ticket! But with Brian Hoare gone, and assurances that 'there was nothing to it', the job was his!

Mike could handle 'Jylland', there wasn't any doubt of that, but needed the engine running to do so. Getting him to turn it off, even with a good wind pushing her along under full-sail was a fight for the lovers of peace and quiet! He just seemed to need that reassuring 'thump thump thump'! Mike was an engine man - be it in sports cars, speedboat or plane, flat out and fast was to his liking. No wonder he and my brother got on so well!

Another thing Mike was good at was being 'careful' - so careful one might mistake it for 'tightness'. Many a time I would see him eating the 'secret' - before dinner, club sandwich at the 'Wicky-up' - when I knew full well he just had to be broke, for I was and we both drew the same wage. Dressed in white large collared shirt, black trousers and those high heel boots of the early 70's, he was out every night dressed for the kill to do the hotel tour again and again - and again! His company was those unable, by fortune of character and face, to collect the company of ladies - for Mike certain could - being Captain of the 'Jylland' helped!

Somehow Mike was financially better off than he wished to let on, and at the table of all who could never afford to go ashore each night, he carefully chose his 'Prince and the Pauper' role - slipping in to both quite comfortable! It would be many years, and far too late for him to realize which he preferred, and if that time should ever be granted him again, which of the two companies he remembered most with affection.

How Mike got his secret fund, or who supplied it, mattered little to us - it just cast him as really unacceptable, not part of the team!

The news, when it sunk in that the Panama expedition was definitely on, was met with mixed feelings at first, but as time progressed the attitude changed to 'let's get on with it then!' Contracts had been signed and sealed and were as tight as a drum - so we were told! Everyone's part in it as clear as the water round which we now sailed - so we were told! So assured, our minds were centred on the objective, that in the month before our departure, the certainty of a successful partnership had been entered in to.

Chapter 15: Off to Martinique

First thing to do was to book a berth in the dry-dock at Fort-de-France in Martinique. The painting of her hull, some chalking that needed attention, and a general once over of her rig. So in April 1975, a happy boat load - full of great expectations left for the ways across the channel!

Martinique is clearly seen from St Lucia, just 30 odd miles to the north. A rock sits apart from the southern shore, named Diamond due to its similar shape. Up its difficult slopes in the 18th century a party of British sailors manhandled cannon. Admiral Hood (dark Dick) thought, as he sat looking at it from Pigeon Island in St Lucia, what a wonderful place to use as a lookout - not only that, with guns set up they could sweep the channel between it and the mainland of shipping - a right pain in the French arse so to speak!

They even gave it a name - H.M.S Diamond Rock. It held out for 18 months against all efforts to shift them. It wasn't until Admiral Villeneuve arrived here with his fleet from the Med, that the insult to the French was deemed too much to swallow. It took many men and a great effort to move them, and in doing so, treated them with great respect.

"Never again will I raise my hat to other than a British seaman!" said an observer from an American newspaper as he watched astonished at the feat. "Like mice wrestling with a great sausage!" he wrote and, as we passed it to starboard, I tried hard to imagine the effort!

The dry-dock here was built also in those times of conflict between us in the 18th century, and built as if the French, unlike us, intended to stay!

Entering the still waters of this dock you notice to port, the railings of a huge gate slid back in to a cutting shaped out in stone. Centred by lines ashore, you await the pumping out to settle you slowly to the ways some 30' beneath you. Great stone steps appear as you descend between the terraces - props are placed beneath you as the movement down ceases - you are at last upon the ways that once held a Man-a-war!

It is only when the gangways are craned to you can you get off the boat, and that you do on wooden boats, for you are eager to inspect those areas that have niggled you - the infuriating small leak you couldn't find being top of the list. I would know more than I wished to know on this subject in the years to come, and if there is an authority in this field, my understanding of such is second only to the reasons that cause them!

A week is what we were booked for and, while upon the ways, we were joined by my brother Brian. He arrived hot after a long flight and angry at not being met - that hasn't changed much, then or now! As to the reasons for Brian joining us, I never did know, and lovely as it was to see and have him aboard, never was told at whose request made him venture from England - to have asked could have been a sign of my disapproval, if that mattered!!

It is never felt necessary for an elder brother to seek approval of one so many years younger and, in the case of Brian and Dennis alike, my words to both were treated with the same enthusiasm as those I first uttered upon this earth! Any consideration for room to grow, let alone have an opinion in the years when fighting for space was important, was survival of the hardest!

The impression on children lasts long and, in an uninfluenced state, makes up their mind about a person which, in nearly all cases, turns out to be a true likeness of them which you later wish to forget. Brotherly love can shield him in forgiveness for the way they treated others. Peel that back, and underneath is seen the very person who gave little all those years ago! If needed or not, his presence just added to the flavour of some fine memories that would be shared in the coming months. I remember him being there - whether his memory of events is as good as mine is not for me to know but, if pressed, I'm sure his conscience would include me to forgive himself!

Returning to St Lucia was no problem, for the authorities knew now it wouldn't be for long, so the visits from customs and immigration officials ceased. What visits we did get were from higher up the ladder, much higher up - so far up oxygen tanks were on hand. Under the glare of spreader lights, jewels flashed in the night air, perfumed ladies drowned the smell of Stockholm tar, and expensive wristwatches gleamed on bare arms.

A cocktail party was in full flow, given and attended by those who always attend cocktail parties! Especially those who wished to show (just in case what they've heard is true) on a photograph of giving his total support to the project - as long as the support means of course, no cash donations what so ever!!!!!!

Such a send-off, I thought, can only be matched if we return with Drake at the helm - and paid for by the government if and only if the P.M. can have his photograph taken with the old sod! We had stymied ourselves by celebrating a foregone conclusion before the battle commenced - between us and a "Go fuck yourself!" stood a lead coffin. The very same man had made the mistake of celebrating an expedition by exposure 380 years before us, when all his success that led to his fortune lay in surprises – surprise, guess who's here! Were there to be any leftover in that place for us???

Chapter 16: Panama and M.A.P.P.

These letters stand for 'Marine Archaeological Project Panama'.

We set sail from St Lucia at 12.00hrs on the 6th of May 1975 with winds light and variable from the east - course due West. The assault craft sent over by Syd on Guest Line were aboard and lashed on the forward hatch – with Mike's speedboat taking up the after hatch and the ships boat hanging from the davits, we'd have plenty to choose from if such a time came to abandon ship!

At 13.00hrs I fixed our position at Latitude 14.00.5 North - Longitude 61.07 West, with the log reading 5.9 miles.

The crew for that passage were -

Mike Atkinson:	Skipper.
Rose Widowson:	Cook.
Roland Sinson:	Passenger.
Brett Sinson :	Passenger.
Geoff Terry:	Crew Member.
Derek Songhurst:	Crew Member.
Brian Hamber:	Crew Member.
Howard Hamber:	Crew Member.
Will Hamber:	Crew Member.
David Hamber:	Crew Member and 'Navigator'.

On taking that role I'd disobeyed all orders received from England which had said, in a warning by Syd to their Lordships at the Admiralty, of "Tricky waters" and of "submerged rocks ready to catch the unaware novice". Novice eh? I should learn soon enough in the coming months that Syd knew more about that subject than the whereabouts of a certain box! Novice indeed!!!

Had I not been confident, I would not have put the lives of the people with me at risk. I knew full well that both Howard and Will put their faith in me, all I needed was the time to prove to myself all the studying had not been in vain!

The job of cook at sea must be the worst job of all. It is a job best for those whose stomach is slung on gimbals - whose feet are as wide as long! In rough weather, they must look in to, and stir, what some above them are disgorging over the side, as if in some effort to make room for what's being cooked below the heaving deck.

Mike had met Rose at one of the hotels he frequented with his friends - the wish to look over the schooner could not be refused, being the Captain. The first bit I saw of Rose started at her feet, followed by legs that seemed to keep coming down the companionway in graceful steps. As the face appeared Mike introduced her, "This is Rose, I'm just showing her round!" With that, appearing behind her came Jim White, architect and Scotsman and one with a firm belief that, by Mike showing her round 'Jylland', he was on to a winner later by knowing someone who knew 'Lloyd George!'

"Hi! How's it going?" said he that would have preferred to wait on deck than enter our domain, and one totally different from the world in which he lived. He trusted Mike with this tall red head as much as he would a Turk with a hard-on in the shower room telling him to bend down and pick up the soap!

"Thanks and goodnight!" she said over our conversations, and was followed in to the evening air by Mike and the Scotsman, dying to find out what impression the tour had done to his chances later on that evening!

It was a complete surprise when Mike said some days later "Rose would love to have the job as cook aboard!" The Tall willowy frame of the ex-Tiller Girl just didn't fit the role of ships cook, but if could - and would - its better having something lovely cooking something rotten, than something rotten cooking something lovely – that in no way is disrespectful of Geoff, which I made clear to him then, for Rose could well die at sea on day one!

Rose wasn't to be tested out in rough weather, for the following breeze and small seas drifted us along quietly - our first days run being 159 miles. Brother Will would have Roland and Bret Sinson with him on his watch - father and son, Wills in-laws, for Will had married Sharman, Roland's daughter just a few months before departing. Roland might have been born in Guyana, but put a headdress on him and you had the perfect face for a North American

Indian. He was the son of an 'Estate Manager', and moving in to his father's footsteps, that is what he had become.

You don't need too much education to understand the first principles of what that work entails, for it involves the common sense to realize you can't do it alone! You need people, and you need to know how to handle them. Roland's greatest asset was that, and wherever he worked in the Caribbean, the mark left by 'Mr Sinson' remained long after he'd left! He was their Boss - Hero - confident - and friend. Amongst such people, Roland was safe - but others now owned the estate he ran then in St Lucia after the death of he that first employed him. Men that think not what they can do for people, but what people can do for them, in such company Roland had awaiting him a few surprises to learn about his fellow man! Buts that's another chapter!!

The confidence my brothers had in my ability to navigate obviously didn't extend to Mike. The position I'd fixed us in at 19.00hrs on the 8th (Latitude 12 41'N - Longitude 68 5' West) was, at 05.00hrs on the morning of the 9th in his watch, considered way out - if considered at all!

The faint glow seen on the horizon to port by Howard at 02.00hrs on the morning of the 9th was that of Curacao. The 'probable' entry made in the ships log then by my brother, made Mike, upon his watch, look at this as 'Guess work'. Knowing land was in plenty to the south of us, his decision was to change her slowly towards it! Just 10 degrees for now to 260 - that by 10.00hrs was now down to 250c - and by the time I was called and told of the change in our heading it was down to 230c - and land had been sighted 'Dead ahead' at 10.35 by Derek!

My intentions of passing north of Aruba had been changed by 'Just a hunch' so that, in those few hours, what lay ahead of us was not the northern end of the island, but a point of land reaching out towards us. Land he had sighted at 06.50hrs bearing 155 compass - was the 'hunch' that said, it wasn't Curacao - but Aruba. Convinced he was right and I didn't know what I was doing, he would then call me as we passed the northern end of Aruba!!

Now surprised to see land dead ahead, another 'hunch' said it was the southern end of the first hunch - so fell off to pass it to starboard. To get back to where we should have been before his 'hunches' came about - would have meant motor sailing in the fresh easterlies blowing that morning. A harder job than rounding the southern end of Aruba, now closing in on us fast! By noon our course was down to 195, and an hour later we had Seroe Colorado light abeam under full sail.

The picture we must have looked from the shore, was a little different than that aboard, for Mike had made himself look a right prat in the eyes of all by thinking a Yorkshire man's 'Hunch' is far better than an Essex man's arithmetic any day!

"Why I wished to pass north of Aruba Mike is because of these!!" and I pointed to a small clump of rocks called 'The Monjes' on the chart. They lay halfway across the Gulf of Venezuela and, in the right position, would tear the hull out of her. "At the rate we are going, we'll probably pass over them in the darkness and if you would like to rely on another 'Hunch', the lights will be on!"

This wasn't home waters where you could count upon such things. We now had to get north of them. So at 16.30hrs we altered course to 305c with the log reading 478. By 22.30hrs and the log reading 505.5 miles, I figured it was enough to clear them, so again we changed our heading to 275c.

The question of whether the light on 'The Monjes' would have been working was confirmed as very unlikely when the major light on point Manzannillo was not! Situated on the Panamanian coast, we were searching for its glow on the horizon in the evening of the 12th, having fixed our position at noon as Latitude 10-32.5' N - Longitude 77-51' with very overcast skies. On a course of 245c, I believed we should have sighted it and asked to be called when we did! By

04,00hrs of the 13th, with still nothing to fix upon, the lights of shipping appeared - so we were getting near to the 'plug hole'.

By passing Portobello at 06.00hrs, it was pretty obvious that the 20 mile beacon was out! Beware of submerged rocks - tricky waters eh? - What about lights and skippers with hunches Syd???

The log when shipped read 1072 miles and at 09.45 on the 13th May, we dropped anchor in area F - 7 days out of Castries. Apart from the little 'cock-up' round the Dutch oil refinery – Aruba - I felt quite happy with myself, helped by a slap on the back with a "Well done!" from Will and Howard, who I'm certain had wondered at times, "Can he?" They knew then they could relax and trust my hand when we had to move her across open water again - so could I come to that. But I wasn't fooling myself for this little exercise had been easy.

Chapter 17: Coco Solo

Roland and Brett would leave us within days of arriving, for them it would be a quick flight back to St Lucia. When our time came to leave though, I knew it would be a battle to windward, for the blissful ease of that easterly wind that carried us here would fight us for every inch of the way back. The square sail that had done its job downwind would be furled now for it would be sails best for 'reaching' that would try and claw us to windward.

As yet, the best course to set had not been discussed, and was really not in the minds of others than mine. We were here to do a job and, if successful, the battle back would be done in the high spirits of achievement and there was no reason to believe we couldn't do just that. The enthusiasm ran high for the search ahead.

Panama is famous for two things - the canal and the rain that fills it. Oh yes, and dictators! For like all the countries south of the Rio Grande to Cape Horn, they breed 'Macho men', that odd strain that runs through the Spanish dago and flourishes on South American soil in abundance.

We stood under the awnings awaiting our next move as buckets of the stuff fell from a leaden sky. Hissing as it hit the sea, heading towards us came rain squalls that stung the bare skin and made you wonder just how much could be held by one cloud.

It was a rather isolated anchorage. When the sun shone there was little of interest to gaze upon, for the shore lay some distance away over an uninviting stretch of water. The movement of shipping through the 'cutting', brought with them vast amounts of fresh water. The rain off the hills that filled the trench then came out with them to murky the delta in which we sat, when the time came to haul in the hook, we were glad to move.

Kindly - which means the pulling of the right strings in the right places, a berth was allowed for us at the disused naval base at Coco Solo. "Follow us'" said a pilot boat, and we headed for Pier No 2 - for the strings pulled in Washington months before, had at last made someone move, but not before a visit to his 'castle' had been made by Howard and Mike to pay some 'respect!' - Papers or no papers from Washington.

Ten miles each side of the waterway is American 'soil', a zone drawn up to protect its lifeline from the Pacific to the Atlantic Oceans. It is a thorn in the side to many Panamanians and many a 'Nasser' has promised to throw the 'Gringo' out. Unlike our 'cousins' who, in 1956, gave a nod and a wink to the Egyptians to cut our Empire off in nationalizing the Suez Canal, we have stood back in a tit for tat confrontation.

The zone is full of dictators that use their small offices to administer bureaucracy if protocol is not followed. A man called Green (Les I believe was his first name) was the American of Anglo-Saxon descent that was standing 'firm in the furrow' for having his nose put out of joint. 'Kiss arse boy!' is what democracy is all about - the only difference between that and a real 'Dictatorship' is: you have to kiss so many more!

The south bank of the ten mile zone is flat and once rather marshy. It was seen to be the place to build a naval base from which to patrol the Caribbean - and would be the biggest seaplane base in the world in time. Obsolete now by progress and American dominance, we followed our escort to pier after pier of empty berths that was once alive with men during the last German uprising.

Concrete jetties with their wooden Dolphins planted beside them were built with that usual 'no expense' necessary attitude of tax payer's money; they then become the sole property of the US navy department who, like our own, flaunt the country's wealth with a flippant mind. Huge, well fed Admirals, desk bound, egg (scrambled) bound, plan not for any future return on investment, for half predicted there wouldn't be one, and the other half tried their best to make that come true!

Pier No2 was just as empty as any, but behind it lay a mass of desolate buildings - workshops and offices, and further still - houses that once held the families of flyers, seamen and ground staff. These places brought back memories of my time in Virginia as laundry boy - for the design was a replica and the layout just as regimental in their squared off plots. Thankfully, these now housed those that administered the running of the canal, for without them, we'd have been parked up next to a graveyard!

Much is spoken of 'American hospitality' and it is true, but I've often wondered if it doesn't stem from its isolationism. A society with a single language raised up in dream world behind the 'Statue of Liberty'. Bring in an outsider from the 'Old' country, and they wish to share their 'Apple Pie and ice cream', not only for stories from outside the city's walls, but maybe because they're bored with the bloody stuff themselves. Food and booze they have in plenty, but a foreigner speaking with a strange accent about things they've only seen on the movies, is a real find!

It wasn't long before our lines were ashore when a few turned in to a group. Those fascinated at our appearance at this deserted spot.

"Hi! Where are you guys from?"

"Have you really come all the way from England?" said another, noticing the red ensign flying from the stern.

"Expedition? Wow!"

"They're looking for Sir Francis Drake!" said a father to the child!!
"The famous Pirate!"

"WOW!" said the child,

One face did I recognize in the afternoon was that of Syd. The rest was his team of underwater divers, film crew and experts in the world of marine archaeology (with or without a degree) and it looked, by what was being un-loaded from the taxis, that they intended to spend the night! Rose would be in for a big surprise too, she hadn't been told of 'guess who's coming to dinner!' either. We just put this slight cock-up down to a lack of communication!! A word that would long be remembered by all concerned. I would spend the next 5 months watching a mixture of confusion, a lack of communication and incompetence that, by the time we left in November, I was not the only one that was left wondering – wondering was it worth the effort.

The arrival of Dennis came (by plane again!) but not with any 'well done' or 'great to see you missed all the tricky rocks!' - but a "Who's taking care of my boat!" sentence.

We were at some ones place the evening my rather grumpy brother arrived - an invite we'd taken up to go for a drink by some American who'd wish to show some hospitality and wish us good luck. Dennis walked in to these proceedings wishing to stamp his authority upon them with the manners of a dog marking his boundary.

"Wow!" I thought, "Imagine how he'd have reacted if we'd said "What boat - we hit The Monjes due to the skipper you hired!" All we needed now was the arrival of Graham and it could well be a moaning trio we had on our hands!

We learnt then for the first time (after a cooling off period of some days) what the set up was that Syd, Graham and himself had arranged back in England. Of course it had little to do with us but, if we must know, here's how he saw it. What Will, Howard and I learnt from him as we sat on a dock out of earshot from those aboard 'Jylland' - made the three non-owners raise some eyebrows.

Graham would be financing the expedition on a monthly basis. That the ship should, from its safe, finance the expedition for the first month till it could be reimbursed - at a later date! Expedition members (that does not include us, or our families) shall receive a small weekly allowance towards their entertainment!

"Do you mean to say Graham has been allowed to back this on a pay as you earn basis, like some productivity deal? Find me Drake and you'll find me a very generous man set up? You were there when Syd told him it was just a matter of jumping over the side with 150 feet of rope! How much rope do you think Graham will give him before payments will find some great excuses to stay at home???"

Such fears put to my brother went un-heard, for in his own mind, such a wimp wouldn't have the nerve to let him down - he'd tear him apart! Letting Dennis in the safe was about as sensible as letting a starving Billy Bunter loose in a pie shop promising he wouldn't eat a thing!

"The money we have, is our concern - our safeguard - our way out of here if things go wrong - or not! Give that up and we give up our independence - our passage back!" How they knew what we had left after dry-docking expenses etc, had been learnt, but never thought by us to be taken in to consideration in this affair - let alone as a 'Loan' to Graham.

A great bit of negotiating by Dennis could really screw things up making life just that more difficult. Planting himself in a hotel in downtown Colon didn't help. There was nothing we could do about it now, but get on with it!

It is needless to say that the money from Graham came as regularly as he did, that being for a holiday to see his family there, or when the signs where good that we were on to something.

Yes, the families were all there, but it was not to be at the expense of the expedition - that was to come from the ship and our own pockets! Syd had been told this back in England, and had agreed to all, but now here, it was a different tune! Plus he had the lack of Grahams promises to make him keep his own. So like a bloody fool, made life difficult for all!

Nearly half of the team Syd had chosen for that 'Once in a lifetime experience!' were young women or girls. Good figures in tight rubber wear with faces to match seemed more important than ability! As expedition artist, he had chosen a Welsh girl - Leslie Bruce. She would have very little chance to show us what she could with paint and brush as time will tell!

As an artist, painting the bottom of the assault craft that now lay upside down on the dock was not really Leslie's idea of creativity, but she did it, and awaited the call, like all the rest of us, for the move. Boredom can set in on idle talent, so she passed her time between such menial tasks and getting in with 'Bad company' - that being, talking with Nick Watterton and John Robinson, as both worked on setting up the man less submersible in an old office area behind us on Pier 2.

This interesting invention was down to Nick, so was the idea of getting an old air conditioner working to make life more comfortable - so comfortable, Nick and the expedition mechanic John, moved in their sleeping gear. Nick, I was lead to believe, worked with 'The Rolling Stones' - special effects making their concerts more interesting - each and every mad idea I would take a guess at, brought about by a good 'smoke' rolled from something grown just south of us in Columbia.

After dinner both John and Nick would take off to a bar, the only one still open on the base. Open to us by an invitation of master sergeant Lou Pinson - shooting some pool while drinking a beer their intent. So why not come with us they had said to Leslie. Back at the ranch after, with the air-conditioner running, they would sit, chat and maybe smoke some of the funny stuff that brings on laughter, even to the bored.

Entering upon this happy scene, stage left, came Syd. It was obvious there was some confrontation by the look Syd wore the next day. There was talk that all three were to be sent packing for reasons not to be shared with us, or the rest of the 'team' who were seeing part of an integral lump of the squad banished from the camp!

Our leader was saying that nearly one third of those that had come there were expendable! This show of pernicious power had me worried - we had not a Shackleton here but a Scott, and we all knew what happened to him! Why was Syd so upset?

Leadership is to lead – a quality lacking in Syd. He had lead three people all the way to Panama and, at the drop of a hat, led them astray and us to believe they were never needed in the first place – so who paid for their air fares?

Emotion had played a part in this rash decision, I was certain. It was plain to me and others Syd had chosen Leslie Bruce for some special attention. The 'Once in a lifetime experience' surely meaning for her something other than she expected. The girl was well over 30 years younger than he, and a man in his late 50's with not a lot going right for him, standing before you in tropical attire, big shorts and sandals, grey hair and goatee beard, sounding and looking rather pathetic, is not really much of a 'Pull!'

With the dismissal of Leslie, it meant the expedition was now without an artist, yes? No, Sweden would come to the rescue in the shape of the lady doctor! Karen Skalsjo, taken on to care for - severe attacks of 'Athletes Foot' - watch out for signs of 'Athletes Foot' - administer warnings as what to do if it is encountered - and, if we did find Drake, to see if there were any signs in his coffin that he actually died from it, rather than the Bloody flux. Karen was also a very competent artist as well as a very nice girl caught up in something that must have bewildered her.

Chapter 18: Portobello at last

We would eventually leave Coco Solo on the 17th of June for Portobello – minus Leslie, John and Nick. A month of idle time wasted while Amundson was pushing on to the South Pole.

If there is one thing I will always remember about that place, it is - sand flies!!!! In the morning and late afternoon, wave after wave would take off from some little fly strip close by. Destination 'Jylland' – purpose? To eat all on board!! Little wings designed only to keep in the air flying teeth. They attacked us relentlessly! Some of us suffered more than others - your only defence was the repellent 'OFF', which you guarded with your life. Poor Rose was driven to despair, her great long lovely dancing legs were a total mess after a week of bombardment. Hospitality from homes nearby was her only refuge, without them she would have gone mad! She was one that cheered the loudest the day we departed.

The run to our new anchorage would take 4 hrs. Aboard as passengers were the Mayor of Colon and the Governor with his son, for a large reception was planned in Portobello. Waiting to welcome us were the school children from the area. Unfortunately, within an hour, seasickness had them begging to be put ashore - Bahia Las Minus saw them depart across a calm sea in one of our assault craft - missing all.

This shoestring run, badly led expedition that would fall apart at the seams in the end, was forgotten then. Lining the shore as we entered the 'Beautiful Harbour' were the children - all dressed in their best clothes. A grand banner was held to welcome us to this once bustling place that now lies quietly forgotten. None of the great guns opened up to welcome us - just the cheering of small voices from the area where our campsite lay. It was some time away yet, and none of us knew then, our departure would be in a very different manner - a manner that insulted the welcome!

St. Lucia in search of:
Sir Francis Drake's Remains

SIR FRANCIS DRAKE

By Voice Reporter

A SEARCH for the famous English Admiral Sir Francis Drake whose body has been buried in a lead coffin at Porto Bello off the coast of Panama, some 379 years ago, began from St. Lucia yesterday. Sir Francis Drake was the first English Admiral known to have sailed around the world in the fifteenth century.

The search taken the form of a Marine Archaeological Expedition which has been mounted after several years of documentary research and on the spot investigations that resulted in reasonably convincing evidence that Sir Francis Drake's coffin still lies buried in the sea bed off Porto Bello.

In an interview with the Voice yesterday prior to the Expedition's departure, the 31-year-old British Captain Mike Allen, one of the re-organisers of the 16-year-old 130 feet schooner Jylland built in Denmark in 1899, members of the expedition will be accommodated, said that the expedition comprises a total of nine persons from England and the United States most of whom carried from Garler's

Wharf here approximately 10,000 people along the coast of St. Lucia.

"We have a good crew and the trip to Panama will take about nine days."

Speaking to William Humber, 31 year old part-owner of the Schooner Jylland, he said:

"We have worked here in St. Lucia for the past two years to finance this expedition.

"I should get William Rambally, one of the owners of the Jylland assures that, for it happened in Schooner before he saw it. Captain decides an under-use on a similar voyage as we are now undertaking.

"We thought the idea was set-backs for about one year, but we are happy now that we are accompanied by him and the crew. He stressed emphatically.

The thrill of it, Anything else could have been done. We have the best of everything to have over the best.

See Page 3

Seen in picture from left to right are Co-Owner Humber and Mrs. Humber, Barrister Maurice Salles Miqueile and Premier John Compton sharing and enjoying a joke on board the Schooner Jylland at Ganter Wharf Vigie on Monday evening.

Coco Solo Naval Base

Alongside the dock at Coco Solo

Alongside the dock at Coco Solo

Alongside the dock at Coco Solo

In Coco Solo heading towards the Panama Canal

On our way to Portobello dinghy in tow

On our way to Portobello

Portobello Harbour from the air,
with Drakes Island on the left and the 3 sisters on the right

Portobello

A crowd of school children, awaiting the "Great Arrival".

Building the camp at Portobello, built with help from the locals

The camp at Portobello

The unloading of Syd's container. Me on the truck, Dennis, Graham Bonney once Bradley, and Howard.

Building the Pier at Portobello – such memories! : Myself, Dennis, Howard and Will.

Richard Price on shovel duty with Geoff Terry just standing by

Planking the pier.

The moon over the pier

A Kiuka where once guns were installed

The Gold House, Portobello

The Gold House, Portobello

The Gold House, Portobello, once full of Gold

Chapter 19: To be or not to be? That is the question

While the Schooner lay to her anchor, invisible in the blackness of night, the crew's eyes would see the lights from the camp ashore. One Man in particular sat, eyes transfixed, slowly mesmerized by its glow. Casting on the deck his clothes, like some spent cocoon, he quietly slipped into the water and swam ashore, pulled towards that light like a helpless moth! It was our dear skipper Mike that crossed the line drawn by Syd in the sand. He had decided it was time to don the uniform of 'The Favoured Few' and figure out the answer to the question. To be where the action is - the nightlife of camp fires and Girls!

Up till then, Mike had hedged his bets as to the outcome of events. Silently he had observed the proceedings during the month in Coco Solo and had calculated during that period that this expedition could collapse before it had got going. He was right too, for there were times I believed, by the sacking of members and Sid's attitude towards us, that this might well never get off the ground. The feeling of not being part of this expedition was made plain by Syd's reluctance to share his thoughts, thus creating a 'them and us' madness. Making a move too soon, could find Mike - plus speedboat - heading back to Sheffield, so an each-way bet on loyalty was his answer! Now in Portobello the expedition was on, and it was time to shift his colours.

Syd would quickly present him a reward for joining his ranks. I happened to notice in the coming days the distinguishing marks of his new company. You see, Syd suffered from an ailment, as did the man we were trying to find - a leader of another ill-fated expedition, Drake! Drake's curse was The Bloody Flux, which did for him in the end - but the wonders of modern medicine would keep our leader from his bed, and on his feet, for it was in that area that caused him most grief!

He was a sufferer of 'Athlete's Foot!' Such was his obsession with this complaint, that those who did not comply with his orders were despised for their shoeless habits! His orders were, that your Powder (Foot, not gun!) shall be kept dry, and with you at all times! A good sprinkling shall be given to the feet each morning and evening. The wearing of socks then shoes was enforced by a stare and Ostracism!

Syd's team were easily recognizable, they all looked as if they'd been playing football with a bag of baking powder. Syd, from the delivered container, had supplied each member with a pair of plastic sandals, so no excuses there! With each pair came their personal tin of anti-foot rot!

Personal favourites were loaned also, for the duration of the expedition, or until he fell out with them, a Rolex Divers watch! I don't know how many of those Syd had, but they seemed to appear like rabbits out of a hat! 12, I later found out was the total 'Given' by the makers for advertising rights, though Syd gave us to believe they were on loan, and at all cost, must be returned - yet another lie!

Such was Mike now dressed - shoes, powder and watch! I felt rather betrayed by this action. To me it was one of disloyalty by shifting his colours to what he thought was the winning side. More though, was my anger directed towards Syd for the creation of teams! Surely we were all after the same result, regardless of what promises had been made.

Both Dennis and Syd now blamed each other for not playing their part, and from Syd came a sense of paranoia that we were here to steal his day of glory. He would throw the blame and point the finger at any misdemeanour, any act he believed treacherous - and later of theft at the Schooner and those aboard! Of course, not to our faces, but to others willing to listen to such a convincing tongue!

None of us believed that it would be just a case of 'Jumping over the side' to pick up a box of bones – none, I suppose, except Graham. He was dragging his heals with the promised monthly payments, leaving us to make excuses to Syd. Syd had given assurances to those of his team, that a small allowance would be afforded to them each week!

Just enough to go buy a beer, so to speak! As the weeks dragged by though the money, coming from a man who wanted some results immediately, would be lucky if they got enough to eat, let alone a beer!

The road from Portobello to Colon was a long drive, a drive that, if made without getting a puncture on its treacherous surface - exceptional! Dennis, still insisting on the luxury of a hotel room, daily made the run in a car he had purchased for expedition use. Cheap it may have been, but not when adding in the constant cost of tyres not made for such roads.

Blow-ups at blow outs was a daily routine I was happy to stay clear of - I knew how the colour of the air would look round him on that wild road - I'd seen him on too many such occasions before. Graham's non-appearance didn't help. "When is he coming? Did you speak with Graham?" met him each day as the promised arrival time had long past. His response was enough to say he hadn't - and in him started to boil the thought that just maybe, maybe he had misjudged the man.???

Getting hot around the collar in the tropics is not wise, it can turn you mad! Very mad, and mad he was getting with the position he had got us all in - nearly as mad as Syd was for falling for the same promise. Syd, lacking in leadership, preferred the role of complaining bitterly in the quiet surroundings of his Bohio to close members. Broken promises made to him - leaving out, of course, the ones he'd made to others round a table in England. Who was there to doubt him, and the muck thrown our way was sticking. His mischief making had brought on the 'down tools' strike by his team over the lack of food and the weekly allowance - 'Jylland's' safe was running the show - like it or not, we had no choice but to keep it going hoping funds would arrive to replace our dwindling assets.

Had Syd been willing to discuss the position rather than stir up trouble, it wouldn't have happened and, having been the cause of it, left it to us to explain to his chosen Lt, John Stubbs the predicament in which we found ourselves. John was more understanding and totally oblivious to what the arrangements were. We were all caught between a rock and a hard place, and he knew full well after our discussion there was little we could do about it other than pack up and go home! All we could do would be done, and he relayed that to all - so it was back to work for now.

'Never hang your dirty washing on the line!' and in the circumstances we found ourselves, it was a case of trying to make things seem not what they were to all outsiders. High on that list was the Guardia National, those sent to work with us whose eyes and ears are tuned to unrest. Any show of dissentient in the expedition could lead them to wrong conclusions.

Having moved our caravans and the old school bus that was my family's home to the campsite situated below the old Farnese fort, we had moved from the protection of the Canal Zone, in to the domain of the gunslinger. The removal of Nick Watterton, John Robinson and Leslie Bruce hadn't done much for a show of unity! There was little for us to do but wait for Graham's arrival - or some promised funds to ease matters.

For William 7 and Helen, not yet one year old, getting used to the new environment was done with that which all children do - 'What's good for Mom and Dad, is good enough for me!' Having some time to wait for direction could be spent exploring this place whose name was covered in so much history.

The move from Nombre de Dios to Portobello was suggested by Bautista Antoneli who, accompanied Juan de Tejada, was sent here to inspect defences by Philip II after the successful raids of Drake and Hawkins in 1585-6. The Italian military engineer saw the need for better fortifications in the Caribbean and, on returning to Spain, drew up plans for such, along with the recommendation of the move to Portobello. The harbour surrounded by hills could be better defended than the openness of the port that shipped out the royal bullion.

Little action was taken on this advice, for when Drake returned ten years later, the move to Portobello was being undertaken at such a pace that only 8 to 10 houses were built - besides the great one being erected for the Governor - all would be destroyed by the English when they took the place. Only after that, did the push start, and Francisco Valverde y Mercado officially founded the city some years later.

12 sites were positioned to defend the city, the fort's walls constructed from coral - a Spanish report of 1607 describes it so: "For ramparts it was found that the best stone was the reef-rock (coral) found under the water all along the coast, because it was soft to work and almost as light as pumice stone. After being fashioned and placed, the sun, wind, and water in a short time hardened it much, but left the stone of such quality that no ball however large it might be, made any effect on it, because it checked the missile without splitting or chipping. This stone was bound and joined with a reddish clay and lime, which made a mixture as strong as the stone itself." The finished article was plastered with a fine white mortar.

In 1975, the remains of these forts were in excellent condition, and an effort to extract them from the jungle was apparent by some clearance of it from the walls.

San Fenando was typical of all forts here, and being across the bay from the town, you were alone by its remoteness from the majority on the southern shore. The view from a sentry box on to the bay was once made when it shone out in its whiteness, but the effect of time and weather now stains them in sooty streaks. The limestone base that once ran out excellent bronze artillery, now have old iron ones to remind us what they were here for. Forts and guns all silent now, but with a little imagination, so easy to be in the real picture of another time!

On the subject of time it was, for us, moving on and little seemed to be happening. Something had to be done! The main reason for being here was the search for Drake - but up till now, all Syd seemed interested in was the filming in and around the forts. It was now July, the anomalies that had been detected by Harold Edgerton a month before, had still not been checked out - just buoys left marking the position of some interest.

This lovely old man from the 'Massachusetts Institute of Technology' who'd come at his own expense with his grandson, had gone weeks before. He was not just a wise old bird in this field, but in others also - wise enough to get the feeling something was wrong in the camp!

Syd seemed to me playing a waiting game, waiting for some promised cash before sending men in the water. Frustrating as it was, nothing could be done till the man who held the purse strings came and, as yet, guessing when that would happen was all we could do. My concerns for the expedition would lead me to start something that, to this day, I have continued - logs of every day happenings to place times as to who said what, and when they said it!!

My first entry reads: "Started this log on the 17th July 1975 - two months too late!! Today has been another un-eventful day. The expedition is lacking in leadership and direction!"

We had been there now just over two months, and the holes appearing by first the sacking of members and Syd's outward contempt for our presence there, had brought about the desired effect. The manners of the gentleman he'd been so keen to show to our families in England did not come out with the container from Wales.

When in the camp, his attitude towards all 'Intruders' as he saw them was in total contrast. His eyes would avoid any contact with the aliens, so silence remained on the lips that just one "Good morning!" would have meant so much to. Never was there any concern for wives or children in this hot and humid atmosphere, and rudely he drove past their 'homes' without so much as a wave of recognition in the car they, like it or not, had provided.

It would be Annette and family that would find the first 'excuse' to rid themselves of such behaviour, and left for England to find a warmer climate. It did little for Syd's cause when Graham heard of their treatment, and just added to his excuses for holding up payments. Howard's wife and family were next to flee his hostilities of schizophrenic proportions, to the safety of the homeland - for in this Republic, such a mind working against you was a thing to fear. Brother Brian was next to go, the inactivity and the wife at home that said "Enough!" being the reason.

Before the whole thing collapsed round our ears we would have to have serious meeting to iron things out between us. Graham had at last arrived from Germany, it being the day I started my logs on the 17th July and another reason for me doing so. It was all too 'hush hush' for me - I was in the dark as to what he and Dennis were saying and the sooner we had a meeting the better.

Strangely Syd was being nice to everyone on the Saturday of the 19th and, as I note, was in the campsite two days in a row. Why, on the Sunday he even spoke to me - though I note in my log "He said nothing!" Maybe all this was due to the arranged meeting with him for Tuesday.

To mediate at these 'Discussions', to stop things getting out of hand and hear all, was Dean Edwin Webster from Panama City. This man was a pleasure to be with. To say he was an amateur historian of the area and Spanish occupation would be an insult to him! To say he was an expert, would be saying he didn't spend much time on his real profession too! What I will say is this, if Syd had half his manners, then where would we have been???

On Wednesday 23rd July the Dean was there to hear all. On a hill overlooking the campsite, Dennis, Will, Howard, Graham, Syd and myself sat and talked. In the presence of such calmness, the air was cleared. "Were we not here? So let's get on with it!" was the outcome. "If you want us to help in the search above or below the water, just ask us Syd!" we said. This offer was eagerly accepted

Syd didn't know that some of us aboard were capable of diving, for he hadn't asked! His attitude towards us on board gave us the impression that, had we offered any assistance, other than what our role was in this show, he would have taken it as an insult. Imagine, if you can, someone other than one of his handpicked 'Professionals' had to be credited with the find?! Graham, at that meeting, made further promises and like the born liar he is, failed to honour them again and again in the coming months!

An excerpt from my log, the day after that meeting on the mount reveals: "24th July. Had our first real working day with the expedition members from England. Dived on a small but dangerous reef, 2 miles from Garote! Rumours were, a 17th Century Spanish Treasure ship sank there. By the location, I can see the reason why this assumption would be made!

"Lifted an old anchor from the seabed off Drakes island - had a problem with the Air bag - Lifting eye parted, Bag needs to be in a net - will make one tomorrow! Had another meeting with Syd which was okay!" – and so my logs went on, for my ideas that it was 'Okay' could soon become not so.

Chapter 20: The Experts

Our working with Syd's team at close quarters in the coming days, showed for the first time just how 'Expert' some of these people were!

Brian Richards and John (call me Mango) Chetham, were two chosen by our leader as experts, in what will leave many, in the years to come, scratching their heads in disbelief at incompetence. Brian Richards, we would find, was not the 'expert' in moving film, but just on the still form stuff, and as for Mr Chetham as sound recorder, their professionalism by shifting the blame caused not only some concern, but a change of nick name from Mango to - "OH! Mango!" by Brian who blamed him for everything!

Camera batteries not charged, hairs on a dirty gate and why they only had half a roll of film with them - each blamed the other "I thought you had it, etc. ".

My mistrust of the word 'Expert' was taking shape and before I would be killed by one, I'd learn never to trust one again.

Syd had gone to meet Prof Tom Muir in Panama on Fri - returned Tues! Then took another 5 days to go and meet someone off a plane from the States, which seemed a rather long time, but then, that wasn't unusual for Syd, he spent more time away from the camp, then on it! In command while he was away was his right hand man, John Stubbs.

Whether John was frightened of giving any orders for the day's proceedings without first conferring with his elusive boss, I'm not sure, but we seemed to be following the same pattern set by the leader, that being - No direction and no discussions. Never in all the time we were there did I take part in, or see any sign of, a meeting where the day's events were discussed, or provided with what was required of the team the following day!

Tom Muir was from Houston, Texas; He was bringing with him a side-scan. To mount that on Syd had acquired the use of a large Catamaran from Ed Carwithen, an American from the Canal Zone who used it himself for the training of diving! What story Syd told Ed about his heritage, can only be guessed, but it must have been something good to get the Cat plus board and lodging when he was in their area. That was as regular as clockwork, as was the use of the poor fellow's phone - in which he ran up a horrendous bill too!

What was bothering me, as we loaded Tom's heavy gear aboard the Cat on the 31st of July, was that Harold Edgerton's 'Finds' had not yet been checked out. Surely, had they done so, maybe - just maybe - we wouldn't need to do this extra surveying? One more thing! Syd had told us that Drake was buried at sea, so what was Dr Muir doing making runs up and down the harbour and, on the 6th of August, having us in the dirty muddy water of Portobello, checking his 'finds' out.

There we were, in six feet of water, right under where the drinkers from 'Romero's' Bar piss in the water, looking for Drake! Visibility 2 feet - finds? Human excrement, an old rubber tyre and spent tin cans lying on top of mud, God knows how thick! So, after wasting nearly two weeks, on Monday the 11th August my log reads: "Spent the morning unloading the Cat of Tom Muirs equipment - Syd gone to Panama!"

On the 12th of August, a rather pissed off Tom Muir went home to Texas.

We were supposed to be searching in an area where, in the presence of 26 ships, the old dog was ceremoniously dumped over the side, and deep enough that the Spaniard's could not get him! We had read it ourselves, and been told by Syd he knew exactly where the spot was, so could someone please explain to me what we were doing under water outside a Bar we used to drink in at night? No!

While we were concentrating much effort on swim lines around 'The Three Sisters', just west of Portobello, we found out that Syd had put up a Reward! '$500 to anyone who can give information leading to the whereabouts of Sir Francis Drake!' Can you imagine what that did, word went out on the drums and everyone ready to make a fortune, or some drinking money, came up with a story so convincing, it made Syd get us to check them out! We should have packed our things and left this madness right then.

A Captain Phil Bowdenhorn from the US special services had me in the water near Los Gallinas on the 31st July, going over an area where he said he saw a lead object about 8' x 4'! I wrote on that day: "I found the area he described on my last dive, and buoyed it. Will get him to check it out tomorrow!" Of course Captain Bowdenhorn didn't show.

Sunday 3rd August, a Bill Yancy came down with Mr Bowdenhorn, he also said he had seen the object described by the Captain, off 'The Three Sisters' this time! So, who gets the $500 if we found Drake? It was for certain he could not have been dumped in such shallow water. The area in question was to the leeward of three small islands. It was obvious that ships would round up behind these for shelter, to await entry in to the safety of Portobello's Forts and harbour. Unfortunately the ground their anchors would hit was not by any means perfect. Full of rock and gully's of sand. A good grip on the bottom meant you were lucky if you could raise it - hence the amount we saw!

As for 'Our' Syd, where was he? Seemed he was always in Coco Solo, never once did I see him in the water.

Friday 15th August: "Awoke to a beautiful morning, Richard Price, Karen, Sharn and myself with Geoff Terry as boatman, to Lavandera Reef to do a quick swim line.- nothing to report! Ran out of bottom time. To 3/S in the afternoon! Heard from a local fisherman about the sighting of an object in the water with a 'Crown' on the top. How much is that worth! Told him to go and talk to Syd - if he can find him!"

Saturday 16th August: "Another day at 3/S. More engine trouble, could only do one dive, terribly angry. Diving team round Drakes Island found Lead ingot! Size 2'8" by 8" square, looks like ballast! Felt very tired today"
Sunday 17th August: "Spent the morning at 3/S finding 10 fathom line and the afternoon doing some swim lines at the same place. No sign of Drake but plenty of lobsters, got one for the pot! The other team at the Salmedina Reef! Syd not here,"

On the point of lobsters, the area round 3/S was perfect for them. On one dive, a swim line, I passed an area where they sat on ledges, huge ones, watching me as I passed by, I went back once, trying to locate that same gully, but search as I could I was unable to find the spot. Found others, but not that large group!

Monday 18th August: "Syd was back! Spent the Day filming with Brian and Mango, I was again at 3/S with a team in the morning and afternoon. Lifted our buoys there as we'd been told a 12 man team of U.S army divers were going to sweep the area tomorrow and help us for a week, didn't want our buoys confusing them. Divers on Salamadina brought up some cannon balls!"

This reef, Salamadina, sits just off the entrance and in the middle of the channel that leads you in to the harbour of Portobello, Nothing marks it except the occasional breaking of water in rough weather. Perfectly positioned to catch you out - and by the bits being brought up by the divers, it did to some poor sod!

Tuesday 19th August: "Heard this morning, the U.S diving team won't be coming after all. Politics, which in this case is the Canal. Can't play in our yard, if we can't play in yours! This threw us out and will have to rearrange program. Fixed the errors on Syd's sextant - Lot of side and index in it"

Wednesday 20th August: "Spent the morning with John Stubbs re-surveying the Anomalies that Dr Edgerton found. Found that some marker buoys were missing, not surprising after two months. Had to lay more down, as checks! Divers brought up a silver spoon from S/reef. Team went and lifted the lead ingot off Drakes Island. By the weight, feels as if it's solid!"

Chapter 21: Drake's Coffin?

It was at this point that rumour would spread that Drake had been found. Syd was all of a sudden back at the helm! All plans (as if there were any in the first place) were changed and all leave cancelled - people were walking around with fingers on lips - why, what was all the fuss about?

Thursday 21st August: "Felt good for a day's work but was completely confused by Syd's change of plan. All confused except

Syd - work stops! Took time off to teach Geoff how to dive - brave lad!"

For the next week very little happened below the water, not much diving went on, but for a little scratching around. Stories were floating about along with a couple of Ferrets from Reuters, that the lead box found was hollow! That it was under armed guard in a 'safe' house in Portobello - which was true!

To us it was a laughing matter. The truth was, it was just a lead weight left over from some rock crusher used when they constructed the canal. The San Felipe (Iron Castle) fort was destroyed by the construction company for its fine material. To those of us who struggled to get this lump ashore, it was obvious what it was! But Syd wasn't going to miss an opportunity and back on centre stage, the limelight switched on his ego, and playing it for all it was worth was what he intended to do!

"There! Is that not a lid?" said Syd, pointing to one of the layers of the lead lump. Try to explain the obvious, that it would be constructed that way for ease of handling, and one would be rejected as a fool - a non-believer of what was plainly the lid to a coffin! To ask the question -"How tall do you say Drake was?" and all manner of abuse would be fired at you!

Logic was not in command here, but a greed for glory when your answers were met with "Could be his ashes!" Maybe they folded him in three, would have been a better answer.

I was to find out later from Richard Price, in a letter he received from his grandmother, that it had been announced on the news in England that Drakes coffin had been found - and the backer behind this venture was the 'Pop Star' Graham Bonney!

Didn't take much working out who put that little story about! That little shit would do anything for the publicity, and it didn't matter whose reputation it would hurt! What was quite amusing – though at the time, had we known, would have been even more humiliating - was that Graham had stated the coffin was that of CHARLIE Drake!

It would be the following Thursday, 28th August, that I would be approached by a man wearing dark glasses. Talking in lowered voice, I was told of a job they needed done. "Bring your own tackle!" said the stranger "There's a certain lifting job to be carried out. You will be met at the dock near 'Romereo's' by another stranger!" It was Syd in a height of secrecy playing silly buggers, not wanting prying eyes to see blocks and tackles arrive at his hideout.

Sunday 31st August: "Took Geoff diving in the afternoon. Syd back at last - takes him a day to run in to Panama and a day to drive back. He went to pick up Malcolm Dickie from the airport, Syd back to his old ways again - like a muddling old woman!"

Malcolm Dickie (Ex-speedboat racer) was another of those Syd had squeezed for free supplies to this expedition, Malcolm's payment was - he'd never get back what he lent.

Monday 1st September: "Spent the day Painting 'Jylland's' topsides. Syd gone to get camera film, spent all day doing so. Not back till 19.0hrs. Arrived at last 19.45 a little tipsy too! Spoke with Richard Price about trying to get the filming in hand. He's the only one who gets going on anything in an organized manner!"

Why I was so concerned about this filming was the fact, that when we left here, these rolls would be the only thing we would have from the expedition. The understanding Syd had arranged with the Panamanian authorities was that any 'finds' would go to set up a Museum. Drake's coffin - if found, would be the centre of that attraction.

Now having learnt in the last few days that our cameraman, Brian Richards, picked by Syd was expert in another type of lensed instrument - rather worried me and my brothers! Which I think was rather understandable. Now! whether or not his giggling partner

'Mango' (And don't ask me where the hell he got that name from) was recording what he was supposed to be, or looking for the B.B.C as he twiddled the knobs, really bothered us!

My God! Years later how we suffered the torment of watching so much crap - hair on the gate! Too blue underwater shots for not using the provided lights! Film speed like an old Charlie Chaplin movie for not charging the batteries up! I have in my attic today, thousands of feet of incompetence!

If by chance, that somewhere in this world today, Brian's eyes are behind some camera, a moving one, we paid for that apprenticeship. It would cost us dear!

I'm not saying that the likes of Tom Morrow (who's father by the way provided our compressors – hence Tom being there) Karen Skalsjo and Sharn Whittaker didn't do what was asked of them; they did so with much enthusiasm and effort.

The likes of Richard Price, was luck more than judgment in picking a good one. Those that were any good, and those that came to learn to be good, deserved a better leader and teacher!

While waiting to get back in the water, film shots were done aboard the schooner of her under sail and coming to anchor!

Tuesday 2nd September: "Spent the morning Diving on Salmedina Reef with Geoff who is doing well! Also along was Richard, Howard and Luciano, Lot of artefacts around. Found some Bar-shot!"

We had with us on the expedition, up to four Panamanian divers, army fellows from their National Guard. Whether it was to learn something about Marine Archaeology or just to keep an eye on us, I wasn't sure! Mostly a nice bunch, but one could never be sure with confidence that they wouldn't turn on you.

Syd wanted to see the old settlement of Nombre de Dios, the port on the Isthmus used by the Spanish before the move to Portobello. The Guardia arranged a flight, and a party of them went down. Returning, they found one of their stills cameras missing - believed stolen by those living there. A quick return to the old port and by sticking a pistol to the chief's head with the demand - his life in exchange for the return of the stolen article, showed what type of people we had with us. They got it back!

Geoff, now donning a diving suit would give us another man in the water. He'd often had thoughts about having a go - I guess the thought that he couldn't swim, might have had something to do it! "Why do you need to swim?" I used to say to him, "Working down there, you don't need to, all you need to know is how to breath and use a hammer, and I know you can do both of these!" Both Richard Price and I helped him don the suit.

Geoff had for weeks, been boat man, just sitting there while the rest had all the fun below. It must have frustrated him so, that one day he wanted to try it! So off we went to a shallow area round the corner known as White Beach, the water was clear and warm there! Geoff and I have always trusted one another, and soon with that trust I got him to stick his head under the briny and sit on the sand! Wasn't long before he was facing it and pushing himself along with his hands in to deeper depths - well weighted down of course!

Now out on the reef some weeks later, there he was bashing away like hell at concretion with the rest of us. Any problem, just slip his belt - blow life- jacket and bingo! No problems! When his air was running out, or he had something to take to the Cat, he would 'WALK' to anchor chain and up he'd go, coming back the same way! Nothing Professional then what was round here?

I told this to some American's learning to dive with Ed - they would not believe it! For knowing what a stickler they are for safety and rules, where even before you can put a regulator in your mouth, you must be able to swim like a fish above and below the water for several miles. Saying we had someone with us who couldn't swim was un-believable! Why, if I'd tried any of that Buddy breathing stuff with Geoff, he would have thought I'd gone all-queer!

I remember once returning to the job on the reef after changing a bottle, seeing his shape heading towards me carrying rather a heavy load he could hardly see round. Where to place his feet was also restricted by a partly inflated jacket, blown such to help his buoyancy. I could see he was coming to slight drop off, a gully 6 feet deep and about as wide! In my interest in how he was going to negotiate this obstacle, I paused to watch! Seeing the gully by the turning of his whole body, he inched forward till he could feel it with his feet, on which were worn boots, not flippers! Stopping there I knew he would be thinking -"Now how am I going to do this?" With that, he started to pace backwards - "My God!" I thought, "He's going to have a run at it!" And run at it he tried - it was more of a wobble really, he cleared 4 of the 6 feet and vanished still holding on to his lump of concretion. Where were the camera crew, I thought, what a shot!

Later, Geoff would wear flippers and learn to swim, no great distances, but could swim. This newfound confidence not only pleased him but me also, for I had another man to help scrub 'Jylland's' hull! It was just that he intended to do one day. Donned in all the black gear, like some frogman going to plant some limpet mines, he stood on the deck, rubber boots on and flippers underneath his arm. These he would put on once seated on the lower section of the boarding ladder, and off he would go!

He was about to, just that when I said to him! "You would find it much easier if you jumped off!" The response to that bit of advice was "Fuck off David!" nicely said - with much feeling. I then continued my chat with him as he was seated pulling on his boots below me. "Honestly Geoff, believed me, you'd find it so much easier than all that messing about. It's just arse over the rail and go!"

He was now telling me to Piss off as well as go try an impossible act - but all the time he was coming back up on deck. I talked him on to the rail "That's it!" I said "Now before you jump, just hold on to your regulator and mask" I didn't think he would go just then, and he hadn't finished the sentence as he hit the water with - "Fuck off-_____!" But decided to complete it when he rose, mask off his face and regulator less. I threw him a line, as he threw me abuse hanging by the Schooners side! That quiet harbour in Portobello hadn't heard so much foul language since Henry Morgan's lot were here in 1668!

Chapter 22: What the eyes don't see!

When Howard Carter entered the tomb of Tutankhamen, being the first to do so since the boy king was buried, who would have dared check his bag on the way out? Not only that, where was the inventory that could say something was missing after he left??

To say archaeologists, on the land or under the sea, are all honest, trustworthy fellows is a hypocrisy that is set upon by the 'closed' ranks of their profession. Enter any of their houses, and adorning walls and mantelpieces are reminders of a little dig here and a little find there. Worth anything or not, they sit there by right of possession.

Those who enter this world of un-earthing our past, do so for many reasons, one is the love of it, and in that sense, it would be rather odd not to see them surrounded by some of that love. The difference between their sort of collection, and that of a stamp collector say is, the stamp collector paid for what he has - the archaeologist on the other hand believes in the finders keepers approach, and as the owners of what is now ancient artefact can't argue over the price, nor demand they put it back where they found it, small nice bits vanish without a soul knowing.

I always believed in what my mother said about honesty – it is the best policy! I still believe that, for you can't be broken like the liar. But my mistake was, I believed such honesty was taught to all. Syd had much to teach me. In his small world, retrospect raises its ugly head on far too many occasions; they can become cornered by their past and the head rests un-easy on the nightly pillow
.

Many an eminent fellow who un-earths history can find his own being pulled apart in a search for the truth. The reputation of a dead man does nothing but make one for he that can tear it apart the best, and they that do so, can well find their own under the microscope by another looking for fame! The problem is, when the likes of Carter die, and little bits that could have only come from Tutankhamen's tomb turn up, he didn't leave any of the answers to how? - - thus leaving himself open to have done some magic tricks with an empty bag!

Whether in a tomb, or alone in deep water, the temptations upon discovery of something priceless, something lost, something no one would miss if you took it home, can for the best of us, be only understood upon being, why should it concern you before concerning others?

A case that came to my attention is one that must be of many such temptations.

It all began in 1961 off the island Giglio, just off the western coast of Italy.

Reg Vallintine, founder of The British Sub-Aqua Club (patron The Duke of Edinburgh) was with a small team, diving off a submerged island called Secci Pignocchi. Down over a 100 feet, they came across items of pottery, cigar shaped pots used to carry wine, oil etc, Somehow they didn't 'feel' Roman, and weren't - they were Etruscan, forerunners to the Romans.

For 2,500 years, those pots had lain there - but what as more exciting, was the discovery of another object. Passed up from diver to diver from the depths, the heavily encrusted object looked very much like a helmet of some kind. Reg had made it very plain to all that each and every item by law, has to be declared to the Italian authorities. Oddly, a German diver with them, only known as 'Hans', obviously did not understand English, and left the island with the precious object, leaving poor Reg in an embarrassing position over its fate.

Giving various artefacts to the local authorities with the suggestion of the founding of a small museum - made slightly less important by a missing piece - I might add. Reg leaves!!!!

Some 20 years now pass, and entering the scene comes a Mensun Bound. Born in the Falklands, but has, after a globetrotting career, found a home in Oxford University studying 'Archaeology'. This young blonde 'tousle-haired' man is just fascinated by the Etruscans and by a chance meeting with Alexander Mckee in his library filled with 'underwater relics' from past 'finds' - one being the 'Mary Rose' - Mensun's eye catches something (if only a coarse handle of a pot) that if, had Alex obeyed Reg Vallintines orders on all artefacts, should have been in Italy!!!

Told where he'd got the object in 1963, Mensun was directed to Reg. A return to the site in Giglio was the talking point. Could Reg remember where the wreck site was? It seemed a problem to the man who was to be made head diver.

With the support of his distinguished colleague Prof John Broadman, a 'classical archaeologist' to boot, and the World Ship Trust, set up by no other than Prince Philip to help preserve ships round the world (for themselves no doubt!) a little expedition was organized.

In the summers of 83/84 young enthusiasts converged on Giglio, paying their own way, and bringing their own gear for - 'some dawn till dusk tough diving and recording!'

In a 150 feet of water, such was this wreck scattered. Your time on the bottom before heading to the surface is limited to something around ten minutes, if not, decompression stops have to be made.

In the process of uncovering a large wine-mixing bowl, decorated with a frieze of dancers, disaster strikes!!! During one night, looters arrive with quote "Portable suction equipment. They just woofed it all up" recalled Mensun in an article written by Brenda Harsh - who obviously knows nothing about the subject, especially to do with airlifts!

Quote: "When Joanna and I went down in the morning it was like a big bomb crater, the remains of the bowl were scatter over the site. Everything gone It almost killed us both etc!" He also goes on to say the men responsible were arrested, and are now in jail - Why says I, for when their apartment was raided, nothing was found! What would the Carabinieri have done then if something had been there - hung them no doubt!

Again quote: "It became rescue archaeology - we had to get everything up as quickly as possible!" but didn't he just say everything was gone?? The delightful objects NOT taken were given to the Museum of Archaeology in Florence -- but hold on, two years ago when someone I knew visited there, nothing was to be seen!

Someone has to be lying here, and the person that can tell a novice, looters using a 'Portable' pump were to blame, seems to me the best person. Anyone who has used an air-lift will know that!

The chances of hitting the spot where artefacts might be are greater than winning the lottery two weeks in a row!! Is he saying someone was down there in 150 feet of water, at night, pitch black, directing the weighted end of a pipeline - opening the valve to let the compressed air in! Where was the compressor? Where did the end of the pipe go? And what were things doing down there that should have been already ashore one might ask?

Let's move on to the mask! It had been just a 'Thumbnail sketch of the helmet in the old logs!' that Reg had shown our Mensun. This was the one object that - quote "Had haunted Joanna and Mensun; Vallintine remembers that a diver named Hans took it, but there were three divers called Hans! Two of them were found but hotly denied having taken it, so the hunt was on for the third Hans, whose surname they now thought they knew" - End of quote. Odd that Reg didn't have any surnames in his logs of three German Hans don't you think?

It then goes on to say that Mensun and his now wife Joanna, scoured German city telephone directories at every opportunity, "There were hundreds" she recalled -_ did she mean cities? For to have meant Hans, would still see them making phone calls! And, I would like to know, who paid for the phone bill?

They, down to the last 13, fly to Germany to find 'Hans ageing and un-well, He was also more than suspicious - had they come to steal his helmet? It had been preserved and kept in a bank vault, an investment for old age' - so says the Hollywood script. Finally he allows them to see it. When they saw it, and where they saw it, is a matter for the imagination, but what they saw was priceless! It is a most wonderful object, beaten out of a single sheet of bronze. Beautifully engraved with Boars on its cheeks, snakes heads terminating the curled up eyebrows. Almond-shaped eyes are formed by the projecting nosepiece, and its dome shape curls down the nape of the neck where it is paper-thin.

Now! I have a National Geographic magazine dated June 1988. In it are TWO photographs of that very same mask - before cleaning, and one after! The shots are attributed to a Paul Arbiter - Ocean Images; Mensun Bound, Mare, Oxford University.

One must imagine then that Mr Abiter took the first photograph before it was stolen! or that Hans cleaned it up after taking it out of the vault, for Mensun says one was allowed to be taken when they were allowed to see it. Very un-likely on the last part. If he did take it before, how come Reg only had a 'fingernail sketch' and not a print to shown Mensun?

One other very odd thing, the patron of the Giglio project was Prince Adam of Liechtenstein, first name 'Hans'. Just another 'Hans', or can we assume in what vault the stolen object lies. I smell 'Rats' - some slight of the blackmailing type. Fellowships at Oxford, etc! Benefactor unknown!
Mensun now refers to himself as Dr Bound - yet isn't one!! All funny, I would take a guess, that if you entered Mr Bounds home, the walls, like Mckees and the rest are covered in artefacts - Etruscan ones!

Kings - Princes - Earls - Lords - Knights - Professors - Dr's - Diplomats wish for a 'Handle' to hide behind. It is their key to enter countries unhindered by the Peasant! It is believed that such men are honest and trustworthy - the salt of the earth! What crap.

Observing Syd was an eye opener in to a world where nothing was safe "Just shout wreck and GOLD! David, said Richard Price to me one day - and in moments someone will appear out of the jungle wishing to assist you!" He would be right too, and not just on that, missing objects - like the mask, were soon to disappear.

Wednesday 3rd September: "Went out with Will, Richard, Geoff and Ariastides to Salmedina. Discovered large amounts of concretion under loads of stones! Back on reef in the afternoon, Cat brought in to load Compressor on board"

Friday 5th September: "Worked the morning getting the Cat ready for compressor. Brian filming that, Went to the reef, got airlift going, really shifts it. Bill Curry arrived from the states. It gives us another diver!
Saturday 6th September: "Another day with airlift on the reef"

Sunday 7th September: "Spent the morning talking with my brothers. Dennis said Syd has been demanding his signature to guarantee moneys owed him back in England. Will and Dennis gone to phone Graham and Syd's wife Jean. Found out a few lies told by Syd about expedition insurance and moneys paid him. Spoke with Richard and John Stubbs about this later and Syd's explanation on how the lead 'Box' was tampered with at Portobello! - Suggestions by him are "That it must have been one of the crew, or expedition members!" is not a nice thing to say - of course it wouldn't have been Syd would it?

Richard Price broke his finger today - real shame as we will miss his workload! Syd gone to Panama City - again!"

One can see here in Syd's reference, as to who was responsible for tampering with Box - as he put it! Crew or expedition members still drawing that line in the sand. In his eyes we were not one of the same, yet doing more than our share of the work!

He wanted to hold off 'Opening The Box' so to speak, till he got some written guarantees about what he thought was owed him. I'm certain Syd still believed something could be inside - if he didn't', maybe we did, so tried using that belief to force us in a corner. But just to be sure of the winning hand, would have a little peek at it first! Hence the tampering accusations.

Monday 8th September: "Went out to the reef in the morning. Bill, Geoff, Doug and Oscar found a nice Bronze Breech Block, and another close by! Syd opened his lead 'Box' today - cameras rolling and much fuss! Low and behold it was as we feared, lead slabs from rock crusher! Dennis got in touch with Graham, found out a few things about our 'Friend'!"

Graham... or was it Syd? Or was it Graham! It was difficult to find out who promised whom what and when. Who really was the liar? It was as hard to find as Drake! Like a couple of tarts they blamed one another while we got on with the work!

Tuesday 9th September: "Will and Sharman left today for St Lucia. Went to the reef, Good day. Two more B/Blocks and powder weight. 16 hours in the water in four days. Syd didn't rise this morning - Hang over! When he did get up went straight off to Panama - what for - who knows for he doesn't tell anyone anything!"

It had been decided here that the way things were going Will had better get back to where we should have to go to earn a living in the charter business after this fiasco. I was sorry not to have him and Sharman sail back with us when that time came. Will was a reliable person, and I just knew he would miss something and I would miss him.

Wednesday 10th September: "Back on the reef! 4 more B`/Blocks. Bronze ring about 5" dia. Lead shot - piece of wood with rope still in it! Syd got back 18.00hrs. Richard got a letter from his Grandmother in England saying she heard on the local news (Plymouth) that we'd found Drake! Grahams doing I do Believe! Pissed Richard off and I don't blame him!

Thursday 11th September: " Back to the reef, 5hrs yesterday and another 5 today underwater, Lot of hard work and not much to show for it today - half a silver spoon, silver buckle and musket shot. Lots of cannon balls, Brian and Mango came out to do a film shot of wreck site and 'Finds'. Dennis went to see if money had come! Behind again. Dean Webster said he'd spoken to Jack Davis who informed him Syd had been trying to raise money in the States. Syd had been told by Davis it wasn't the right thing to do! The Dean said he is powerless to do much, but would keep an eye on things for us!"

Friday 12th September: "Another good day on the reef, 5 more B/Blocks, Moved some of the large mortar shot, making good headway through the concretion.

Found large heart shaped deadeye - was told there has only been one like it found before! Spending 5 hrs. daily in the water hammering, the effort gives you a headache"

Saturday 13th September: "A good day again, 8 more B/Blocks, making 16 now , 2 came from under the cannon, which we intend to move, Also silver buckle, Syd did some filming then off to Coco Solo, Ed's place I guess ! Cooked a pig in the evening at the camp. Syd back and happy, wish he was more like that every day!"

Monday 15th September: "Back on the reef after a day's rest for all, gave my sore throat time to heal, Got under the concretion, Moved the large iron cannon with air bags. Bill Curry found a silver coin under it. Brian filmed the lift, found a nice blue bottle in the hole I've created by the moving of concretion. Syd has gone to the States, Reason, they, whoever they are, are trying to take The Bonham Richard project off him. Fears it's the work of Tom Muir!"

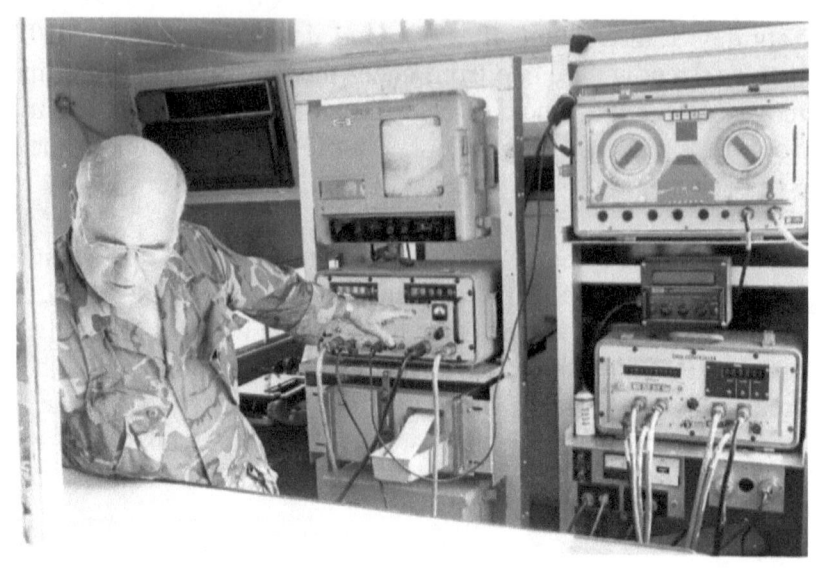

The pavon. From Coco Solo. Why we needed it God only knows

Professor Dean Webster, Marine Archaeologist with the readings from his side scan

Dr Dean Webster with his side scan

"Daring" Dick Price

"Sir Francis Drake's coffin" said our Syd

The raising of a very small but heavy Drake

Breech blocks used with the first rapid firing small cannon
15 of the 17 found by me on Salmedina Reef – Two went missing!!

"Mango" and the Teledine underwater camera – is there any film in it though?!

Mapping the location of the cannon before it was lifted

Malcom Dickie, Panamanian chap, Mike and Karen, getting ready to dive

Cannon being raised from the sea bed

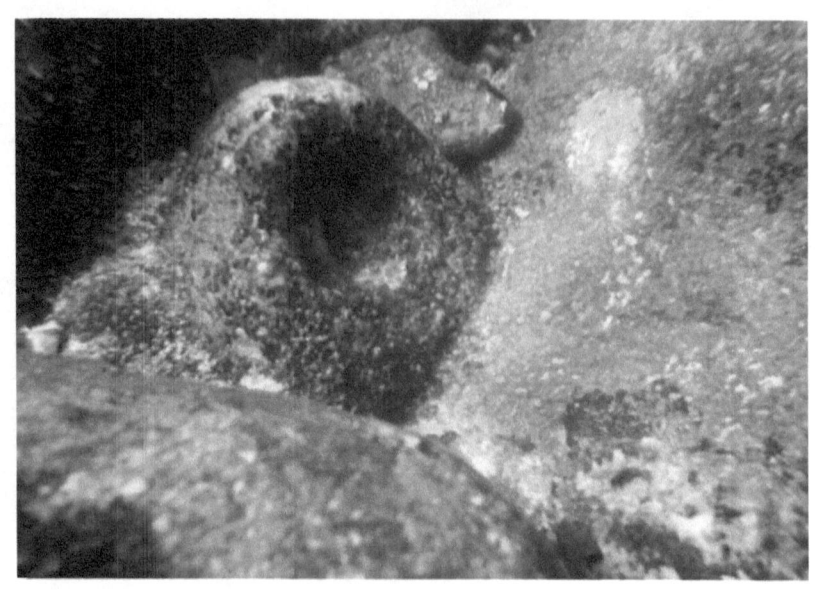

Recovered cannon ball

Karen Skalsjo and John Stubbs aboard the Pavon.

The loading of the air compressor on to the cat lent by Ed Carwithen

A bunch of Guardia sent to watch over us!!

The Wignall group on the pier we built. From left to right:
Top: 2 Panamanians, Brian Richards, another Panamanian, Syd Wignall, Mike Atkinsons and Tom Morrow.
Bottom: Karen Skalsjo, Sharn Whittiker, John Stubbs, Adele St John Wilkes Best of the bunch sitting in his Kiuka: Richard Price

The cat, so low in the water with the compressor on board. Bad boat handling said Syd

The raising of the Compressor from Salmedina Reef

The raising of the Compressor from Salmedina Reef.

Jeff Terry thinking about jumping in the water

Now we know why Syd was happy on Saturday, he was off to the States for two weeks. Didn't know about that decision till he went Mon!

Tuesday 16th September: "Brought up a few more artefacts from, the reef. Silver spoon handle - bone buttons, Lots of large lumps of concretion ready to raise!"

Wednesday 17th September: "Raised the concretion broken off yesterday, also timbers we pulled out from the hole, A lot more down there! Found 4 buckles, one real nice one Geoff brought up. Hack money and two coins stuck together, One more B/Block making 17 in all. Sharn and Adele St John Wilkes left for home this day, Brian Richards took them to the airport! Richard Price has been laid up for a couple of days sick! Up and about today, feeling a lot better!"

Sorry to see Sharn Jones go, she was a willing worker and nice girl caught up in messy business from the very start. As for Adele St John Wilkes - it's who you know not what - Daughter of Bill, who at the time was deputy chairman of the council for Nautical Archaeology (you scratch my back Syd and I'll scratch yours one day) she was rather aloof and distant. Training in Archaeology and there for that purpose under Syd's wing! I'd learnt, she went to Texas last year to gain some knowledge and by doing so got a position in a university! What really hurt - we paid for it with never a thanks or goodbye!

Both girls were around 20, but very different. Adele is probably somewhere now, an expert! If she did learn anything in those months (and I can't for the life of me think what it could be other than 'How to mope about in the tropics') it could have been, how not to admit you could ever be wrong! For her teacher was one of those breeding that say 'I've only been wrong once in my life, that's when I thought I was wrong, but was right?' His and her field is the perfect place to hold on to such righteous theories, for those that can prove them so wrong are quiet in death!

Thursday 18th September: " No guesses where we went today! Brought up some canister shot still with its packing in tack! Richard was up and with us today. The other team of divers have finished at 3/Sisters and have decided to do some towed searches. The Buckle Geoff found yesterday is Gold!"

This buckle measured about 2"x1l/2" and was highly decorated, something of real workmanship!

Friday 19th September: "Didn't work today, need to give my cuts and abrasions time to heal, John Stubbs did some surveying out on the reef, Brian filming him doing so, Fixed the airlift on the Cat, ready for tomorrow!"

Saturday 20th September: " Gave my sores another day off, Bill, Geoff and Richard out on reef, took Ed Carwithin with them. They found more things in the hole I've been working on, Flea combs - bone, Pair of matching shoe buckles, sheet lead and a 6" mortar with the spout on. Should move the other cannon as it covers artefacts!"

Sunday 21st September: "Bill Curry and Richard on the reef, I'm still too sore to go!"

Monday 22nd September: "Went back to the reef, First job we did was move the large cannon, Found a piece of timber in the hole in good condition, but can't place it from a ship! Pieces of buckles found. Nothing on Syd's whereabouts yet! Heard Graham was arriving Tues - tomorrow! Went to spend the night with Pat and John Rinchick, to leave from there in the morning for the airport, had two flat tyres on the road"

Tuesday 23rd September: "Got up at 03-OOhrs to run in to Panama City. Met Graham and some good excuses, bought some charts, Went round to see 'The Honourable Dean Webster' for a chat. Discussed our problems after with Graham, Dennis and Howard!"

Wednesday 24th September: "Went back to the reef at Salmedina, Found some very nice pieces of Gold, What looks like collar studs, and a small length of chain of some beauty! When I showed Richard - who still is unable to dive, due to his broken finger - which I might add, frustrates the shit out of him! - his eyes lit up, saying the last time one was found like this, it measured 11 feet long, and was sold for 25,000, Made around 1740. Maybe the rest is down there or in the concretion sent to Panama, Also brought up a blue stone, could be from a ring. Two silver buttons a buckle and a wooden section I've been clearing! Good days work - another 5 1/2 hrs. in the water!"

Thursday 25th September: "To rough to work on the reef! Had a meeting with Graham and my Brothers. Still no sign of Syd! Mike went in to Coco Solo about Mercury engines, Came back with them both!"

Friday 26th September: "Back on the reef, Bill found a lovely Gold earring or pendant. Geoff found a lead weight. Nice buckle in perfect condition, Raised two large lumps of concretion - one weighting 200 lbs. and other, 100. In the smaller piece can be seen another nice buckle, Still no sign of Syd!"

Saturday 27th September: "Again out to the reef - only 4 hrs. in the water today. Oscar (Panamanian) found another Gold piece, looks like a rim to a bottle. Lots of musket shot, brass button and piece of buckle, Looks like a bloody shipload of Haberdashers gear went down! Had Ed and Barbara Anderson come out with us! Two more Guardia came yesterday; Luciano has left for a while - trouble with students in Panama City. Probably shot a few!! John and Pat Rinchick, also Henric and Dee Knudsen came down in the evening, Lou Pinson didn't make it!"

We met some lovely people in that area, none more so than these I've just mentioned. John's main pastime was fishing, he lived and breathed it. To earn some money, he worked for the Canal Co, You could always be sure in the back of his transport was a rod, He caught something from 'Jylland's' decks once while 'Just dangling a line over the side' that he couldn't get to the surface. This was in Portobello as we lay at anchor, fought the thing for hours, was it a large Ray or shark, couldn't tell and never did find out for the line gave way. Henric (The Dane) Knudsen, same name as 'Jylland's' past owner, but no relation, worked for a shipping agency, his wife Dee was Panamanian and a lovely girl, always ready to put you up for the night, if ever you were in town.

Louis Pinson was a master Sergeant in the U.S army, we met him due to the fact he was in charge of the Bar on the Base (or what was left of it) in Coco Solo, as I have said before. Through the months he gave us lots of help, even the lone of a pool table for the campsite.

Went out with him one night in Colon, showed me the old haunts once packed with sailors of the U.S navy. As Howard myself and Lou sat one night and watched a floor show in a large but empty bar, Lou pointed out "It was early yet - later maybe the girls will do two numbers, Years ago you wouldn't be able to move in here, didn't matter what time it was either! See those guys?" he said nodding to the band, "They have been playing here as long as I can remember - and for some really beautiful girls too!"

The guys, three black and in their 60's, were brass, drums and Piano. "Just watch em!" said Lou, as if something was about to happen, a girl came on rather shyly and started singing a number in one rhythm, while dancing in another! "Not the girl, the band!" pointed out the sergeant. The fellows were playing a tune they'd probably played a thousand times over, backing as many girls too! They knew the music inside out - right side up and upside down. They didn't have to look at one another or be counted in - it was just a job they'd done over and over again for the last 40 years!

The girls? They mostly came, then and now from South America - Columbia, the main source! There looking for a man or even a husband to take them away from it all. Lou had spoken to a women behind the bar when we first entered. Sitting, sipping a beer and chatting to her like an old friend, This woman was in her mid 40's Lou told us, he knew her when she came here as a young girl, did the same show too. Now runs the place.

The girl on the stage singing finished her number, which I'm certain she'd never heard before in her life, and made way for the next act! "Thank you ladies and gentlemen" said a sleepy drummer - For your delight now, we have all the way from Bogotá - (Little roll on the drums) Rositiaaaaa!" And a dear thing appeared, nearly tripping over an awkward pair of high-heel shoes also to sing a song well known to the band, but of which she hadn't a clue!
Try to imagine "I'm In The Mood For Love" being given a Rumba body reception!

Wherever those girls are now - I do hope they got what they wanted from life, not just what they were after that night in Colon! I shall always remember that place and the man who took us there!

Sunday 28th September: "Didn't go to the reef today, Did a film sequence with Jeremy Green, Took Dennis, Graham and Margarette diving, Helen, William, Sue and Pat round to White beach Swimming! Still no Syd!"

Here appears in my log, the name of Jeremy Green, He just turned up one day, out of the forest with his girlfriend Sue - just the way Richard had predicted. He came with an air that he was in some way, expected! 'You will know him when you see him!' sort of thing - or, he had just got lost for the last two months and had now found us! It seemed that others on the expedition knew him, for he also was in to the Marine Archaeological world. I guess the word had spread of us finding Drake and some wanted to be there at the kill for whatever reasons.

It rather seems there is a love/hate relationship between people in their chosen professions, Mirror, mirror on the wall, so to speak! Love them if they find it – and hate them for finding it before you.

Here also applies as the saying goes "Don't talk bad about another on your way up - for you could well meet him on your way down!"

Syd (Our Leader) was away, and for all we knew had abdicated the throne. Coming down the hot dusty road, was a younger, bearded man - unthreatened too to grab the crown and glory while the older 'Expert' slept.

John Stubbs, Syd's right-hand man, gave the impression he was expected and welcomed him to the camp to stay awhile - and he did, with his girlfriend to eat our food and holiday with our hospitality in the sun!

Personally - I thought Jeremy a likeable fellow and very able in many things. Would work for his food too as the coming days would show. But on the return of Syd some days later, through the smiles and talk between them, one could see and feel the resentment Syd had for this younger intruder - one who maybe, was more apt at his job than he!

I also mentioned on this day a girl called Margarette. She had arrived from Germany a couple of days after Graham! A good friend of his, I was told, one he just wanted to show what he was involved in!

I was to find out the following year just why she had come. Graham had tricked her in to investing some money in the project. That's why he wanted me to take her out to the reef to show her Gold and silver. Didn't tell her though we could not take any of what we found! Poor girl, who earnt her money in the oldest profession on earth, to be rooked by the little shit!

Monday 23th September: "Water too rough to work on the reef! Went to the Carrening cove instead to try air lift in shallows - surprised how well it worked in 6 feet of water, Mud deep here now, not as it was in years past. Did some film of it working, but unable to continue due to fault in camera - magazine sticking it seems! Syd gone now 2 weeks. Richard went to the hospital, came back still with plaster on, Wish more had the mental energy he possesses - be plain sailing!"

Tuesday 30th September: "Had a good day on the reef, after a talk with the boys. Oscar found a lovely Gold ring. Hack money concreted together and bronze object that can't be recognized. More concretion sent to the surface! Dr Reina Torres came down lunchtime and stayed the afternoon. Very pleased with what we're doing! John Rinchick has arranged a fishing trip tomorrow, so those going, went to his place to spend the night as it will be an early start!"

This was only the second time I'd seen Dr Reina Torres, The first was when we arrived back in May! She was Director of the Museum. What I'm sure prompted her interest all of a sudden, was the raising to the surface of Gold. The real indication as to some ones true Archaeological interests!

Wednesday 1st October: "Got up at 04.00hrs and went fishing out on the Falcon Bank, an area about 30 miles due west of Colon, Caught about 3OO lbs. of fish for the pot! Tuna - one 45lb Wahoo and 25lb Barracuda! Syd got back at last. He spent the night at Dean Webster's. Graham leaves tomorrow, so he, Dennis and Howard will speak with him there when they drive to the airport! Lou Pinson picked up the pool table, need it for stock checking - will return it later! While we were away, two small signal guns were brought up off the bottom near the campsite. Jeremy Green seems to have taken charge of that area. On whose orders I don't know, but I think he will do a good job! Bill brought up a sword or dagger handle - looks brass!"

The fishing we did that day, had to be the best I've ever done with rods. A friend of Johns had one of those typical boats loved by Americans, High wheel house above the main one - two chairs on the stern with belts and very comfortable, and very essential when fighting a big one! Those fights can go on for hours, Dennis got the big bite and fought it for quite some time with the skipper backing up, keeping an eye on the line. Then all of a sudden the line went slack! Dennis's face dropped as if he'd just received some disastrous news. What he brought on deck was a head of a Tuna the size of coffee table, cut off as clean as a whistle! What a place to go for a day's fishing! The camp had fish with everything for the next few days.

Thursday 2nd October: "Went out again to the reef, the hole I've been working in is just about cleared out now and all concretion gone to the surface! Two small cannon were found on the southern reef. Graham left today!"

Friday 3rd October: "Had the misfortune of the Cat sinking, Got a bit rough out on the reef, water filled the starboard hull through hatches not fastened down, and in a matter of moments, over she went! Managed to get all diving equipment off before she went down but of course not the large compressor. Towed the Cat to a Bay near Drakes Island and will go about getting it righted. Mike, John and Bill recovered the compressor. Will drag it out tomorrow! Syd returned to the camp today having been gone now 18 days - some leader! Full of praise to all for their efforts - left shortly after for Coco Solo though, grabbed the chance to run and tell Ed what we had done to his Cat!

I guess why so much praise was heaped on us then was that Syd had met Dr Herrena Torres while in Panama on his return. The finding of Gold and Silver by 'His Team' was indeed worthy of some kind words.

Saturday 4th October: "Raised the compressor and righted the Cat, Soon had the machine running. One of the Guardia, (Santana), rushed to hospital having gone too fast in one of the Avon's, Cuts on hand and chest! Syd came and was soon away, Hospital also; Brian Richards has foot problems - John Stubbs with elbow pains! Heard about a wreck down at Maria Chiquita -will check it out!"

The amount of time this so called 'Leader' of the expedition spent at the camp was rather farcical. As for direction - it didn't exist! People were just going about on a day to day basis of - 'Do what you think best' and the real purpose of the expedition - lost! All emphasis seemed directed at wreck sites and what they may reveal!

Sunday 5th October: "No diving today apart from Richard Price taking a team to recover Cat canopy frame. Had a letter from the Governor of St Lucia - Sir Alan Lewis - wishing us luck! With another leading us, it might be of some use!"

Monday 6th October: "Syd in Coco Solo again last night, Returned 10.30 this morning, Jeremy Green took the surface camera apart - might have fixed problem!"

Tuesday 7th October: "Decided we might try and film the Black Christ Festival on the 21st of this month. Need to get something interesting on film apart from fish and forts! That's what Brian and Syd did this morning, filming round the forts. Someone today squirted oil over Jeremy Greens bedding and clothes while we were away - I have my suspicions as to who could do such!"

Wednesday - Thursday - Friday, I spent in Coco Solo trying to get certain supplies for Jylland, for we should be leaving in the near future. Some of her Ratlines needed replacing and small stuff for that job was hard to find! '. On the Thursday, a team checked out the wreck at Maria Chiquita, Brought back some once silver plated 'Apostle' spoons and news they saw 13 cannon down there!

Saturday 11th October: I spent aboard 'Jylland' fixing some gear. Portobello was celebrating the 7th year of this revolution. Any excuse for a chance to party is their motto, and a revolution is as good as any I guess! The countries in South America must be the world's centre for this type of conflict. All to do with the Macho Man image, the big hero on horseback started here.

Sunday 12th October: " Lou Pinson came down today - brought with him beer and food for all. A fellow, Mike Bolton and his wife came down to see us. Mike works for Bob Marx and dived in Port Royal- Jamaica! Had a chat with him! "Shout wreck and Gold David" said Richard "remember!"

I used to live on Scilly. During the dark winter months, a very quiet place to be. Not many visitors around. Not until some poor little lost bird hit the deck, rather than the sea! "My word!" a keen eyed 'Scout' would shout "Isn't that a 'One under Par birdie, what's the hell's he doing here!" (I know I'm getting off the point rather – but bear with me – I shall return.) Soon the word would pass round the country like wildfire that this other rare occurrence on the golf links on Scilly would be seen!

My God! in a matter of days the place was running alive with all types of people, people who seem to be able to take time off from work at the drop of a hat - as if it's written in their contract. All travelling by train, boat and plane to Scilly with the most expensive cameras, wellies and foul weather gear to see this poor little windswept sod!

Back to the point! Before me, sat the same type in the shape of Mike Bolton, Word had got out that their 'Hobby' was found in Panama - Gold and silver! Both he and his wife sat at the table telling of their 'Find's' in Jamaica. How he came upon the treasure in Port Royal Harbour - of the Emeralds from the mud. Some of which now, hung round the neck and wrists of the storytellers set in chain and silver bracelet as a sign of proof to such a story, but of course, one to show the 'Honesty!' of our guest's also!

The time I spent on The Isles Of Scilly, that little nest of islands off the Cornish coast, would, long before I worked on a wreck site, involve me in the meeting of others that would come to those islands in search of another Bird - This one being a Goose - the one that laid the Golden Egg! Around those treacherous rocks lie many a ship that never made it home, some full of great wealth too, like the

'Hollandia' and the 'Association'. Men wearing different suits would dive to the depths, with all manner of ways with them on how to conceal 'The Coin". Both wrecks had much of this on board and divers that worked on them had written on their mind, not on paper, that all were due a share of that wealth over and above their weekly wage or agreement!

One could easily recognize a diver, with arms sleeves rolled up in the local Pub at night; the same sign was on him, though in a different form as the two in Panama. One would think, when you heard another say "He has Divers Wrist's!' that it meant in some way of strength like they say of Jockeys. No their sign was a mark left by the stuffing of the best specimens up wet suit sleeves! The higher the mark, the higher the rouge! Oh yes! ...I can well imagine the temptation. Who would know you say, as for the first time since it sank beneath the waves so many years ago, your hands hold a most beautiful object, an object too, of immense wealth!

The waters are dark and no one can see you, so why not! Finders keepers -What the eye don't see etc, are good old sayings to help fuel the dishonest embers that lie within us all. But once you have sold your soul, you'll spend the rest of your life living like a pimp on its earnings!

Monday 13th and Tuesday 14th October, I spent running around getting gear for 'Jylland', things needed for our passage back to St Lucia!

Wednesday 15th October: "Dean Webster was here to do some filming - talking about the history of the place, we had spoken with him about us filming the coming festival on the 21st. He went with us to see the priest in Portobello - and we got permission to do so! Jeremy Green has been doing some blasting with Verhillio!"As I have said, the Dean was very knowledgeable on this area, He had written a small book in 1970 called ' The Defence Of Portobello' which I found very interesting. He had spent much time on the subject and was keen to share his findings with those who showed interest!

Since 1502 till 1821 this area was the possession of Spain. The harbour at Portobello "Belporto" was first entered by Columbus's son Ferdinand on that date in November, But not until 1597 did the Spanish move from Nombre de Dios to Portobello after an inspection of the area by Bautista Antoneli, an Italian military engineer sent out with Juan de Tejada, Antoneli had been employed by the Spanish to inspect all fortifications and defences in the 'Indies'. Nombre de Dios with its sandy bay was easy to sail in and out for the treasure ships, and likewise for those wishing to attack the place, as Drake and Hawkins had shown in 1585-6 and again in 1595. The place was not easy to defend nor the Royal bullion awaiting shipment! On that ill-fated expedition in which both died, the changeover to Portobello was in progress. The Camino Real (First Road) would now be a somewhat shorter path for the Mules from Panama City to walk. This pathway through the thick rain forest was paved throughout its length, a three-day hike for the traveller, but a week or so for the 200 or more heavily laden Mules!

It is easy to see why so much attention was given to this place by Pirates, when one reads of accounts of what passed through here during the annual Fairs. Wedges of silver like heaps of stones lay in the streets without fear of being stolen. Sugar, tobacco, Alpaca wool and spices. Bulkier goods went to Cruces and down The Chagres river to the fort at its mouth - San Lorenzo. From there by sea to Portobello to await the Merchants from Spain. Some twenty ships, half merchant half Galleon, would come and trading would commence for the next two weeks or more. The Galleons in 1708 carried out 40,000,000 Peso's and as a Peso = 1 oz silver which = 8 Reales (Piece Of Eight) a calculator will tell you just how many tons that was!

Through this wealth, Spain became the powerful nation of Europe through the 16th and 17th century's, much to the envy of their neighbours who spent much time and effort depriving that nation of vast fortunes made on the returns of their investments!

On the subject of the Black Christ festival, we had heard something of this during the days before. Portobello's inhabitants now, I guess, number no more than 2,000 people. We heard that on that day between 30,000 and 70,000 would be here, filming that would or could be rather exciting.
Syd wasn't too keen. I suppose as keen as we were with what we figured he'd captured on film so far. To us, the expedition was soon to finish - Syd long ago resolved himself to the fact that, unless Drake was seen in the bottom of his glass, this expedition was doomed to fail also!

Syd was becoming exhausted with it all, like some trapped Hornet in an upturned glass that was weary of trying to sting all around him, yet couldn't escape from his prison. Yet in some funny way, I was feeling sorry for him now, walking round head rather down with the fire in him going out. Even after all he had said and tried to do - I felt sad for the man! We thought we couldn't lose anything by trying to film this. Reluctantly Syd went along with it!

Thursday 16th October: "Drove to France Field (or was it Francis Field?) to pick up Dennis. Had a talk with Syd about Black Christ film and Graham!!!!! Back to Portobello. Spoke with Syd again - went to town with him - Dennis and Howard, reason? To look over location for shots! Syd's birthday today - had a beer with the old sod later!"

We had learnt from our chat with Syd in the Fort some weeks before (which I'm sure he'd forgotten all about) to be careful of another act - the showing of remorse - the pleading of innocence - passing of all blame, and the showering of praises for all we had done here, was well known to us. Come tomorrow, a new man would appear from his tent, certainly not the one we were now having a beer with. He was singing a song we had heard before - all very familiar were the words and tune, but all as false as the hair on Elton John's head.

We knew this sincere show would be pissed out on the sand by the beer he was now drinking! That any agreement of co-operation he might then give, was as useful as the paper he would wipe his arse on the next morning as he emerged from the only flushing toilet in Portobello. Which, by the way was on our campsite, built by those he sat across the table from.

Yes! Syd was a treacherous old bugger all right, one that lived by the knife, and thought, as they do, behind every tree, stood the one that got away! Any assurances not to hinder our idea of filming the coming event, was taken with a piece of salt. He still held great sway with he that held the camera, threats to ruin what little reputation Brian Richards, or of 'Mango' Chetham had, could easily happen in the quiet of Syd's Bohio.

In the world of his choosing, Syd still had plenty of 'friends' to take care of 'mutinous' members. As for our own standing, whatever shit he'd wished to throw, would be a wasted effort - and Syd knew that! Many a gentleman, with a sack-full on the blackguard, has found to his utter dismay trying to defend himself from a small handful first thrown - what he is carrying over his shoulder, doesn't quite stick like the lump on his back! ---- We'd just have to wait and see what tricks - if any, Syd had up his sleeve for us.

Friday 17th October: "Did some filming aboard Jylland in the morning. Went to Colon and the bank - expected money not there yet. It came later that day, too late to return and draw out! Up to the first of Oct, Graham was $7,800 behind on budget. The first of November another $1,400 is due! He has let us down! Helicopter arrived to do some film shots of us at sea under sail. Wish someone had informed us. They were asked to return tomorrow!"

One can see here, just how organized our expedition was! Helicopter from the Panamanian army turns up - lands at the campsite and we not told what for. It was too late in the day for us to prepare for sailing.

On the mention of moneys being late and behind on the budget - That little shit of a Pop Star Graham, had let us down miserably. We had run out of excuses trying to defend his butt - Syd had every right to be pissed off with his failed promises, but none more so than we!

The only ones to have upheld their side of the promise - and more! Syd would later in England, try to recoup from this man, some which he thought due to him - but had not figured of having to deal with a man with as much honour as that born to himself! For here were two from the same mould. The only slight difference being - Graham was a younger shithead - and could move faster than his opponent!

Saturday 18th October: "Up early to prepare Jylland for sailing. Weighed anchor at 08.00hrs leaving Portobello under sail. Helicopter arrived 10.30hrs - Lot of time wasted by Syd not being here last-night. Arrived to start then organizing things after plans had already been made in his absence!
Same old song! Syd having had his say, then left for -- guess where? ....Yes! Coco Solo, where else!"

Sunday 19th October: "Spent the morning 'Dressing' Jylland for Tuesdays Festival. Howard and the boys are renewing the ratlines! Helicopter returned to do some filming here, and then make a run to the 'San Blas' Islands. My wife Sue and son William went along! This expedition is fast coming to an end. It could have achieved much more had the leadership been motivated better. As for Drakes coffin!.....The most obvious place has still to be searched. Little time has been spent around "Under the rocks where Sir Francis Drake was buried!" That area between Salmedina and Drakes Island. I must try and rally this bunch into one more go at random swim-line searches....and effort!!!!!!"

My frustration that so little time had been spent looking in this area, was very hard to bear. I know it was deep - over 100 feet, and time down there was short. But all seemed right - the depth, where it would be hard to locate this rouge by the Spanish and raise him. The

distance from the town - the island named after him, enough room for the 26 ships to anchor - so why were we not looking there! It seemed as if all had given up, especially our Syd. Only once had we dived in this deep spot, a search on July 28th at 130 feet, so why nothing more? We spent so much wasted effort on hearsay, caused mainly by Syd's offer of $500 to the man who comes up with the right answer! It seemed as if Syd from the outset didn't want to be the man to find Drake - then why come this far you asked yourself!
No discussions, no analysis, no theories, no tactics, no opinions and no direction - just a case of - Well! do as you please attitude - who gives a shit anyway. It prevailed all over the camp! I didn't know then, we would never get back in to the water!

Monday 20th October: "Went to the church in the morning after fixing the lights for filming tomorrow night's scenes! Did some filming in the church of 'The Black Christ' on his carriage! Lots of people arriving now all dressed in purple - walked many miles to get here too! Syd was more of a hindrance than a help.

Guardia riflemen arrived to watch over the camp during this period. Heard that half of those that come to this festival are a bunch of thieves, so we can expect between 15 and 35,000 'tea-leaves' around in the next couple of days!

This figure carved from dark wood, was a present from the city of Cartagena in Spain to its names sake in Colombia. The story goes that the ship carrying it there stopped first in Portobello. On trying to leave the harbour, three times they were unsuccessful due to foul winds. The always-superstitious sailor took this as an omen that something aboard was preventing them from doing so! The finger was pointed at the Christ figure and it was thrown overboard in haste!

It is said it floated ashore to be claimed by those living at Portobello as a sign that is where it was intended to be in the first place. The year was 1658.

During the great plague of Cholera that ravished this area in the 1800's, the people of Portobello prayed to their figure of wood to save them from the death that was sweeping the Americas. It is said that not a soul died, when on the 21st October 1821, it was officially announced the plague was over!

Each year on that day, it is celebrated by thousands who come for whatever reason - by the sounds of it, half to repent their sins, and the other half to make a few! It seemed to me, seeing the many walking in their purple robes, carrying small crosses on their shoulders that these could well be the ones with the most to repent! A few hail Mary's, then all's okay for another years thieving.

This life size figure of Jesus is - for most of the year, kept in a glass case in the Parish church of San Felipe in the town. Now, and for the next couple of days, it stood on the large carriage, for all to see and walk round, while members of the church decorated it for the big day!

People were arriving in greater numbers and the steady stream of Pilgrims on foot filled the square. A mass of long flowing Purple robes walked the streets, or sat taking refreshment on the grass or on the many wooden picnic benches set up for them! The air was full of a strong spicy smell of meat Kebabs as they roasted on the many fires to feed the growing number of disciples. Stalls selling the cool drink for the weary traveller were scattered amongst all - while just as many merchants sold a souvenir, or a gift for Their Saviour upon his carriage inside the church.

It would be to the church that all these worshippers came first after their long walk to go down on bended knee at the open doorway, then to enter the cool darkness in such a fashion. With pained faces from their ordeal, they would approach what they had come to see - then touch his carriage, or say a prayer before him. It was the finishing line to a great Marathon, now they could join the happy throng outside to celebrate that surely 'Jesus' had forgiven them.

Some were in tears, some lay on the benches in San Felipe away from the hot sun, to sleep while a soft breeze blew through the church.

It was to this church that we had brought Brian Richards and Mango with orders to 'Shoot All' – such an order one would not give to the Guardia – just in case! With fingers crossed, and eyes on him that he did so without saying 'Oh Mango!' once, the camera was pointing at a this rather strange scene, one not filmed before.

Two weary men entered looking about to drop from the long walk. They came upon the doorway, and like all before them - fell to their knees! The look of pain was on their faces, and stopping to grimace in agony as they made their way towards the figure on all fours, they gave the impression of a great wrong done, and now the punishment to fit that crime was about to happen!

Slowly, ever so slowly, they made their way, crying for forgiveness - no! Never - never will they do such a thing again, if just this one time they could be shown mercy, their faces said. Boy! How thankful they were when the wooden figure didn't strike them down -- again!

"Did you get that Brian?" Howard asked - "Get what?" said a rather bewildered fellow, who had obviously missed the lot! But why? If the camera had been pointing their way - had he also missed the point why we were there? My fears for the man's competence had long been in doubt, now his common sense worried me.

"Right! Just you stay there!" said my agitated brother pointing to a spot on the floor. " When I tell you -- start filming!" With that Howard went over to the two now lying on the long pews taking a rest, and of course very relieved the Son of God had spared them.

"You will know him when you see him!" and for all they knew, standing above them, talking in what well could have been Jewish, was a stranger. He stood above them pointing his finger to the door, which then beckoned them to follow. Were they being cast from the church? Without protest, they followed, in greater pain now. "Why - is he telling us to get on our knees and enter as before? Was the 'Jesus' not ready for us then - did he want another look at our eyes before making up his mind whether to smite us dead or not?"

Those that came before him a second time were not actors, but real people with a greater fear, one of losing their life - rather than just the part! And this time, Brian did get the shot out of the fear of losing his! But who could tell how good it was. As we had no surface lights, the night-time shots inside the church would have to be done with a lash up! One using the underwater system both Brian and Mango thought were un-necessary. The Teledyne camera Syd had managed to persuade the U.S Navy to give us (hold it - the American taxpayer that should read) didn't need it, so they said! Well of course they were both wrong, and like so many other things connected with this expedition, it was too late to do anything about.

This only lighting we had, we'd run off a portable generator we'd stuck in a back room of the church. Taped heavily at joints to stop the penetration of water, it needed the same to keep the bulbs cool! Only short bursts could we dare to use to lighten up the nights scenes, otherwise we could have a fire on our hands - fire and brimstone - a church in flames - and the whole expedition crucified - Syd - our leader, nailed up after first being made to carry the cross round the town. Thinking about that - no! Someway he would worm his way out of that one. Our dear beloved leader would be behind the crowd and the first to cast stones!

Tuesday 21st October....." Lots of work running about with camera and lighting! Shots in the Church in the afternoon and evening. Many, many thousands of people in candlelight procession following the carriage round the town. Syd giving us more trouble. Scene inside the church at midnight very Pagan! Rather than religious"

Yet again we see here, Syd's interference. The day had started well; all had been motivated into doing their best. The generator had been carried to the church and Guardia were assigned to us to assist in our need to get through the crowds when necessary with equipment. That to these men meant a liberal lashing out with the family heirloom! Passed down from one brute to another the 'Prizzel' is a nasty man's idea for a whip. What was once a Bulls prick, is stretched by hanging a weight to it till around 3' long, and those hit with it say it stings like hell.

The scene in the town that day was one of great excitement. Estimates varied to the number of people there, 40,000 - 60,000, who knew? - a bloody lot is good enough! The whole town was bursting with an eating and drinking crowd, a merriment of white - black and the mixture that comes from both! Cuna Indians with that distinguishable haircut of the native South American had come also, more for the piss-up than for the occasion.

Some of these short but healthy looking men were worse for the wear having had one too many - and one was too many! Drinking is no good for them, as it's not for their northern cousins. It's sad to see such a good-looking man in such a mess!

This area is a very wet place. The average rainfall ranges from between 118 inches to 237 inches a year! When it falls, accompanied with thunder that, with a little imagination, sounds like one is on the lower gun deck of a man-of-war, it comes down so hard you just have to run for cover or drown on your feet!

With us positioned inside the church, taking shots of proceedings, the carriage was being prepared for its parade round the town born on the shoulders of around 40 strong fellows! We had been told - "It has never rained on 'The Black Christ'" yet outside was the storm to prove them wrong - and I, me, would be the first to see it happen!

People who couldn't get in to the church, found cover wherever an overhang of a nearby building afforded it. Packed like Sardines in a can, another broadside of thunder boomed in the torrential downpour! Was this a fanfare from a different trumpet - Could it be

God was dispersing the crowd with his personal hosepipe to make way for his son! No! - surely not-- but wait, is it not easing as the now raised platform is making its way to the door? Has it not stopped? I stood quite amazed for only moments before a betting man would have won, or lost a fortune - it stopped - totally. Without thought for a greater meaning, we grasped it as a sign of a good time to move the Genny and camera before it came down again. So with Guards in front, pricks in hand, a way for us was made, and we rushed to the schoolhouse to set up the only land camera the expedition had.

The second floor was a perfect spot - one we'd picked some days before. Here we would await the passing below us of the mass of people carrying candles behind their Saviour while others prayed at its passing, throwing gifts and money at his feet!

Whether Brian was getting all this on film, was just a matter of wishful thinking, but for now we had to assume he was, and must treat him with kid gloves, for we still had to return at midnight to get the finale. We couldn't afford to upset him, but it seemed Syd was intent on doing so - why? - who knew? I had the feeling Syd hadn't expected this festival to be up to much - and really not worth the effort! Now seeing, maybe he could be wrong, to prove to us he was right in the first place, he'd have to do what he could to sabotage proceedings! "Shut up Syd, and sit down!!" - he didn't like it much - but we were past caring about his feelings.

With the passing of 'The Cristo Negro' below us, and the Genny now back at the church, we could take a break for an hour or two. Still it had not rained, a fact that struck me as I went aboard the schooner for a quick nap. It still wasn't raining when I returned at 23.00hrs and made my way to the church. Would they manage to get back through the crowd by midnight - the deadline! Stops round the town would represent those that Jesus made on his way to be crucified, but the figure must be in the church by then, so we waited! The noise made by that crowd as it entered, was that which came from the mouths of those that watched Christians being fed to the

Lions, that same deafening roar of approval from a crowd watching heretics burn! All the time the camera rolled those of the crowd below us pointed to the lights, now aflame! It mattered little now, let them burn we said, for we had nearly accomplished the last scene! An even greater roar went up, with applause too, as the carriage came to rest. The festival was over for another year, and happy we had done our best we retired to our homes, letting the crowd continue through the night in celebration!

We would do some more filming in the church the following Sunday. A service in thanks for the 21st Oct a beautiful day of peace after that stormy night and the rather fanatical crowd. Sunny was the weather with a fresh breeze blowing through the church. Silhouetted against a bright backdrop stood Nuns singing. Their habits clean and white caught by the wind. A wind that would blow away all traces of the last few days orgy to leave it clean and in peace for another year!

When Howard and I tried, some two years later, to make something of this little film we would be frustrated by lack of expertise in the camera work done by Brian Richards. Shot after shot ruined by either 'Hair on the gate' caused by not cleaning the lens - and the use of 'Flat' batteries making it look like an old Charlie Chaplin movie.

I'm not sure if Syd knew just how amateur one of the 'favoured few' was. If he had, he wouldn't have needed to try too hard to ruin it, for Brian had made a better job of it without him!

We have the short film we made! If it tells one anything, it is - just how much importance to thought Syd gave when selecting the cameraman! A man, one must remember, that was to collect and record the only material we would be allowed to leave Panama with!

Still, right then, I was not aware of the future, of just how bad the work was! We had done all we could, and now it was time to concentrate on our departure - to plan the voyage back to St Lucia and to prepare the schooner for sea!

Wednesday 22nd October: "Went to Coco Solo to get some gear for 'Jylland' - no money in the bank, so couldn't do so! Took Jeremy Green and girlfriend Sue to Colon, they're on their way now to Peru! John Stubbs, Tom Morrow, Mango and Malcolm Dickie went to get customs clearance! Can't see getting anyone back in the water again!"

It was also now plain to see, that indeed the camp had been given orders to break! In the coming days Rolex watches were collected (except one from Brian Richards, who had managed to lose his - only later did I wish I'd lost mine also!!!) and Sandals burnt! Syd pulled the lid over his own coffin, bidding all goodnight with the departing words "Every man for himself!"

Our leaders casket would be born to Panama City to an awaiting Jet with cries coming from within to the Panamanian Soldiers that held him high - "You are all direct descendants to the King of Spain!"

Brian and Mango filming

The Fort

Fort with watch tower close to Portobello

Fort with watch tower close to Portobello

Richard Price. A good Man who led from the Front

Karen Skalsjo. Such a nice girl. A doctor, who later in the expedition became a painter - and totally confused by it all

Brother William

Brother Brian

Jylland at anchor in Portobello

Dr Dean Webster tucking into a crab supper

Mango, Dr Dean Webster, Syd, Rose Widowson, Pat Card and Jeff Terry

Karen, the Doctor come artist

Mango filming at the fort

Brian Richards and Adele St John Wilkes filming Syd Wignall

Chapter 23: To be or not to be - I've forgotten

"Sitting at the table, sat a man deep in thought! His ears were no longer interested in the conversation, nor could his eyes focus on those that were talking. A far cry it was from the atmosphere round the camp than when he first came. The months before had been all fun and games for him, eating, drinking and merriment with the girls, all of which hadn't cost him a penny! Yes - that was his type of party alright!

The point of it all hadn't really concerned him. What it was all in aid of meant little to him either - the benefits from this expedition he would take on the daily basis like the man subbing his wages each day just in case the firm goes bust before the end of the week!

It wasn't Mike's fault that he was a man that knew nothing about loyalty - he'd never known what the word meant! The selfish attitude of doing what was best for Mike, and getting close to those who would afford him such, was not his fault totally! Others inflicted with the same disease that couldn't educate him in 'The Right Thing to Do son!' were just as much to blame. Mike had learnt from an early age how to get what he wanted. He felt no shame in how that was achieved. From crying - sulking - promises and bullying - all stages of his life had born the fruit he desired!

From a family of wealthy store owners in Sheffield whose money helped mould him, came a man who got what he wanted and did what he chose! "No Mike! you are not having a new T.R.7!------- You want it, you'll have to earn it!-----If you go in to the store and work all Sat morning, then we'll talk about it, right son!---now unlock the door and let me in there's a good lad!" Such words ringing in his ears reminded him of how he made his way from childhood to adulthood and what concerned Mike right then was how he would do so again!

Another free meal in front of him bore no taste, as surely as it doesn't for the man condemned to the Gallows. The mind is on survival, looking for a way to escape, no matter what the cost!

To him this had been one long party, one which was drawing to an end - people had already left - making their way home like remnants of Napoleons army! Each with their version of events - minds made up as whom was to blame for the route!

Those talking to him from the table that once held Syd's hopes of glory, had in their pockets, an airline ticket and passport stamped 'This Man May Leave'. Mike could not join in their happy banter - nor, as he had done many times, taken centre stage in such chit-chat! The reasons for that had gone home! His concern was for himself now - totally!

Mike rose from the table and walked out from beneath its canopy of banana leaves. Today he wouldn't eat all his dinner. The day had bothered him from the start! Syd, gathering in Rolex's and unused foot-powder, was done with the charm of a defeated General stripping all rank from the sleeves of his men!

Malcolm Dickie, ex-speedboat driver and supplier of so much free-bees to Syd from the family firm, was treated like the rest of his team now - all had failed him - all were guilty of treachery, talking behind his back and planning his downfall - any sound of laughter now was aimed at him, and with the anger of psychosis in him, Syd sat with the remains of his army, or went to Coco Solo to tell others of the Plot against him! Yes! Mike had to go for a walk, to get some air that would clear his head, make him think straight too!

He walked down the long wooden jetty to sit at the landing stage on the end - his feet resting in his speedboat. Those that had built what he sat on were preparing to leave this place. He had seen the activity of supplies going aboard from the shore, not at any great pace but he knew he might wake one morning to find 'Jylland' gone, a thought at which sent a coldness through him!

There was no feeling of remorse, of guilt in him as he lowered his feet in the water to wash off the remains of his old company. No pride would he have to swallow before assuming his position back on board, for Mike new nothing of such things - if a few tears would have to be shed to get him and his boat back to St Lucia for nothing - then so be it!

It was a good performance, one worthy of a good Thespian too, but really there was no need for such theatricals, my brothers and I have always been ready to forgive and forget - at times to our great cost! Did he really think we would have left there without him? Did the storybook life by which he led read - "And those he had deserted, by the same fate, abandoned him!"

No Mike, we were not such people, we had learnt from a humble upbringing, that to get things done people must stick together, to share the good and the bad times with your friends as you would your family! -- Sadly some forget too easily that hand of friendship - some prefer to take you for a mug instead, rather than return it.
They lose out every time!

Thursday 23rd October: "Got some money through - only half of what we need! Sue, William and Helen leave for England next Tuesday. Found out Syd has been selling some expedition equipment! Doug (American) bought a Bang Stick for $50.00 - and two Rolex watches! I thought they had to be returned!

Friday 24th October: "Spent the day running around for supplies - Pitch for Jylland! Took Sue and the children to Dee's - they will stay there now till they leave!

Saturday 25th October: "Had Ed Carwithen's divers down here today - final test before they pass exams! Should have sent Geoff along to show them how to run under water! Had a couple come down in answer to our request for crew to St Lucia. Gave a Barbeque for locals in the evening at the camp. Expected 60 - about

200 turned up! Don't know where they came from. Lou was a great help!"

This party was to say thanks to the locals for putting up with us. Brian Richards filmed this with the lights used as before in the church - just needed a bit more tape round them! Lou Pinson came that night and showed how to cater for a large group - having done this sort of thing for the Army for all those years!

Sunday 26th October: "Went to the church to film the morning service. Beautiful day - lovely singing! My Helens 1st birthday today, so popped in to see them at Dee and Henrics!

Monday 27th October: "Sues birthday, did some shopping in Colon - little presents for home"

Tuesday 28th October: Sue and the children left for England today. Pat Rinchick gave us a lift to the airport. I returned by bus and then back to the camp!"

The decision for Sue to return home had been a hard one, but news had reached us in a letter on the 23rd Oct, that her stepfather had suddenly died - a heart attack as he sat outside in the front garden. The uncertainty of what lay in store for us after this disastrous episode, also added to that decision to return home.

People's lives are full of 'what ifs' and looking back on it, I could say 'what if' Wilf Phillips hadn't died, would Sue have left, rather than return with us on 'Jylland' to St Lucia, she probably would, but would it have saved a marriage that from that time onwards was in contest with my attentions on another 'Woman' -- 'Jylland!' It can't be answered, for it didn't happen - what did was, that from that time onwards, due to the failure of this expedition and the lack of some contingency plans if it should happen, my life would be controlled in the effort to save one, at the expense of the other!

Wednesday 29th October: "Howard and Dennis in Colon trying to sort things out! Syd back from Panama, said he didn't achieve much there film wise! Will return tomorrow!"

Thursday 30th October: "Things on 'Jylland' running smoothly - Ratline down and changing halyards. Bill Curry making four strop blocks for the Boom guys! Derrick fitted the new bilge pump! Syd went to Panama to do some filming with Dean Webster!"

Friday 31st October: "Went for a run in assault craft to Isla Grande. Wreck there in the last few weeks. Steel yacht went down we'd heard. Lovely trip down there but found nothing of worth aboard! Got back to find Syd had been ranting and raving about us putting air bottles aboard 'Jylland' - Rushed off before we got back, to see Reina Torres - again! Started to water schooner in the afternoon! Lot of rain in the night! Howard and Dennis got back to say money has just come through for the expedition's airfares. Syd has been telling people Graham has refused to pay them!"

Whether or not Syd had in him this streak of Paranoia from birth or that it had been caused by the weather and conditions there is hard to say. Just maybe he was more like the man than the man we never found - it would be interesting to have Syd's chromosomes checked - YYX.. Syd too never had any children - like Drake! What was intolerable was the inconsistency of the man. We knew vicious lies and accusations had been cast at us by him, yet to our face he was as nice as pie!

Here again on this day, while we were away, he starts his ranting with the imagination of a thief that feels all his ill-gotten gains are rightly his, and will protect them against the 'robber' far better than the rightful owner! The continuous whinging program, the running to Reina Torres like some spoilt brat from the playground with his hand in the air shouting 'Miss, guess what!!" was not showing anything other than his lack of leadership!

The wreck we went to check out that day - in which I might add, it being the only time we, and some of his members took time out to dive on anything other than ancient sites! - had gone down some weeks before hitting the cliff face at Isla Grande. Whether he relied on the light at Point Manzannillo to be there, who knows, but he wasn't far out on his navigation if he did! We were told there were guns on board, and this to us was worth checking out! There was no secrecy behind this mission - Syd was aware of it and made no objections! We made that decision to go on the plain understanding and our interpretation of the same orders that governed the whole affair, that of - use your own initiative! Never once did I attend, or was asked to attend a round table of discussions concerning progress reports, or what our leader required of us. I say us because had not Syd, on the fort, in the company of Dean Webster, taken up the offer of the Schooner's crew to help in the underwater search under his direction!? If meetings were held - they were done in secret, with just his 'High Command' present. And if their orders were too top secret for the rest to know, then they did an excellent job in keeping it from us, and he should have commended them for it, not as he later would, condemn all!

Why air bottles were aboard Jylland was simple to answer (had he asked) it was from here we departed for our run to Isla Grande in the early morning - one must ask again the question - why was he so upset at this? Had he already got plans of dispersing them around Coco Solo as he was doing with other pieces of expedition equipment?

His friendship with Ed Carwithen (diver) and the favours he owed him, not to mention the large phone bill he had run up while staying with him would suggest there was some truth in the rumour!

That run to Isla Grande on the morning of the 31st and the dive we had there would be our last off that coast. It was plain to all that this so called expedition was over and like that of Drake and Hawkins, the same squabbles between Wignall and Bonny descended here to destroy any success that could have come out of it!

That run up that coast on a beautiful morning, both craft with engines running smoothly at last, was one I'll always remember. A flat blue sea shining in the morning sun as we sped across it, over the area where much wasted time had been spent underwater in search of Drake between The Three Sisters.

On towards the reef at Garote, the air so sweet and fresh after the heavy rains of late put a new life in your body. Past the reef we ran, across the shallows of sandy bottom that once was land. To seaward of us, small islands that had resisted the sea, lay in groups and as un-inhabited as the thickly forested land to starboard. So shallow was this water our progress was slowed, but only once did we have to lighten the craft of bodies to push her gently across a bank of pure sand before we were back aboard! Engine down and soon on the plane again towards Manzanillo!

We found the wreck eventually, close under the cliff face in a Gully. A mass of steel plates mixed with a shape that told you, this was a yacht at some stage in its life. The area it was in, had something to do with the quick destruction, even on such a calm day as this, a surge in there was so strong that to turn one of her plates all one had to do was pick one end up, and the sea would do the rest. If guns were aboard, we didn't find any! What we did get off her was her anchor and chain, and a load of old junk we later inspected on Jylland to discard overboard there, wondering why the hell we'd bought it back in the first place!

The run back was just as lovely, but spoilt when we heard of the demented wails of our leader!

As for the airfare issue - Syd had again jumped the gun by assumption! That what was about to happen is what one could expect from him, if the roles were reversed! Being that, what he expected to receive was what he would dish out to those who had performed their part so badly! Syd, in such a rush to make his own name in history, spent little time on judging those that might help him climb to such heights. Expedition leaders in the mould of the great Shackleton, that achieved the impossible, was due to their great ability at picking the right men for the job, for he knew his success depended on them, and they who went, being of the same sight, knew theirs lay with him!

Could anyone honestly say, from the team he strung together in Panama, that one could expect Syd to brave the Antarctic seas in winter, to sail 800 miles in the James Caird a mere ships boat! To cross the unknown mountains of South Georgia, in an attempt to save his men stranded on Elephant Island! No! Not our Syd, if it had been up to him, Frank Wild and his lot would still be there - a heap of bones!

Syd had not the ability to pick men or women of the quality needed. Those good ones he had with him, were, more out of luck than judgment. Instead his judgment went on what they could give him, then without thanks, move on to the next provider, cursing the last for not having given more - even if it was all he had!

Dear old Harold Edginton saw what a mess it all was and couldn't wait to get away! And we, for our part knew that had Drake been found, Syd would try and dump us as soon as could be arranged!
This we had seen in early Sept, Dean Webster had told us he had been trying to raise money in the states at the time a certain lead 'Box' had been found! For hadn't the news been 'Leaked'? Was it not then that Syd 'Demanded' signatures from Dennis for money he said was owed him! Had he not had a little 'peek' at his hand before trying blackmail! Had he not flown to the States under the pretext of 'The Bonham Richard' project, to spend two weeks returning in silence on what he had achieved!

Oh! yes, we knew our position all right, If Syd had his way, we had about as much chance of sharing any success in this expedition as the thoughts of a 25lb turkey does at Christmas about planning some new year celebrations! All that is plain now, but in the turmoil of it all then - not apparent!

Saturday 1st November: "Spent the morning clearing the decks of yesterday's rubbish. Carried on with the watering. Started time checks with Chronometer!"

Sunday 2nd November: "Up early to do last of film shots aboard 'Jylland' under sail. Moved Brian Richards in to positions we knew were her best angles for shooting from! Took out people from Coco Solo who had helped us - back at 16.00hrs. All enjoyed it!"

Monday 3rd November: "Worked on Jylland in the morning - had words with Syd. He gave us a list of more things he wants paying for! Howard and I drove to Colon! A message awaited us from Graham - Thus! "Tell those arse-holes and Bastards I've been trying to get in touch with them all weekend!" Howard rang him to ask, not only what he wanted, but not to use such foul language - un-twist his knickers - and to whom was he referring to from the safety of many miles!? It was a series of ultimatums to Mr Wignall! Now all we have to do is pass it on in a more civilized manner!

Graham could be a nasty piece of work - both he and Syd suited one another! The problem was we were stuck between them. Both had lied to us about who promised who what! It was a race between them from the start to see who would beat the other for the skulduggery prize! Just who would have who in the barrel first, hands at throats screaming abuse for domination, while that which the other wanted to stuff him in, rolled down the hill, smashing itself on the rocks below! Bloody fools! Now the fight would intensify further, as an added cause now became vengeance. They would roll around on the legal mat for years - and both come out losers!

Climbing over the backs of others to get where they wanted to go, was their sport! The spotlight of fame they both briefly stood under hatched an ego far greater than their talents! It would become master of feeling and thought! Both now, lay licking their wounds in oblivion! Despised by all in their field of chosen professions!

Tuesday 4th November: "Lot of running around in the morning. Spoke calmly with Syd in Portobello about yesterday's phone call with Graham. Syd agreed to release film in Miami, camera and equipment also if Graham would settle outstanding bills owed to him in England -- once of course they had been checked! It is only right that Graham should do so! Went back to Colon to call Graham. Told him Syd said he'd call Miami and at the same time call his wife Jean, asking her to send his bills on for checking! Graham assured us then; he would settle accounts after checking he was responsible for each! I hope that's the end of it now! Truck came to the campsite to collect Syd's container!"

Wed 5th Nov...."Colon Day- Met Syd outside the Y.M.C.A. Went with him to Dee's house - was there when he phoned Miami and wife Jean in Wales! Took Syd to Ed Carwithen's place - Howard and I drove to Portobello - and again back to Colon. John Stubbs, Tom Morrow and Brian Richards went to Panama to get tickets for home. Syd had asked that they pick him up after at Ed's, but they never showed - could have let him know!"

For Syd to have been left stranded by his two most trusted confidant's any time before this, would have been un-thinkable. John and Brian, with confirmed tickets to safety in their back pockets, could now say "Stuff you Syd, we're having a night to ourselves!" Having to be present while Syd made phone calls was nothing to gloat over for Howard and I. The part of trying to settle the problems between Graham and Syd was very tiresome. Seeing Syd fall from his perch, in spite of what he had done and said in the past months, was all rather sad - a strange thing to say but true.

My brothers and I are not ones to kick people when they're down! It was also odd that, it was us, Howard and I doing the clearing up of the mess - Dennis had taken a back seat in all this now - it was 'Our' schooner again - 'Our' problem. I don't like to say it, but I know it true, that had we found Drake, air tickets would have been in our hands too - and I also believe such perfidious actions by the Three Musketeers, be the very reason we didn't!

Thursday 6th November: "Returned to Colon - met Mike at Ed's- Plymouth needed a new pump. Got one, fixed it and Mike returned to Portobello. Howard and I got some supplies for Jylland. Howard rang Graham to find out if he was satisfied with Syd's call to Miami yesterday. I hope that's the end of phone calls to England"

Friday 7th November: "Finished our shopping in Colon and returned to the camp. The crane that arrived to load Syd's container wasn't man enough for the job. It was down to manpower with the aid of the Plymouth! Syd was not there to see it done - just those he had abused got their shoulder behind this lump to relieve him of a headache!"

For the next week it was a matter of making final arrangements to leave - clearing up the campsite of our existence there! With Syd's container full, that which was left would be sold. Richard Price and Graham (an American crew member recently taken on) took the alloy assault craft to Coco Solo where they were sold to a Fred Clarke along with some air bottles! Howard and Syd stayed together on all these arrangements to see all was fair!

Friday 14th November: " Went to the camp this morning to find a problem! Heard no one could leave the camp by order of the Guardia. A Breach Block has gone missing!

It had been left lying around with some other finds that should have gone to the museum in Panama long ago! Syd said he picked it up - put it in the locker, and from there it vanished! So now here's Lt Virgilio Morones saying we all stay here till it's found. Syd is, as usual, running around like a chicken with its head cut off! Spoke with the Lt calmly and told him our intentions! Got his okay to run in to town! Later, we gave permission to the port Captain and Lt Morones to come aboard the Schooner to look for the missing B/Block! Of course they found nothing! In fact they didn't bother to try hard - Guess they had a good idea it wasn't on here!"

Brother Dennis has booked his flight back to England for Monday - shame he's not coming with us - tried to persuade him, but no good!"

These bronze pieces, of which we found 17 on Salmedina, were the size and shape of a large beer mug, even to the extent of having a handle. This Block was placed in the guns breach, with a wedge driven behind it to hold it in position. They were the earliest form of rapid-firing! This Block was loaded and primed, as were many others ready for close quarter fighting!

Left lying around the camp for ages, in tanks of salt water, the once thought worthless objects were of no interest, not until one of the team told the Panamanian overlords they would fetch something in the region of $300 to $400 each! Only then were they collected and counted - the money factor coming in to play, rather than the historical one!

This little incident could easily get out of hand - knowing whom we were dealing with! Any minute of any hour a team of gun happy chappies could swoop on us and pull the Schooner apart - happy looking for what else we might have stolen! We had already been cast by the Director as the bad boys in this movie! He, that in my opinion who was responsible for its loss, would for sure, under pressure, point his crooked finger again at us!

So what had happened to the missing piece? My mind quickly remembered - it had only been a week before that we'd loaded Syd's container - and Syd, not being there to help in the operation - could not be held responsible for what went aboard if during that procedure if an inspection was made -- clever! So if it is anywhere, I'd bet it's just another 'find' finding its way to room in Wales.

It wasn't until recently (1995 in fact) that I learnt what had happened to the last hoard of artefacts from the Museum we were then re-supplying. Priceless objects in gold, from the days long before the Spanish came to this area, were stuffed in to the bag belonging to the last Curator before he made a quick exit during the last revolution! All he left behind were some Elephant tusks!

If the same idea was on the mind of this new Curator - she might well order in the army to stop us stealing something before she could!
I would love to see if any of those objects we so honestly gave, are still available for the public to view! Not on your Noriega Life?!

Syd knew all this back then, and I guess felt what I feel now - that all that was brought up, would go to make up a nice retirement pension for another!

There is some argument that these 'Lost' objects on the sea-bed, have no rightful owner. That the wearer then, so long ago, probably stole it anyway! Those lovely pieces in gold we found could surely persuade those with such thoughts, that by that same right, what was within their grasp they should grab with both hands!

If I had a second chance, and knew then what I know now, would I have taken the objects I found! It is difficult to say! If they have vanished like the last lot, and in private hands is a most handsome gold shoe buckle - then it should surely be in Geoff's, the finders, than anyone else!

Sat 15th Nov....." Last bits of clearing up to do before we can go! Saw Dennis in Colon to settle up phone bills run up at Pat Rinchicks -$500! All from having to call Graham! Dennis said he'd see that Richard Price and Pat's airfares would be waiting in St Lucia when we arrived! Port Captain came down to give us clearance - first time he's worked on a Sat in Ten years!"

It was a shame Dennis would again refused to come with us - he missed out on so many memorable trips - and would do so again! His long standing girlfriend Pat Card, who he would later marry, did come with us, along with Richard Price, the only man in Syd's team! He had proved time and time again all the qualities that the other men lacked - Had the likes of Richard been leading this expedition - much more would have been achieved!

Sun 16th Nov....." Got back to 'Jylland' in the early morning - had to get out to her by Kiuka (Dug-out canoe) seas being a bit rough. Aggravation still going on ashore about payment of things promised by Syd. Just discontent in general! Lot of rain, which filled our water tanks! Had advice from the British Consulate to leave as soon as possible before they (Guardia) give us any more trouble! Oscar was on board till late - he knew we would be leaving soon, but we couldn't tell him just in case! Oscar was the nicest of all the Panamanians that worked with us! Got the anchor aboard 20.10hrs and departed quietly on a dark night under sail!"

Chapter 24: It's the leaving that matters

It is not the coming that one should be remembered for, but by the way you depart! We had slowly, during the last couple of days, cranked the windlass bringing home the chain, a fathom or so at a time as not to give away our intentions. The night we had decided on, Oscar and his army friend had jumped in to their boat, yet again leaving us in the late hours. Our eyes had shown this was the last time they would meet, so said a farewell under the glow of the cabin light. For months now he had been with us, and though both knew little of the others language, it was an un-necessary requirement to form a friendship. We cast his line off with a wave and the inflatable sped off - to circle us once, as if to take a last look!

All was quiet now, and sure of no more visitors, all lights were extinguished. 'Jylland' now lay invisible from the shore, and any eyes told to watch our movements, would find her black hull impossible to pick out against the backdrop of a darker forest. With our eyes getting some night vision, the small scope of chain left, was brought aboard slowly. Soon we were up and down, and sucking the anchor clear of the thick jelly like mud, the raised staysail turned her for the open sea.

The months spent here would play an important part for such a departure, for we had travelled over its waters so many times and guessed we knew it well enough for leaving when we did - yet still we were alert - eyes straining for the shoreline and ahead for Drakes Island! Once pass that and we knew we were clear, putting some miles between us and Portobello before day broke was important knowing the people we had been dealing with. Visions of an inflatable charging towards us, with orders to stop us, was not beyond reason, what we needed was some sea room and a sea that would make it impossible to catch us in one. Eyes will play tricks on you, and you will see what you want to see, and as all wanted to see - the outline of Drakes Island against the skyline. You have the best forward, those you can trust, for it was upon those who guided the helmsman course as much as the compass.

Though I'd swung the 'Jylland' some weeks before to check for any changes in deviation, and found nothing, relying on an instrument, rather than our eyes here, none would have risked.

We saw it okay, its familiar shape close to starboard as we slipped past it silently - we knew we had plenty of water under us, for we'd been under it plenty of times, but it felt good to get it behind us all the same.

Relaxed, my mind dwelt now on the past. It was a far cry from our 'Coming' some 5 months before, where our arrival was met with a great reception, as if cheering home some conquering heroes! Here we were leaving like a dog with its tail between its legs. Some hero! Not only had we lost a small fortune in this folly, but more important - we lost some dignity!

Syd would later write yet another book - not was it to be on the Best Sellers list, nor was it written by 'Sir Sydney Wignall' about the discovery of Drakes coffin in Portobello! Just a Book! One about Spanish Treasure, with one chapter on The expedition in Panama!

Did he mention in it that the reasons for failure were in any way connected to his leadership! No! --- Nor, in the Nick Watterton case, where with one blow, he wiped out three members of his chosen team did he say a word! Nick, a very clever chap in electronics had brought all the way from England a camera that had it been able to function, would have done all the deep searching in and around Drakes Island - that area of importance! It was not the switch from 240 volts to 110 that was the problem - it was the cycles! Syd had failed to check this out when we paid for him to come out here for such a purpose!

Nick, who had paid his own way, was rewarded for such incompetence by being fired for other reasons, to bury Syd's mistake! And in the fury of a madman, Nick could take his friends with him! Leslie Bruce and John Robinson, for they also were aware of who was responsible for the Cock-up!

Did he mention the only reason Adele St John Wilkes was there was because her father might be able to do him a favour one day!

That Sharn Whitaker was a waitress he had recently met in a restaurant, and a pretty one he wanted so to impress! Sharn was a nice girl - a hard worker who got not a mention.

That the only reason Tom Morrow was there was in return for his father's influence in supplying us with the compressors from the States! Tom gets a nice write up from Syd - even a photo of him underwater too - Dad will be very impressed and well satisfied for his contribution.

Did he write down that he convinced Brian Richards there was nothing to filming - once you can use one camera, you can use the lot!

Was there any mention that he who pick's a man who likes to introduce himself by a nickname of 'Mango, must himself be questioned? John Chetham now refers himself as "Hello I'm - Oh! Mango". Another handle given him by his partner Brian for failing to keep camera batteries charged!

Of John Stubbs, his right hand man - a man willing to stick his head in the sand rather than face the truth. His position was - "I am a nice fellow - please leave me that way!"

Had Syd realized his true potential, that of a getter! thing's would have been different. Syd was good - nay great in getting!
Get people to give things - Get it organized! - Get some commitment! - Get in to Countries! - Get out of countries - Get on the phone! - Get on the T.V! But unfortunately, the getting didn't stop there - and should read - Getting a good leader!! Then - getting his arse out of the way, so that those that have been got can get on with it!   But he would continue the getting okay, in a different way --- Getting people upset - Getting easily annoyed - Getting to ranting and raving - Getting Paranoid - Getting to set others against each other - Get the Gin out   The last, and most annoying 'Get' of all with this man is -- that he gets to sit down and write about it! Getting all the praise!

I haven't seen Syd since. Even after all he didn't achieve - and blamed us for - we were willing to help him in his case against Herr Graham Bonney! For Graham was to us, just as responsible for the failure! But I guess Syd thought it a waste of time - and I can tell him it would have been - Graham Bradley has had more people looking for him, than looking for Drake.

No! The last I heard of Syd (Before his latest Blockbuster) was, a program on T.V about some expedition being organized to find The Loch Ness Monster – again!   The team were to use Micro-light aircraft - swooping down from the surrounding hills the very moment of a sighting! Cameras ready in hands - divers would plunge in the water alongside the beast and prove, once and for all -

that Scotsmen! - After a bottle of a fine malt! - not only like to recite Robbie Burns - and long to settle old scores with their Sassenach 'Bastards!' down south! - but also on such nights see strange things floating ore' the wa'er!............. after which, follow them to bed, to change in to Elephants, pinkish in colour too, climbing up walls!!

This sort of expedition sounded just up Syd's street - and it was him I was told, trying to get it together! Yet another chance to get a good story I suppose. I just wondered who was going to be thrown in the water from a fast moving Micro-light - Brian or Mango??

Some 30 years after that little event in Panama, I was given a book written by Syd called 'In search of Spanish Treasure'. I found it difficult to read for the contents were so far from the truth it hurt! I sat wondering, was he the same Syd I knew - for it was pretty obvious that this author was never there! It was only then I realized after looking in to my own logs and memory of events the truth! He wasn't - it was all made up - or based on hearsay!

He blamed all but himself on its failure and praised all could do him harm.

He stole their limelight - he cheated them of any leadership - and the hand that should have been in control, pointed its fingers at others why it failed.

On page 182 his wild utterings are insulting to the man Henric Knudsen - the man we purchased 'Jylland' from. Syd's account - quote " ...where she lay derelict, without masts, on a beach in Denmark." Such a lie - if ever Henric read such nonsense - entangles us all in his web of deceit.

His whole account of that ill-fated expedition is flawed! Photographs can't lie - but captions can! 'Whose origin remained unidentified' referring to Drakes false coffin on page 206. At the time he wrote his book - he was fully aware of what it was! WE DID the moment it was raised!!!! He repeats his lie on page 176.

'Poor boat handling' he claims for the photo on page 156! Look on page 144! One can soon notice how low the cat sits in the water! Hatch covers on the starboard side were loose - no way of fastening them down without nailing. Something Ed Carwithen might not have liked. A sloppy sea as we shipped our mooring buoy on Salmedina Reef - filled that hull in moments - how do I know? I was there - unlike Syd.

Page 166. Note there are but 15 Bronze breech blocks in this photo. We found 17 on a wreck site that Syd claimed on page 212 - he knew was there - quote "I knew that a Spanish galleon had struck the reef in 1746!" On that same page he writes - quote "was solved when three of the Hamber brothers decided to learn to dive in order to fill my depleted ranks. Thus Howard, David and William Hamber --- etc.!" Syd knew as much about our abilities as he knew about that wreck site. William was not there at that time - but another William was - Bill Curry. Who never got a mention for all his hard work.

A tunnel indeed on page 215 - 'one which we liken to those dug by escaping prisoners of war in world war two' What a load of crap! I could go on - and on, but I'm breathless!

Just one last thought - I just wonder where Dr Reina Torres de Arauz is today. The last director of the Panama Museums fled with all he could carry!

Chapter 25: Panama to St Lucia

The San Blas coast was but a day's sailing time from Portobello, and once we had cleared the harbour we set our course for it. In the clear waters we knew were there, and anchored under the lee of one of those islands we could dive on the hull. A small leak needed to be checked round one of the skin fittings before pushing on further. We had heard how lovely that area was - a clutter of islands of sand, brush and coconut trees. It was just too close to pass without a look, leak or no leak!

Drake had lived among these islands in the 1672/3 expeditions - raiding Spanish vessels whenever the chance arose. Once inhabited by the Cueva Indians they - since the early 17th century have been occupied by the Cuna who came from the mainland Drake became friendly with them, as did others who used them as guides in attacks against the Spanish! Rather a warlike little bunch and after their treatment by the Spanish - thanks to them came when in 1726/7 they destroyed every Spanish settlement in The Darien!

Our course through the night would be 115 degrees compass. With the wind WSW force 3. At 06.30hrs we changed this heading to 150 compass - the log reading 38miles. By that time people in Portobello would be rising. Some would be looking out and saying "The schooner - it is gone!" -- some might even be saying later - "Fancy that, they didn't even say goodbye –well, well, well!!!" And sadly, we could never explain why!

The decision we had made was to head for the most eastern end of this chain of islands known as the Holandes Cays. Those to the west were inhabited and our fear was our arrival there might get back to the Panamanians. The San Blas come under that flag, and a flag that some might think we have insulted. Angry people don't listen to reason, and the main reason for our wish to stop could well be misinterpreted under the circumstances. Slip in quietly, get the job done, and hopefully leave un-observed was our intention. Little did we know that others eyes were watching us in those early hours!

It was on the morning of the 17th of November that we saw to the south a chain of islands low on the horizon. White water breaking to seaward told of a reef we must clear. We skirted these looking for a break - one had to be there. We had charts - but nothing in detail of this area - it was a good man aloft now and one to steer us towards an open passage. There it was - no white water - just the deep blue of the channel and in a matter of moments 'Jylland' was slipping across a calm sea under power. At 10.10hrs we dropped anchor in three fathoms in the lee of a small group of islands - the nearest but a stone's throw away!

Stretching to the west lay a string of these Cays, all of different sizes, and shapes. The biggest no more than that of a football pitch, all covered with coconut trees - some with a sprinkling of thicker brush. The one directly in front of us was no more than 30 paces across - and round! The perfect island from stories of the South Seas, just as perfect as one imagined one to be. Coconut trees were growing close to the water's edge, due to the very low tides in these latitudes.

All we could see were un-inhabited - not a sign of a soul around but us! There we were, anchored in the clearest water in the most beautiful setting unchanged since Drake was here and long before him! Everything was clean and clear - the sky - the sea - the pureness of green - the blue and the yellow sand. When there does not exist such places as this on earth for people to gaze on as we did then, the un-touched beauty, a beauty that outshines all the so called wonders achieved by man, then man will have stolen from their children the chance to appreciate perfection.

I dived on the hull in the afternoon to inspect the after toilet skin fitting - it was as suspected, leaking! It would have to be fixed before we left - also a check on the whole hull before we could depart on the haul to windward.

I never expected then, diving on 'Jylland's' hull would in the years ahead, become a daily routine for myself and for the crew that could don the suit. This slight leak on a skin fitting would be by comparison trivial to what we would experience in the future - it was to be the start of a five year apprenticeship of an underwater shipwright - specializing in the 'Leaks' department.

"I think we've got company!" said a voice as we sat there in the afternoon sun relaxing for the first time in months. Heads shot up for obvious reasons, but it was not what some expected. Far behind us was a small sail, each tack bringing it closer and clearer as it beat towards us. Soon the naked eye could make out the Spritsail rig and that of a lone sailor aboard his dugout Kiuka!

"Here comes someone ready to barter" you said "Someone ready to slog against the wind to his fishing ground with the patience of expectancy driving him on - knowing the run home with his catch would prove his good judgment." "Get up the old rope boys, here comes our Lobster dinner!"

During a period of rigging new halyards in Portobello, we had been told by some locals "Don't throw away any old rope - if you do go to the San Blas - exchange it for lobster with the Cuna"

So now being thrown up on deck was that which we intended to barter with - and by the looks of another tack - would have the Indian alongside. Displayed before him - as irresistible as 'Hawks Bells' - the finest cordage in the realm! The thought 'Frying tonight' and full of buttered Crayfish, we watched from the taffrail our fisherman coming in for the kill!

I was really quite amused at the way he came alongside and the ability he showed in handling his awkward craft. He was aboard in a moment and sat on the handrail just looking, the sail on his Kiuka still raised, shivering in the breeze just in case his coming might not be one of welcome and a quick departure envisaged.
.
The hairstyle of all these Indians, women and men, is the same. The black shiny locks that cover the ears are cut in a fringe at the eyes. Skin is olive colour and seems totally unaffected by the sun!

Before us sat a man in his mid-twenties - untouched by the modern world - unchanged in appearance since the days his ancestors helped freebooters like Capt John Coxon who in 1680 attacked the Spanish gold mines on the Pacific shore, or assist Drake in his quest for riches and fame. All that came, left free to leave with that which would help create our modern world.

What wisdom told them, that to have hoarded their share of that which the white man craves after - would give them no peace? That just as surely on some dark night their throats would be cut like that of the Spanish - cut for 15% by their merciless friends. No! --- here was the pure example of the naked man, one who can walk un-afraid down a street full of pick-pockets and cut-throats and come out the other end alive. He that has nothing to steal, or nowhere to hide that which was not his!

There, sitting on our schooner was the son of a greater intelligence, someone surrounded by real jewels - and still living in Eden. While the rest of us lock our doors - safes, and bank our wealth to hide it from a bunch of thieves and Pirates, sat what God intended us to be!

It was time to parley! - "Get Ben!" Ben, an American taken on to help on the trip back to St Lucia, spoke pretty good Spanish, so would do the interpreting! - "Tell him Ben, if he gets us lobster! Mucho - Mucho! then all this fine rope he sees before him will be his! That when he returns to his village, his people will sing his praises, ones that will continue round the campfires long after he is gone to the happy hunting ground - tell him Ben - tell him!"

I don't think the translation went quite like that - and by the way he moved slowly off his butt to look over what we had on offer, he gave me the impression he didn't give a shit about the happy hunting ground - or being spoken of long after he'd dropped off the old perch!

I started to worry a bit about our dinner by the way he picked up the coils - opened up the lay and threw them back on the hatch. This fellow knew more than we'd given him credit for and the one Spanish phrase he said to Ben, didn't need to be translated - "CRAP" is crap in any language! Thus spoken he resumed his seat on the rail - puffing on the bribe of a cigar we'd given him earlier!

We had showed our hand, he had seen our need for Lobster by the way we'd bothered to save such crap rather than tossing it over the side! We had even gone to the bother of having it ready on display - such was our desire for some spiny creatures. No! - he'll play this one real cool like - give no sign he wants anything really - just popped by to say hello like all friendly Cuna do!!! He had noticed something though - something we were unaware of at the time. An old sail was the focus of his attention - not one from the schooner but something from a smaller vessel. . We use it for covering up the Boston whaler when touching up the hull. Apart from a few splashes here and there, the sail we'd recovered from a wreck was in good shape. We knew that - so did our Indian after testing it with a few hard jerks! "He will get us Lobster for the sail" said Ben. With our appetite back for some seafood - we struck a deal!

Springing in his dugout, he continued a course to windward, its sailor handling his craft with ease in the good breeze. Between the islands ahead of us making for the reef went our Cuna and in his boat, all he would need to sow up the deal -- Bow and arrows, or the long spear with its barbed end.

It hardly seemed to me more than ten minutes before the shout went up "Here he comes!" and coming he was too with the wind up his tail. Rounding himself up alongside, we could now peer down upon our dinner - seven large Crayfish flew over the rail to thump on the deck - followed closely by the pitcher. Either this fellow was some mighty good fisherman or there were a hell of a lot of Crayfish on that reef!

His last action before he was gone was perfect - with the sail rolled up under his arm, he went back to that heap of crap picking up a coil. He would take it off our hands according to Ben - all of it!! Running before a good breeze was the last I saw of him - probably laughing to himself - free as a bird and far better at bartering than us! The tale round the old camp fire that night would well be at our expense - drowned by Cuna laughter about looking dumb to the dumb and how it bears fruit to be so!

The sight of the lobster on the deck, and the speed in which he got them, made us anxious to go check the area out! So in a much shorter time than our Indian had taken - we were upon the reef. We caught another six beauties in a matter of minutes in water so shallow you could stand up in it! It was like picking apples off a tree - our friend must have thought us very lazy - or very daft! Lobster is all we ate that night - too much really!

I awoke early the next morning. A bed on deck under the awnings was the only spot to taste the atmosphere! The day had not broken, and through the islands shone an orange moon - not a white one you see on a winter's night in northern climates - but a warm moon of the tropics. Not a breath of wind as 'Jylland' lay on her chain. Slowly I watched the day break - the orange light changing to deep red as the sun made a move upon the horizon. It was just the distant hills of the coast blocking out its view for the moment. Every minute islands once invisible appeared down that archipelago. Take it all in I said to myself - for I shall soon be gone from this place - maybe never to return - so look and remember!

Our first job that day was to complete the hull - stem the small flow of water entering round the skin fitting. Two patches were applied and all was now ready for a departure!

"What's this - our friend returning!" said a voice. The sight of a sail and its rig suggested it could be the case. The glasses though showed more than one aboard, five heads at least sat in the dug-out - brought his family no doubt to view the 'Lazy Ones'. Creeping up behind them and blotting out the coastline was a rainsquall - one of those that can fill your water tanks in minutes - so what was going to reach us first, the Indians or the rain?

The Cuna family did, but only just, and it was not our friend after all. Leaving the ladies and children in the Kiuka the two men came aboard fast before the squall hit. Father and son? - could be! With the rain now upon us, and falling as it does in these parts, we in the shelter of the awnings were rather concerned about those left in the dug-out - not that it seemed to concern the men-folk. Cowering under the cover of modern Polythene was a much older tradition - two ladies and their two mites quietly accepting their role laid down for them by men a thousand years ago! "Tell them to get people aboard Ben?" we said. Very reluctantly, and after much calling and beckoning of hands, the children were passed up, followed by a shy mother and what we believed to be her daughter - she looked too young to be married!

The love for bright colours, as with all Indians - is apparent with the women. Coloured beads round ankles, wrists and neck are worn. Round the waist was tied a sarong, mauve with a gold thread in its weave. This same material is on the sleeve of the blouse and also in the head-dress. . The blouse bodice is made of many small different coloured cloths - stitched together to form shapes of birds - animals or signs long forgotten. Some wear gold - as rings through their noses - or on their arms - safe to do so now - the fear of those that cut off arms and heads for it has passed - for now!

Under the arms of the ladies, was what they had come to trade with, Molas, the name given to the coloured patchwork of cloth. Feeling at ease with us, they laid on the hatches the hard work of many hours with needle and thread done by a grandparent, for they were old! For $2 00 I bought a whole outfit of their dress to fit a young girl. – a second or third generation one - but bright and clean - the Molars where on the garment still - not stripped off and sold as they do when they travel to Colon. There is quite a trade in the Canal Zone of Cuna handy-work - Molas in particular! They range in price from two to twenty dollars each, depending on age and quality of stitch-work. Most of the older ones being the finest - many today are just made for the tourist and with that in mind the women's work is not so fine, nor likely to be worn with pride by a loved child. Sold now to be framed as a conversation piece for the worldly traveller.

They sold what they had and stood smiling and happy. The squall had left and before they departed, we asked them to pose for a picture. These people have a shyness of such things - a certain fear - is it the fear of the spirit world, seeing their faces appear on paper - or facing the lens, the one that resembles the barrel of a gun? "Stand still, I would like to take a shot at/of you!" Having a Polaroid on-board, a cast off from our filming days, someone took a shot and passed them the blank sheet! The look on their faces as, before their eyes appeared the very image of those they knew, it was amusing, each one laughing and pointing at the other. We found a zip-lock bag, placed the photos in and handed them as a parting gift. Clutching it, the family left happy running before a good breeze!

Employed by the expedition back at Portobello, was Emanuel. Dennis, my brother, always one for things to be spick and span, had given him the job of raking the beach area round the campsite, and in general, to keep things tidy. Emanuel, like many that lived in the area, was of Negro origin. The first of which were brought over by the Spanish sometime after its first discovery. Those that escaped their brutal masters, set up communities in the forest and along the coastline once enjoyed by the Cueva Indians, the original owners. Once in great numbers, they disappeared - probably worked to death - as did many before them under such masters!

Called Cimarrones, these Negro slaves, now free, helped Drake attack Mule trains loaded with treasure crossing the Isthmus to Nombre-de-Dios in 1572/3. In the ensuing years, the Spanish - knowing full well the cost of having such rebellious people ready to take sides of any that should come to attack their treasure routes - made a move against them, burning their villages to bring them to the negotiating table. The thick forest made such a move impossible. In 1579 a treaty was signed so that when Drake returned in 1595 he found a settled people, a people with their freedom recognized, brave and loyal to his Spanish Majesty.

Whether or not Emanuel's ancestry went back that far, not even he knew for certain - but from Africa he certainly was.

Richard Price, who had made for him a Kiuka (Cost-$40.00 U.S) asked Emanuel once, "Why don't you (the Negro's) sail your Kiuka's like the Cuna!" - "Why!" was the reply "Because they never taught us!" They used instead, as they had for a thousand years before - the paddle!

Emanuel was a nice fellow, loved fishing. Once a large Turtle came ashore close to the campsite - before it could get back to the open sea he was on it, and it came ashore - dead. The locals were coming down with wheelbarrows to carry off its meat - of course, leaving some for us to try - as we did and to realize after, why its meat is so much admired by those that live here!

Richard - who was one of the last to leave the campsite, arose one morning to make the early rounds, entering the toilet, facing him was an empty spot where once he sat contemplating life! Emanuel, fearful others would have taken it before him, had taken it home. Whether he knew about the need to plumb it in I don't know - but if he did, many an admiring eye would have seen him on his throne. Portobello had no running water you see – nor any sewage system! We had created both at the camp – water came from two large storage tanks held on platforms above – Emanuel had left those!

I sat watching the Cuna family pushing on to the west, with their skill and a few Dollars in the pockets. Soon though, they would be wet, and gone forever from my view (but never my memory) for coming again was a black cloud loaded to the gunwhales with water. It was upon us in a mighty rush and the opportunity to get the salt from our bodies was taken. The power of the rain falling that day actually hurt - stinging the skin. Trying to apply a little soap was waste of time; it was washed from your body to lather on the deck, hosed down towards the scuppers in a rush! The 15-minute shower cleared our heads, and fresh, we thought it time to leave this little corner of Paradise. Oh! I could have stayed alright, part of me is still there I guess - the un-westernized part before so-called civilization caught me!

With a flat sea and the time at 16.00hrs on the 18th November 1975, we raised anchor and left. Our course was set for Cartagena - Colombia!

To leave such a place as this, I did with reluctance! I loved the solitude that allows a mind to dwell on the greater importance. The pureness of the sky, the sea and its people. A people that live but a few miles from the sea-lanes of the modern world, yet are unconcerned and untouched by the rush for dominance and power. Two worlds do exist - and while those that live beyond the two tropics speed onwards towards the abyss, there still lies pockets of resistance inside the arc of the sun.

I for one crave little for what the industrial society thrusts upon us, nor is the voice heard that cries, No More! For above the tropic of Cancer and below that of Capricorn, still lies the attitude of the Pirate!

I watched from the stern of our schooner the islands dip below the horizon far too quickly. How odd, that just a day and a half can leave such a lasting impression. Why? It can only be its remoteness - the undisturbed beauty of a never changing face. We were now alone on the Ocean, there was no point to look back and wish, but pull one's eyes away. My destiny lay elsewhere!

For us, the passage to Cartagena would take a day and a half to cover the 176 miles, mostly under engine through lack of wind. The sea was flat calm reflecting a lovely moonlight that first night. Fixed our position at 06.00hrs on the 19th at N9-50' W77-22' - Course 072 compass. The wind came light out of the North and all sail was hoisted at 08.45hrs.
With an increase in its strength 2/3 and backing to the N.N.W we secured the engine at 13.30hrs.

With the wind up and down in its force from that quarter, we sailed till it fell away completely at 22.00hrs, having covered only 27 miles in 8 hours - but who cared about speed on such a day, only those I guess who wish to be elsewhere.

I would remember some years later such a person. We were returning on one of our day trips from Anguilla - the afternoon saw the winds light and working her back to the anchorage in Marigot Bay - St Martin, was all concentration without an engine. This part of it I enjoyed, as did all the passengers we had aboard - bar one - and there is always one! He continually kept looking at his watch and asking some of the crew - "How long before we get back?" - then would slump down next to his wife to ruin her day with a bollocking for pulling him along on the trip.

'To return approximately at 16.00 hrs' it had said on the Brochure - and though it was obvious we wouldn't be back early, we would certainly meet the approximate requirement.
Up again he got, leaving his wife lying back on the sun bed. Hands on rail looking ahead - then at his watch - then at the water - then back at his wife. Today was just not his day!
His dress suggested that of 'Good time boy' - clean white short sleeved shirt - shorts to match with a fancy trim and white slip-on shoes. A large gold watch, a ring and chain necklace hung from the body that later in the evening would be life and soul of the party round the bar

We were making way - just, but not fast enough for the American go-getter. Even if I could have started the engine, I wouldn't have (it was out of commission at the time) spoilt the party for those asleep on deck just for one miserable sod.

"David!" I said to our engineer sitting on the taffrail - "Find out what his problem is?" He returned to say our friend must be back to the hotel to receive a phone call from New York by 17.00hrs. - broker business, a deal of some sort and very important it was to his happiness in life on this earth! "Well David, get the whaler and run him and whoever else is unhappy with life ashore!" He was the only taker - phone call to New York eh? - We should have dumped him over the side just to prove the point he might well raise later while under the influence when saying --- "I could swam faster than da fricking boat!" -----

'Fricking'!!! now there's a word that amuses me - used by Americans and is acceptable in certain quarters of their society other than what they really mean - 'Fucking'. Now some might say "Oh no - the word is 'Frigging' - Frigg, the wife of Odin and goddess of heaven, might be offended that her name was used in vain! - but fricking - there is no such word - accept by the remnants of a Puritan society who shudder at the thought of using the real wording.

Back to sea!

We fired up the engine and lowered all sail for the wind had gone completely. At 23.45hrs Isla Tesoro was seen fine on the starboard bow. At O5.00hrs on the 20th November 1975 we dropped anchor in the inner harbour of Cartagena!

It seemed we had cured the leak in the hull - bilge checks every watch showed little sign of water a factor that would decide which course to take when we left here. Were we to follow the coast to Aruba - Caracas then north?- or Jamaica - Haiti - Puerto Rico then south. We would decide that in the next couple of days - but for now it was get alongside the Yacht Club for water and Diesel. At 09.00 we went stern-to - got squared away and some of the crew deciding to take a tour of the town.

This city, once the strongholds of Spanish dominance in the Caribbean, has changed little in appearance - at a guess - in 300 years. The walls that ring the town and the heavy batteries to defend this part of the Spanish realm are still in prominence. Now, masses of gaily painted buses ply back and forth to the surrounding villages bringing people and produce to the huge market area. The amount of produce is staggering, fruit and vegetables piled upon stalls - much of which lies on the ground. The earth is obviously very fertile in these parts so allows its inhabitants an indolent lifestyle. The air had a smell, one that in such an environment is just as ancient - one of dust, sweat and a pungent urine mixture. Gone suddenly, as the breeze brought the only relief - the smell of cooking Kebabs!

This place, once built to keep out thieves, is alive with them (nothing has changed - just a different thief!) again the only man safe is he that is naked - but would be so in Jail. Anyone walking the street wearing gold or anything of any value, would have it snatched and gone in a flash is the artful dodger. Money, if carried, should be spread about and never in the back pocket - tight arse jeans can give the whereabouts of a single note to a trained eye! If you happen to see a thief - and are the type that likes to give chase - you could end up dead or in hospital - for waiting to block your pursuit is a knife, aimed by an accomplice for that very reason - just like ol' Panama.

Moneychangers are in abundance, ready to give you a far better exchange rate than any bank. Mike was the one to fall for that one. "I saw him count it out in my hand!" said one trickster about another. "One note at a time - how he did it baffles me!" went on he that was caught by greedy motives by a man who knew how to pick his prey. The sleight of hand trick had caught Mike, but he was not streetwise to see it, nor poor enough to check his change!

I knew Mike, and I honestly liked him, but what I found in him was a lack of sincerity, of open honesty with those around him. I would not say he would lie about things but the character role he portrayed deceived you from the truth.

The case of the moneychanger is but a pure example. Some weeks before, and obviously Mike had forgotten - he had pleaded poverty - that he had been ostracized by his family for leaving the business - cut off from his inheritance by choosing to go his own way. "Come share our food Mike!" - we had said "Don't worry about it - we'll get you back!" With the rest of us having to watch the budget for what could be a long haul back to St Lucia - here is our pauper with money to change - and, not too concerned about the swindle! Such actions drove him from our hearts for the 'All for one and one for all' meant nothing to him!

Hindsight I guess is what makes older people turn cynical, especially those who have been taken for a ride time and time again! My father used to say, whenever there's a knock at the door, you can bet on it someone wants something - never to see how you are or - can I do anything for you today Mr Hamber? I don't like to be associated with any party - club - organization - church - it is hypocrisy run by the best of hypocrites.

There's a statue in this city, one of a large pair of boots. Under it is written "I love Cartagena as much as I love my old boots" This old explorer had no doubt visited 'The Las Vegas' club! We had gone in for a beer after dinner and just like Colon, every bar one enters sits a nest of ladies ready to partake in some fornication. No messing - no small talk - no foreplay - hands go straight to the point - that being your balls not your wallet! By this very short leash, they will lead you to the bar - table or upstairs!

Trying to 'Chat-up' foreigners is not a problem for them. It's done with a certain 'feel' for things that are more important than words for the male - and female!   Prices range from $40.00 for those with the cash - to those without though, goes the Christmas ditty ---- "If you haven't got a penny a ha'penny will do, if you haven't got a ha'penny, then I'll fuck you!" - that's only if they like you though - we would have to be liked a lot.

Now 'Jylland' carried many things on board - but one was not a dispensary! An itching crutch and other lower part problems was something not really wise to leave these shores with, but we were men - not wise men, like those that follow stars or read books on seaport diseases - just men, more handsome by the look of those that sat there with a few bucks to spare and plain Jane at home.

Imagine, if your able to in this think alike world, a group of girls sitting at the bar expecting another bleak night. The weekend was still a couple of days away before things might liven up, so they sat chatting and laughing - mainly at the expense of stupid man. There ages ranged between 15 and early 20's - some maybe younger, but it didn't matter - the rule was - 'If you're big enough - you're old enough - and the sooner you're big enough the better for you'll have more years at work than the late starter.'

Looking around them for customers was a waste of time, the few there they knew well - they could grab their own balls for a change - they also knew it was their only asset they could put their hands on right then - no! - they would have to wait till they could rub together something other than two hot balls. Certain it was going to be a slow night the door opens - and bingo!!! In walks, not one - not two - but seven good-looking tall (compared to them) 'Americanos' to buy a beer! Why all seemed to have lost their way in the night - and come with that appealing look of 'Help me' innocence. "Bloody Columba!" was the cry. OH yes, we were liked all right!

There is another statue in this city, this one is the lovely form of a naked girl - a single feather in her hair held by a headband to tell us the bronze work of art is an Indian girl. Dancing in front of me to the tune of 'Mexico! Mexico-o was that statue, thighs like Tina Turner that held the figure of a beautiful maiden. No schooling could train such seduction - this was straight from the heart stuff - thousands of years old stuff and danced with one purpose only - to continue those raw gyrations on a worn out bed! The price of a man's soul right then was $40.00, but Satan wasn't around to sell oneself to - I found out later - too late, I wouldn't have needed to sell my soul!

That first night in there set the standard for the next, as round our table came the girls for a laugh - a chat and no business. They'd guessed right - we had little cash - and morally banned from paying for sex! Get rid of all that and underneath you'll find a person with other things on her mind. How easy it is for the morally righteous to condemn the actions of these girls. Not educated to earn a living by other means - but earn one they must. Just to live or support a family who must turn a blind eye to how their daughter earns a living.

The standards, under which her ancestors were raised, were set long ago by those that came here with a sword in one hand and a Bible in the other. The Roman Catholic priests would demand from their 'Children' payments to support a greater house - never to question or reject a dishonest donation - but instead bless the child who gave the most.

Here, as in all the areas that suffered under the purge of so called Christian ideals lies the symbol by which all those false prophets earn their dishonest living - perpetrators of a prostitution that use the Lords name to pimp by!!

I read some years later, a ship un-loading containers in St Martin, heard crying coming from within one crate. Upon opening, inside were found girls, most dead from the suffocating heat from the passage from Columbia. These poor pretty girls are much in demand to fill the whorehouses - some I guess might have been bound for the Japanese Club on the Dutch half of this island - ironically once a chapel! - I thought about those I'd sat and laughed with when I heard the news. I prayed it wasn't the Indian Princess or any of her friends that suffered in such terrible circumstances. I would bet this - when it comes to entering the gates of heaven - I'd put my wager on a prostitute being allowed in long before some of these so called men of God!

We were leaving the next day so didn't intend on staying late. We had decided on taking the northern route - Jamaica and Port Royal.
That though was not on my mind right then for again on the dance floor was most of the crew getting to grips with the music - arms and legs thrusting in as many directions as a bunch of sky-divers realizing they'd forgotten their parachutes! Centre stage, and right in front of me was Pocahontas. "How about $2.00 now and I'll send you the rest when I get home?" If only I'd got Mikes trousers on I thought - before I could suggest the proposition of a down payment - another girl jumped between us - who - in the routine of the dance, slipped her knickers off, placing them on my head! By giving something once so very close to her - she had staked her claim!

I learnt from past experiences what a late night and one too many beers can do when the next day you're riding a roller-coaster that doesn't stop! The sea movement will mix your stomach in to a violent cocktail. The bar you lent against the night before becomes the lee-rail - and you won't leave that like you didn't the other! You hang on yawning - the sign that says something must give soon. A dear friend with a cast-iron pot for a stomach is doing your stint at the wheel - bless him - till he talks of breakfast - juicy bacon and a nice fried slice! Your eyes try and concentrate on the only thing stable, the horizon - then a whiff from the galley hits you and bingo!! Never again you say.

The ride in the taxi wasn't far to the schooner, the girls seemed determined to come see it - and bundled themselves in giving orders to the driver where to go! Oh! dear, this could be a late one, I thought.

There was an argument going on when we arrived, one of the girls was in a heated discussion with the Taxi driver, both facing one another standing their ground.

The last sentence he spoke could well have been his last - had the other girls not grabbed her - for the girl had a knife out in wink of an eye! Bravely the man jumped in - slammed it in gear and fled, knowing full well the lady intended him to bleed! The cause of this clash was over the fare he was charging us for the short ride. When losing his case that petrol was dearer at night, he reverted to calling them names - names by which he was best known I might add "Children of whores! - Gringo Fuckers!" etc.!

The girls stayed aboard that night. None would have to call home to tell parents not to worry! - or make excuses "I stayed at a friend's house - honest!" These girls had long ago been cast out of the house - fending for themselves and taking care of their friends. Sticking together, not too far from a call for help by a sister! Not in our company would they need to worry about the sadist or men with strange desires - but instead sleep safely in the arms of a brief encounter!!

I awoke the next morning to look at the sleeping face beside me. No, it was not that of Pocahontas, she was not aboard, and maybe it was just as well, it may have made leaving more difficult and memories more longing. Instead it was a sister, the one who had laid a claim on my head, then later defended us against a man out to crook us!

I didn't wake her, but lay instead gazing at her face! "What? - I thought - young girl, goes on in your mind when the eyes open? - how do they see life? - do they see things that make you envy others? - what do you see when you look in the mirror? What you are - What you think you are, or what others think you are eh?" Only a sheet covered us, just! Most of her fine figure lay revealed before me motionless. The brown skin of her ancestors showed not a sign of blemish, nor a change in colour as one sees on those from northern climates - those that turn themselves over on a spit in the sun till done!

It was her breathing that showed any form of life in her, it wasn't the silent breath of a normal healthy person, more that of an asthmatic. The wheezing sound of someone that finds over exertion very tiresome! Certainly a handicap in her way of life!

She in her sleep was not to know the feeling of sadness I felt for her, to worry about what the future holds. Why I would feel like that, was hard to say, in a few hours I would be gone - never to see her again - so why the concern? Well she might be the daughter of a whore and a fucker of Gringos - but it was not the fault of this poor thing beside me!

"It was time to go!" I said to myself, for the skylight showed morning was here. I had to look at the horizon ahead, not to dwell on the emotions of the present - something that I have no control over.

Moving as silently as I could so not to wake her, I pulled myself from under the sheet, slowly lifting the lifeless arm stretched across me. Escape was not on my mind, just to leave the girl in peace while preparing to leave. The leg that stopped me was an awake leg - one thrown to hold on to mine. The brown eye that looked at me said don't leave - yet the arm I held could never hang on to what it would never own! I held that small hand with its clean unpainted fingernails. I now seemed helpless - yet would have struck down another last-night. Who will defend you my girl I thought!

Her face turn - both eyes catching me in a sad reflection of the truth. The night was gone and the memory soon will follow. I held her face and longed to tell her things that were not true - that I'd be back - to wait for me! Yet it would have been a lie - and she would have known it, and maybe resented me for it! She held me close with arms that showed a different passion --- then!---as if a switch had turned, she relaxed and the hands let go!

To perform the role life had forced upon her, emotions can't play a part - the stress of too many broken promises - leave to too many broken hearts - it would destroy her! I could see now the change of expression in those brown eyes - it was back to business - wipe away the what ifs - what may have been!

We departed late from Cartagena - 11.00hrs on Sat 22nd Nov. The reluctance of the girls to leave made it difficult for us to get underway! Some I know would have come with us - with or without a passport. They were there waving long after their faces were unrecognizable! Maybe still are!
I wrote in my log that day 'definitely a place to return to' It is now nearly 40 years and I never did! It was not just the girls - the whole place was intriguing - the atmosphere.

Chapter 26: Just a run across the Caribbean

Our run to Port Royal Jamaica would take us a little over three days. Due north would be our course for some 400 miles. With the wind constant, light to fresh, from the N.N.E - to N.E we had to motor sail most of the way. Such is the sailors life I'm afraid - when you want it out of the S.E, bang! N.E is what you get, and you can depend upon that as surely as night follows day.

The alternative course for the Punta Gallinas headland would have seen us stripped of all canvas, motoring some 350 odd miles right in the teeth of the trades before a change of course to Aruba could happen. The chosen route was done hoping the winds would have more southeast in them - they didn't, leaving us rather frustrated. Punta Gallinas is the area from which come the Guajira Indians, had I read 'Papillion' earlier than I did - I'm sure I would have stuck out for the southern route. Put the hook down in some quiet spot and maybe get a little of the reception he had some 50 years before. Had we all known what reception was awaiting us in Jamaica, I wouldn't have had much opposition. But that was the hindsight we'd all like at times.

The usual squall with its strong gusts ran us down from time to time. Always hard to tell what strength the wind will be in these small storms - but one better be ready for them at all times! The darker the cloud, the heavier both rain and wind. At night, the peril of these gusts can pounce on the un-prepared ship and its crew. Old sails and bad rigging, you could soon find being towed over the lee rail, or be on your 'Beam ends' and gone if the rig can take more than the vessel can handle - as was the case of the 'Marquesas' some years later with the loss of so much life! A keen eye during the day is important, but at night it's a cheek to the wind, the change in its temperature is your quick warning to duck! But always let prudence be the better part of valour when what sail one carry's through such squalls! At night the rule should be, get it down!! It's easier and quicker to re-hoist it again than it is to bend on a new one - that's if you have one!

The squalls we encountered put our maintenance program to the test, and the extra care of the novice was caught lacking in certain quarters. The loss of the fore topmast at 08.00hrs on the Mon 24th, was due to a bottle screw un-winding itself having parted its seizing. Hoisting the flying-jib un-aware of the lofty problem, the extra pressure on this spar was too much, and Bang! - breaking it off at the hounds. Lucky for us the halyard held its weight and so didn't do much damage! Could have caused havoc with the all headsails otherwise. This sail we never flew in squalls, and rarely the outer, and it wasn't a squall here that snapped the topmast, just a good morning breeze. Now we would be without it till a new mast could be found.

There was though, a lot that day, squall after squall coming out of the N.E. One was the cause of the starboard running backstay to part on the following morning. The lurch from a beam sea put pressure on the Bulldog grip at the hounds, cutting through it like a knife. A bad way to rig it, which we later rectified with an eye splice in the wire. We rigged a tackle and reefed the foresail for the rest of the passage - and learnt another lesson!!

At 06.40hrs on that morning, being the 25th. The 'Blue Mountains' of Jamaica were sighted, and it was 15.15hrs when 'Jylland' dropped her anchor in 9 fathoms at Port Royal. Some hours before entering Port Royal, a helicopter had been circling us! Sightseers or photographers we thought, for the machine had no markings.
With the innocence of the honest, which always travelled with us, the thought that we were under surveillance by an anti-drug patrol was not even considered - We were in for one big surprise!!!!
We carried with us a certain amount of weapons, the last addition a .38 given to Howard by Syd in Panama with a request - "Just shoot some bastard for me will you?" We were all aware of the hijacking of vessels along the South American coast, running drugs north the purpose of such evil sods. Going to the assistance of a life raft neatly placed in your track, one better have more than just a heaving line in their hand! Waiting to board you, would be a bunch of thugs ready to thank you with a bullet in the head! It had happened to others - but wouldn't to us!

The decision to hand our weapons in here was due to the very fact that it was once British, and not down to from whence we had come - Columbia! It was a wise decision too! 15 minutes after we came to our anchor a customs vessel was alongside. The amount of firepower we gave them I think took them by surprise and confirmed to the already suspicious ashore what we were! Little did we know, the hour we waited with the Q flag still flying, gave them time to organize their men, discuss tactics and load machine guns! With the trap nicely laid, cars out of sight, four heavily armed officers in each, the health inspector could now be told - "Go and give them clearance to come alongside Morgan's Wharf".

There is nothing quite like watching those who believe in your guilt scratching for clues! Trying to prove themselves right in an attempt to prove the policeman's golden rule - 'Everyone's guilty of something!' When you know full well your honest answer is totally ignored by he looking for the 'Truth', you are depicted now as a real 'cool' bastard. It can be fun playing the game of 'Cat and Mouse' just as long as you know who is which.

The oddness of a lack of bodies ashore wishing to take our lines, wasn't noticed at first, in fact it was nice for us to come alongside somewhere quiet without the hassle of the usual nuisance wishing to take your lines for a fee. All that soon changed! The very minute those lines secured us, the welcome they had planned all happened at once. Cars came screeching to a halt from all angles, discharging grim looking faces with an attitude problem. 'Bullocks!' to the "Permission to come aboard Captain?" -- and as for the little saying in the front of my passport, which states ' --without let or hindrance' - go fuck yourself! Coming over the rail was the cast out of 'The Black and White Minstrel show' and not singing 'Ole Man River' either.

"Oh! Charlie me boy!" I thought "Never will you get to see the real face of men - the same men that would be on guard as the band struck up 'God save the Queen' when you stepped ashore from the Royal barge! Nor would I want to change my role for yours, for the snarl on their lips would be all smiles but for the chance to kiss your arse!" We were in the real world, a world where all are guilty until proven beyond doubt - innocent! That might take some time by the look of it too!

All were ordered to stay where they were until each in turn had to accompany two officers to their cabin. Contents of lockers were inspected, and anything looking suspicious questioned about. Pill bottles - containers - boxes all gone through. It was here somewhere - they knew it - just a matter of looking that's all. Having found nothing worthy of a "Eureka!" in any of the cabins, the search continued forward.

It was in the sail locker they found what they were looking for - hidden under canvas and rope! The hand pulled out something soft, wrapped in dustbin liners and pulled in to the light of the forecastle, proved beyond doubt they had struck 'gold!' 5 - 6 - 7 bags of the white stuff followed one after another from their hiding place, each wrapped carefully (as any Cartel owner knows) in a roll like a long black soft sausage. The handling of such was of course not new to him, and was the desire of many a white lady flying in from Canada in those days.

"If what you're holding is what you think it is - said my brother Howard standing next to he that held the catch - "--how much is it worth?" ---- "Why one roll is probably $250,000 worth" said the black, happy hunter. "Well then - why not keep one and say nothing about the rest!"

The fellow could hardly contain himself with such a blatant proposal under such conditions - crawling alive with officers, and his superiors too, here was one real cool bastard offering a bribe as if it was a mere biscuit on a plate. Having had to refuse for obvious reasons - Howard tells him it's not what he believes it to be - Cocaine! - but something used in fire extinguishers. When men hold in their hand what they believe all the world is looking for - the first rung to promotion - and what happens!

Happy they would soon return to arrest such arrogance for drug violations, they left us a guard with machine-gun to stop any attempt of a breakout while an analysis of what they had found could be done.

The frustration that must have tortured our accusers as each test failed, we never saw, but as we waited for the results that took a long time coming, we smiled inwardly at what must have been the scene. The snorting that gave nothing but a violent headaches to those willing to give it the 100% stamp of approval - the cursing - the total disbelief at what they knew to be right, wasn't - it was something I'd loved to have seen.

Whether the black inspector that returned 6 hours later was drunk with excitement at the find or pissed from hours of failure trying to get high on Magnesium Potash and Fire extinguisher powder I don't know, but he was one angry cookie! He was born for that uniform just as surely is the Leopard is to his coat of spots! Denied of a kill, he was just as vicious! Hungry in his pursuit for a pound of flesh, any thought that we might just be telling the truth after all, was alien to him. Honesty does not exist in his world, and those that remind him of something he can never be, repulses him!

For the next hour he grilled us below decks, looking for an answer we didn't have. "What do you know about Iowa?" said the sharp question directed at Bill Curry - a Seattle man and as honest as the day is long. "Only that it's an American State!" said Bill confused at such a silly question. Either this piece of shit was thinking of taking a holiday later in the year - or it had some significance to the case! "Don't be a smart arse with me man!" retorted a drunk, bewildered by the only reply Bill could think of!

"What of you? - why are you with these white people? - you are one of us, tell me what you know???" - three questions in one as his head turned to Julie, his brain still with Bills answer. Julie was from Trinidad. She, like many West Indian women still live under the threat of the men's world. It consists of a good beating to make you tell 'The Truth', and a good raping for not telling it quick enough.

Feeling awkward answering such a racial remark in our company, Julie searched for words, keeping her eyes averted from his threatening stare. I watched as her finger draw, meaningless patterns on the lounge table, her embarrassment at being under the spotlight so apparent.

For an hour the guilty had interrogated the innocent, and it had been fun watching him digging for water in the desert - but it was time to call it a day, it was 23.00hrs and all were getting tired of his abusive remarks. This man and his colleagues - so certain we were responsible for trying to make some money illegally, departed, with what little manners they had left in the afterbirth between their mothers legs. It was time to tell him to charge us or leave!

There is nothing more insulting than to condemn others of taking a bribe when you know the accusers 'Arse-pocket!' is bulging with backhanders! Nor can you expect justice and sympathy from a psychopath who believes all people to be liars other than he! He brought back memories of my childhood - and that of the 'stolen' pen days! "You are wanted in the headmasters study boy!" rang in my ears. "COME OVER HERE BOY!" ----"WHAT HAVE YOU DONE WITH IT?" ...."THE PEN BOY! THE PEN! ----WHAT HAVE YOU DONE WITH IT?" As I received no apology then, I'd expect none from this moron.

A century ago, the law that protected that headmaster, would have had me bending, the cane ready to beat some truth out of me, leaving me scared in body as well as soul. He then, was as unworthy to be in such a position as this enforcer of the law was - and given half the chance, would have had us in a nice little cell to beat some sort of confession from us. It eases their conscience you see, makes them sleep better knowing there are no honest people.

I honestly believe in that saying about 'Pissing in to the wind' that one day it will come back to hit you smack in the face! It's the same as reaping what you sow - or looking only for the evil in others. We all have it there, evil that is, and if someone is allowed to dig deep enough it will rise up and bite them all in the arse!

The demand to charge us or leave brought a voice from above! God?----It certainly said something that made the drunk rise and push his way past his henchmen and up the companionway! No goodnight gentlemen either and sorry to have caused you any inconvenience from this man. No! that would come from the big white boss who had been listening to it all at the skylight and made his own assessment. An American voice too, anti-narcotics boss who didn't show his face, preferring the dark surrounds of the deck to hide his identity! Maybe it was God!

"Enjoy your stay!" he said - and they were gone! It was too late to do anything now, so all hit bed and all hit it at the same time!

We would spend three days here after passing our entry exam! The people here are just as friendly as other West Indians; it's only those in authority that are a pain in the arse! No different to any other country I guess. Those that decide on a career in governmental departments must expect that, when they jump on such an escalator. Their eyes get trained to look at those behind them. Fear of being overtaken and suspicious of all ahead of them, they rise not as servants to the public, but subservient to those up the stairs. Many a third world country that dabbles with democracy falls flat on their faces in the shoving and pushing for positions. Many trip over the leader, who himself lies in a heap having missed the point to it all.

Jamaica, like other once British possessions, has suffered greatly coming to terms with self-rule. Oh! I know much has been written about the 'unfairness' under the British, a twisting of words and deeds to fit all rather than the few who mis-used their position. I know the teaching of our history now leaves out the great heroes and the good men, but dwells instead on the evil whenever it can be found by the do-gooders who live in safe havens to preach from. One need only to talk to the elderly folk of poor origin in this region what life was like under British rule! The answer is unanimous in its praise rather than what has replaced it. They knew where they stood - like the Baron or not - they all preferred the safety of his castle walls!

There is a plaque in Port Royal to a fair and great man, Lord Nelson - who died in his efforts to secure our Empire. The tribute has not been torn up, harmed or covered in graffiti as would happen to a perpetrator of evil! It says "Here once stood Horatio Nelson - let all who stand in his footsteps, remember his glory!"

Our first day to roam free here proved fruitful. A spar was found on a stretch of beach not far from us, and that a few locals would tow it round to us for a small fee! It proved to be a Telegraph pole of some length and with some work with an adze, better than that which was lost - but the preparation of it would have to wait until we reached St Lucia, for now we'd stay Bald- Headed! More important was the wire to repair the fore shrouds and running backstay. Again we were lucky and swapped a demand valve for two lengths of appropriate size - with some small wooden blocks thrown in! The afternoon of that day saw Bill Curry and myself stripping broken gear and splicing up the new wire!

Of Bill Curry, there is much to write about for our lives were intertwined throughout the years we were in the Caribbean. When a person has the same interests as your own, it's easy to become friends. Bill had a hate of engines that matched mine, and constantly we were at loggerheads with Mike over this! We both liked the challenge of working her under sail alone in all conditions. Bill was a seaman of the highest quality in my opinion, small though my knowledge of such men was. From navigation to the splicing of heavy wire, making blocks from scratch to the stitching of canvas, Bill made all seem easy! You can tell more about a person working with him for a day, than you can talking to him for a week.

Bill was a big man - 6'4" and not an ounce of fat. Such a size at high school put him in trouble with the sports master who believed all men that big should play the game of 'American Football'. Had he been of average height, he would have been left alone to get on with his studies, of which he saw, more important! Bill would prefer to play with a violin than a ball, but no one would dare call him a sissy! for doing so. His attitude towards sport was - that it is a game, and should be played in the same spirit. To come off the field laughing with friend and opponent alike - not to play with the mind deranged by some fanatical coach whose instructions tell you to go out and kill another mother's son - or at least maim him for life!

Bills response at the invite to play a game against the local Port Royal football team a game was met with the same enthusiasm as the rest of the crew! Most of us hadn't played a game since leaving school and those that made up the numbers - Graham, Bill and Ben - Americans, only knew one rule - that they couldn't handle it! So once more the old allies joined forces -- The playing fields of the local Garrison the battleground!

The 27th of November 1975, being a Thurs, would go down in the annuals of history as one of the biggest laughs had by white men and black men in the competitive world of sport! 4 - 3 down and only minutes left to play (thank-god) a high ball came over in front of their goal, the ref, a local black guy, took his eye off the watch for a moment, keeping it on the ball instead. Running in shouting "My ball!" he nutted it in the net, blew the whistle and declared a draw! Which about summed up the atmosphere the game was played in! My brother Howard was the only real player on our side, but even he refrained from the daring stuff of other days on this pitch! It was a cinder track that one sliding tackle would have produced bone! I was wearing a pair of Mikes Rugby boots and for days after, walked like a cripple for playing on that hard ground. Still we all enjoyed it and laughed about it for days after - surely that's what it's all about!

The next day though, when the Port Royal police, hearing we had a football team on-board (Surely he meant a comedy team) sent a representative to challenge us to a game that evening, a -- "You must be joking!" came out of a lot of weary mouths! Plus, it wouldn't have been fun playing people without a sense of humour! Each move we made might have been seen as a plot against them and the holding of the ball too long, disrespectful to the law. Somehow, I just couldn't see the Ref knocking one in against them without spending the night in the cooler!

It was now 10 days since we left Portobello, and we were not to know then it would take us another 15 to reach St Lucia! Howard was getting rather agitated and anxious to get it done with! Getting back to his wife and children in England was the only thing on his mind. Frustrated and angry at how things had gone in the past few months got him down!

Why, with all the promises of success and effort put in - didn't things go as planned? - Why was Syd so negative towards the main objective - had he been warned by voices in the night not to touch Drake!? It all bothered me as well as my brother. Both of us didn't know Syd was a self-destructive schizophrenic that liked to build things up, and then take pleasure in destroying them before it became their master and a monster like Frankenstein!

The silly move of this folly in Central America had cost us dear - and the future looked very bleak! Financially we were broke, and we found ourselves hobbling home on a shoestring. Leaving us here in Jamaica, to fly home was what he wished to do and had he done so, the cost of his airfare would drain us dry!

I didn't have to remind my brother something he already knew, but talk about we did on the evening of the 27th. Had the money been available - I'm sure he would have gone - and I for one would not have stopped him - for the foul mood he was in was better ashore and not aboard to make a hard task more difficult! I found myself at times seating in Frank Worsley's chair! Praised for good progress across the chart and blamed for a foul tide.

The crew of the 'Endurance' at the time were camped on pack ice in 'The Weddell Sea' moving N.W in the drift. Hundreds of billions of tons of ice being moved by a greater force, yet the Captain who fixed their position each day received the quietness from some who in some way thought he was responsible for going astern! Not that I could ever be of the quality of such a man - but I could well imagine his feeling each day when grabbing his sextant!

When the 'No Option' clause presented itself - Howard in the manner well known of the British that, though they might moan about the position they're in, that others (to their cost!) see as a sign of weakness, they will fight to the bitter end once the guns begin to fire! Having used up that right, Howard resolved himself to the task ahead!

Friday the 28th saw the rigging repaired and on Saturdays we took on fuel and water! It wouldn't be till the afternoon before we could depart! Only one man working on a Saturday at customs was the problem - but that's typical of the attitude in an area where work is what women do and furthest from all men's minds! Job satisfaction is thought to be the size of the wage packet at the end of the week!

I would like to have seen more of 'Xaymaca' - the name now extinct as the Aboriginal who used to live here. Columbus located this Island on his second voyage in 1494 - on the 3rd of May to be exact. 16 years later - when the 'Lads!' arrived from Spain, they soon put the locals to work! Death came by working 12 hours a day - 7 days a week. When the British relieved the Spanish 'Gods!' of this place in 1655, not a single Indian remained alive.

Old 'Captain Henry Morgan' himself, of so many Hollywood Pirate movies, sailed out of here with his merry men to attack Portobello in 1668, and again to have another go at Panama City two years later! --- Winning both away matches each time! The amount of cash he stole from other thieves, earned him the reward of our first Governor here. See how far a little hard work and honesty can take you?

It wouldn't be for some years before the English saw the real value of the Island, so brought it under control and Morgan with it! Through the Morgan years of 'Rum! - Bum! - and Baccy!', living in the northern hills; were the escaped slaves from Jamaica and Cuba who called themselves 'The Maroons'. Those that had escaped their harsh Spanish rulers - who, like their countrymen in Panama, had downed tools and fled to the forests rather than die digging dirt.

In 1738 a tract of land was granted these people by the British - which they cultivated and built on it two small towns. The coming of the sugar plantations which replaced the Spanish mining for precious metals, also saw the coming of some cheap labour - more slaves brought over from Africa.

Legitimately purchased with a piece of paper to prove ownership. The arrival of these people was resented by the old slaves - they saw trouble in it coming and bitter hostilities on all occasions, it divided the 'Free Jamaicans' from the imported Negro. It was like asking the haves and have not's to live together under the same roof - 'Freemen and serf', both the same colour yet totally different in their positions in the new Jamaica.

Runaways would find no haven in the freed slave's domain, and a prejudicial atmosphere prevailed long before it became fashionable to talk about in our own society. When that time came to set free the 'new' slave, the only place left for many to go, would be to the mother country, whose short sightedness left them without a piece of their own country.

The internal peace on this island, Jamaica, has been seriously disturbed on many an occasion and it continues to this very day! The cause is over the same issues too - the haves and the have nots. You will find no 'Yardies' able to trace their ancestors back to the 'Maroons' - but to the streets of Kingston and from a hovel they could never call their own.

With our guns back on board, rearmed and having cleared customs, we set sail at 15.00hrs streaming the log some 20 minutes later - Wind N.E force 2- course 110 degrees compass - Goodbye Jamaica!

Chapter 27: Hispaniola

The course we would take from Jamaica depended entirely on the wind and its strength. If we could slip through the Windward

Passage North of Hispaniola on a calm night under power, we would do so. It would help when the time came to turn south, getting as much Northing in as possible on our eastern track. It wasn't to be, the wind increased to 5/6 N.E at 20.00hrs with the log reading 24.8. It was still blowing as strong when we entered the passage sometime after midnight. Our track now would have to take us south of the island.

It wouldn't be a comfortable night; quite a sea was running in the channel and meeting this motor sailing, threw much of it aboard. For me to suggest we put the helm up, letting her fall off under sail alone would, I know, have met the approval of Bill, but not those wishing to get this trip over and done with!

In my mind were the bigger seas off Portugal, the ones which she handled with comfort, but those memories I knew, would not have gone down well with my brother especially - all he desired was a bee-line course for St Lucia, then home! It hurt me to see 'Jylland' punching seas, and I was straining as much as she was waiting for another blow up front. It was at times like this I'd curse having an engine aboard and would willingly cast it over the side. We were making 4.5 nautical miles over the ground, but to me, the fight - the stress and strains on her beating to windward - just wasn't worth it.

This is the penalty you pay for having a Captain aboard who can't realize the qualities of a sailing vessel and a brother in a hurry! Both preferring to fight the elements with modern power. When we had decided to take Mike back with us, his position as Skipper had also been given, for one really couldn't go without the other, it would have been rather humiliating - and that wasn't necessary, for Mike was a good Captain in many senses, but for some reason couldn't understand how a zigzag course could be faster than a straight one at times!

The clew might have gone on the fore-main anyway, but to have argued that point of 'I told you so!' on a dark wet deck at night is not on your mind - what is 'get it down' and fast before it's beyond repair. It's only after you say to yourself "Fuck it!" - frustrated that you can't prove the point the extra strain for being sheeted in so hard, put upon this sail - plus to have done so, would never have proved the others wrong!!

I know it was badly made at that point, the sail-makers relying on the strength of modern synthetics to hold it. The boltrope used was nylon, it ran inside the tabling of the leech - loose! - round a large cringle and stitched only 3 feet along the foot! Of course it pulled free at that point! But by later experience, and what rags I had to use to sail her in, such a sail that parted that night would never have gone had we been off the wind. Furled, it would have to wait for attention in Santo Domingo where a spectacle iron was made, replacing the cringle, and the boltrope stitched in place properly.

Not trusting the reefing points till an inspection in daylight could be made, both foremain and mainsail was struck now, along with the outer jib. This set of virtually new sails were now deemed untrustworthy!

At 12.00hrs on the 30th our latitude was fixed at 17-25.4'N. Log reading 89 miles. Wind E.N.E 2.

At 18.00 we fixed our position at 17-31'N, 74-56'W. Course was 050 compass. Wind N.N.E 1, Log 113 miles. We'd obviously been pushed by wind and current further south than we would have liked, so took the opportunity in the light airs to get some north in. With the wind still light at 04.00hrs on the 1st Dec, the shore of the island of Haiti was sighted.

Once free of the Windward Passage, we caught an easterly going current up to 1 1/2 knots along Haiti's southern coast, which helped our progress, up till then it had been slow to say the least - averaging just 5 knots!

While we travelled along its southern shore on a December day in 1975 - Columbus was looking at the northern side in December too, but nearly 500 years before of us on the 6th in 1492. He named the whole of this place 'La Isla Espanola' (The Spanish Island) for the lands reminded him of the area around Castile. Later to be called Espanola by the Spanish and Hispaniola by the English! He also crossed the Windward Passage coming from Cuba and experienced the same N.E winds as us, but with a S.E course as his heading, and a current to assist the slow 'Santa Maria', he made better headway than we did! And, I guess, had a better suite of sails at the end of it!

The first ever Europeans to settle in the Caribbean did so on the Northern shore of what is now Haiti, at a place named Navidad. It was also here he came in contact with the friendliest of all the Indians he met! They walked as naked as the day they were born, and had they wore clothes to protect them from the sun - would have been as white as the people he left back in Spain. So where did these people come from in the first place to inhabit these islands? - from the north I guess, and over many hundreds if not thousands of years ago. They didn't have a chance to tell us either, and were not around long after old Chris found them.

As I looked at that shore, and had my eyes been that of one of those gentle souls, I bet they would have remembered their homeland with ease, for the whole place seemed asleep in time! The coast turns south halfway along this island. A promontory of land jutting in to the Caribbean for over 20 miles. The strong current to the west washes against this headland turning some of the flow in an easterly direction. Nature's forces have been hard at work trying to round off this stubborn horn whose solid rock resists its work. Once 'Isla Alto Vela' was joined to the mainland and fought such a good fight that the sea decided it should be left alone! It sits upon the sea over half a mile from the shore defying not only the sea to get past it, but any sailing vessel heading east!

On the 2nd December at 03.00hrs a light was bearing 140 degrees compass, our course at the time was 110c. At 06.00hrs Alto Vela bore 149 true! By 08.00hrs the decision not to run between the island and the mainland of the Dominican Republic was due to a good force 4 from the East and what we assumed would be a good set of tide against us. Our charts of this area were not detailed enough to show whether or not other rocks had resisted the sea and lay just beneath the surface to catch us.

About that time, out of a blue sky, came something that would make up our minds not to tempt the passage -it came in the form of an aircraft, a light craft, painted in army style! It circled us low, making a few passes, buzzing like a Bee as if warning us away from some danger! Whether this intrusion made any mark upon the sub-conscience judgment at the time, I don't know, but when I now reflect upon issues past concerning 'Jylland' - strange happenings - visitations of Ghostly presence etc -- all cast aside then with a "So what!" or relevant to some close call! I find it hard not to believe that fate is closely connected to a Guardian Angel -- someone up there deciding the shots! Heading now 155 compass, sail could be put upon her to assist the engine. Reefing the foremain, due to the damage, and main to balance her, we took on Alto Vela!

As with all headlands, or any object that restricts the flow of air, the wind increases - a good drawing fire is a prime example where a throat is formed in a chimney for that purpose! As wind is the prime mover of the Oceans currents, the increase in strength at that point will make the seas respond accordingly. Deeper will be the troughs, with higher crests than elsewhere as all join forces to round off the agitation.

By 09.00hrs the wind had increased to 5/6 from the east as 'Jylland' poked her nose round the corner and with it the seas became short and rough! A double bell-ringer was a sign of angry water! The Schooners forward bell would ring once when we forced her against heavy seas, but here they would give two sounds occasionally as she rose and fell down from a high place!

An hour later, having cleared the Island the wind started to fall in strength to force 3+ - East as we remained on our heading of 155c!

At 13.00hrs with the wind backing E.N.E force 4, we tacked the Schooner to the heading of 025 compass!

By 14.00hrs Alto Vela was again in view bearing 320 True - course was now 010 Compass- wind still E.N.E 4 with the log reading 307 miles!

At 16.00hrs with the wind easing from the same direction we passed Alto Vela to Port on a course of 025 compass! We had in fact, made a little over a mile to the east of our position 8 hrs before. Ten minutes away by the Boston whaler, was where we were at when the clock said 08.00hrs! Some were not happy with Worsley's navigation!!!!

At 20.00hrs we altered our heading to 040c, and to 050c at 22.00hrs with the lights ashore of Barahona bearing 355 True. Log read 341 miles!

The pilot book on the area speaks of an easterly set close in to shore! This we were hoping to catch, but being night off a strange coast, how close we could approach was by judgment! Not having radar or any fixed lights to plot our position, navigation was done by dead reckoning! Close in enough to catch the current. With Puerto Viejo De Azua bearing due north by the compass, our course was changed to 120 compass at 23.00hrs - the wind was east 2/3 - the log on 345 miles from Jamaica!

The 3rd of December was Bill Curry's birthday, and it will be remembered long by celebrating the passing of Alto Vela once during the night heading south, and again going north during the day. From midnight till a fix could be got at dawn, we had kept a course between 120 and 130, keeping her close hauled in the 3/4 easterly wind, hoping the current would sweep us along. Bill, on watch at the time had fixed our position at 06.00 hrs. as 17-36N 70-51W, but couldn't believe his eyes that the fix said we'd made 60 degrees of leeway since going about at 23.00hrs the night before!

No matter how many times he went over his figures, it didn't put us where we expected to be!

At 07.00hrs we went about on a heading of 020 compass with an easterly wind persisting 2/3 and a log reading 375 miles! The set of current was much stronger than anticipated okay, and worse - it was westerly.

Howard was one rather pissed off owner during the morning when the news reached his ears we'd been carried downstream during the dark! With Alto Vela to port some distance, and no mistaking it! He still insisted I take another fix to confirm Bills - and noon did nothing but prove Bill was right - or both of us wrong! Which could have been the case had it not been for the perfect outline to the west of our very close friend - 'Alto Vela!' Thus making it four times we had been within gunshot range.

We would this time bring 'Jylland' as close as possible to the shore in the afternoon to try and look for that elusive drift east - they wouldn't be telling un-truths of such a set to us would they? We did wonder!

At 14.00hrs Punta Salinas was dead ahead - distance 1 mile. 10 minutes later we went about to head 140c on the port tack- and at 15.30 back on a starboard tack, bringing her again in close to the beach - so close we could have hailed someone ashore - had anyone been there. Not a soul was seen on the rather desolate place. If there was, they must have thought we were going to anchor we were that close. At 18.00hrs we went about with the wind backing to the E.N.E. Motor sailing now we could raise 100 degrees on the compass, to 090c as it backed further to N.E at 20.00hrs.

And that was the trick - keep her close in to grab the set to the east, for it was there okay, and that of the wind, which follows the coast in that direction up to Santo Domingo! At 21.00hrs Lu Caleta was sighted and at midnight with the log reading 457 miles, wind now from the north 2/3 our heading being 055c, we went about for the last time to head 270c outside Santo Domingo!

Un-able to enter at night for lack of a chart, we hove-to in a northerly breeze to wait daybreak!

At 07.00hrs on the 4th December 1975 we passed through the breakwater and at 07.20hrs we came alongside the west bank of Rio Ozama dock, clearing customs 10 min later- fully armed!

Chapter 28: Dominican Republic

The atmosphere here reminded us very much of Cartegena. The smell in the air and the same faces of an old Empire hang around as if people are waiting for it to return. It has the same apathy of its merchants, the jealousy and mistrust of all leave them sitting there while their harbour is void of shipping and the great city falls to pieces round their ears year by year. The strong vein of Spanish blood - the remnants of the population that came from that country is seen in the colour of their skin. Founded by Columbus in 1504, on his fourth voyage here, it is the oldest European establishment in America.

The old Cathedral in the town, certainly once held the remains of the old Admiral when his lead box of leftovers was transferred to here from Spain along with his son Diego's (The second Admiral of the Indies) coffin in the 1540's. In fact, quite a few of the Columbus family were buried here - Bartholomew (his brother) lies in the Monastery of San Francisco and Columbus's grandson Luis, the third Admiral was interred with his father and grandfather in the same Cathedral. Spain ceded the western part of this island (Haiti) to France in 1697 and when forced to give up the rest of the island nearly a hundred years later, decided to take The First Admiral bones with them. They carried to Havana what they assumed to be his remains, and buried them in the Cathedral there in 1796.

In another hundred years though, Spain lost yet another island, Cuba - and the old boy, so much on the move in life, was just as mobile in death so it would appear. In 1899 a box was transported to Spain and buried in another Cathedral, this one in Seville. But it could well be the coffin of his son Diego that was removed, for in 1877 the vault from which it was first taken, was re-discovered and - next to it lay another! It was so inscribed, identifying the remains as "The illustrious and excellent man Don Cristoval Colon". During an examination of its contents, some of the ashes that fell to the floor made their way to Genoa, Pavia, Rome and New York, in the pockets of our old and trusted friends - the Archaeologists!

An engraved silver plate in the bottom, under dust and some ash not taken read -- "The last part of the remains of the first Admiral, Don Cristobal Colon, the Discoverer". So if it was the Ashes of Columbus that remained behind in Santo Domingo - and it can't be proved one way or the other - was he moved or his son Diego? If it was him, then some has gone to further fields, as seems fitting!

This island was once the most fertile in the West Indies. Noted for its plantations of sugar, coffee and cotton. Later from the mountains, Mahogany and different kinds of Dyewoods were stripped for commercial wealth after the gold, silver, copper, tin, iron and rock salt mines were unproductive! The political turmoil and unrest in this island would turn away the long-term investment that might have brought some stability here. The malaise they have been brought up under is an inheritance of uncertainty for the future, passed from generation to generation too. Caused by Spain ceding the western part to France, who in a mad rush on 'Liberty and Fraternity' a hundred years later, freed all slaves in Haiti.

The wisdom of that 1794 National Convention, far away in France, by a committee who gave little thought to the consequences of their action, is a sorry tale that would repeat itself time and time again by such righteous people of all nations! Who, safe from the great fan, shit their ideals on others with an arrogance of spite! 'Madame Guillotine' delivered the same attitude of retribution by 'Free' people upon those responsible for their present position, with a vengeance in the New Republic! So would such terrible minds carry out upon their oppressors in Haiti, the thanks for their deliverance in the same manner! European governors and plantation owners would suffer at the hands of those wishing to establish their own Monarchy and rule in Haiti. Nearly Christophe, who became king in the northern parts, and Petion who declared another Republic in the west wiped out the whole of the white population! When the 'King' died in 1820, the whole became what it is today - a bloody mess!

Though the eastern half, proclaimed by strength of arms by France in 1795, stood unsure of its position after 1815, it decided to rise against their western oppressors in 1844, to proclaim themselves also a Republic!

In 1861 they reunited themselves with Spain, but in 1865, after two years of insurrection, declared again independence! Offered to the United States to become their benefactor in 1871, it was turned down by the Senate! Since which, it has been in the hands of one despot or another intent solely on his own greatness and wealth!

Such is the island, once inhabited by such 'Gentle and honest folk in the whole world' as Columbus put it, so governed!

I wouldn't get chance to see much of this place - much to my disappointment. We had pulled in here to get fuel mainly. The fight against wind and tide from Jamaica had used up more than expected. Also a few repairs to sails had to be made, so a walkabout that day was not on the cards for me.

Ben, our American taken on in Panama as crew, would leave us here; work in the States was calling. We would visit the town in the evening, find a small bar and wish him well and goodbye over a beer, for our plans were to be off again the next day!

The taxi driver that stopped to a group of people flagging him down was not governed by the laws stating how many he could carry, but one leaning more towards that of physics and mechanics! Like - if it was physically possible to get them in - then mechanically possible to move afterwards, then that's all that mattered.

Counting the driver, 11 of us solved the first half of the question, leaving the large old American car to prove the rest! The laughing attitude of the driver, held in the driving position only by a firmly shut door, decided to give it a try. Old American cars were always renowned for a rather springing suspension system and the bumpy streets would put a car (well past its sell by date) through a most vigorous test!

A report to the Admiralty.

"All metal coming in contact with the ground i.e. - Sump! Gearbox! Front and back axles! Front and back bumpers! All exhaust fittings and much of the whole cars outer bodywork! sounded in a satisfactory condition"

"Though we grounded many times, causing grave concern for both the safety of the vessel and its crew, much credit must be given to a most powerful, if not noisy engine that dragged us across pure rock at times! If there was but one fault, it was in the lighting system, a fault pointed out to us by a policeman (whose other job of lamp post support, seemed more important) he stood, legs crossed at a junction that had brought us to a temporary halt. While stationary, and the driver speaking in one word sentence Spanish to the man whose orders were 'Don't leave your post!' there was noticed standing next to the policeman - a girl! Who upon request through the open window entered the car by it - thus making us 12. Laying across those in the back that couldn't stand up to give her a seat, we sped off with our driver occasionally throwing his hands in the air concerned only about police interference".

"I should like here to recommend to your lordships that all future car designs should contain headlights that can be wound down from the inside while underway. On full ahead, under such a heavy load, lights point skywards and under times of war - gives something to aim at for an enemy aircraft!

While I also understand I am indulging in your Lordships patience and most precious time, I should like to take the liberty to bring to your noble attention, the bravery of one - Don Juan Dago Diego! The willingness, at great risk to his livelihood to run us to our destination, was done in the spirit that gladdens the heart! His "To hell with it all!" attitude was like a breath of fresh air, the scent of which has long been lost in the pigsty of our mundane existence at home! His disregard for his own life and safety was matched only by our own, though he had most to lose! When asked to stop by the local militia, whom I might add, can be totally ruthless! He did not abandon us, but stayed at his post till the end. Some thought this due to the fact of being unable to move anyway! But I would prefer to think otherwise!"

"If it pleases your most worthy minds, that an honour should be bestowed on such a people. No greater one could be given than to leave them well alone - not to teach them the good customs of our realms, but instead let them sink back in to a world of un-Christian people, that they may find what was here before! That lost formula that made an extinct race so gentle, so friendly, believing in their maker and living a life as he intended!"

It was to 'The Green Parrot' that our taxi flew. "Just a bar!" we said, but taxi drivers have their friends, so to his he took us! Last in, had to be first out, it was the only way of extracting yourself from the Sardine position! It was an upstairs bar to which we had been driven, one with the usual loud music so distinctive to white South Americans of Spanish descent - lots of brass played between a hurried sentence as the singer delivered the lyrics to a song without a melody! Probably a love song, one about the 'Inquisition' where one must endure the pain of torture stretched out on a rack before true love can be appreciated! Or..... it could have well been about freedom (Always a popular subject around these parts) being released from the torments of the Inquisitor who enjoys his job!

Either way we could have been back at 'Romero's' in Portobello where the same fiery music blasted us and kept awake half the town.

The usual cluster of girls was there ready for 'business'. Taking it that they were the reason we were there, they joined us as we sat down. We should have brought with us a letter of introduction from the girls in Catagena - it would have saved them trying out the only English they knew, which related to the lower half of the anatomy at the junction where right and left legs meet!

Only one male was there apart from the bartender, a young fellow in his early twenties, he - like the ladies sat down at the table as if expecting us. Had the news reached here from the 'Las Vegas Club' quicker than us - which would have been too difficult? I would guess it wasn't for a free beer or some idle chatter that he sat down, but to parade himself as another option to the female companion!

Not taken much notice of, sitting Macho style on a back to front chair, he butted in occasionally demanding one of us to Indian arm wrestle him. Mike would pass him on to me, and I to Howard, and Howard on to Geoff, who told him to piss off - so round the table his challenge went, passed off by us as "Who gives a fuck about trying to prove a point!" I guess we might have missed the point to it though - some people have strange ways of showing and communicating sexual desires! His climax might have come from squeezing something different! He moved his chair back from the table after he had no takers, letting the girls have the floor!

I thank god I've always been attracted to the fairer sex! The long finely shaped legs of a woman whose proportions match the figure. The back that shows not bone or muscle out of place and could never belong to another but a female. The well-formed bosoms where I clung to as a child, will always turn my eye! For in such loving arms of a mother, you nestled safe and warm remembering the first thing you ever saw! Men (Some that is) spend one day fighting to get out of a hole - then spend the rest of their lives fighting to get back in!

The fine line a child walks in its years towards puberty is a knife-edge in which half of that person can fall either side of the moral right! Such a person away from loving guidance of family and a mother who's pure and only devotion is to your wellbeing, can allow others to lead you down a road of un-natural perversion! The irresponsible parent that fawned such children sets an example easy to follow by dumping on society or in to the Public school system, their contribution to the human race! Those with clean hands and a clear conscience of what life in a cesspool is like are delivered to us from such 'Fine Establishments' to follow their betters in to another Public places (Sometimes Public toilets!) to be our leaders in Public life. Such poor bastards (and many are), wanted by a parent only as an heir or a boast - lay broken hearted alone in the dark dorm! Nothing but a Fag for their elders and to be buggered by their 'Betters' - all to make a Man of him!

Many an unwanted skeleton lies in the cupboard, brought about by desertion of hard parents. Tutor performed many an un-natural act or elder on a bewildered child who would wonder why no one came to help! To some, the memory of that abuse will haunt them for the rest of their lives, a bitter taste in their mouths of what childhood meant to them!

It is January 1994 at the moment, a 'Back To The Basic's' idea is in the minds of the Conservative party. Just a little thought from those who haven't the foggiest idea what it means but believes that our drift from a good society to a bad one, is due to this reason! How can a voice from the Public Platform be heard or believed, when the speaker is so obviously lost in his search for reasons.

The issues of morality have set their roots deep in our society, and those that cast the seeds to make 'Gentlemen' of us all, didn't read the instructions on the packet nor were they concerned about the long term effect of such selfish behaviour! For 250 years, the Public school system grew and flourished, bright heads blooming in our meadows and 'picked' for position of prominence! And who did the picking we might ask - - those of course who did the sowing! The

Archbishop picks the Bishop - as the leader in Government picks his Cabinet! "Can you keep a secret?"...."Hope so!"...."Well you're in! Take a seat!"

Unfortunately, our leaders are not picked from a common meadow, but from a field of cultivated thought!

I cherish the memories of my childhood and give thanks to the sanctuary of a poor but happy home! When the time came for me to enter the period of adolescence I was not confused by others, nor misguided by a warped mind as to the role I should play in the 'Herd' - but left instead to fall the right way up in a morally safe haven! I entered the world a boy and didn't disappoint my parents when they found I preferred sleeping with my opposite sex! In this modern world where the emphasis is on 'Freedom' - 'don't knock it till you try it!' - 'The Gay Movement' etc.!

A parent's job to isolate their children from the wicked world outside and from those who wish us all to be so tainted to ease their own conscience is not easy! I have four, and so far all seem to be 'The right side up!' But I am being penalized for fathering two girl and three boys with their sexual hormones in place! My efforts to give them a fair chance in childhood, is being attacked on all sides by Satanic forces that control the media and our education - eating away at little minds while our backs are turned, are dirty suggestions, dirty movies and dirty people in high places who have lost control of the situation - yet they talk of 'Back to the Basic's' - back to what basics do they mean, the ones that govern their lives or ours! The word alone can conjure up many meanings for a 'Get out clause!' by the shifty politician. Basic pay for basically everyone is but a starter!

Sorry about that - I do go on at times! Where was I? Something to do with my preference of the ladies I do believe!
Sitting next to me was a rather pretty, if not slim girl in her early twenties. Though the speech language barrier between us was complete her closeness didn't need any interpretations! Who talks anyway during an ancient act of intimacy - which was what she

certainly had in mind for us! Wallet full or empty, she was taking this Gringo home!

I've found myself waking up in some strange places during my life! Here I was again, wondering what the hell I'm doing here. Why didn't I go back with the rest last-night I thought? I knew they wouldn't leave me here in Santo Domingo - though there have been times later I wish they had! My thoughts at the time were, I had to get back to the boat. I lay there trying to figure out what time it was and how far I thought the dock away, trying to remembering the taxi ride.

The girl next to me still lay asleep, just her head above the covers facing the opposite wall. I studied her one room flat as I searched for the ticking clock I heard somewhere. Last-night with candles burning, it didn't look too bad, but then candle light can do that to a place. It was clean and tidy, but poor, no furniture in the small room, just things to stand things on! On one of those 'things' stood a very small television - quiet now, but last-night a black and white picture flickered round the room. Continuous lines wandered up the screen, destroying the face of some man screaming abuse in a barrage of long sentences. He sounded like a Spanish Peter O'Sullivan at the end of an exciting horse race - one without a horse or a race.

The walls were covered in the usual things girls can't ever have, photos of idols of her ideal man! Women it seems, no matter what country they live in, decorate their walls from an early age with pictures. Movie stars - male models or those from some band they swoon over. They imagine the character of their choice to go with that face on the wall. It seems as if it's an intimate personalized photo of a love they all so desperately desire! Given a chance to meet in person, or just see him from a distance in a crowd, will drive them to the point of hysterics, that when they return to their small room, an even greater love and longing will be bestowed upon the image! None of the 'Posers' I knew.

The windows were the Jalousie type, their shutters shut now, but still let in enough light to show it was daytime out there - but what time I wanted to know! I had to wake her to find where the hell that clock was!

She turned, surprised first, and then smiled! Some girls, especially those that hide themselves behind a lot of make-up, can look disastrous in the morning. Here, you get what you saw the night before, no war paint smudges on a face that would have discredited the plain beauty! I pointed to my wrist where a watch might be and backed it up in English that I needed to know the time! She replied in Spanish and turned to reach under the bed, revealing her naked back.

Though she was slim it didn't have bones protruding from it as if she'd gone through a mangle at some stage in her life. She had a fine figure, one that really I hadn't noticed the night before. She spoke something as she found what she was looking for and rolled back with a large wind-up alarm clock - so that's where the ticking was coming from. She repeated the sentence in Spanish and then turned the face towards me like some school teacher wishing me to remember the short phrase - and repeat - "Its 10 o'clock". It must have been what she said but my reply at seeing the hands of - "Bloody hell its 10 o'clock! - I must get back to the boat" must to the girl been a seemly rather long English passage for such a short Spanish one!

We had battled for some time the night before as each tried to make the other understand what had just been said, it broke the silence! The small bit each new of each other was totally useless for any conversation - "Can I have so many beers please - good morning - good evening - goodbye etc.!" didn't really help very much, and was as helpful as her contribution in English. I've wondered sometimes, just how long it would have taken for each - locked up in that room together, to emerge fluent in the others tongue! The morning light that shone through the shutters has lost its meaning to those that live in the night. Her room was her world, and like her friends, she knew those on the move outside, lived in a different one to her own. Her hunting time came when the sun dipped over the horizon, only then was it necessary to stretch the limbs and prepare themselves for the gathering of the pack.

"Getting up now - why? - Come back to bed dear" was certainly on her mind, her body trying hard to change mine by pulling herself close! Now most people, when they visit foreign shores, leave with something to remind them of what a wonderful time they had - for maybe they'll never return! Photographs - postcards - jewellery or a piece of clothing leave with them in a bag for home. With me would go the memory of a girl, longing to be loved and ready to prove, she was better in the art of making love than any I'd ever come across again! Whether it was me she held, or the thought of one of her idols on the wall that drove her passion to such lengths, I couldn't say, but there was a determined effort on her part that the memory of this encounter would keep her satisfied for some time.

Now, I know when Moses came down from Mount Sinai he had with him two stone tablets on which Ten Commandments were written - the main ones that are supposed to govern and enrich our lives. Now you could say, if you've broken one you've broken the lot! Or for each one broken if you like, you lose a stripe. Not many of us know that (Except Michael Caine!) the Lord God made many Commandments to his people as they trekked across the Sinai desert. Laying down the laws to Moses from inside the Tabernacle! Just read Leviticus and Deuteronomy and you'll see just how many that is. Only then you can add up how many you've broken! I had broken two on the one- to- ten chart - the 4th, not to work on a Sunday - and the 7th, committing Adultery! Both of which I'm not very proud of, especially the 7th!

Ignorance of the law is no excuse they say, and I don't presume to use that plea if I have to put forward my case, for I knew I was cheating on a dear wife then, even though it was far from home! I could blame it on circumstances, education or a need to satisfy some sexual desire, but at the end of the day basically (Back to Basics again!) that's what it was! Confession over with!!!

Having again broken the 7th, I really had to go and made the sign indicating a steering wheel as we dressed. I really would have preferred something to put on that would blend me in to the morning scene than that of a goodtime night-owl. An old straw hat say - dusty Jeans a broken down pair of Cowboy boots - a mule to pull or something. As it was I walked out in to the bright sunshine looking like I'd just come off stage from some Pop concert trying to outdo Elton John - I felt a right Prat!! People looked at me as if I'd just descended from some holy spot - a spot where all are rich and wear rich brightly coloured clothes - clothes without holes too!

Her hand movements said for me to wait where I was, and walking off, she hurriedly crossed the road, entering a house opposite. It was a different scene than what the evening before had shown, so much so it could have been a different street even. The light of the sun showed a tired rather run down area. The suppressed atmosphere on the people as they passed me, reflected on the buildings that looked as if little investment had gone in to them since this island was a whole nation - a rather 'what's the point' attitude prevailed everywhere. "No wonder she slept all day!" I thought - "Who wouldn't living in this place" it was rather depressing.

I stood there in my 'going out clothes' - not much to brag about I know, but still making me feel a bit like The Sultan of Brunei in a Social Security line-up! - or maybe more like the man whose dog is doing a crap in the middle of a busy shopping Mall, and you just dying for a hole to climb in.

I knew it was VW beetle long before it came over the brow of the hill. The engine first has its own tone - then the distinguishing shape of the roof came slowly in to view. It was what was on top of that roof that made me wish the girl would hurry back, for as it came on I could see it was the Police and the vehicle was packed solid with four burly, well fed Gorilla's! Out, no doubt, on the lookout for someone to have a workout on. The four pair of eyes scoured the pavement opposite. Un-concerned about the road ahead, the driver seemed as eager to spot the 'Rabbit' before his mates, so paid little attention to the Highway Code.

As any hunter knows when loading a gun, you can't wait to get the quarry in your sight to give it both barrels! Too feel the power in your hands delivering death and destruction to where the sights are pointed. Most sportsmen have a preference to what game they enjoy the most, and in civilized communities a season has been designated, by law, allowing them to let off steam! For without a law, all species of animal, fish and fowl would have long departed, leaving their destroyers with the final solution, that of facing one another across the smoke of war! Un-satisfied as always, whether it was size of the 'bag' - not enough left hand choke or not winning 'The angler of the month award' they sit dejected, some pissed off, they cannot claim as having --- 'Shot the last living creature on earth - apart from 'The Last man' award!'

This weapon, the gun, does not weed out the strong from the weak, nor in the hands of such men as was about to pass me, the good from the bad, it just becomes a bigger stick to beat the people with! As 'The four horsemen of the Apocalypse' drew abreast of me, I just hoped what they were looking for kept their eyes in that direction, for I began to feel a little like some staked out bait. "Bugger it!" I thought for I saw their heads turn, slowly - as if all joined by some hidden wire - "Currrbloodyrumbaaa!" said the faces as it settled in my direction, and it didn't take a genius to figure out who was the centre of that attention.

Even slower went the car now down the hill - the brake lights going on and off - as if an argument was ensuing between the driver and his mates about whether to stop or not - an argument concerning whether I should be allowed to hold a sensible conversation in the very near future! Should or should they not take me for a little ride, letting this 'Fucking Gringo!' Know where he can stick his American aid. The car that blocked them from my view was enough to distract their attention and with the mentality of the Anthropoid, I was forgotten as quickly!

The old '52 Chevy that gave me cover, pulled up next to me, the back door swinging open. In the front sat the girl telling me obviously to get in - quick! Our driver was a young lad about 18, who I found out after some lessons and deduction, was her brother! The Chevy took off with the enthusiasm of the young, always ready, whatever the age of the car, to give it the gun!

Whatever the girl said to me on our run back to the dock, I didn't understand, but she spoke anyway in a tone that was kind and soft that seemed to say she was sorry to see me go. I had no money to pay her, this she knew - I wished I had, not for the night, but to help her out! We said our goodbyes, each in our own language as if making the point of something that could never be, and as I turned to the gates, the old car moved off!

Chapter 29: Onwards to Puerto Rico

We left the quay at Santo Domingo at 14.10hrs on the 5th December. Streaming the log at 14.20. With the wind from the N.E and our course being set at 110 compass, we stopped the engine ten minutes later at 14.30hrs being under sail alone! At 15.00hrs the log was reset.

While in Santo Domingo a small Baltic called 'Fremad' was moored behind us. The owners where American who had done some refitting in Heybridge Basin of all places. Their last port of call had been Ponce in Puerto Rico and had bumped in to Dia and Mary Neale. We had decided to head there! A passage of about 190 miles to give them a surprise! Having done 20 miles in three hours the wind started to head us, so at 18.00hrs the engine was started to keep us full-and-by on 110c. By 02.00hrs on the 6th with the log reading

67.5 miles, the seas as we passed Saona Island in the Mona Passage were rough! Throughout the night and the following morning the wind continued E.N.E. At noon, with the log reading 111.5 miles we fixed our Latitude at 17-45.7'N. We had made less leeway than first feared. At 14.00hrs the coast of Puerto Rico was sighted through the heave swells from the N.E. With our course 90c as the wind died away in the evening we brought her up to 080c. At 20.00hrs with the log reading of 148 miles we dropped all sails in the calm air! On the 7th of December at 02.00hrs with the log reading 175 miles, we made our approach to Ponce harbour - dropping anchor half an hour later at the Yacht Club in 5 fathoms!

'Jylland's' engine had a very distinctive sound. It must have woken Dia from his slumber like some familiar call. We had seen 'Maica' at anchor and dropped ours close to him. Squaring all away, we sat on the deck to see appear in the Sloops cockpit a form. It stood on the stern and began peeing over the side. It had to be Dai - or Mary would need a closer inspection! Our outline in the darkness was well known to him and a closer inspection couldn't wait till morning, so hauling Mary from her pit and jumping in the dingy they rowed across. Ducked beneath the gunwhales, we listened to each confirming to the other it could only be us as they drew closer! The Welsh accent, un-affected by any mid-Atlantic crossing was strong and clear - "It certainly is her Mary - I wonder when they arrived!" The sound of a bump against our side and oars being shipped told us they were beneath us.

"They're probably all asleep" said Mary, a lady wishing not to disturb our peace and ready to leave the reunion till the morning light! "There must be somebody awake!" was the reply of a determined voice ready to board. He was about to do just that, but was repelled with a chorus of 'They'll be a welcome in the hillside' by those who knew the words. The waters round Ponce Yacht club sounded like Cardiff Arms Park come rugby time, Dias loud distinctive laughter in winning form!

We were not ready for sleep just then, and with Dai and Mary had just woken from theirs; we sat talking filling each other in with what they had been up to since we last met in St Lucia. Sadly we were to learn that Doug Nesbitt had gone missing. His Yacht 'The Aware' had been found ashore on the Island we'd just left; blood stained and stripped of anything worthwhile! So the story I'd read in a small article while in Panama stating Mr and Mrs Nesbitt is offering a reward for information concerning their son Doug was true!

We had met him in St Lucia where alone he handled the 'Aware'. Considering his handicap - leg wounds from Vietnam I believe - he hobbled about determined that they would not hinder his life. It appeared, while in Antigua for race week, he gave a couple of guys a lift - whether or not they were the cause of his disappearance - or suffered the same fate by others unknown we never knew! Whichever - Doug did not deserve such - and those who would do such a thing - may they rot in hell!

It just brings home the vulnerability of the small boat at sea in these waters - you can prepare for bad weather - but never for bad people. Since Columbus, the Caribbean has been nothing but a hive for evil bastards ready to cut a throat for a buck! The rule is --- and heed what I say! Whenever you come across a small boat that looks like it needs assistance - stand off - and have a rifle and shotgun ready - tell those aboard to stand up - then tell them to jump in to the water. If they don't obey immediately - sink them!

We spent two days chatting, doing a few repairs and deciding on our next leg. To get as much easting as possible was what we had in mind before falling of south - and hopefully get some sailing done!

I didn't see much of the island, the weather being against any sightseeing - very wet!!! But this island would see the coming and going of me many times in the future. Little did I know then that not too many miles from where we lay at anchor - my future sister-in-law Sandra lived. Mayaguez and its neighbouring village of

Bourqueron was the area. Her husband Phil Ark practiced Oral dentistry!

I will butt in on my journey here and go forward some years!

I would find myself in Phil's company waiting to catch a small plane to San Juan - instead of the one Phil was going to fly me up in. An amateur flier with a share in one, the weather got in his way of showing me Puerto Rico from a different view. I had Phil's company though at the airport till the stormy clouds passed, and it was thought safe to leave. "See that guys face over there" said Phil, nodding in a direction behind me. I turned to see a group of people standing at a small bar area. "Which one?" I asked - "The swarthy one!" said my companion. "Right," I said "do you know him?" I found myself looking at a rather good-looking fellow in his 40's wearing some sort of uniform. "No!...I was just thinking about going up to talk to him about his Jaw!" Puerto Rico, like the U.S, its benefactor, has no 'free' medical care where patients are more or less delivered to you on a plate. It's all down to salesmanship, the right approach and how to deliver a well-rehearsed line. Whether you live well or starve, depends entirely on pushing your product on the un-suspecting customer who believes your sincerity is exclusive to them! A signature to commit them to an un-necessary piece of equipment, or entice them in to your Parlour, is done with the same subtlety as my old teacher the Bible seller.

"Why! - what's wrong with them?" I said, studying the man's face as if some deformity was apparent. "Oh, he has what we call"- - and went in to some medical terms to explain the man's unknowing discomfort and imperfect features! He went on - "Most of us you see have problems we are unaware of in this department, due to one reason or another. See the squareness of his jaw line? I bet it makes a snapping sound when opened wide!" I found I wanted to give mine a little test, for it often did when a mighty yawn was underway - I didn't just in case Phil heard a familiar sound and an appointment would be suggested for my next visit!

Phil's profession is no different than any others in this mad world of the hard sell. It is part of the American way of life that has enveloped the rest of us. The success of yourself, company or country lies solely with a gift of the Gab - a bribe, or a threat if it can't be done with a quality product alone! Scruples must sit on the back seat with your heart and conscience if you're going to win the 'Salesman of the month' award!

I would like to have spoken with Phil more on the subject - how one executes the punch line after his self- introduction to the future patient, but I was off in to the high blue yonder leaving me to my own imagination as to its outcome and conclusion!

I could well see Phil asking him "Excuse me, do I know you from somewhere?"............."What do I do!!!! I'm a doctor!" Before the fellow knows it, he'll be rubbing his Jaw and looking at himself in the mirror of the airport gents, opening and shutting his mouth far beyond its normal range of safety - and capable, in the open position, of inserting a small coconut!!
Having planted in his mind the suggestion, the noise of the clicking sound he now hears becomes a bit unbearable, and he reaches for the introduction card Phil left with him.

If he has the money - time and ego, he will end up with a broken jaw that has been reset more than once! Passed on to a dentist friend, who can give him just the teeth he wants to go with his new jaw, and then to a throat specialist who informs him his bad breath is due to a bad set of tonsils. Removed - for the second time in his life - he sits broken to the chair and open to any suggestions now that might save his life!!! This finds himself upon the table with a surgeon about to give him a 40-year body service - a book on the Human anatomy open on page one before him!

This good-looking fellow could well end up in an intensive care unit being spoon fed because of Jaw problems. The most expensive drugs being administered to assist internal complications, while being pushed around in a wheelchair!!! This due to years of wearing the wrong shoes and the chiropodists being brought in too late to 'Save him!' Monthly, he will lay upon the operating table for the removal of a growing 'Lump' on his right buttock, the wallet once removed, that which made up the 'fatty' substance will be milked off - and a much thinner one put back.   "Thank God! they will all say - you were medically well insured!!"

Back to 75! and also of an Island long before the Americans were involved! Whereas this island was considered the most healthy in the Caribbean than that which we had left - Hispaniola (That island was deemed the opposite for Europeans! After the gold and any precious metals were stripped from that island, Spain was not bothered about its future and less enthusiastic about fighting for its possession, hence readily gave it up to France) Puerto Rico though, was a very fertile place indeed, and of a kinder climate, was a different proposition!

The production of sugar, coffee, tobacco, cotton, fruit and vegetables, was very great in the 19th century. Though 14 times less in extent than Cuba, it produced one third as much - and three times more than Jamaica which was as half as large again. Something worth fighting for was not to be given up without one, hence the intensive fortifications in its capitol San Juan de Puerto Rico on its north coast.

It was Columbus who put this place on the map of Spain in 1493, and again with a thoroughness of the Old Testament commandment, the Roman Catholic's extirpated most of its Indians to make way for their own brainwashed society of Christians! The fires of Hell have long been fueled by the souls of such men, who interpreted Gods word with wicked intentions of self-elevation in mind!

For 400 years this island flourished, guided by such reverence and direction! People by ignorance that others should gain, the church suppressed education that when a census was taken in 1873, of the 495,806 whites - 31,219 slaves neither could read or write - in fact, couldn't reside here up till then unless you declared yourself of that faith - Roman Catholic!

Such actions, the wish to keep others in the dark ignorance of illiteracy was done for reasons of self-interest. To hide from others the secrets of your genius, or in such a case as this, to conceal from the people the actions of those who carried out that evil in his name - for had the past been a history of goodly deeds by holy men, the story of their acts would surely have been one worth reading for its inhabitants!

Spain received its just rewards for being guided by the Holy Roman Empire, and the loss of another Dominion was the price they had to pay! It is odd that we the British alone stand condemned for the slavery issue. Spain, like other nations that gained much from this misery, keep their mouths firmly shut, happy that the finger is pointed our way. Yet if suddenly, the descendants of those un-happy lot were to give thanks for their deliverance to the new world, rather than be suffering the greater misery on that dark continent - hands would shoot in the air for their share of the praise.

The United States of America - flexing its muscles in the opening rounds of the international scene, had purchased St Thomas and St John's from the Danes in 1868 - at a rather knocked down price too as soiled goods, caused by the great Hurricane of 1867 But a stubborn Senate, remembering its constitutional promises, refused to ratify the agreement for some years - meaning, that lot were replaced by those with an Empire on their minds.

Puerto Ricans, learning rapidly to read and owing no favours to their suppressors, wished to throw off the shackles of the old Empire dying in Europe. With the help of 'Teddy-boy' Roosevelt and his Rough Riders little escapade of Cuba fame, the plains around another San Juan were swept of any resistance and after negotiations with Spain; this island became a toy-boy to big daddy in Washington in the Treaty of Paris in 1898! As the once mighty Spain lay dying, others unconcerned went through their belongings choosing for themselves the finest jewels.

The aid from the U.S each year, has made that knock down price a pig-in-a poke. Millions are passed on to a people that, had Americans used Spain's system of ridding oneself of the future 'Thorn in your side and splinters in your eyes' analogy, Puerto Rico would not contain any people of Spanish origins. They didn't, and it is today, still in the hands of those whose hearts are still in Castile.

Chapter 30: St Croix

We left here at 10.00hrs on the 10th Dec, making the most of the light E.N.E breeze. Our course was 105 c. The wind continued light from that direction all day and progress was slow. We had decided to pull in to St Croix briefly, to take on fuel. Where we had been in Ponce, getting on fuel was not possible.

At 13.15hrs we were alongside in Christiansted having taken 27hrs to motor 101 miles due to lack of wind. 3.7 knots wasn't by any means a great speed! It looked a pretty place from what I could see. Gaily painted houses lined the waters of the harbour, well-built and of a respectable character worthy of its past owners, the Danes! 24 miles long and 8 miles broad was what the offer said, and a 'Sold' sign went up - the buyers the U.S.

Again the Puritan attitude of those that first drew up the American Constitution was at stake. That, which stated, neither to meddle in others nation's affairs - nor to bear arms against thy neighbour - that all nations should be free etc.! etc.!. Of course it was said when a large un-touched cake of land stood before them - the Pacific still a long passage by sailing ship away. Never was the day visualized when such a vastness of land would not be enough for their needs, that a need to expand the 'Empire' should ever come about.

Even reading the small print, a reason could not be found to break from the binding contract as the Senate fought with its conscience over first the 'Indian issue'!!! Defending themselves against 'savages' was the answer - armed to the teeth by Washington brave white men massacred in great numbers - men, women and children whose only crime was - being there! Such clear wording had received its first blot!!

Drawn to this land of the free, would come those who had their own idea of what freedom meant, and what the old boys who drew up the agreement were really on about. From humble backgrounds many rose to the seat of power and wished in the egotistical state of the 'overnight millionaire', to show off to the old world that strength!

The mighty wealth of a united nation after the bloody civil war would expand beyond all decency, and the wisdom with what to do with such power was left to those who created it! Led by the genius rich, the nose of government would be pointed where their masters bid. To flush out some prey, corrupted by a pat on the head and a share of the spoils as the prize, buying another country, though ethically wrong, did not break Constitutional rules. Time and a little friendly persuasion of getting a large wad of notes in the back pocket of the morally conscious soon cleared up that issue. With the question answered by precedent, all cases concerning the interference of other countries affairs were carried out in the manner that was proper to their own understanding of the rules i.e. - if you've got enough money, you can buy whatever you want, that includes the world, for he who holds the purse strings holds the power! Thus with the shrewdness of a grand master and the ruthlessness of a Mafia Godfather every move to dominate the world would be taken!

From a safe distance from bomb and gunfire, a greater wealth would be created by the opportunity of war, for the Constitution now is your 'Get out' clause for partaking in other nations business. The time to enter the conflict was crucial and calculated to perfection. With an arm round your shoulder, a voice behind a thin veil of that 'Special Relationship' demanded certain conditions along with his loans! "As it is every man's right to be free, so be it true of all nations!" etc.!

"Britain must give every assurance that the nations within its Empire be given the right to self-determination!" What Bullshit!

For 50 obsolete Destroyers our 'special relation' wanted the use of certain Caribbean ports for a 100 years, bartering while our nose was being bloodied!!! Loans to buy food and materials of war went to the bottom of the Atlantic, as German and Brit wore themselves out in the opening rounds. Not till it was sure we could rise from the ashes of this conflict, and Germany was on to a loser, did our friends move in to support - not us, but the democracy and the free world they would inherit! It was a Special Relationship alright, worthy of the one King David had for Uriah!

To America went the spoils of war! While Europe lay in ruins - bleeding from the great battles - U.S citizens slept well in houses untouched by bombs and grief! Generals won honours - men were claimed heroes and dead - and politicians made plans to pick over what remains of a once great nation.

As you can't buy your friends, you can't buy countries! By your ill-gotten gains you will be despised by all for how you acquired your wealth. The American Empire was not won upon the fields of battle, and the Laurels of Bay tree they covered their brave in, were home grown, placed upon head and uniform by the dirty hand of deception. Many a brave American boy would die in the service of his country, the reason for his death not clear. Many would return head bowed heroes, tormented by defeat of a useless cause. The Moron attitude of its leaders, who were raised on 'hustling' for a living, would state "American Forces are not involved other than in an advisory capacity!" A nice way round the Constitutional issue! Total hypocrisy!

Its involvement in all countries, without commitment to all is done by envoys with a large bag of money but no foreign policy. It's an

Empire run on shady deals, on concessions, on manipulations and threats. Winning is all that's important, how it is achieved is immaterial, for in America there is no place for losers. To capitalize on friend and foe - to administer its influence and punishment, the high chair of The United Nations is the key that allows it access on foreign soil as Champions of the free, but who's real aim is only, the best interest of - their America - their freedom - their rights - their wealth - their laws - to hell with the founding fathers principles - for when all is said and done - did not they have things their way?

"You can fool all the people some of the time!" etc.! Wise words that fall on deaf ears! There are many in this country, and in Europe, that understand their ploy. And many that will not forget what "A special relationship" can mean to them! Having driven all Nations back to their own borders, the roosters are coming home to rest! Britain, shorn of its Empire and power to administer the rule of law, have fallen back to join the ranks of Europe! Leaving America to deal with the mess created by that folly 'All nations have the right to be free!'

Freed, nations had the right to choose which form of Government they preferred, and went to he who gave the most aid. The old globe, showing the sun never setting on our Empire, was marked in red - it would turn to that Communist colour in many places! It would cost America far more to stem the red tide than ever was made when they created it.

The money to be made by freeing the slaves of any Empire, never happened, other than outside their own country. Bribed Governments were overthrown leaving another with his hand out or else, attitude! The only imports from free people were drugs and crime. Jamaica, for one being a classic example of a real thorn in their side!

America is broke, with a national debt running up faster than you and I can count! It can print its own meal ticket on the count of its superior force of arms! While the status quo remains, it is free to continue the rule by blindly following a crooked path! But all of us have to sleep at one time or the other! 'Having run out of petrol! - you can't expect a push to the next garage from the hitch-hiker you just gave the one finger sign to five minutes ago!'

The selling of St Criox to the U.S took from future generations of Danes, the nice idea of place for its people to get some sun without having someone asking you for your passport and - how long do you intend to stay! The French and the Dutch had the right idea, they retained their little gems in a silver sea by making it part of their realm. Both travel freely back and forth unhindered. Not us - all given up without a fight, yet how hard we fought for it eh! The only place Brits can go to be sure of catching a tan without being moved on, is on a couch in your front room with a sun lamp turned on. Great foresight and great negotiating wouldn't you think?

Having taken on 100 gallons, we left at 17.30hrs the same day! The weather was wet and calm, so again it was bloody motoring.

Chapter 31: St Lucia at last

Our course from St Croix was 120 compass. No wind to help us but with no current to head we were making better progress across a calm sea, speed around 5 knots!

It is this time of the year the prevailing easterly winds are affected by the 'Northers' as they are known here, Strong weather patterns across the American continent pushing down in to the upper reaches of the Caribbean bring strong winds and squalls, Not that we would mind that for a change! At 06.00hrs on the 12th with the lights of Saba bearing 060 true, we had some squally stuff out of the N .N.W but nothing to raise hope or sail!

A large bank of shallow water lies to the west of this island. In the next couple of hours we would catch some fish, the first in our passage back. Two large Tuna and something large enough to take our heavy line! Replacing it, we hauled in a rather big Barracuda - which is good to eat, but not from this bank! They have a high copper content absorbed in the flesh from eating their prey that have passed it down the chain from the bottom feeders - so we were warned by those whose intent it is to conserve the ever dying sea and its species! Catching fish brought a sense of fun, and broke up the usual procedure of things. To see the wonderful colours of a Darado as it breaks the surface, the beauty of them enhanced by the water! Good to eat, but a shame to kill!

By 08.30 we were abeam of Saba, distance 15 miles. This island is nothing but a top of a mountain, and like the rest of the chain - Volcanic! Conical in shape, rising 3,800 feet to the summit which is on many occasions covered in cloud, Some years later we would come here in 'Jylland' to spend the night. It has no harbour but on its western side large buoys have been laid for visiting craft, The seas round Saba can pick up quickly and heavy swells smash against its side with terrific force sending spray high up the sheer face of this rather strange place to live. The night we were there was not very comfortable, rolling like a pig at times. Had we an anchor down I think we would have left, but hanging on the buoy we stuck it out knowing we could soon slip out line and leave if it got worse!

It is a Dutch island with pretty painted houses and neat gardens, that's if you can get ashore to see them. Landing is tricky if not impossible with a sea running. Only two towns exist, one called Top and the other Bottom. Top is a village that sits on the ridge of an old Volcano, and Bottom, the main town lies in the hollow therefore one has to go to the Top before reaching the Bottom. Though it might be a precarious place to live, and I can't for the life of me think I could put up with sitting on a sleeping time bomb where every rumble of thunder had me on my feet thinking this is it! It is probably one of the few places to live in the Caribbean where friends and relatives would leave you in peace.

They have a small airstrip which is carved out at an area called Hells Gate! If you miss it you enter it, for a 1,000 ft drop at both ends to the sea below awaits you! Sabans they say, make fine seamen! I've heard that same claim from many islanders in a boasting competition, but to live here and survive fishing out on that bank, with its testing sea, then to be able to get your catch back upon a treacherous shore I would say - "If you aint any good your dead!"

Saba, in its isolation from the outside world, and a social attitude of a past race, has led to much inbreeding. Such enclaves of old white families still lie dotted around the Caribbean determined not to mix. Through lack of the fresh blood of their own kind, and not willing to intermarry with the black, the signs of degeneracy are plain to see in all areas. I didn't see any blacks on Saba and as we walked this place, we would see, offering us lace and wares white girls and women caught up in the sad realization of that dilemma! Descendants of a once fine ancestry, wearing a mask not of their choice but one now that held little beauty to the eyes of the beholder

I heard the story, that on a visit from a Dutch warship, the men were requested to go ashore to pump (to use the expression) some new blood into the island! If the tale is true, and I heard it from more than a good source, it was rather a strange one and certainly not considered with wisdom, for surely such a request would assume to the men that waiting on the slopes ashore were all the islands maidens ready and anxious to be served by a bunch of seamen! It was like ordering your men to sexually assault a mentally retarded institute, to retire leaving the incapable to take care of the mess!

I know many a ship carried more than just its cargo to foreign shores and the genes of many a sailor run through the blood of an overseas bride - but it happened by chance not orders! Anyway, the reputation of such an order to the Dutch, would if carried out, have done little to bring in new blood to the island - not unless the men folk of Saba can bear children.

Just after noon, the wind lifted slightly from the W.N.W so sail was raised at last, On a course of 140c at 17.20hrs we were abeam of Redonda and by 20.00hrs were passing the island of Montserrat, Our speed a little over 5 knots!

As usual, the wind fell away during the night leaving us with a flat sea and a lovely moon.

At 06.00hrs on the 13th December, the island of Dominica was close at hand, a most beautiful sunrise appearing between the mountains of that wooded island! Our course was now 170c and to join us going south came two whales. Blowing hard like a couple of marathon runners, they closed with us as if to re-join the pack.

The hard punching to windward was all behind us now, the further south we came, the easier the conditions with wind and sea. At 16.00hrs the wind was coming straight at us from Fort-du-France, Martinique! Such closeness to St Lucia brought Mike out like a flower with the first rays of spring sunshine on its face. It was home waters he was in now and with the radio-telephone in hand, he called in the hope of picking up someone he knew to inform them "We were Home!!" For me, I would have preferred the silent approach instead.

Having cleared customs, we were alongside the dock at Ganters Wharf at 22.30hrs, taking us 3 days short of a month to get back, It had been an interesting trip, if not trying at times, but certainly one I'd never forget!

Chapter 32: Picking up the pieces

The practice of fishermen, in the days of sail was to beat to the windward for the days catch, running home before it, sorting and gutting what they had caught. Had we observed this rule and obeyed it; we would never have gone to Panama on our fishing trip. For not doing so, we paid the penalty of the long slog to windward home - our holds empty too. Our arrival, under the cover of night, was about appropriate. I'm sure things would have been much different though had the news of our 'Find' been true. The very news that had prompted the then Governor of St Lucia, Sir Alan Lewis to send us a telegram saying 'good luck with best wishes' you can bet your bottom dollar, it would have been him that Mike had got on the radio, not Michael Bagshot. With it would come the request to save our entry in to Castries till the daylight hours so they could bathe us in its glory! Might even have a band playing to welcome home 'Their Boys!'

No, I'm afraid, we had returned empty handed to those who had heard the news long ago, and had blown the candle out in the window soon after. The wasting of his time on a telegram would certainly not be repeated in a little car ride down to Ganters to say "Hard luck old boy! - glad you got back okay!!!" Grahams 'Leak' to the media had left us with the egg on our faces, okay, and we felt the silence from those that would have otherwise been ready to grab us by the hand. We were lottery winners who's arses would have been willingly kissed, lovingly too by our new found friends. Some must have been sitting in their offices wiping the very thought of it from their lips!!

What to do after the mess was not going to be easy. The easy way was to have got an airline ticket like Howard, and to retreat back to England and lick my wounds. But who would take care of 'Jylland' - who could you expect if her owners deserted the ship. He had gone within 5 days of our arrival back in St Lucia, and as it stood then, had no intentions of returning. My dreams and hopes for the future were at a low ebb and just how we were going to pick ourselves up, it was difficult to imagine.

No one likes a loser; the dock we had laid alongside was the first to show its feelings for such. Scott - the other partner with his American pal Doug that ran things at Ganters, asked us kindly to move off - which we did, not wishing to upset the situation for we may wish soon to return. As for 'Jylland', who had suffered from the sweating and soaking in central America, a dry-docking should have taken place - check the hull over and whack on a coat of paint before any future plans could be thought about - but there was nothing in the kitty to pay for that.

The idea of carrying paying passengers to Martinique on a three day excursion was an idea thought about, but not with decks that needed chaulking badly. She was in need of a good overhaul before anything could take place - if not underwater, then certainly above, so with no complaints from those left with the job, we got on with it.

While the ever willing Bill un-shipped her topmasts and went over the rigging, I pounded the chaulking iron on where I thought the source of the elusive leaks originated. For those who have spent time on this task - they'll know what a frustrating, head scratching, thankless task this can be. To add to your misery, if it rains - you're buggered. St Lucia in December can be very wet, rain hitting the water like bullets as it buckets down.

Awnings up, you're protected, but soon it makes its way towards the area of your attention down the natural sweep of the deck, or blown in the gusts straight underneath them. The wind in those squalls has blown out your fire under the pitch pot and until the sun dries all - and the wind is gone, you might as well forget it! At such times, it was get on with another job that the damp conditions in Panama had done to us. Jackets round the main-mast and Samson post had split from swelling wood, so it was down to the forecastle, pull out some canvas, and get stitching!

The anchorage at Vigie saw the coming and going of many boats, from the beautifully kept charter ones like 'Circe', the live-aboard floating home like 'Mystic', to the touring Camper with a keel - the old 'Northern Lights'. She was the home of Ann and Jimmy Griffiths, an elderly couple that had decided to 'Do' this part of the world at the slow pace in a craft as old as they were. An old double-ender, full of baggy-wrinkle and rigged for comfort not speed.

I sat looking at her one day, my attention taken by someone in a dinghy under her stern - obviously inspecting something, Jimmy, a ships surveyor, wasn't too happy with. An area back aft saw him leaning over the stern rail in some discussion with the person in the small boat. I saw them row ashore and for the moment the thought of them was gone as I got lost in my own problems of ship maintenance. I saw Jimmy return alone, head out to his craft - and return again - it was obvious he had taken a measurement, one of those measurements when you can't get what you want. His usual happy face suggested to me, a problem!! This time when he had tied up his dinghy, he headed our way. We would soon learn what his problem was and as luck would have it - be able to help!

"You wouldn't have aboard some large screws - something slightly larger than these," he said, holding in his hand a 4" bronze one that looked as if it had been a problem removing and unless one used a hammer, wouldn't go back where it came from. Jimmy's eyes lit up when I said – "Hold on I might have something that will do" for he really didn't expect that response. When I returned from the forecastle holding a 6" coach bolt, I could have named my price - though not bronze, where it had come from proved the quality of its galvanizing and perfect to pull in his ends to the transom. Before he had chance to say - "You wouldn't have anymore" for fear of his luck running out - I said it for him,

So for two people, our trip to Panama hadn't been a waste of time after all, and had I held the coffin of Drake in one hand rather than a number of fastenings from the dock at Coco-Solo in the other, I know what Jimmy would have taken.

Tucked away in one part of that cove, anchored before and after, with some 'just in case' safety lines ashore to the trees that bordered it, sat 'Rose Salters'. Her 40' hull had seen better days, and Wally her owner now, had intentions of bringing her back to life. But at the pace dear old Wally moved, he would need many of them if his intentions were to do the job himself! I would guess Wally, a Canadian, was in his fifties and living alone on her at the time, the one thing that struck you about him, was that leisurely gait he had. Rowing his round frame ashore, was his daily workout, The small two person fibre-glass dinghy moving ever so slowly across the still waters to the dock, to be just as casually made fast before he thought about landing himself ashore. Even for his size, it made him easily 'missed'. There were no sudden movements to make his position known. In a world of rushing people 'finding Wally or Waldo' was our game, and a trained eye spotted him 'mingling' with the fore or background. You could be working away on deck - an empty dock beside you - look up and there he was, come from out of the blue standing there just watching proceedings.

His daughter came to see him once; we saw the dinghy going past us well down in the stern as dad gave her a tour of the cove. She wasn't a big girl; it was just the smallness of the craft that had her hands so close to the water as she held on to the port and starboard rails. She seemed as elusive as her dad though, for we didn't see much of her either!!

He asked me one day to go aloft - check out 'Rose Salters' mast, I doubt if anyone had been up there for years, if they had, it was only to do what I was doing. The mast was in fine shape, but the rigging certainly wasn't.

I happened to be looking once for the anchor of 'Mystic' - slipped when Tom Judd its owner, had left for one of their weekends away, and on returning, couldn't find its buoyed line, "While your down there - came the voice of Wally over the rail - would you mind checking my anchors!" Both forward and that aft, showed by the long growth from the waterline to several feet beneath it, that they hadn't seen the light of day for many a year. Where's Wally now, I sometimes think to myself, and did he ever get her finished?

The anchor belonging to 'Mystic' I never did find - the murky water being difficult to search, and of course, the rough position given me by Tom where he slipped it, rather guess work. But our assistance would come to that family of a much greater urgency on another day, and leave both the husband and wife teaching duo so very thankful. We'd seen them come racing in as we sat one Sunday afternoon chatting. Early for them too, as the usual time for the returning 'from a weekend away up the coast somewhere' was around sunset, No sooner was the anchor down and Tom was in the dinghy racing towards us - something was up, and that something was - he was sinking!

Throwing an air tank in the whaler, a few tools and some oakum, we ran out there to see the wife and his two children looking rather concerned and worried about the first time of hearing water rushing in the hull rather than past it. Those used to seeing dust in the bilges, panic slightly when water is spotted. We were used to it, and as the future would tell, totally a home with such a sound - not happy, but at home. Being made of steel the little schooner rigged 'Mystic' either had a big problem, one you couldn't nail a patch on, or something small. It was the latter - leaking stern tube, that when Bill stuffed some oakum up it with a screw driver and it ceased flowing - all Toms family were now smiling, for they could sleep in comfort till the morning when a better assessment of the problem could be done. "Yes, you can run your engine, but not in gear!" and so saying left them till the morning.

The cutlass bearing that had gone was behind some concrete put there where the shaft came through the stern post, and getting at it meant swinging a hammer in a tight spot, We could do it alright - and did - and not only that, charged Tom half what it would have cost him when we totalled up the hours spent- the bonus we wanted was - two loaves of sour-dough bread, I used to smell his wife cooking while I smashed concrete. They were happy, and so were we, eating the best bread I've ever had, then and since.

If there is one place left on this earth where one realizes the importance of friends, its life aboard a boat, The very fine, thin skin line between you and a long swim, or seeing your home sinking before your eyes, makes you realize just how important others are when the 'big' surprise you didn't reckon on happens. People that live in solid walls that don't drag their anchors, nor get blown towards a Lee shore with a useless engine, never experiences that feeling of total thanks he has in his heart for the person that comes to your assistance - many times a mere stranger too. Safe in your warm home, a good gale blowing outside, there is little to concern you about the good argument you've just had with your neighbour - nor he you! In fact, you may not even hear the wind, for your mind concentrates solely on how you can upset him further. If the same attitude adopted on land was taken with you to sea, you'd be a dead man - or one standing up to his neck in water, and not a spare pump in sight.

The sound of running water entering a boat can be a fearsome sound for the beginner. But life aboard an old wooden girl just wouldn't have been the same for us in the coming years. How many times I would spend either outside or inside directing someone to the spot you can hear the flow. I wouldn't like to say I just wished I'd got a pound for every hour spent. Hours would be taken sometimes searching for that mysterious leak - "It's about there!!!" you would shout from the inside of the hull - he outside hearing your voice - while you inside can hear his bubbles. Up the hull he lets his air bubbles flow where you shout from, and if he's sharp eyed, he will see some enter with the water - then bingo! - oakum and patch and you've got a few more bilge hours, but not always.

Life was hard enough during those early months - harder still without any money. One small job came our way, and having nothing to do with boats, we could ask a price for our services without the need for favours. It was a diving job to - looking for, and raising if we could, a car! It had been driven in to the water by its owner, who claimed it was an accident - yet he had failed to convince the insurance company it was a total loss. Thus they wished us to check it out, and if possible raise it. It was Mike, Bill and I that went across to search for it, and from the tyre marks left in the grassy wide verge, it was just a matter of following the line out underwater. We found it without any difficulty laying upside down in 15' feet about 50' from the shore - five more feet was all the driver had needed and it would have gone over the edge of an area dredged for an extension of Castries harbour. It seemed to me, this was what the insurance company thought was on the mind of the owner - and knowing the fellow had been trying hard to sell the big Chevy without success - guessed foul play.

We couldn't do much that afternoon and to lift it, oil drums would be needed and strops made, so we returned to the schooner. As Mike had to go with Will the next day to check out Martinique - Bill and I took on the task. The first thing was to try and get her turned over, a job made easier if she'd been in deeper water, 15 feet with a car close to that in length, our strops would have to be short, and we'd need something big to pull her over and out, Two oil drums close to her back chassis, then filled with air from a spare tank, up she went, back-end first. All you need sometimes is a little luck to make a hard job easy, and round the corner, as I waded ashore to the gathering crowd of the curious, came my luck! Four bloody great wheels bouncing under the weight of something used in the road construction business. Waving down the driver was no problem, yet from a distance, I believe he thought I was one of his fellow countrymen, bollock naked, emerging out of the harbour.

Stopped, he was as interested as to what caused the crowd, as much as the crowd, and would certainly, for nothing, let alone for a few bucks, be part of the action and show just how powerful his machine was. A line to him, and slow ahead, and up and over the small bank she came. Job done, Bill, Mike and I got $265.00 U-S, paid the next day too, and seeing though it was Christmas Eve when we received it, all could have a better day.

In amongst that crowd of onlookers, I later found out, was the person who 'Lost control' of the Chevy, On an inspection by us when we found it, it would seem at first by the lack of 'anything' aboard, no paper, empty glove compartment, that it was indeed as the insurance company had thought. We could have so easily 'tipped' it over the side and none would have been the wiser - but would we - even if he'd asked for a 'favour' - hard one that!

'Dan! Dan! was a very fine man, and a very fine man was he, All he wanted was some peace and quiet, a boat and a bit of sea!'

The first time I met this quiet unassuming fellow was on our return to Castries from Panama. Creeping up, out of the darkness towards the dock, Dan couldn't make us out just yet, but by the sound of 'Jylland's' engine, he knew we were a Baltic. Why? Because Dan owned one too.

I saw his single outline standing there and didn't realize the reason was to take our lines, Dan didn't know we knew this area like the back of our hand; and before he had the chance to say anything, I had thrown the bowline over the bollard that had acted as a table for his glass of wine - smashing good shot! Mike had put her in with ease that had Dan very impressed by the lack of all the shouting that usually goes with a Captain not sure of his crew! Dan's Baltic was called the 'Sonja' and with it he ran up and down the islands carrying anything he could put aboard that could be taken off the other end, General cargo was Dan's trade, that - not-got-too-much to say cargo. Get it on, Get it off, Get paid, and go and have a beer trade.

Dan was an American by birth, but in him somewhere lay that urge to get on the old 'Briny' ocean, take a chance at something you've never done before, and won't be happy 'til you've tried it, We would get to see Dan on most occasions when in port, and if not see him, hear his 'Pots' agoing hard astern, or that gentle 'thump' as he headed out for sea. Dan had a daughter Meg, and like father like daughter, was very much as the genes would predict. Meg had come down to see how dad was fairing in his chosen life, and I would say - proud of him too - win or lose! I would spend my 34th birthday in their company, for they came aboard that night for a session of 'yamming'.

Christmas Day 1975, would see the arrival from Germany of Horst Dueter and his wife Martel. News had reached us that the filming we had insisted on of The Black Christ festival had turned out good. Horst, a director of T.V programs in that country, and a friend of Grahams, was willing to put it together!! Problem was, he needed more shots. As Panama was out of the question - Horsts only option was St Lucia!

It was thought, who's going to notice the difference between one Palm tree and another. What would turn out was not the difference between trees, more the difference between cameramen! It wouldn't take much to realize from the very start that this fellow knew something about 'Hairs on the gate' and which end to point at the subject, and it would stick out like a sore thumb when eventually we got to view the finished article.

Had we known then what we know now, we would have said "Horst, you're here, but forget it. Running around setting up shots, hiring Felix to put on the 'Purple', then getting him to carry a cross round the island - is going to be a waste of time - so enjoy your two weeks holiday!" And really, that's about the only two people who got anything out of our 'good' idea. When he and his air-hostess wife left on the 15th Jan, we had fed them, bedded them, entertained them with money we really didn't have. I can't remember them once paying for a thing, and why? Graham had said "Have this one on me!" A phone call by Will to Dennis and Herr Bonney on the 26th December with regards this matter, came back the reply from Graham "I've been trying to get in touch with you for two days!!" and from Dennis, nothing but a lot of old crap, said Will - which meant - you handle it!

Money worries were pressing, and the need to get her back to work was imperative. The intended cruises to Martinique was an option, but getting her ready for passengers and back to shipshape, was a full time job for the much depleted crew. Mikes input never was anything to shout about and getting less as if it was a new year's resolution he'd made, his time aboard was going to be as short as my temper was by seeing him using us basically as a hotel!

A very large spanner would be thrown in our spokes and ideas concerning Martinique. It came in the form of a telegram on the 5th Jan! From Dennis it said "Phone me 6 o'clock their time!" Doing so came back the news "Have got work all year round for 'Jylland' in Nassau - very good money - will let us know more in a couple of days!" I write in my log-book on such 'wonderful' ideas _ "Let's hope there are no hitches or false promises as there was last time - it could finish us if it's the wrong move!!!!

The next day, Will decided to call Howard in England to tell him of the phone call from Dennis concerning Nassau, In Cornwall now with his wife, he was 300 miles from the scene of the action in Essex where the future of 'Jylland' was being decided - but some 5,000 miles closer than us to check it out!

I write on the 8th of my real concerns about this deal - "We could lose everything if this doesn't come off, I think it would be better to stay here - work the season till maybe April, go on dry-dock, run up to Nassau, then if it doesn't work out, come back here and we won't be broken - I just hope Dennis realizes that!!" - Did he? like hell he did.

A letter arrived from Howard on the 9th stating 'Things not all that good back home!" - didn't say what things - was it with wife, or work! I also hear, after years of him backing off, Dennis and Pat were getting married that very day! "Whew!" says my log,

It would be a stormy affair, a right old distasteful brew they would mix up together too. Out of earshot of those it would concern, deals were being struck - promises made of a rosy future to his new wife, and with her blessing - as a condition in the pact she made with him - 'Jylland' would be the prize - a 'Jylland' without us!! How such an influence by her on proceedings came about - I would learn in Nassau!!

By the 12th of January, and nothing from Dennis concerning the Nassau deal, we decide to press ahead with the trips to Martinique, and on the 13th I heard, it could be a month before it was finalized, So with that now at the back of our minds, a planned cruise to Fort-du-France was on for the 19th, and to get her ready - all leave was cancelled - except Mikes of course!

Any activity aboard something 'Jylland's' size attracts attention. Unshipping or shipping her topmasts is for boat people, something to stand and watch - and if never done, admire the ease in which brave hearts dangle aloft without any form of safety harness. My harness has always been my hands and to rely on any other means, obstructs my movements. Anyone that won't go aloft without a harness shouldn't be up there in the first place.

I would be disturbed, not this time aloft, but as I worked on deck - the nice task of refurbishing our heads. In the next couple of days, they were in for some heavy pumping. A little verse here on heads I read aboard the 'Deliverance' once.

"Pause if you can spare some time to peruse this awful rhyme. Remember those swimming near, wish you would wait till they were clear! And when you have done your duty, to preserve this thing of beauty, Press the peddle for a while to see water gush forth like the Nile, Now work the handle to and fro and soon your order it will go. Repeat the process as required, until your arm becomes quite tired. The final touch is with the brush, thus avoid a maidens blush. All this the Captain asks you for, departing thought - don't close the door!"

"Hello there - I'm sure you won't remember us, but we met you once in Denmark - Middelfart" standing there on the jetty - for we were now back on 'Doug's Duck' - was a fair maiden and a man dressed in smart white clothes. "I'm Margaret Havers and this is my husband Doug - we met you some years back when searching for a Baltic of our own". I seemed to remember such a couple due to not forgetting a pretty face and the fact one doesn't meet too many English there.

Work stopped as I tried to recall them and to listen to their obvious enthusiasm about 'Baltic's'. I was soon to learn that they were part of the large gin palace that had slipped in to Castries that morning. Doug was in fact the Captain of 'Lac 11' - with its helicopter pad an' all. He looked the part too, bearded like some old 'Titanic' skipper ready to go down with his ship.

It wasn't long before dropping anchor, when speeding towards customs went something that had Mike's jaws foaming at the mouth with envy. It was one of those 'Donz' boats - an all-Italian job, a Ferrari on water made as a must for all of those countries crooked bankers. Returning to the mother ship, it then sped our way and docked. Two crewmembers, dressed in the essential white of pureness certainly looked the part. That 'Donz' could pull a lady from several miles by the sound of its engine alone. It was Mikes dream machine - I could see him coming to rest after parading himself round the bay - jumping ashore after waking every sunbathing beauty up! What girl wouldn't want to seat back in those plush armchairs and go for a spin!

Doug and Margaret had slipped in quietly on this same craft and we hadn't noticed it 'parked' over the other side of the dock. It came at a pace not to attract too much attention. It is odd, and to me very annoying to watch the reaction of people when wealth nears! It has a great affect upon most, thus to flaunt it is its main purpose. Mike had noticed the 'Donz' as he came back from the 'Wicky-up' - and the betting's were, it was 'Club sandwich' time. I saw him standing, looking over the side of the dock, then turn and walk pointing at something I couldn't see, yet knew it must have been something amazing by his facial expression. "Have you seen that?" he said, not realizing those that had driven it over sat on 'Jylland's' deck.

Having introduced him, it didn't have any affect till I walked across the dock with its drivers! Hearing and seeing is believing, and it was only then did Mike say - "How do you know them?"

Of course both returned later that evening, the 'Donz' lighting up the dock with its underwater lights. Both wished to show their album of 'Svanen' being converted to a Barquentine in Denmark. Much was being spent, and it was obvious they wished to be more of a part in that conversion. Margaret of the two seemed totally in love with all to do with old sailing boats - the smell, all their own of Diesel and Stockholm tar, it was the perfume to appeal to such a lady. Fill her pillow with oakum rather than feathers, and she would sleep like a baby.

Being a Sat, they were due to leave for Martinique the next day, but on hearing we were to cross over on the Monday, Margaret asked was it possible to come with us. And of course it was.

Margaret would not be the only passenger I knew on that trip. On board would be my cousin Chris, girlfriend Edna - and my uncle, his dad - Howard. The same uncle that sat in our front room at 36, not knowing who I was, and caring less to be where he was then, but not now - right now I was his nephew - and one who didn't have one gene of him in me! It was a little too much to ask that a sea wash him overboard, and the way he had planted himself on the hatchway amidships, with little intention of moving, the old sod wasn't likely to grab one.

It was an early departure - all passengers aboard by 07.15 and under sail by 07.35. Arrived in Fort-du-France 12.30, 5 hours for us being about right. Carrying mostly locals with relatives in Martinique, they departed once cleared, to go do some visiting and to do some shopping of things they couldn't get in St Lucia - which in 1976 was about most things.

'Lac 11' came in an hour after us and missed the chance to get some sailing shots - leaving Castries late, they thought catching us up wouldn't be a problem. The 'Ferrari' came to pick up Margaret and those who wished to go over and take a look at what they were missing out on. I didn't bother, nor was Billy in much of a hurry to look at the palace - we slung our hammocks on deck, sitting under the awnings in peace.

We got underway the next day at 11.20 - first another visit from Margaret and Doug to take those who hadn't seen the boat for a tour - Bill and I got out of the first chance, and felt it rude to say no the second time. They would get some good shots of us when we left, for a fine wind was behind us. It would be one of the best sails I ever had in 'Jylland'. The wind was strong out of the N.E and she was in her element punching all before her like some happy Dolphin.

I sat with my brother Will in the netting under the jib-boom. That day was worth all the hassle and hardships. Seeing her coming at you with a 'bone between her teeth', as the saying goes, made you feel great to be alive, and kept in you the desire to have more days like it.

Sailing right up to entrance to Castries harbour before starting up the iron lung, we arrived back at 17.15. All those that came, thanked us and I did really believe - meant what they said - and if we persisted with such passages - we could make a go of it!! What was standing in the way though were other people's ideas. Wooden boats that don't leak are either pretty new, or in a boat shed! The trip to Martinique with spray coming aboard, had found places that needed attention - that area being above the forecastle. If we were to continue with these passages that were the area, we the crew would find ourselves - so it was for me, another round of pitch-pot and oakum. I had the hatch covering boards off the next day and worked late doing what was found necessary and what only another good sailing experience would prove if my efforts had been successful.

Thurs 22nd of January saw us without enough for the planned trip for the 23rd and pushing the idea was important - but first before any commitments, Will was to call Dennis for some information regarding Nassau. I would get the response from that call on the 23rd, which did rather make me shake my head in wonder of my brothers total lack of understanding and what's more - odd statements as to our financial position! He, Dennis, was first going to Germany, then on to Nassau - would phone us from there on Tues 27th. Will told him about Martinique runs, with the response from Dennis 'Not to use the sails!' I write that day "That's okay then - I still have fears of what might happen to us if it's left up to him".

We received a phone call from Dennis and the word from Will - late Tues evening saying - "It's on! Dennis is waiting on contracts which he'll get tomorrow - will call when he has them". I write - "Must remind Will to ask Dennis about sending us one!"

It is now January 28th, and now with the news is out of the bag, and the wise or un-wise decision to go taken, but not confirmed, our eyes and attention is set in that direction. Howard, not committed at home and un-settled in any work, is contacted, and of course will return to make up numbers - for we certainly couldn't afford to pay anyone. I'd hoped before coming, he might have contacted Dennis, and approved such a decision by a meeting in Essex - or Cornwall, for our fears of the loose cannon in control, still worried us.

Before anything could happen, and due to funds having dried up by not working, it was pressed upon Dennis that monies must be made available to us to pay for the passage to the Bahamas - fuel and food and something in the kitty as a safeguard.

We would eventually leave on the 6th March without a penny coming from England.

My logs during this period ring out like inhabitants of Lucknow awaiting the arrival of Havelock's army. Mike was not coming and had moved off in early February - Howard arrived 5th February and hadn't seen Dennis, nor been able to get charts for Bahamas by - lack of trying!
On the 7th Feb, an offer to us to do the film 'Pirates' being filmed in Malta by Roman Polanski, worth - I write, #40,000 - was doubtful, but didn't close any doors due to our fears. I also write that day - "Cable-gram from Dennis saying money won't be through till the middle of next week - so it looks like we'll be here for a few more days yet" - wrong again, I should have made that week's!

Such was the time pressing on, no contracts and no money forthcoming, Will says, maybe he should go to Nassau, check things out. He should have gone and not told Dennis. The consequences of not doing so were just waiting round the corner, along with the answers that had puzzled us from afar.

Where did the money come from to get us moving --- Roland, Sharman's father. So at 05.00 hrs on the 6th March 1976, we eventually left and in a way happy to go, for all the frustration of awaiting phone calls, and listening to a bunch of excuses were over!

The crew in St Martin: From left Bob Curry, Jackie, Dave Marchant, Anita Bowman, Tony Heath, Helen De Grooth, Geoff Terry, and me

Anchored off the West Indian Island of Saba

Me, building a fife rail in St Lucia before going to Grenada

Me at the helm, with Bob Curry and Passengers - Sailing off the Coast of St. Martins

Brother Howard and Bill Curry sailing in the Bahamas

At anchor in Rodney Bay, St Lucia – April 1980

Geoff Terry Sailing in St Martin

At the Helm

At anchor in Marigot Bay, St Martin, French West Indies

Under Sail in the West Indies

Chapter 33: Nassau

The passage to Nassau, considering all things, would be a memorable one. It certainly started well, a good wind in the early hours that continued for most of the day, it saw us cover 48 miles in 6 hours, Mike hadn't come after all. St Lucia was to be his home from now on.

Brother Howard, as eldest, took command of her and as for the rest of the crew for that passage it consisted of, Brother Will and Sharman, Derek Songhurst and Julie, Geoff Terry, Bill Curry and me - plus Gloria, Sharman's mother, who had decided at the last moment to come. In all sense and purposes, it had all the makings of a happy cruise, and it was!

Having left Castries at 06:00hrs sailing off the anchorage, the N-E blew force 4. By 09-10, Diamond Rock was abeam, and we'd averaged 7.5 knots. Strengthening to force 5, we were doing some fine sailing that by 13.20hrs, Cap St Martin was abeam, and we left Pointe Des Fours abeam at 16.12. By 0.600hrs of the 7th, we had put 128 miles on the log. Calms behind the hilly area at northern end of Martinique (Mt Pelee and friends) slowed us, and again the high points of Dominica took the wind from our sails. The first night out was to be a bit of a roly-poly affair in those calms, and for the first time, and certainly not the last, bilges became a word that was constantly on our lips, and very much on our thoughts.

The morning of March the 7th was typical of those Caribbean ones that makes you feel so happy to be alive, A fair wind was picking up friendly white horses, clear sunny sky, and around you a host of islands, some near - some distant. Having left the 'Iles Des Saintes' earlier to port, the island of Marie Galanie and those east of Guadeloupe sat before us to the west, plus in the distant to the north, that of our destination for the first leg – Antigua.

It only takes one to spoil your fun, as far as I was concerned, and I can speak for Billy too on this. Working her to windward was fun - but to make English Harbour, a tack or two was going to be necessary.

"Tack!!! - What for?" it was my brother Howard who, having heard of such utterings, didn't very much like the idea, and was insistent upon getting the iron lung fired up. I write in my log - "Howard gets very-agitated if we have to do any tacking what-so-ever - it really spoils things! I don't think I could do another passage with him. I thought we'd got rid of the engine hero!!!!"

I for one, was in my element, here we were upon a beautiful sea quietly working her to windward under sail alone. A steady wind on an open ocean, the perfect chance to see just how she performs - and also, to learn. No! - Some see another goal to life, all straight lines from A to B and can really get pissed off if you zigzag a bit. So at 13.00hrs, not wishing to 'Spoil the fun' of another, we fired up the main engine, motor sailing towards English Harbour. The wheel now to me, meant little, before it was alive - part of you and you part of it right down to the rudder that answered your questions - I gave it now to he that didn't quite see it that way.

We still had to put some tacks in before we reached Freemans Bay. We dropped anchor in 3 fathoms at 17.40hrs on the 7th March with the log reading 190 miles,

Bilges were a problem, and though we could keep pace with them with what we had, another source of pumping had to be found. It showed the need to get on dry-dock now and should have been a priority before the run up here. It certainly would have made life so much easier.

As the centre of the 'Yachting' society, we thought getting charts for the Bahamas would be easy, the reasons soon became apparent, for charts are not things easy to come by out here, hence are guarded objects, just like the life-raft, you never know when you might need it - and without one, you can bet your life you'll want it.

Before leaving here, checking the bottom over to try and find a problem was necessary. The clear waters of Freemans Bay, needed for such a search to solve one, gave us a few more! To anchor outside, you are caught in the surge, and a strong one it is! Before we had chance to rig some relieving gear - the morning of the 8th saw the head of the windlass blown off like it had been hit by a large shell. Had it not been for our massive oak Sampson post, the whole lot would have been dragged to the hawse as the anchor checked our rate going astern. The head that holds the arms - all cast iron, had to now be fixed before the anchor could be raised.

"What a day!" I write - "First the windlass arm broke - then the compressor broke down, also taking water like mad!" The compressor broken down, left us without means of topping our air tanks to inspect the bottom, the 8th started very black indeed for us. It certainly put our minds to the test.

The forecastle of 'Jylland' was large enough to stock all manner of bits I thought, and hoped, never to be needed. While Derek sorted out the compressor problem, Howard and Will found files and tapping tools to go with some large bolts of re-fix the head down and did the job that looked impossible without assistance from shore.
Billy and I got on with trying to rig relieving gear and transporting down our main cable a large shackle, our kedge anchor to act as some sort of spring. That done, and with the compressor going, it was over the side searching for what must be an easy thing to find by what was coming aboard.

The difficulty here was again the surge, you had to keep with her as she raced first one way, then the other _ very, very tiring work - but thought we had found something we caulked and patched. I write later that day "What looked like a black day, might not be so bad after all.

I must look round here before we leave; it has some many nice old forts and outhouses. The only trouble is, when we do stop, there is always something to do that is urgent!!!

Having rigged shank painters to our cable, it relieved the strain, and our minds in that area, but not the leaking problem. Still we were taking water badly and the old deck pump with its 4" bore that Dennis had given to Gordon Swift in Maldon, was sorely missed - seen as something old and out of place in his modern mind, had he been with us then, he'd have realized it was worth more than a small fortune now. Something Gordon knew when he grabbed it willingly from the arms of a novice!

Such pumps are not worried by debris that blows apart the modern impeller - what goes up the un-filtered end, ends up on the deck. Such is the learning game, but the one to whom it would be a lesson, was - unknown to us, about to give away more than a pump

Both the 9th and 10th saw us persisting with the search for leaks while Howard and Will searched ashore for some means other than our generator to shift water. They found inside the harbour, an old Baltic that had been wrecked some time back - and though not as big as we'd have liked, saw something right then we had to have. While they tried to find someone whose authority it was to name a price, Billy and I spent some frustrating time going over and over her hull as it raced back and forth before us.

A good idea at the time can turn to a bad one - in time! For those who are still around when (like the pump) it proves it wasn't, you do indeed learn a strong lesson. When the 'Hog' had been put in to 'Jylland' in Barbados when under the command of Brian Hoare, her lines had been destroyed somewhat. When money was plentiful after the good season in St Lucia, and we were about to head for Panama, it was thought while upon the ways in dry-dock, that if straps - metal ones 2" wide 1/2" thick were placed diagonally across her planking outside and beneath the water line, it might hold some of her shape. Un-fortunately, none knew the stress and strains of such an operation upon the hull.

Both Bill and I confronted now the error of our ways. Metal had been buckled by her bulk, and fastenings dumped in to her frames.

had pulled. In to these movements, we saw our air pass, not all, but some. Patches of lead nailed over rammed oakum - was a makeshift arrangement, and each time we came aboard, minutes had been gained to our 'Bilge Time' - but we were surprised just how little it was. Only a good dry-docking could really sort us out. That was impossible, and not till we could reach Nassau, was that likely to happen. It was, for us a case of, do best you can, and hope it doesn't get worse.

This arrangement of iron straps to hold her 'Hog', was an idea I would read many years later, not new! When Joshua Humphrey's, designer of the old 'Constitution' back in the late 1700's noticed the strain upon her ends, he had in his mind for her sister ship the 'United States', diagonal 'Riders' to stiffen the big frigates lengthways. He saw the idea work when she slid down the slipway - barely moving. Large new ships moved 2 feet or more, and at sea this could increase as the waves picked them up amidships leaving her ends jutting out in the troughs. With money and timber, they have in her restoration at Boston's navy yard, fitted old 'Ironsides' with Humphrey's idea found in old documents he'd left. We would also have done it the same way, on the inside, but without a major movement of layout to fitted cabins it was impossible to do, What we did though, showed the movement might be checked with a greater increase in rider size.

It is only by experiment do you learn, and I'm sure, had the restoration team not found Humphrey's papers on such things, they wouldn't have been allowed to interfere with her structure as they did. For us, un-restricted by committees, we could do as we pleased, and if had the time and money, would have fitted these riders, not on top of her ceiling as they did in the 'Constitution', but notched across her massive framing. We saw the problem of such 'Hogging' and how to contain it through the eyes of 'Chippys' - what a door hangs like without some bracing. To get her lines back, would always be on our minds, and yet another 'Cheap' idea would be tried some years in the future with grand results too!

By the 11th, I'd given up on the leaks, for Will and Howard had got the pump from the wreck, and with it installed and overhauled, would add to our system, and relieve the problem we all shared of "What if the generator packs up on us!!"

Before leaving St Lucia, one of those classic craft had stopped by as it did the rounds of the Caribbean. 'Dyarchy' with her owners Sue and William (Scrap) Batten had made the passage from England on a trip in a lifetime promise. With them was their daughter, and friend, and of course flying out to see them, would come others as they toured the area before heading back home around May. We were invited aboard when she came in to Castries, and I must say 'Dyarchy' was my 'cup of tea'. Oil lamps burnt in the open arrangement below decks, and the oak barrel seats followed the taste of all that met the eye.

Her rigging had so much linseed oil and varnish mixture applied to it through the years, that water would have to penetrate a smooth coat before ever reaching the wire shrouds. She sailed handsomely off her anchorage when she left for Antigua, and who knows, we had said, we might see you there. We did, and on the 10th of March they came over in the evening for a drink and to say farewell, for we had planned to leave on the 11th.

Like many places, due to work-load, seeing Antigua was no exception. I would see the museum and the inside of the 'Admirals Inn' briefly and who else but the very man who was the cause of 'Jylland's' new shape - Brian Hoare. I would have loved to have invited him over for a beer, but prayed instead that those deserving such a fellow would get him!!

4 days we had been here, and apart from getting a deck pump, didn't achieve much else. At 19:00 hrs. of the 11th March, we left this surging area, and departed setting our course for St Barts under sail. It was a lovely night, and with a fair wind we made good progress for the short passage - around 100 miles to Gustavia. Pumping was required every half an hour to keep her dry, but we were never

anxious and dropped anchor in 5 fathoms at 09.20 hrs on Fri 12th March.

There is with all the French islands a sense of order without the presence of it. The casual homely atmosphere is nowhere more apparent than St Barts. One policeman is enough to show that Guadeloupe (their new Devils Island) will be the place those that upset the status quo will be sent. Like all their islands, it is part of France and the big stick theory prevails over all. It was once our way of keeping order in far places and is still the French way.

Being a duty free port, 'Lou Lou's' is the name of the Chandlery and will supply you with most things - not charts of the Bahamas though. I was determined to get off 'Jylland' while here and take a walk. Of all people to come in that very same day was Dia and Mary Neale. On their way to Martinique to be slipped first, then to go on down to St Lucia to see us. So for a couple of days, we had their company.

Why, I'd like to know, can the French get hold of an ordinary building, shack or hovel, and make it the place to go. One small bar we visited with Dai one evening, had a young black boy singing as the beer and duty free wine flowed. Nothing special to look at, but different than if it had been run by anyone else. The air was full of the same duty free cigarettes that would have even healthy jogging Americans inhaling it as part of 'the thing to do!' It is all down to doing it their way - and bugger the tourist.

It would be with Bill, that I made my break away from the chores of 'Jylland'. It was the 14th now, and we'd made plans to leave that afternoon, so if we were to see some of the island it better be in the morning. I'll always remember that walk, Bill and I pacing out along the road north, to return past the small runway that brings in the people that want to get away from it all. We would see some who have - and still do their thing, problem is they don't come here to do it; they live there and do it amongst themselves - which alas, brings that look only inbreeding can. Here too, like Saba, it is all around. Someone should have a party and invite those from Saba for a week!

We didn't get any charts from here as we had hoped, but did get some cheap spirits to raise ours. St Thomas was where we were bound now, they were bound to have charts that would allow us to run through the many islands rather than go outside. So at 15.30hrs with us heading to the north, we left St Barts with Dia and Mary heading south, to somewhere we should be going – dry-dock.

I write on the 15th March "Did a lot of thinking today. I have my fears about Nassau not going right! It could mean the end of my dreams," What dreams? Dreams of happiness I guess, Dreams where others also laugh. 'Jylland' was to me but a home in which all should feel 'theirs' - theirs to be as much as mine and to take us on in such spirits as far as we could go. Such dreams others do not have and I knew waiting for us was a brother who didn't see it that way. To him dreaming meant owning what you haven't got, and seeing others dreaming about what he had. To shatter mine to achieve that aim. was what I feared lay ahead.

It was a lovely night on the 14th of March; the moon shone throughout as a soft ENE breeze pushed us on under sail alone giving us a speed of 5 knots. At 06.00hrs of the 15th, while on watch with Geoff Terry, I write "Sighted U.F.0!" Something in the eastern sky that still today baffles me. It was like the body of an airship or plane fuselage passing between two large banks of cumulus cloud - very fast and very far away, Geoff, at the helm with eyes to the front, only caught a glimpse when I said, "Did you see that?" Who knows eh!

It is around 100 miles to St Thomas and we arrived at 13.00hrs on the 15th, dropping anchor in 5 fathoms and the log reading 375 miles since St Lucia. It was sometime since I last saw a traffic jam and as I sat on deck looking ashore, I was quite content to be where I was! I had no reason or wish to go ashore and mingle with such, and being told we were not allowed to without visas, suited me fine. It would be up to Bill to do the necessary even he was quite surprised to find charts of the Bahamas unavailable here. It would now mean, instead of an interesting passage slipping between islands north, stopping here and there maybe, we would run up them outside using the large scale chart – it was all we had.

There really was nothing to keep us here, so we left this busy little American place and its protocol at 11.00hrs on the 16th. We intended to sail as much as possible and as long as the sails were pulling, I didn't have Howard complain about speed. It is a busy area for shipping, many a cruise ship out of Miami ply the route, and some passed us like huge piers all lit up. A good wind to kick us off gave us 6 knots and it continued when at 18.00hrs the log read 415 miles. Fixing our position at 19.00hrs as 18.45'N 65.39'W

It would take us a week to sail the distance to Nassau. Sometimes we had wind sometimes none and we sat flogging around in bad visibility. We celebrated Wills birthday on the 22nd, but upon arrival, those celebrations would soon be forgotten when the news of what Dennis had in mind for us reached our ears!!

Through the centuries the Bahamas islands have seen first the English settle here in 1629, and the comings and goings of the French and Spanish till a peace treaty was signed in 1778 in favour of the British crown. Even the Americans made a play for them during our little half-hearted war and invaded New Providence in 1776, which they abandoned shortly after.

Many a royalist, after that war of independence transferred the remains of their property here and set up shop! To encourage commerce, Nassau the capitol, was declared a 'Free port' in 1787 - a small thank you for their loyalty and a gift to help those that backed the wrong horse to get started.

Of course the debate has gone on for centuries too, as to which of the islands that Columbus first saw - Watling? - San Salvador? are but two under close examination and I'm sure the argument will continue longer than the claim as to who owned them after. We do know for certain that they were inhabited, and the Indians are now long gone as is the names they had for their home. Luca'yos is now Baha'mas - Lucayo is Abaco and Guanahani in 1492, is San Salvador today.

It is the Gulf Stream that cut this group of islands adrift from the mainland. It runs at a rate of between 5 to 6 miles an hour at its maximum northwards between them and the Florida coast. The Bahama Bank, on which all the principal islands sit, is 300 miles by 80 with a depth of no more than 30 feet, yet the drop-offs at its edges would leave an anchor dangling on a full scope of chain pointing the way to a bottom only. It was this, for the want of a chart, I would miss, and like many an opportunity, once missed, never to get again, The Bank is alive with fish and that Lemming of sea the Lobster who, when for some odd reason they go for a walk, those fishing for them will fill a boat in a day. Protecting what is theirs by manmade borders is impossible, and other countries like Haiti 'Poach' from this garden on the basis of - there's plenty enough for everyone!

As chief depot for the blockade-runners to the confederate states in the American civil war of 1862/64, such sums of money made went up dramatically. 300,000 pounds of imports vs exports of less than 200,000 in '81, saw in '84 the figure - imports at 5,346,112 pounds vs exports 4,672,398 pounds. Such figures from such misery are not new, and the Bahamas would administer to its neighbour further surprises whilst under the protection of Britain and its own constitutional rules. Slaves, booze and now drugs sit in transit to flood the American market It is too the old 'Wreckers' home that many a racket came, and with them, many of people who'd use it as a base to wreck their own home.

Moored to one of the large buoys that held much bigger vessels, I viewed Nassau with a mixed feeling of apprehension. Being caught here even before clearing customs came the smell of a trap. I had not the trust of my brothers word that "All's well!" to relieve my anxiety, and if I'd listened to my instincts, we'd never have come. New Providence and Nassau its capitol lay before me - flat and uninteresting, that without some construction put up by man, an uninterrupted horizon was possible. A breakwater, which seemed to be made entirely of Conch shells met my eyes, bleached white now by the sun's rays. The amount was proof of the Banks production of that species and showed us Conch was eaten in large quantities here

The openness of the whole area would show that winds unobstructed could be a problem, and in the Hurricane season, a big problem. Between New Providence and Paradise Island, (its small but close neighbour) large chains lay on the channel bottom to catch the boat that goes for a walk during such times. Bill and I would, in time, check them out, holding on against a swift current and using the same chain to pull ourselves along.

Paradise Island lies like a shield, protecting Nassau from the Atlantic. I would guess half a mile wide, and 3 long. Some nice homes sit there now, but at one time just one sat in its isolation from the main land, for it was owned by someone whose name I can't quite remember other than he owned many a race horse, many a home and one would bet - many a politician. Since those days, a bridge now links the two, with hotels come hotel/Casinos flooding the area.

Clearing Customs on the 24th March, it was to this Island we moved, laying alongside a concrete jetty who's Dolphins protected our hull from its hardness. In the next few days I would learn some things that even though I was prepared for the worst, still struck me dumb for words. No cock-up surely could better the Panama one. Surely it would have taught Dennis a lesson about trusting others - if not him, us for trusting what he told us to trust. Really! - I under estimated my brother's big surprise for us by a very long mile.

The news first from his lips to Will and Howard the day before, was when they met him going ashore to clear customs - it came as if in a way to soften them up for some worse news to come later! It was that our dear sister Phyllis had died, died last week as we picked our way north in the misty Atlantic. Dear Phyllis gone! Too many doctors saying take two of these a day and not asking or caring if it was two too many. The blow of such news did deaden the next bombshells he had in store for us. The anger of the living soon made us forget our sisters passing.

We were up early on the morning of the 25th March, and in Will and Howard's company I sat as we talked about what to expect before Dennis arrived from his usual 'place' ashore. As in Panama, it was expected of him and by him to stay apart from us when the 'News' wasn't good, and remembering that episode then, the similarities of that experience left me in little doubt there was some over ripe stories about to hit us!

You can get to tell through the years that behind the small talk there is something on your brother's chest he wants to get off! If it be a heavy burden, where blame is wished to be shared around, or as it would turn out here, he wished to rid himself of our presence. Getting down to the nitty gritty, didn't take much prompting or prodding for him say what was on his mind. The trouble was, he didn't, instead - in the heat of the exchanges of views, he lied!! Such was the expected prize about to happen for Dennis in Nassau, that this little lie to his brothers, of all people, would go un- noticed and mean for little in a big chest of pure Gold.

Such perfidy does not go un-noticed, and would be well rewarded - in time!

He stated to us in that first meeting he had 'Borrowed' £15,000 from his new father-in-law to get this project started. Promises that had obviously been made to Pats dad Tom, on his, not our behalf, to see it through to a successful conclusion unhindered by our interference. It was only us - Will, Howard and myself, that stood in the way of my brothers guiding hand and by outing us, one way or the other was what he had in mind!

It all seemed a simple thing to do so many miles away, but face to face with those he wished to share no part of the coming fortune, he was faced with those who, if told the truth, could spoil his plans.

In the heated debate as to why, if Tom Card had lent such a sum, none came to St Lucia as promised; was met with other excuses and when realizing we were not going to give up without a fight, having every right to leave this place unhindered with the 'Jylland' too - Dennis came to see the arrangement put to him was the only way out - a decision that he would fight against in honouring during the next few days.

On 'Jylland' paper on the 26th March an agreement was drawn up between us stating - 'It is hereby agreed that we four brothers namely - etc., etc. - do henceforth divide all monies earnt on the schooner 'Jylland' five ways. That is two fifths to be taken by Frederick Dennis, and one fifth each to etc.! Repairs shall be equally divided, and also any 'DEBTS' incurred in connection with the said schooner!' It was also agreed that we three should be paid weekly from any profits. Sounded good, but before Dennis would agree to sign it. Another heated argument would ensue - this time about what he wanted.

Promises to stay with her, getting her ready till she got working were made, and he signed. I honestly believed, getting such an agreement with him would ease the feelings between us. Again I was wrong, for the full story behind the small lie was about to unfold itself - something he would have preferred not to come out.

The name Claus appeared upon the scene during the latter part of March. Late for the Christmas one, and in time, the arrival of this Claus seemed in some way just as important to a happy occasion, due to arrive Sat 3rd April from Germany. I wondered what this man's role in the set up was, but failed to get an answer. Germany and Graham Bonney's involvement had something to do with it - but what, and just how deeply that went, I had to wait upon.

The day we heard he was to arrive - the 31st March, saw the leaving of Gloria back to St Lucia - and I wished then we could have taken her back in what had brought her here. This lovely woman,

Sharman's mother, had I know, enjoyed the trip. Her life's story is, like all true stories, far greater than fiction and if not known as honest, it would be difficult to believe!

Having thought we'd sorted our differences out with Dennis, we played out our role preparing 'Jylland' for the work she was about to do. Bill. Curry had agreed to stay on as the role of Captain and had asked if it was okay to get his brother Bob to join him, for if 'Jylland' was to be in the hands of Dennis, Will and Sharman wouldn't be around, and following Howard and myself back to England, would be Geoff - maybe Derek too.

The constant attention to painting, oiling and rigging - plus an engine overhaul went on as we awaited the news of all's well on the work permit front. Money as always, was our biggest problem, the cost of getting here - owed still to Roland - but now on a promise, had all gone. If Dennis, as he had said by 'borrowing' 15,000 from Tom Card to set this project up, either was not going to honour that debt, or hadn't got it! If he hadn't then where had it gone - for even food money was not forth coming from him. Anybody knows that people can't live without food.

Pressure to release something of what we thought he must be sitting on, brought us some wages - $5.00 each - and as it was on April the 1st that came about - we were too happy for something to worry about the fool's day present!

It would be April 5th before I found out Claus didn't arrive. Something to do with him 'Awaiting his luggage from Italy!' - Had he sent money though - for we all received $20.00 each. Not much I know for the work we were doing, but that was bound to change soon, surely!! What did come that day was the 'Phantom' one of Mike Burkes windjammer vessels, Bill and I would take a run out to see her later that evening, The 280' four master schooner was alive with the swinging 70's people, who all sounded American, determined to enjoy themselves. Rules - if any seemed to matter were - "The Captain requests the following shall apply"

(1) Do as he does, not as he says.
(2) All smoking of any funny material shall be done to windward, thus giving all a fair chance to inhale the wonderful aroma of Columbia!
(3) Applies only to the finest looking ladies amongst you, and that is, your Captain will be willing to discuss them only after he has fondled your fine breasts! - private parts! and rung your bell at least 8 times a day!

The certainty of some connection between Claus - Graham and Dennis, slowly emerged as the days dragged by. All aboard were getting rather tired of being kept in the dark, and for Will, Howard and myself not to be able to tell them, it wasn't easy - for it would have showed up the differences for certain of problems between Dennis and us!

The differences of class structure between Julie and Sharman, started to show cracks under the strain. Sharman was brought up with Julie's culture catering for her, and both felt rather awkward - if not, finding it impossible to work/live together. On the 11th of April, Sharman, who had taken the role of cook, while Julie was left with the cleaning and laundry position, called a halt, refusing to boil another potato! – That's assuming she could find one. Julie would be confronted by Will the following day, about not changing their sheets and not taking the dirty ones to be washed.

Such was the feeling of wife and girlfriend, it would end up with the obvious, and one had to go. So Julie it was that left for home soon after leaving a man behind who found it hard to forgive or forget who it was that gave him a lonely bed! The once friends that had made this trip out to the Caribbean un-attached, saw things differently now. The once 'dry' sense of humour Will liked in Derek was no longer appreciated by the victor, and the best man at their wedding just counted his days till it was time to part company - preferring Julies now to theirs. In time, Julie would be reunited with Derek and become Mrs Songhurst in England. For me, it was a rather sad ending to a fine beginning - over what - women! Women or money, one or the other will always be the cause of someone's grief! I would have thought Derek would have said goodbye when he left on the 4th June, he didn't, nor had he let it be known of his intentions, for he'd gone before I knew it.

It would have to wait till the 13th of April before I write - 'some very enlightening' news was told us. Dennis, feeling just maybe he's smelt a rat at last, tells us a little more of Santa Claus' involvement - hard as it was to believe then, I find it more difficult to say now. He said he actually gave this fellow the £15,000 on a promise he could arrange all the work permits for 'Jylland' in Nassau!!! The who, how and whys just had to wait till it sunk in. It is usually and mostly the greedy that fall for the big con! Conmen thrive on them and sleep well in the knowledge they get what they deserve. My brother had just finished a waltz in the jungle with one, now - like a lover of the quick step, has fallen for another who offers him the world'.

Extracting from him over the next couple of days - the truth and nothing but the truth, was done as he pointed the finger of blame elsewhere - mainly at Howard for all that went wrong with Hamber Bros and this little episode was the only way 'HE' - DENNIS thought was going to put it all right. The sums he came up with - the loss on the Panama project - 'Jylland's' conversion, Wickford, the home he wished done his way and now this 'loan' (as we still believed it was then!) had nothing to do with him as an individual, but in his eyes, was seen as a joint decision. 'When a good idea turns to a bad idea, it wasn't my idea at all!'

My fears of coming here on the say so of Dennis were proving my instincts correct, and for not listening to them - being more assertive with certain demands, I would pay the penalty. What I believed the future might hold was now dashed by this disclosure. Any hopes of leaving here now would have to be put aside till we knew for certain of the outcome. I'm afraid that was not the case in Howard's mind. On the I5th April, Will and I had a few heated words with him, for he again had it in his head about 'shooting off' home! To what? Why? How can you at such a time? It was for me total capitulation -

but then, I had seen it all before in Jamaica, and it wouldn't be the last I'd see of this single minded attitude when it was time to pull together. Shouldering the blame thrown at him by a distorted Dennis maybe had some truth in it - but it was the fault of all, not one.

Howard, knowing his brothers business like attitude - trust everyone accept his own blood - should have checked this deal out before coming - should as the eldest, kept a firmer hold on the reins of his younger brother's appetite for spending, but this was not the way out. It was to me as if he wanted part of the action - only if the action proved it worthwhile - other than that, it's yours'!! Lock-stock and bleeding barrel - for now anyway!

There was no consideration that such news of his returning home again would have on my own marriage - and his arrival wouldn't take too much to imagine what Sue would have thought. It had been 7 months since I'd last seen them all, but for me I wasn't prepared to leave here - nor 'Jylland' till something was settled.

Still nothing by the 19th of April when Bob Curry arrived to take the position alongside his brother if and when, we left. A tall fellow like Bill, but dark haired instead of Bill's fair mop. The hair also was rather long, and accompanied a beard. He looked rather as if he'd come to join a band of Fur trappers, or a group of Mountain men out on a quest to find some bears to shag, rather than shin up some ratlines. But under all that hair (and as ships barber I talked him in to parting with some in time) was one of the nicest fellows, and like his brother, one of the most loyal of people you could ever meet.

There are few people you can rely on totally, whether in honesty, or never to desert you when the chips are down. Here were two brothers that without knowing them, life would have been poorer. Bob had been in the air force, been through a marriage, and wanted to get out to breath a bit of fresh air before deciding his future. You can tell more about someone working with them for an hour, than you can talk with them for a week – a year even! I would, in the coming years, do both with Bob, as I had with Bill. I guess you could say, that he that announces the arrival of wise men, could fall in to the trap set by such a statement, that it takes one to know one.

'Jylland', if anything, was a great testing ground for character apart from anything else. You just had to get on, or get off! We all have standards, some high some low and much depends upon what you value most. Parents put us on the road and from then on you set your own standards, or can be guided by others as to what is expected of them if you're in doubt in anyway. Hard work - cleanliness - honesty - and integrity, with a touch of common sense, and not in that order was what you wanted - oh! Yes - one mustn't forget another important factor - with very little pay at times – never show anyone you're willing to shovel shit, eat it if you have to, and the person jumping in beside you, is the man you're looking for. If you didn't know whom you were when you came aboard 'Jylland' - you did when you got off! Ask any of them.

April was coming to an end and with it still no sign of Claus. Permits to work also showed little sign of turning up. Who came upon the scene more and more, was a fellow called Doug Prudden. Doug ran a water sports program - parasailing and speedboats etc. A white Bahamian, Dennis had met him when he first came to 'Check' things out. With nothing left of the £15,000 to get us out of this mess, Doug had been turned to for some assistance by Dennis - which means a percentage! Doug had been led to believe 'Jylland' was Dennis's and his alone - and when asked by him for help in this permit problem, Doug saw a chance to make a buck (and nothing wrong in that) for something he thought was just a matter of a phone call -. Wrong! Both in assumption and colour!

By the 23rd April, to find out more of Doug position in all this, we asked just how much so far had he invested in 'Jylland' - $2,300 was the reply from Dennis. Far less than half what had kept the whole schooner and crew here since our arrival a month back. Accounting for the rest, started up another confrontation. The agreement we had all signed looked, by such figures, a bad one now, my share of this debt now stood me owing $460 - having had only $25-00 of it!

Much of it went on Dennis's living ashore, and even if he would have moved aboard to cut costs, the thought of it made me judge such consequences. It would have been a little unbearable to say the least due to this mess up.

A good example of my brother's lack of understanding and feeling for others position was when he decides to paint 'Jylland's' inside bulkheads. 4 days after explaining to him our fears of debts, that 'Jylland' needs food money, an important ingredient, he spends $20.00 on something un-edible, starts rubbing down walls, and goes about his task as if waiting for someone just to say something un-towards. I write - 'Dennis has started to get the walls rubbed down and painted - waste of time and money. Spent $20.00 on paint when we have nothing to eat tonight. He had agreed to spend no more on 'Jylland' until we are working!'

I was livid with his arrogance and by the actions of his body and smell of his attitude; he was looking for an argument - a chance to blow his top as before! The proverb 'It is safer to meet a mother bear that has lost her cubs, than catch a man with his folly." or words to that affect - is so true. Living close to such a person was hard to bear, and it seemed then, harder to get away from. I also write! "Had to borrow some money off Bill, Bob went over the bridge to get some food, just enough for tonight!"

It was during such troubled times, a little light relief came upon the scene. It came in the shape of a 51' yawl, and aboard 'Sapheadra' were Ed Hartmann and his children - young Ed the second, Caroline and Kathy. We'd met them in St Lucia - a stop off on their tour of the Caribbean. Ed, divorced, but with the looks and money that said it surely wouldn't be for long, was a nice fellow. He had done one of those things we all wish to do, but leave for too long, and that was to spend some time with his kids alone.

Where better to do such but upon the briny ocean where dad's presence is essential to your own survival - not just an object to lean against for money. Ed was out of Annapolis, a partner of 'Hartmann and Kane' lawyers. This family firm had provided a fine old home whose lawns ran down to the Chesapeake and like so many there, a jetty for the boat of your choice hanging on it bits.

 I would know all this, for in the un-predictable future, I would visit him in the city of Americas Marine academy. Ed had three girls - the eldest Debbie. She was soon to join him again to help bring 'Saphead' home, but wasn't yet aboard when Ed wished to take those of us who wished to go out for a day's sail.

Sunday the 3rd of May was the day planned, and to get away from all the hassle and heated discussions surrounding 'Jylland' was what I needed. Only Bob, Howard, Geoff and I went. With Laurie and Cameron, Bills wife and son here now, he didn't come, nor did Dennis - again missing out - and for Will and Sharman, Sunday meant a day off of everything. As for Derek, he too stayed aboard, all thoughts directed to Trinidad and Julia now.

 Sapheadra' was a drop keel yawl, drawing only 5 feet with it up, 11 feet with it down. After 'Jylland', her helm seemed to have power steering and she could point so close, it made you wonder if an engine was at all necessary. 10:30 was our departure time and the run down to Green Cay and Rose Island was made on a lovely day. Swimming, eating, drinking and chatting, one forgot about the grey clouds that hung over our berth at Paradise Island. Such days as this one, was what I craved for, and all I wished for to happen with our schooner.

Had he that had upset the dreams been aboard and seen for himself what life can hold, just maybe he might change his ways. But that was too much to ask, and in reality, could never happen, for with my brother 'Double dinner Denny!' as Billy Burrell used to call him, he'd miss out on the quality of life by the quantity he'd try to eat all at once. Arriving back at 17.30 and staying aboard for an end of day finale on the old 'box', it was a day I needed to get me through the coming bleak period. Ed would leave for home on the 14th, and given half the chance, I would have gone with him.

The unpredictable mind of Dennis really came out on the 24th May. I write – "Dennis said to me this morning that he is thinking of going home too if we have to wait much longer for the work permits. I don't think we should all leave the ship for some stranger to run - at least I won't! One minute he wants us all out the way so he can run it, now he wants to leave too. It just doesn't make sense. We've lost enough, if we all leave, we could lose her too. However hard we must fight, we must do it together!"

Together is a word I choke upon!!!

The end of May would see us in the same position as that of the 1st. Permits turned down, Doug talking to lawyers about his rights and a great smell of bribery and corruption in the air. Howard had said on the 31st, a Monday, if he can get some money for a flight, he's off! I was rather surprised, if not, a little hurt to find out when I returned from a daily swim on the 1st June, he had - and had! Gone before another argument and didn't say goodbye, I write "Howard had got his flight money - really was a bit sick at him leaving. He left on his 8th transatlantic passage. If my Sue finds out he's home she is going to be so upset!" It was a pure case of 'I'm alright Jack!' and difficult though it was to take - I was glad - for it was one less in the ring. What Sue would think of his return, I would have to confront when it happened - but it could be taken by the 8/1 ratio, my caring was the same. But leaving here without some things clarified was just not right to me. I write on the 2nd June "Went through some of Sharman's old wedding photos in the afternoon - my love really takes a lovely photo! Didn't like to look at them too long - heart pangs!"

Derek would leave on the 4th, another crew-member gone - and another that didn't say goodbye! On the 11th I would here from my brother of a shouting match - not with us for a change, but one with Graham over phone! About what? About him backing out of a 'Promise!' What promise? A promise I would learn from a brother who now wishes to share his problems - and very enlightening they are too!!!!

The man in question, 'Claus' - he that had failed to show and in whose hands Dennis had put £15,000 in used notes was someone Graham had met on a plane! So enthused and taken in by him was our Graham that he persuaded Dennis to 'Borrow' (remember it is still borrow) money on the basis that if all went wrong - he, Graham, would guarantee the outlay. Hearing such words from a brother, you stand back and eye him in wonder - wondering if you have the same parents - even come from the same planet! To have taken the word only of someone so devious and un-trustworthy as Graham had proved to be in the Panama expedition was hilarious if it wasn't for the fact that my brother sat before me, wearing the same clothes as his partner in this crime!

Both had failed to inform us as to the underhandedness of this idea - knowing full well our disapproval and total rejection of such a proposal. Both had deceived us, conned us, just like they were conned in the process. The greatest insult was that one of those in this dealing was my brother! A brother that had led us in to a well-laid trap yet didn't see - wished to see, he was putting his own neck firmly in the snare!! What a plonker!!! Was I now privy to whole truth of this fiasco? - was I hell! I would much later learn that the £15,000 was not indeed borrowed - but that it was a wedding gift! One old Tom Card had given to all his daughters to get them started in married life! So not only had Dennis dragged Tom in, but his now wife Pat - who by such a loan, now believed she and her husband had every right to call the shots!! What a to do, and what to do about it? Any thoughts now of leaving here, following Howard home had to be put on hold.

Mid-June would see still no permits forthcoming, and Doug's lawyer Keith? was having talks with senator Lockheart - who promised a meeting to discuss our position. So all one could do was sit and wait it out putting one's mind to the always never-ending list of jobs to do aboard the likes of a craft 'Jylland's' size.

It was private money that built the bridge linking Paradise Island to New Providence. To pay for it, motorists and walkers alike paid a toll. The idea being, as soon as it had paid for its costs, it would become a free bridge. Where the money came from who knows - but as Paradise Island was the location of a string of hotels come casinos, mostly run by the 'Mob', it doesn't take much thought to figure out who put the cash up to get the punters to the tables. The cash flow created did not go un-noticed by those in government, and when it came time to hand it to them, instead of a becoming a Bahamian peoples asset, it passed in to the hands of another crook, an elected one who decided for now the toll shall stay! And I wouldn't mind betting it continues to this day - 40 years on.

We would walk over that bridge when one found a spare buck, for 'The Bridge Inn' would have a happy hour in the late afternoon. Two for the price of one attraction. Cheaper too than on our side of the channel - Boy that was nice, the first one hardly touching the throat as the ice cold one did the business of cooling you down. Then it was sit and chat whilst listening to some older black fellow play a good piano.

Under the bridge was where all the action went on. When the wind changed, Chalks Airlines 'had' to change too. The small seaplanes they ran out of here to Miami charged against the strong current to get airborne. Sometimes hitting pretty good swells, spray in all directions before parting company with the sea. I've seen it stop them too, having to go round for another run. Seaplanes, what a wonderful idea gone to seed. The pillars the bridge was formed on, made leaving Nassau for bigger boats, those with tall masts, impossible. People heading south could cut several miles off their journey if they could squeeze under. On the New Providence side, one would have heard if not seen, the arrival of something out of the past.

An old working Caribbean schooner, bare of any topmasts but alive with bodies. Out of Haiti, it was seen heaving ashore lines in all directions, followed by that usual necessity of certain cultures to scream louder than the man next to you and certainly louder than he that might be ashore taking them. A big old girl, that once surely must have been painted white, had sailed over the banks from her home to pick up anything cheap that was on offer.

Who knows what she carried, or whom in this corrupt area, it was impossible to tell, but you did know it was wise to bring the dinghy aboard, and nail down anything moveable till she left.

I sat watching her get underway once and for all the screaming and shouting, it was done none the less with perfection. Under sail alone - for it was obvious that's all she had, she was going back the short way under the bridge from whence she came. Her cargo then, was plastic, plastic bottles, cans - barrels - a real 'container' cargo, all collected and saved from the rubbish grave. She could have ripped her keel right off and still make it home with that amount of floating material aboard.

The old skipper would have to beat against wind and tide to get her out, put in a couple of tacks too in the short turning area. But he had done this before and knew his craft well as it would prove! He was nearly on one of the pillar bases when he put her helm down, followed by much screaming for the staysail to be let go. Slowly the big main threw her nose in to the current as she slipped ahead passing the concrete with inches to spare. More screaming, and up went the headsail again as she went through the wind - with the foremain too now for some added power, she forged ahead and the once odd, dirty craft, now under full sail, looked something else, rather lovely in fact, even the out of place wheel house unnoticed now. One would have learnt much alongside that old fellow __ probably something about sailing as well as life!

Chapter 34: Lifesaving

'Sir' Lyndon Pindlings government is held in power by the corruptible with great new ideas on corruption. Democratic elections meant, breaking the arms and legs of those who can't be persuaded that the threat is for real. Cars go out at election time, collect the old and hard of hearing, and bring them in to put their cross where the chauffeur points his finger - getting home is then their own problem - the thought being, they probably won't be around come the next election. Such a wonderful man has been knighted by our own dear Queen - and is the longest reigning head of state in the whole area, if not the world.

A relation of his came up with a wonderful scam - the hotels and casinos, creating a vast amount of rubbish, complained of the local trash collectors reliability - thus a private business was to be formed to fill the gap. To do the job the contractor would have to purchase vehicles from the states - real ones, not the open lorry of unknown age that broke down, and in real terms, a bigger load of rubbish than what they were carrying. It would turn out, that what the operator of this contract would buy from the states was something discarded as passed its useful life there, and thus-purchased all by the scrap ton!

Breakdowns occurred on so many an occasion that it was thought necessary the government take over the business - buying out the 'contractor'. His 'fleet' of lorries were then valued at what it would cost to replace them - as new! Those setting up new democracies round the world, especially poor Africa, come to such places to see how they're run and go away rubbing their hands, hardly waiting to get back home to call for a 'general democratic election'.

Our evenings ashore would consist mainly of going places where money was not essential. Our night out might mean a walk round the Casino watching Americans fulfil a craving - to see just how quick they could fill another - the slot machine. They all were 'conditioned', it would seem, to lose, and none seemed unhappy at doing so, their smiling faces emptying tubs of quarters like alms to the needy.

All the 'front' men - croupiers - were from Britain. Accents and the James Bond bit going down well with the ladies from the states. Yet behind all, watched the American connection through the eye of the camera.

Anyone who had hang-ups when it comes to talking with girls, will soon part with them in our company for it was always the company of girls we enjoyed. Nassau, or rather Paradise Island, was alive with the American - short holiday trippers. Another country and another accent was a signal for many a girl to throw caution to the wind when the urge was just too great.

He that has a fetish for the sound of broken glass goes berserk with happiness when let loose in a large greenhouse! For he that had already condemned himself by breaking a commandment, breaking it again and again is not difficult - nor would be the boasting of it. I will say, it is the hardest to keep and would turn many a so called saint in to a liar if the truth was known - and many a saint handing in his halo if the chance came his way!

If I am to be saved, it is by my deeds! One chance to redeem myself happened my way, and my efforts to try and save another's life, was not done for a reason to cleanse myself. Every afternoon the crew used to walk through the whispering pines to a lagoon created in front of the 'Holiday Inn'. It was our well-trodden backdoor entrance to swim in the cool waters of the Atlantic. It was out of bounds for any other than guests. The lagoon created by a barrier of placed rock, used to heat up rather nicely, yet swimming across the entrance, one was hit by a sudden current of cold water - one that could make you speed the stroke up.

I happened to be out near that entrance when I saw and thought, floating before me was a large brown box or something similar that had come in from the ocean. The closer I got it seemed like a body - but rather still! The nearer I got the more certain I became of someone was in trouble, or that he could hold his breath longer than most without the aid of a snorkel - it was not in his mouth!! Before grabbing anyone in deep water - especially a half drowning big one, make sure first you can make it to the shore with him - otherwise! I decided to swim first beneath him to look up and see his position -

doing just that, I saw his mask wasn't on his eyes or nose, but on the forehead, the snorkel dangling useless. Up I went, fast, turned him over, making for the shore with him in tow.

Bob who was with me at one time, had gone back to the beach, and all shouts of help got lost up in the hubbub of shallow water activity. The fellow was a big man, as I've said and he floated well, but I didn't know then he was already dead! I just pulled him one-handed for shore, whistling and calling for some assistance.

You think you can swim, and I was pretty fit too then, but you try pulling a heavy load through the water for any distance - that 100 yards to the beach seemed never to come to me, and having already burnt some on the swim out here, my energy was draining fast.
Now and then I let my feet drop, hoping to touch bottom, but it wasn't there. I couldn't believe that I wasn't noticed!!

The lifeguard perched high on his chair had eyes on the girls, I knew that, and would be more concerned about his appearance than what he was paid to do! It was my whistle that Howard recognized, it is as good as your voice to he that had heard it from our years together - it is as un-mistakable as his was, or that of Wills, and on hearing it, he was up and followed by Bob and Co, ran out to help drag ashore the 'dead' body.

I left it to them too, for I had had it - totally knackered by the long haul. Letting go of him, I was relieved to feel my feet hit ground, and I waded ashore and hit the beach.

There was one mass of bodies round him, so many now I couldn't see him. The lifeguard had now taken control, and by words from spectators I heard as I lay there, was given credit for having got him in. Others who said "No - some other person pulled him in!"

It was later that evening, concerned about 'MY Body' I had to enquire at the desk in the Holiday Inn, of the outcome - for I still wasn't sure - or I should say - wished I wasn't sure if or not he'd made it. "Yes, the man saved by the lifeguard this afternoon! - Came the reply from the girl - "died in the ambulance on the way to hospital!"

They would say that wouldn't they - look rather bad any other way. "Yes - while our lifeguard was eyeing up the crumpet, he failed to notice a man in difficulties whose heart stopped beating when he hit the ice cold water out there. So caught up was he in what he wished to do with all those white girls, he still failed to notice another struggling with the body for some 78 yards! We intend to get him a taller chair!"

The poor fellow's wife, I heard, had gone out on a shopping spree to Nassau for a few surprises to take home! Poor woman would carry home a bigger one!

Chapter 35: The Flagler's Inn

Al Collie and the V-I-Ps. They were then the band that played in the 'Flagler's Inn', and one of the best bands too I've heard. One didn't have too much time to sit and listen due to funds. Beer money was one, maybe two, then home - a short walk past a small marina close to the Hotel. Bill Curry had recently had a tax rebate, and with his usual - what's mine is yours attitude, wished to buy the beers that night.

This he had failed to tell Geoff, who still assumed it was a one each and hit the road night as per usual. Little to say, he was rather taken aback when Bill ordered - "The same again barman!" and another full glass joined the slow half left in his hand.

Not wanting to see Bill broke, and us drunk, I departed for home alone leaving them - Howard, Bill and Geoff at the bar! I heard later the story after an out of breath Geoff came running aboard - with harsh - very harsh Anglo-Saxon words which translated meant -

sexual intercourse between two people whose parents/if known, were not married and he - Geoff wanted to find them.

Geoff, so it turned out, had been a little uneasy when Bill had called for a round, and with me gone, had called for yet another. Unease had now turned to a relaxed period; sure all was taken care of. Returning from the gents, a further glass stood next to the half empty one. Downing half, he settled down to enjoy an unusually rare occasion, 4 large glasses of cold beer, and no signs yet, it was drying up. There was a very good chance, thought Geoff, that to-night sleep would come easy in a pissed state! But he had missed out on the conversation between Howard and Bill in his absence - a visit in which Bill had in the meantime settled with the bar.

The joke was - Bill had believed for some reason, it was Howard that would settle accounts - and vice versa. Assuring them both he was broke - was what they already knew, but it was nice of Geoff to confirm it anyway for the prank to work. With barman well out of earshot, Howard would thank Bill for the night out - and a very surprised Bill would say - "What do you mean Howie - I thought you ___!" etc.! Letting it sink in as to how they're going to get out of this one was done for a while, till Howard says __ "Hold on - I've just seen someone I know. I'll go and borrow a few bucks!" - and departs leaving Geoff and Bill together.

Before a minute passes Bill ups and says "I can't let him do that!" and leaves-as if to stop Howard asking an embarrassing favour thus leaving Geoff alone - alone too with what he believes is an unpaid bill - a very big one in the circumstances. Sure they would return not deserting a shipmate, turned to a slight worry as the awkward minutes passed. He wished he'd taken a bit more time over the glass of beer now; it was very nearly empty now by the rush to catch his mates up in the drinking department. He daren't finish it off case the barman, now looking at him constantly for the nod of 'Fill it' might say "Another sir?" or worse - present the bloody bill!

"Where the fuck are they?" he thought - sweating now, yet not too much, just in case the barman might say "I can see you need another sir!" Certain both Billy and Howard had forgotten him, or had done a runner, he starts to look now for the right time to carry out his own hit and run tactics, but he is also certain the barman is on to it, for he keeps looking at he that is constantly looking at him. As for the barman's role in this - he thinks that the one his mates left behind is a queer, for every time he looks round, there's this white guy eyeing him up - watching every movement in an odd sort of way. This guy was queer okay, one way or the other.

It became a cat and mouse game, one sweating about what to do, the other - what he thought this white guy would like to do. It was shit or bust time, and seeing the fellow turn away at the far end of the long bar, Geoff makes a fast dash for the door - and freedom. Certain they'll be some pursuit, he gathers speed, runs right past Howard and Billy who had been watching him secretly from outside, and past both he believed were them, swearing like a madman in the dark.

The two lovers, walking together gathering the evening air, had been cautious at first about going out at night - tales of muggings, movies of rape and violence had done a good job on them back home, and it had kept them in most times here. But slowly - ever so slowly, they had ventured forth from the Flagler's Inn. Tonight they were going to be very brave and walk to the Marina through a dark grove of Pines, but a short distance from the hotel. Its boarded walkway had many craft tied stern to and most, if not all, were motorboats having the essential chair and fishing gear most Americans wish for in a boat - other than a fridge! It was a quiet place, softly lit to give a sense of peace and tranquillity.

That was soon to change, for barely had they entered this dark stretch, when behind them came the sound of running feet, heavy breathing and obscene language unheard of but for television. Both were certain of getting a good raping, who would be first, was anyone's guess! - Yet the unknown figure fled past them and vanished in the general direction they were heading. It was best, they thought, to return to their hotel - he could well be waiting round the corner!!

Geoff had mistaken the taller of the two for Bill in the dark surroundings, and realizing the mistake, gathered greater speed.

Chapter 36: Oh Well

The end of June was just around the corner now and still the position on our work permits had not been resolved. A letter I received from home and Sue, was rather upsetting, News Howard was back again I knew wouldn't help matters. Dennis receiving one from Pat saying Sue had been under the doctor, which had been held from me in hers. I just had to get home - permits or not. The 23rd of June would see me arranging a flight on borrowed money from Doug instead of what I'd have preferred - earnt by 'Jylland'.

The 30th of June was my departure date, and leaving here would not be the ideal way to get out. Dennis was in some state of confusion, anger boiling about what he'd do to Claus if ever he got his hands on him - helpful! It only reinforced our fears of his total incompetence. Threatening to 'Burn' her if all goes wrong he was - real helpful, especially as he said he'd speak to Ray Alstone about it first! Ray Alstone by the way was our insurance agent at Lloyds. What did he expect Ray to say "Yes Dennis by all means - burn her when you want - just let us know when and where the loss occurred and we'll settle!!"

He had still not told us all the story, for on the 27th June, the day after the good idea to burn her was thought of, brother Will and I sat discussing the crazy situation. Will suggesting the slight possibility that Graham was in some way involved. By the shouting match Dennis had with him over the phone, something was up! Was it - could it be it was used by Graham to repay the money he/Graham owed the German Prostitute over the Panama loan - we did wonder!

As for Will and Sharman's position, being left in Nassau broke and having borrowed money from Roland to make such a passage - going home would be very difficult - if not highly embarrassing for them, The word would soon get out, if it hadn't already, and the 'told you so's" would be too much to take. I had offered to sell my share in her if Doug was interested, and with the proceeds, settle accounts. There is no interest in a 'dead' horse. When it came time for me to leave to catch the midnight B.A flight home - I said all my goodbyes long before during the day. It was hard for me to go; for I wanted so much to come home knowing all was okay. It could well be also, that this might be the last chapter of my involvement with her. I was wrong!! Very wrong!!

Chapter 37: Jylland April '77

It would be Nine months since I left the boat – and Nine months of getting little done. Sue and the children were on Scilly and had settled in with Nora at Porth Loo, while I found myself dragged from there to Essex in an attempt to find out some answers. In those months I achieved nothing but listen to excuses as to who was to blame for the position we found ourselves. Someone had to return to the 'Jylland' – Geoff was home, so was Dennis who organized this whole affair. So here I was!!

Got up to the sound of Negro voices making coffee in the galley. I remember when it was to the sound of my old friends - many days past now! It's a darned shame to think things couldn't have been different – all because Dennis wanted us out of St Lucia." Thus I wrote on the morning of the 29th.
A lot had happened since I last set foot on 'Jylland'. Talking with banks – the work on The Black Christ film – recordings – the Panama film – all really nothing to show for it other than keeping people off our backs with promises of success.

I was now returning in an attempt to help get something achieved back in Nassau. We were not only in a worse place, but were in a worse condition. 'Jylland' badly needed dry-docking in a place where you can get things done properly – proper timbers and men who could do the right job. Money stood in our way of preserving a part of Danish beauty – let alone the wild sea to get her back there. That we wished desperately to happen!

My flight from Luxembourg left at 14.30 on Thursday 28th of April – stopping shortly at Santa Maria in the Azores. It arrived in Nassau at 20.30 local time where brother Will met me. 'Jylland' was out on an evening cruise so I had to wait till she returned before meeting up with Bill Curry once more. Bill and I always got on well together. We saw eye to eye as far as the schooner was concerned – and on many other subjects. Seeing him again, seeing Will again, I soon forgot my disappointments left at home and the sadness of leaving my family was put on hold as we sat chatting over the subject of our problems in Nassau.

Will had on his arrival to convince Doug that the schooner had been transferred to his name. Dennis had done the same deal here as he had done in St Lucia with Bob Elliot – gone home leaving our schooner in another man's hands. What debts he'd left had to be found out and only Doug had the answer to that. Will and I intended to find that out as soon as possible – plus come to some agreement on a contract with him.

Unlike Bob Elliot – Doug was willing to co-operate once he saw all was above board. As for 'Jylland' then – she was working thank goodness. Taking out passengers on a fairly regular basis – but was it enough to keep her – let alone those she kept. Bill had his wife Laurie and young son Cameron there now – rents for apartment had to be met – plus wages for crew and Bill. Will and I arranged to meet with Doug to discuss what Dennis had promised him – and what bills he'd run up while there! We set a time for Monday 2nd May.

The usual niggling problems all boats have was never new to us. We had to fix them cheaply – or buy something new. Nassau was no different to any other place away from the manufacturing world. Cheap things were bloody expensive – and expensive things out of most people's league. It was back to mending sails for me – and to get a generator running properly. Two days back aboard – saw Will and I stripping down that to try and find the problem! Without the deck pump we got in Antigua – we would be up to our armpits in water – or debt in purchasing a rip off! It seemed like the starter motor – a new one would cost $428.00 – so other things had to be checked first – three days later it was found out to be bad leads – and so we were back in business.

Monday, the day Will and I had arranged to meet Doug, came – but not Doug! Saw him later – no excuses or apologies. Manners mean nothing anymore. It would be the next day before we sat down to discuss things and most of what we wished for he agreed to – too easily to for us. His books on accounts Will had gone through – and found them as hard as Dennis's to understand – and Dennis didn't keep any right? It had to be a case of one step at a time regarding this. First was the contract – then accounts.

For Will and me it was banks again. Traveller's cheques had to be changed – and without a bank – you are f--ked! We went and opened an account on the 5th of May in the Nova Scotia branch – its manager there Chester A. S. Hinkson. We had to unshackle ourselves from Doug Prudden's total control – for now we intended handling the money coming in.

Being away from the warmth and sun – you have to be careful at first of getting too much too soon. Difficult on a boat – where all work is on deck and looking upwards. I suffered my usual bout of the red nosed Reindeer syndrome. Up or down – the glare gets at you – off sails or water. Noses are your biggest problem – the sun's rays attack the larger ones – it acts upon them like paint stripper.

Will was due to leave for a break in St Lucia to visit his wife on Sat 7th May. That would leave me alone for some time aboard during the nights as watchman – I didn't mind that so much. I think I have said before in this saga, that I always felt comfortable aboard – even though some things had happened that were hard to explain.

The 7th came and Bill and I took Will to the airport to catch the early flight out. Hoped to return on the 22nd – two weeks' time.

When things seem to be going good – passengers lined up and our affairs with Doug in some order – there is certainly something is round the corner to spoil your day. That which brought a halt to our progress in the early part of May was little we could do anything about.

Mother Nature decided May that year would have a wet start to it – very wet. Cancelled trips due to washouts in morning or afternoons were the order. The $9^{th}/10^{th}/11^{th}/12^{th}$ and 13th –"Still the same old weather – I wrote – not so much rain today though – Bill had to pay the crew and send them home".

What we needed was not only a break in the weather – but also a break in the size of passengers we were taking out. Prospects were good – 'The Flavia' a cruise ship sent us some, but she was not in every day – Tour groups showed signs of interest. A past manager of 'The Malabar' a hotel in St Lucia (Clive ?) came on the 16th. He now worked for a Canadian travel firm – 'Fiesta Tours' and had with him some from that business who wished to arrange a deal – it raised another problem that had to be sorted out on speaking with him.

The day before, he had found it impossible to find out how to book tickets for a trip out on 'Jylland'. He wished to show the company he was with, giving them a first-hand experience – just like the old days in St Lucia. We also walked round once to see how the 'Club Med' was coming on. They had indicated they would like to use us for two days a week - but could we last out till December for such a happening?

What we wanted was time – time for all ideas to materialize and get a sound program running. The thing was, we had little choice but to wait – you couldn't pack up 'Jylland' in a case and move on like some busker with a guitar. She was 100 tons of responsibility!

Another point to frustrate the situation still, was work permits – Bill received a summons on the 16th too. It stated he must appear in court on the 24th May – reason? That he was a skipper without a permit.

On the 17th I had a meeting with Doug on the issue of the work permit and while at it – he brought up the point on the contract we wished with him. 20% of gross – or 20% of net plus wages! He also wanted some guarantees on monies laid out already – plus wages for last year's hard work. I could make no comment, not till others had been talked to – yet I made notes – 20% of gross - or net of nothing is --nothing!

We had to be careful of upsetting Doug in our vulnerable position – it was not in our interest to do so nor a desire in any way to cut him out of the business. Run properly and in time, there was plenty there to keep all happy. St Lucia had shown us that.

On the 19th – we did what we had done in Spain. Showing 'Jylland' off to a bunch of school children – under sail this time. Taking her down to King Georges Wharf, we took them for a two-hour sail at running costs only = $200.00 – they loved it as most kids do. Those children today will be in their 30's and probably ask themselves at times, whatever happened to that 'big boat' we went out on. Well! – corrupt officials of that island chased it from port to port and harried by all for a part of the action.

Those that remember that day – will never see their children have such a memory. She was never allowed to make a penny before someone wanted 10 cents.

I have mentioned before about rain – the truth in the saying about it never rains but it pours is so right. Our troubles hit us like wave after wave not cloud burst after cloud burst. On the 21st May the usual starting of the main engine to make the run home – something happened that would test us yet again and the skill of all in getting her through another crisis.

No sooner had we put her in to gear – then seen skipping up and out of the water astern was something large – it vanished quickly – but was followed by 'Jylland' being shaken. Shaken as if being grabbed by the stern post by a big whatever – to death!!! We had lost one of her two bladed props. Stemming wind and current, we were making half a knot till it could be confirmed alongside our berth. A mile of torturous shaking by what we had yet to confirm. Waiting for our passengers to leave – Bill and I went over the side to take a look.
On deck we sat quiet – what now – what next – just how much can you take? The evening trip had to be cancelled and with Howard and Graham coming out to see how things were going and to conduct a group of Germans on a tour – things were bleak.

The first thing to do was call home – Annette informed me both Howard and Graham had left – blast! Returning from Bills house – who was aboard – my brother turned up as I was calling him. "I brought the spunyarn you wanted," he said – 'It's not spunyarn we need now Howie - said Bill – it's a prop!" Howard never was one to get flustered – "Oh well – he replied – we'll talk about it tomorrow!"

It came – so did Graham and Will – both rather disappointed at the news. Howard would ring Henric in Denmark – luck was he was home – and would ring Fredricshaven about a new prop the next day for us. Good old Henric – I always wished he'd come over and gone out with us on his old girl – he never did. Probably would have had too many happy memories remembering her as she was when trading in The Baltic.

Bill and I had gone over the stern first thing the next day – and put one fear to rest. Getting the prop off without dry-docking her first was easier than we imagined.

Taking off the hub, we rolled the props out by turning the pitching handle. Once aboard we could study the broken stub. What was first apparent was the state of the bronze – the bigger area looked like the inside of one of those rocks you find full of crystals. The only good bit was the area we'd had welded in Martinique before our Panama trip.
It was obvious that for two years – we had relied on that alone till at last it failed!

Those in Martinique that said they were capable of such work – weren't! Not heating the whole piece in an oven beforehand – not x-raying the finished weld - it left us in this state. Mike Atkinson, believing the slight crack in that prop from her hitting ice many years ago should be welded – made the mistake of trusting the word of incompetence.

Far from he that should be looking at it and us pointing saying "Well – what you going to do about it?" – which would be a shrugging of French shoulders and waffle – it was left to us to use our ingenuity.

The 23rd came and at 10.30 the tour group arrived. We could do little but give them plenty of Rum Punches while Graham sang a few of his old hits to keep them happy. It just wasn't worth the risk of going out – though they pleaded for such. Later after a call to Henric – we found it would take a month to get a pair to us. We thought then, the only way out of our problem was to put the props back for safety – then get a boat to tow us back to our berth.

The following day though, and after a thoughtful night in bed, ideas came from those undaunted by mountains to cross, nor willing to await the helicopter to get them over them. I write on the 24th – "Doug came down in the morning and we spoke about getting 'Jylland' back in to action, so left our talk with him for now. It's going to take a month to get a new one so we thought hard about the old - and where there's a will – we decided to try and fix it.

Howard and Will got Doug to run them about for materials. They put 3/16th steel where the blade was missing and tapped bolts into the break – welding the bolts to the steel. They tried to tin lead on to make up the thickness – but had the wrong flux." Instead another steel plate was shaped - fixed and filled with lead to balance it. That was achieved in the morning of the 25th – I write – "Got up early and started on the prop. Howard and Will shaped another piece to fit like a shell to the main one to give it some flair. We had to get that welded, then made the weight difference up with lead melted and poured in to the hollow." - it was then a matter of sanding it all down with a covering of fibre glass to protect it from electrolysis.

On the 26th and with a coat of anti – fouling on it, it was difficult to tell the good one from the improvised one. Waiting for the rain to stop, and when it did, with fingers crossed, Bill and I fixed it aboard, now to test it. With putting her ahead and astern for several minutes – a check on it showed no cracking. It would seem we had done a good job – seem!

While in our gear – Bill and I would check out the Hurricane chain that ran from Paradise Island to the mainland – large and encrusted, we hung on pulling ourselves across against the strong current that runs between the two shores. It looked okay – then so did our prop. We had to test one – and hoped never to have to test the other.

It was five weeks now since I left Scilly. I'd written Sue on many occasions and sent what I could to ease my not being home. I heard from her many times and on the 27th quote – "She hopes I'll be home soon – so do I!" But that wouldn't happen for one reason or another until July – though at the time I never thought it would be that long – nor did I want it so.

The day of reckoning had arrived concerning the prop. Graham had gone to pick up the German tour group on a nice day. Springing ourselves off the dock using the engine, the prop stayed with us. All seemed okay. Slowly and using the current 'Jylland' headed for the open sea. It was only when we started her up – put her ahead did

Howard see what I'd seen – something skip across the water and vanish in to 100 fathoms. A look said it all between those that knew. While others loved every minute of the trip out and back – we stayed silent – dying to get over the side to see what had happened.

Limping back this time was made easier – due to slack water. Though slightly pissed off – our thoughts were lifted when we saw what we guessed might have happened – bolts sheared – and better still – no damage to the hub. What did hurt was the trip with 50 for the next day had to be cancelled. That day being a Sunday and that weekend a holiday till Tuesday. Always happens on weekends. If plan A didn't work – then plan B would or bust all apart – then we'd have no choice but to await the new ones from Denmark.

The usual helpful people who said we'd never do what we intended – were just as helpful the second time round. Experts in pessimism – those that would still be using clubs to get their dinner said we must go to Miami – that instead of "Go to hell!"

They are the types in this world that learn to use what others invent – but have not the brains to invent it. I write on Sunday the 29th – "Doug came and said we could probably use a workshop – so Howard, Bill and Will took off - but people there kept saying it won't work and call Miami – the short of it was – we don't think it will work and you're not using my workshop to find out." We could do nothing then but wait until Tuesday.

Having nothing to do till that day – we could have our talk with Doug about his percentage and his role regarding 'Jylland'. That was Mon 30th. Doug Prudden gave me the impression of a character typical of those born in warm climates.

Rather lethargic – life is easy – leave it till tomorrow – a one big holiday man living in a holiday resort where from its easy proceeds – he could get up when he wants to do what he wants – and Mom says "All's okay my boy – can I get you your breakfast now?" The Anglo-Saxon in him had been driven out by an easy existence –

leaving him more like a sunshine playboy! Not that I didn't like Doug – I just found him hard to understand.

He had an appointment that afternoon – spear fishing with his pals, for that was what he was good at and liked doing on weekends or holidays – so had to make that rather than business. We thought he should get 16% - the same as we – and so putting that to him – off he went to think about it - underwater!

Returning later, he said he'd accept our proposal on one condition – he wouldn't have to 'Mother' – as he put it – the catering side! Work, one can see by his willingness to accept our conditions – was not what Doug liked! We preferred it like that anyway – so it was settled. Doug would give Will his books to go over the next day.

Tuesday 31st arrived and as Howard and Graham were leaving for England at 18.30 – we had to move on getting to a friendlier workshop and get done what we thought would do the job on the prop. Howard and Bill arrived back aboard at 17.00hrs with the job complete – except for balancing - fibre glassing again - and a coat of paint. He wouldn't have time now to find out if it worked – for he had to pack and be off.

Though not a thing of perfection like plan A – Plan B's looks gave you a certain confidence by its massive construction. The broken hub had been flattened by hacksaw and file during Sunday/Monday. Done to accept a round thick mettle ring! Bolted to the bronze, these bolts now had the plates welded to them. Only shaped for a head work – astern – she'd have to rely mainly on one blade!
Thus once more my brother was off before me to England. I'd have loved him to stay – get the schooner up and running - but as he had proved, on the trip back from Panama – his company pushed me beyond my limits of patience at times. When he was ready to go – he went, and trying to stop him was a waste of time.

I was never sure if he had any sympathy for my position – he never said so – nor gave me any indication he ever had. I had to get used to it – leave it - or lump it!

I often think at times your life has already been written for you. It's just waiting there for the main character to be born that's all. You arrive and play out the role with perfection – the great disappointments – the tragedies – the shock of it all – those you meet never forgotten, those you wish to forget! There were no ambitious chapters in my book, of a character striving for success – money his aim a desire for fame – just a character that drifted along as if knowing the beginning – the middle – and that the ending had already been determined and little you could do would change it.

The joy of so many roles which I played has given me an understanding of each, an appreciation for those you meet, of genuine souls – 'the salt of the Earth' as we say. Such people, where your hand can do little but be held by theirs - not to be kissed by them, but show to you the truth of their person. I have pictures in my book, like books do, that only a picture can portray, for words are difficult to find to explain the scene or the person. We all have a book for us – in us – but just how many have pictures of cherished memories?

Wed 1st June came with us working on completing the unfinished prop, sanding down – glassing and painting. Bill came down early on Thursday – 07.00hrs. He was as anxious as I to get it back on and give it a whirl. By 08.30 it was on and put to the test – a more rigid one than last time too. Time would tell, but we were pretty confident it would stand. The weather turning on us and with only 4 booked for the evening cruise – we cancelled.

It would have to wait till the next day, the 3rd before we could test Plan B – and much to our delight when we returned to the dock, it was still with us. A check over showed no movement what so ever. Too early just yet to say we'd done it, we would have to wait awhile before we say I told you so. After 3 years though – and there till

Martinique dry-docking in 1980 – I think we could justify that claim. I was only then did we have those made in Denmark shipped out to us.

I had been suffering from slight stomach pains on and off since being there. Twinges that hurt badly for a moment – then gone! On the morning of Sunday the 5th June – Will, Bill and I sat drinking an early cup of coffee talking over the prospect of carrying shipments of cargo in 'Jylland' other than human ones – when such a pain came on such as I'd never experienced before.

I felt odd too, then in a moment I lay on the deck rolled up in a ball, clutching myself. Both Will and Bill stood wondering what the hell had hit me. Laurie, Bills wife, had been a nurse so Bill took off to get her. But when away, the pain was so great it made me sick - and in moments, as quickly as it had come, it went. I felt as right as rain when Laurie arrived but she insisted I get checked out at the local hospital, and came with Will and I. It took ages and, but for Laurie's presence, – I'd have said to hell with it and left.

The doctor said it could have been the Conch from last night and gave me a shot – and a bill! I think it was kidney stones and she had taken a calculated guess. I hit the sack early that night – mainly due to feeling drowsy from the mysterious shot I'd paid for.

The next day the 6th was a Monday, we had 50 Germans from Nassau Beach Hotel for the evening cruise – they loved it. I stayed off the Conch Chowder that night – just in case. The Germans though, swallowed it by the bucket-full, washing it down with a gallon of Rum-Punch! Such a boost in passengers at that time of the year was important to our survival. June isn't the best period for tourists.

Brother Will would leave us the next day, back to St Lucia on an early flight. He entered my cabin at 07.00hrs and we said our goodbye yet again – always sad for me, for Will was, in his way unlike my brother Howard. I knew that Will felt bad about leaving us in our situation, but from Howard it was more an awkward farewell, as if troubled by his desertion – it showed on his face and in his handshake.

Will was trying to set up some deal there with John Gold – Cap Estate manager – to use us to build on Cap – using the schooner to bring materials down from the States. It sounded good – and in Wills hands rather than Dennis's – we could be pretty sure such a deal would be gone over with a fine tooth comb! I too was hoping to get home - but couldn't find such a good excuse to have to leave Billy with it – and wouldn't! Bill and I would have long discussions concerning the schooner. Both were concerned about the future for her. We would have loved to get her in to some sort of program other than prostituting herself in this cut-throat business. Trading with 'Jylland' was one answer – the carrying of general cargo as a museum piece – anything to save her demise and the inevitability of a watery grave that so many had let happen.

Just maybe this might be answer – and the hope of it hung on Will and his talks with John Gold.

The weather continued to play havoc with our bookings in June; the 8th – went out the evening only 13 aboard – no wind. On the 9th – It rained for 24hrs – cancelled all bookings! 10th – Brightened up – but too late to do anything about it! Weather closed in again in the evening. It broke on the 11th after a wet start – and we went out with 24 on board. This pattern continued throughout June and was frustrating to say the least. I also had Doug to contend with – he was acting up at times.

He had it in his mind for some reason that he was nothing but a messenger boy now. 'Happy' as he was called – was hustler for Doug's para-sailing business. I found it rather odd that he was coming out with us more on the evening cruises. Was it to check on a head count, – then report it to Doug? If it was – and it seemed pretty obvious it was – Doug must have been quite surprised at our honesty. Within a few days, 'Happy' was happy, and so was Doug – we didn't see him again.

Chapter 38: Homeward Bound

You meet some odd people at times – people you'd just to love to know what their real game is! Such an odd couple turned up at the dock one day. They looked like they'd stepped out of 'Who Dunnit?" movie. A right Sidney Greenstreet and Peter Loire partnership too. I wrote on the 16th June – "Had two visitors in the afternoon – a 'Corky Huffman' and a 'Blair Sutton'. A couple of Americans who wanted to start a trading business with the South American countries. (Oh yeah!) They lost their ship while under tow in Chesapeake Bay and asked would we sell 'Jylland'?

They gave us a name of a shipyard in Virginia that they highly recommended. Said they'd "bring the name of it back tomorrow" They did too – never could find it on the map – somewhere on the 'Yankee Tank' river! Can't remember the name of the yard though. Corky and Blair, where are you two now? I'd guess many places! At the bottom of the Chesapeake? Claiming Diplomatic immunity whilst rotting in some South American jail for drug smuggling? – or retired from the CIA and living in a safe house.'

You could never tell whom you were talking to in such a place. Open mouths can lead to open prisons.

I'd have to wait for two weeks before I could grab a flight home. The 10% ticket I'd got from Air Bahama – had it been in the hands of another I knew – it would have been torn up and thrown away, replaced by a certainty of a seat. I would go down to the airport, wait to see if there was spare seat, and go back to the schooner. Checking beforehand was a waste of time. Monday I was told "Now - If you'd been here on Saturday, you'd have been okay – there were 70 empty places then!" I'd called that Saturday and told "Sorry – not tonight!"

I would eventually get out on July 1st. Leaving Bill there was no joy. Surely it was only right I thought that one of the brothers should be beside him. He'd moved his things back aboard from the house Laurie and he had rented. Laurie and Cameron had gone back to the States on the 30th June. Not sure if they'd return – she missed home, and Cameron had to think about school.

Though I had mixed emotions about leaving – I had a long trip ahead of me to think about – Luxembourg – London – Essex – Scilly. As I took off that evening – I wondered if and when I'd be back.

Chapter 39: July '77

I would arrive back in London via Luxembourg on the 2nd of July. I wrote on that day – "Called Sue – she didn't sound too happy to hear from me, which made me sad!" I could understand that – 'Jylland' was tearing us apart and there was little I could do about it other than give up!

I would spend a few days with friends in Billericay, and when Howard arrived on the 4th from Cornwall by train, we talked over Nassau and the cargo idea Will was dealing with. It was pretty obvious something had to give. Passengers were few and far between at this time of the year in the West Indies and Nassau, why go for the sun when it's outside your back door. Poor Will and Bill and I had been given the job of getting her paying for herself in the wrong season.

What Graham was hearing - and, in retrospect, he should never have been privy to – was a scene not to his liking. Now hearing of our dilemma, it was giving him every excuse to back out of any responsibility. Support from the only person who could keep Mr. Rich off our backs till we had some time to get moving out there, was draining.

He was pleading he was broke – but had flown to the States by Concord. I never heard about Bruce Johnston coming over till Friday the 8th – when back on Scilly and in a phone call from Howard who said quote "He was a bit sick at the money being in spent on the Barbecue for Bruce Johnston! – He's broke eh?" That, fixed for the 9th – a Saturday, turned into a washout. Two people turned up!

Graham, in his role of Star – and wishing for centre stage, had left out those who could have made it fun – and would have invited those who would have eaten the wasted food – and shut Bruce out of the limelight. I'm afraid our 'friend' Graham was as faithful as Miss Collins on a casting couch!

Arriving home on the 6th – Helen was in the front garden waiting my arrival and both Sue and Nora in the back. Something was amiss. I write on the 8th – "Have felt rather sad inside these last few days – I can't explain it but Sue has been rather cold towards me – just a feeling I have – my fault I suppose!!"

I guess it was too – I'd been gone too long and for too many times. 'Absence makes the heart grow fonder' – oh yeah? There is another saying that should go with it 'Fonder for another'.

The strain on our relationship was faltering – what love we had for one another was being pulled apart by circumstances. Was she ever unfaithful to me? – I doubt it – but could I judge her if she was? – me, the man with more than one woman in every port?

My stay on Scilly this time would last a little over two months – though I was never sure if and when a phone call might have me away again. It was a period of waiting to hear of developments both sides of the Atlantic, and until that happened, I could do little but potter around the house fixing the bits that make women happy.

Landlords have had many an asset enriched by the tenant with talent. The builder, who earns his living in construction, spends much of his spare time doing the jobs round the house that is not in the agreement.

Outside maintenance is their responsibility, naturally, but when it comes to making life inside the property bearable, for the many opinions on i.e. - decoration – the odd shelve here and where to hang the picture, happiness is made by the person who makes it.

It is hard for a woman to stare at something she wants fixed yet is not able to do so. She doesn't look at the roof, nor has much to say about the colour chosen for outside doors or windows, that is down to the Landlords agent and the maintenance contractor – the man with little taste and a lot of paint left over from the last job.

How happy and grateful was Nora to have the jobs done, which I got stuck in to during my time there. Wilf had not time enough to take a deep breath, other than his last before he could organize himself. The back shed was a mess of timber - odds and sods dumped their till time would afford him to sort it out.

Islanders are a bigger bunch of Magpies than mainlanders – every scrape is horded a-waiting that time when just such a piece of this or that is needed.

A large piece of flotsam seen by the ever-searching eye, struggles ashore with it and lays claim to yet another plank! With the determination of an Ant, they fight it back to their home – or hide it till they can return with a trailer. Some of this I would use around the house – and the rest stack in some order.

Mr and Mrs Alf Jenkins of Old Town lived there in a Cottage of an ancient design. An original Cornish styled one that sits above the harbour. Stone walls, thick and painted white were covered in thatch. Windows were small and sash made to fit both down and upstairs. To jump out of a window and hurt oneself from upstairs – one would have to be very small indeed!

The small front door with its little porch, led to little rooms where just a little fireplace was needed to warm the little front room. Everything was little about it – all except Mrs Jenkins!

Would one paint such a picture of such a place and as your subject, paint a thin lady of the house? No – she would have to be round – a large jovial face beside her happy little home.

Mr and Mrs Jenkins had but one son - John! He lived on the mainland now and like his dear Mom - was big. How they got round the house without tripping over each other I don't know! I did meet John when he came home to visit during certain periods, and just like his Mom, was a smiling nice person.

John was his Moms pride and joy – the great love of her life which showed when she spoke of him or to him. She beamed fairly proudly and must have been the fuss of all fusses as she watched him grow. The other love was for his father, Alf.

Alf, when I knew him, was in his 70's and the perfect match for a big woman. Being that, Alf was half her size and half as likely to be boss of the house. Not only did he love his boy away, he loved him more when he was home. Then John could get the boat ready and the two of them could go 'Strangle' a fish together as Alf used to say.

Alf suffered badly from arthritis – so badly he had to have two sticks to help him along. Handling his boat alone now was not only difficult but also dangerous. On summer days in Old Town he'd sit on one of the benches facing the sea and watch his boat hanging on her moorings. He knew under certain ledges out there lay a good sized Pollock – one that had taken up the spot Alf had hooked last time John was home.
They do that, and Alf Jenkins since he could remember, caught fish in certain spots year after year. Transits taken by a certain point off

St Agnes and a rock on Scilly and – "Wait for it – got it 'av 'e boy?" Fresh fried fish for dinner yet again. Secret spots they were too – shared with only those he liked.

I'd met Alf on an occasion when Nora and I stopped in one day on a walk to Old Town through the Nature Trail. From my coming and goings – not staying put in one place beside his family, I was at first to Mrs Jenkins the sort of person that her imagination had decided upon. A good for nothing vagabond, worthless of consideration and a mainlander at that. That opinion would change in the weeks, and as it did, I was to be allowed to take the position of John in the boat, and be mate aboard with her Alf.

The boat was typical of many around Scilly and in Old Cornwall at that time. This old girl – half decked forward now, probably served in the transport of crew ashore or the taking of custom officials out to vessels awaiting clearance. In Scilly, it was good for taking out fishing parties – or small groups to visit other islands before the bigger parties and bigger boats came.

Driven by a petrol engine from an old Morris car, once getting it going – a trick in many cases once its starting procedure was known – a tickle here and a gentle knock with a hammer there – off she went with a putt-putt-putter!

On those sunny summer days, Alf up to it, he would often call me over the phone, and off we would go- to 'Strangle' a fish. Why even he'd share with me his 'secret' spots, and talk of the days long before then they knew Mackerel would feed in a frenzy on un-baited hooks even. Alf in his younger days would pull with oars only, a line in each hand too – and stop on the occasion for a strike.

Those old men now are sadly gone – they just leave us 'Youngsters' to tell of how it was – that's if we can find the time or someone to listen. Alf Jenkins was the last in a line of such men on Scilly – men I had an understanding with, those that enjoyed life even though it was hard. Fish on the table meant food, a happy wife to cook it, blessing both fish and heaven that her man had come home safely.

Fish now is looked upon as money - cash to buy at a shop that the catch afforded them. I went fishing many times, with those that loved it for a sport, – and those who took just enough. I also did it for a living later – wrapped up in the greed to feed – but that was in a later period of my life.

During the first couple of weeks home – the phone stayed rather silent. Things in the pipe line hadn't moved yet to cause rumblings on the mainland as to what was happening. That would change soon.

Towards the end of the month, on the 26th, I got a call from Graham. Dennis was round there, and both wanted to know what was going on. I'd kept in touch with both Will in St Lucia and Bill in Nassau by mail and could do little, or say little till some news worthy of passing on came! Unsatisfied with something they never did – keeping in contact – they would call Howard! It was pretty obvious that, once again, some pressure was being brought to bear.

The very next day, so anxious to get some news at first hand – Howard called me to say Graham would like him to go out there - Nassau – 500 pounds from a man broke – yet willing to pay Howard's fare to get some results. On top of that – Dennis wanted to go with him. I considered it a waste of time and money and was rather concerned about Dennis going.

A call to me came on the 28th from Will in St Lucia asking me to tell Howard that he wouldn't be in Nassau till the following Monday or Wednesday, proved the point - but why call me? – Call those concerned! Richard Price arrived on the 29th – so I left speaking with Howard on the subject till the next day – and I'd just missed him when Sue said she'd just taken him to the train.

The four days that Richard spent with us, took my mind off things concerning Nassau. There was nothing I could do till Howard returned anyway, so Richard and did the usual things that people do who haven't been to Scilly! Walking St Mary's and visiting Tresco for one.

The one person I'd stayed in contact with from the Panama expedition, - from then till now, was this person of many talents and as the saying goes – it takes one to know one - our interests and thoughts ploughed the same soil.

One spot he wished to visit while here was the grave of Sir Cloudesley Shovell at Porth Hellick. He was washed ashore there when his ship the 'Association' went down in dirty weather on October 22nd 1707. 2,000 men died that night when four out of five of his fleet vanished beneath the waves after they hit the western rocks. He was one of only two found. Many a story has been told and retold of that fateful night. Like all tales, they get stretched by people's imaginations and the truth that lies in there somewhere must be sorted out. They say Shovell had a man hanged for informing one Captain – "If you don't know where you are mate – maybe I do!" This man was reported to be a Scillonian – and if he was, then he probably did know better than the Captain, who like the rest, thought they were near the French coast 70 miles away. He should have known better - kept his mouth shut and eyes open for a something to hang on too.

They also say that the Knight Shovell, was alive when he came ashore – if anyone would it had to be a knight, how else do you think he became one. Survival of the fittest and the fittest reach the lifeboat first! There is also the story that a woman killed him for the lovely ring he wore! Swore in a confession on her deathbed to a clergyman that such was the case, – and in proof showed him the Emerald ring she had taken from the Admirals finger. If she did, where is it today?

It was never given back to the family! It either makes out the clergyman to be a thief – which is not beyond any stretch of the imagination – or makes for a good story. I heard Wilf say he knew who had the ring – and that it's still on Scilly. Heard also that the arrogant man was dead when he was found on Porth Hellick – had to be or close to it. Not many women would tangle with a man still standing after swimming 10 miles. Fingers puffed up by the always cold water round Scilly – she would have had to cut the ring off the dead or dying man's hand. Who knows the truth?

It was the death of Sir Cloudesley and the loss of what he carried home (The latter being the more important than the former!) booty from a bit of pillaging in the Med – that made murmurings turn to demands that something must be done concerning longitude. 7 years after his death, Parliament set up a Board of Longitude – offering a very large carrot indeed to anyone who could come up with the answer as to how all produce that gets stolen – gets home safely!

A very hungry man named John Harrison solved the question – yet every obstacle was put in his way by those that thought only educated men have brains, and if every country bumpkin is allowed such rewards – what will become of them? And by the way – it took the King – the King that Thomas Pain called a sot, and a drunken brute in his 'Common Sense' that all Americans fell for – to put matters right.

The grave of this old sea dog lies above high water mark on the bank in this quiet cove. A wet area behind him is covered in fresh water reed and the home of many a migratory bird when on their move. It is a peaceful place and when birds are in song, the mixture of their music with the sounds of the Ocean, Mr Shovell could not wish to rest in a better grave. Let us believe he deserves it!

We did a lot in those four days – going out with Alf from Old Town fishing off the Gilstone Ledges and getting some too. Shrimping and the usual walking. We even spoke of work – if things didn't materialize as planned. A friend might have a job coming up in the Orkneys, diving – was I interested? Richard called him in Kishorn and got the answer – he'd know more about it in the coming weeks and would let us know. So come the 3rd of Aug, Helen and I walked to see off our guest as he left on the afternoon boat.

Richard called on the 15th – the job in the Orkneys would now start in the New Year due to the weather. Would see if anything was going on in the Shetlands!

It was the 16th now – Nothing from Howard or the others as yet! They say no news is good news, and not wanting to interfere with that idea – I hoped when I got something from them it proved the saying correct.

When the 17th came – and Howard called having just got home from Nassau. It seemed at first glance, that just maybe the news was worth waiting for. Quote – "Howard rang me – just got back – filled me in on the main points of the trip to Nassau. The main one is that 'Jylland' is leaving Nassau September 1st for Florida. If Billy Ross and his friends like the idea of building in St Lucia, and see no problems there (they are going down in two weeks) – they will buy half of her for $110,000, then we'll run her together! – So it's another step taken – long time between steps though?"

Knowing it would take at least two weeks before any firm decisions could be made, I had to sit on hold and just hope.

St Mary's is shaped like a figure eight. It is only by the position of Tresco to the northern quarter and Gugh and St Agnes to the south that the sea hasn't broken through making two islands of it. On the gap lies Hugh Town – holding both together in a mass of stone buildings. During the Napoleonic wars, a wall was built round the smaller end with gun emplacements positioned for the defence of these islands.

That end has since been known as The Garrison. A flat grassy area on top is where many of the islands events take place. Soccer during winter – cricket in summer plus the yearly carnival. What also goes on there is the school's athletic meet.

The 28th August was a lovely day – perfect for such an event. William, ever the competitor, had been practicing his run up for the long jump, knowing he'd have to get it right to beat his main rival, Joseph Badcock. The 60 meters would be decided by who got who's nose in front at the line – either could win it.

Those events plus throwing the cricket ball and the three-legged race - The Langley-Williams Trophy for the 8/9 year olds, would go to he with the most points. Williams's nose was slightly longer than Joseph's that day and he thundered home first. Had my boy not bothered to practice his run up, he might have won the long jump too – taking off a foot behind the line – he managed 10'10" – Joseph taken the event with 11' 2" ahead of him. Good old Joseph pipped him again with the cricket ball. The three-legged race, for some reason, both he and Joseph had decided to run together. Thinking they couldn't fail – they did, third and that by power alone! Why William won the trophy and not Joseph, must have been due only to the running event. It was fun to watch; yet I'm not a one for laurels – you can't have a winner without a loser and those that see the sense in honouring the winner (8/9 year old here) are fools.

Is it not hard enough already for the loser – or losers - to stand and watch a presentation that thrills a few – yet for the majority – may bring resentment – hatred even? Such a young winner can find the jealousy of their rivals hard to bear. Disappointed Moms and Dads stirring up the pot with "You should have won it!"

Why do we have to love and honour those who are already honoured enough by the gift, is beyond me. It is the root of all trouble!!!!

William, in his love for sports, – decided golf was one game he definitely wished to play. The local course on Scilly – and much to their credit – said yes to him joining the club.

The fee for the year was two pounds. What a wonderful gesture – what a great way to give a young boy a good start. Not many clubs – if any clubs in England could match that in helping the young.

Determined to better himself, he would become the youngest ever to win the men's title there.

By the 15th September, all hopes for the cargo carrying of materials to St Lucia were dashed. Those willing to invest in the venture thought they could get a better return elsewhere – I was very disappointed, yet I said at the time I couldn't blame them for that thought.

Such a decision now meant it was time for me to make one. On the 17th I would catch the boat across to Penzance and meet up with Howard in an attempt to clear up what went on in Nassau – and afterwards decide what know? First though – before leaving Scilly I gave Alf Jenkins a much-needed hand to get his boat from the water.

He and I had gone out many times in the weeks I was home, now with me about to leave, and autumn approaching, such days were over. I loved every minute of it, for it took me away from the problems I had now to confront.

Chapter 40: September 22nd '77 -

We would arrive at Emsworth at 17.00hrs – the drive from Kingsbridge being a pleasant one. At 55 years old, the Rolls doodled along singing still as sweetly as ever. I remember one old gentleman touching the peak of his cap as we passed through one of those villages in Dorset. I often wondered, was it for whom he thought might be driving – or was it for the car?

Writing on the 24th I note from my log a passage! "I suppose in years to come I shall read this and think – what was I worrying about and I should have let life just take its course!" - 24 years later I have now read it! Life did take its course alright – and not one I would ever have imagined at the time!

Richard had spent two nights with us aboard 'Chinkara' and left for Macclesfield on the morning of the 23rd. I still had hopes of getting a diving job with him – certificate or not – but there seemed little chances of work there – though he would call me if there was!

What to do work wise was a problem – money was in short supply, which is okay if you're on your own – but not with a wife and two children you'd like to support! I had three choices open to me – go back to Essex to the place I knew - where it was pretty certain I could get something from those I knew.

Work here in Emsworth boat yard – or go back to Scilly and decide to stay put this time.

Keith had seen the foreman in the boatyard – and yes, if we three wished to fit out a boat for a price – it was ours!

The 'Stag 28's - in their different stages of completion lay round the large shed – several teams of workers were aboard each fitting out cabins, their decks off to allow space to bring in the bulkheads and do all one could before the deck went on.

They say, never say you can't do anything till you've tried it – and as far as John Duncan (the foreman) knew – here were three experts in this department ready to have at it!

Fooling people some of the time can be pretty harmless fun – but making yourself look a fool – the biggest laugh can be on you! I'm not saying we couldn't do it – more than we hadn't – not as a job of work.

From where I saw it – it looked more complicated than it was. First, Howard and I had no tools needed for such a job – nor the money to go out and buy any! Keith had his and said what more do we need? Nice of him – but not an ideal arrangement.

Where would we live – again Keith had the answer – 'Chinkara', where else till you can afford a place to rent! It was a friend ready to help out – but at first I was very apprehensive about the exchange of favours, and wished for a way out! Howard had to make the return trip to Cornwall on the 24th. Rachael, his daughter, was going in to hospital to have her tonsils removed and Sue wanted him home! Being a Saturday, and on a toss of a coin to decide whether I go, or not with him – it came down to, if I could get a seat, I'd go!

It was the way I'd wished for too – I needed to see Sue and my children desperately!

Thus it saw my brother and I leave Havant on the 09.55 bus for St Austell. Price – 6 pounds fifty pence – time 10 long hours!

The 26th of September 1977 was a very emotional time for me – it was also a time in my life – though I didn't realize it as such then – that I was reaching out for a helping hand – someone to make a decision for me. My pride, stubborn as ever, wouldn't allow me to ask would it!

It was a Monday and I sat on the 'Scillonian' thinking over the past and future happenings - an extract from that page about sums up my feelings – quote " - sat most of the way over and I'm still thinking about the best course to take concerning the future. My great failing is my pride, but swallow it I will if I have to. What a long hard road this has been for the last few years. I'm now looking for some flotsam from the wreck of it all when maybe there is none. Perhaps I should give up now with what I have and forget everything!----"

Two words – just two words, that's all I wished for - "Come home!" When I had spoken to Sue on the night of the 23rd over the phone from Emsworth – it was what I wanted her to say – it would have made my mind up for me, but it never came.

When I left there on the 29th – after just three days – the course of my life was to change. Though Sue was to plead for me to come home in two years' time – it was too late.

I had found myself floating in a wreckage of ideas and failed expectations. Sue and the children were the only thing at that time close to me to hang on to – yet by keeping my emotions pent up –

and my cries for help quiet, both Sue and Nora never knew of it! Due to pride and future circumstances I was drifting further and further away with each coming month.

William had been home from school sick for two days, it had made leaving Scilly even harder for me. Like all boys bedrooms, here and there lay the favourite toy and a collection of childhood imaginations. By other boy's standards – it was bare by comparison. As a father I felt saddened and rather ashamed by my inability to have not provided more. I kissed him goodbye with a very heavy heart before I left for the quay and the boat that afternoon.

Helen, still too young, and still not used to me being around long enough to be missed – came with Nora to see me off. Leaving Scilly that day was the hardest I'd experience – it was as if I knew I was leaving a part of me there – a part of me that will always be there – and a part that can never leave no matter what – for I was torn in two!

Howard and I would leave for Emsworth the next morning by bus – arriving Havant at 18.30hrs. Keith met us, and that evening we spoke about the boatyard work.

There was of course the nagging problem of 'Jylland' to consider. She was still in Nassau and with Bill Curry wishing to get home to Seattle and Laurie, for the forthcoming birth of their child – who was to take his place?

Chapter 41: Boatyard Emsworth '77

You never know what you're capable of till you try. "I could never do that" you hear people say. Some honestly doubt their ability – while some say it for other reasons, out of laziness and to boost the other man's ego as he does the job for them! 'Our England is a garden and gardens are not made – by singing oh how beautiful and sitting in the shade!' wrote Kipling – so true!!

On Friday October 14th '77 – I had the chance to test my capabilities for one simple reason – I needed the money! The last 20 pounds I had in the world, I'd sent Sue – whether I could get any more, was down to me – a few tools and some common sense!

Factories, whether it be boat building to car making ones or as far a-field from Scotland to Cornwall – each has its characters that seem to be pressed out of the same mould. Gingers – Chalkys – Curlys – Paddys – Jocks – Taffys – John – Fred – Toms – all you have met before – the joker – the serious – the quiet – the good the bad and the ugly too!!

This shop was no different than what I'd been in before from Wernicks to Armstrong Whitworths – and all in all, the best people I've found to be around. They have little or no possessions to talk about – nor dress in a manner that brings upon any feeling of jealousy. Old trousers and suit Jackets that had seen better days, hung on them till the bitter end. They worked hard – talked hard and didn't tolerate fools! They would look up to someone better educated or wiser – but if looked down upon – he that would do so was finished.

Those that struggle for a life and a living are the salt of the earth. For some the factory floor is their home away from home. It is their excuse to get out of the wives hair - her nagging voice about not making ends meet and the general turmoil of council homes. Once out the door, walk or ride, its clocking in and - "Morning George?" with life outside soon forgotten by the hands-on process.
You'll find that most people who do the most overtime have in the most cases, the most demanding wives! Overtime is a great excuse (and accepted by both) to get out the house faster than you did when children came between you.

She in her domain is happy to get him out the way, especially for that extra bit on the side, and he is happy because such might get him a bit too – which is rarer than he expected by her performances in all manner of positions many years ago! In to this world – I was about to enter again.

Geoff, who had visited us would leave for Essex on Monday 17th and after seeing him off, it was the start of my second day. We'd had a good weekend together, a little fishing for the Mullet and a lot of talking for the mouth. I never realize just how much I missed the chats with my mates till I see them again. I guess we were all cast in the same mould too!

During the next several months, working round the yard became easier as the weeks passed. Procedure was just a matter of figuring out the best and fastest way of doing something. Being on a price, it was up to you how many hours you put in. For the first time in many a year, I collected wages paid by someone other than ourselves.

My first week, though only 45 pounds drawn - was a great feeling to have. That first 'Stag 28' we had worked out – paid us about 3 pounds an hour, it was completed on the 26th and on the 27th – I picked up 131 pounds – total wages for my part, 176 pounds. I note that on the 17th – my second day at work - we reckoned if we really got stuck in to it, we could finish fitting one out in two weeks.

I was out by a week – for we got it down to a fine art by the end and finished one in a week – that was with working late plus going at it Saturday and Sunday. At 900 pounds for each contract, not bad, one had to be careful though not to push on too fast. You could not only spoil it for yourselves – but for those only prepared to work at a certain speed – cutting their price and their friendship at the same time could happen. So long without any money to talk of – Howard and I were prepared to push hard and make as much as we could. For Keith though, after the initial burst of speed, the pace Howard and I were setting he was reluctant to keep up with. On the 24th of November I wrote – "Well, a couple more days and we'll have finished this 'Stag' No 044. We're not going to make much on this – all the waiting around for fittings didn't help, plus we should have put more hours in. Howard and I were willing but Keith wasn't". He didn't need it you see – what with Frankie working and the berth they kept 'Chinkara' in at the yard cheap, plus he had no family to support.

For Keith, working hard and for many hours at a time it was unnecessary. It would lead to a strain on our friendship, for on the 18th and 19th Dec, he was subdued – sulking for some reason. Howard thought it due to him and Sue not inviting them down for Christmas this year as was normal.

He had a little 'say' come the morning of the 19th -- he'd made up a job list so he said, as to who does what – quote " -----I (David that is) do all deck fittings etc., so he thinks he's doing more than his fair share – silly boy!! It could have been an argument – but he was justifying his few days of bad moods, so I left it at that – he was a lot happier when he'd got it off his chest!" unquote!

It was a tight spot to work in at times and of course you couldn't help but get in each other's way, but what could you do about it. We knew this work would come to an end – and didn't want the work to end a friendship! In fact Keith and Frankie did come to Cornwall after all – Howard and Sue asking them down – they even came across to Scilly on the 28th December for a couple of days too!

Every phase of the fitting out process was on a contract price – 600 pounds for painting – so much for skin fittings – deck fittings etc.! By the 7th of December with all on 044 completed, we got No 048 ready to go, and did in the first 8hrs what took us 24 on the first Stag!

We would meet some nice fellows at Emsworth boat yard. John Duncan for one – Will Charlton – Bob Sutcliffe names of those and others who made my time there memorable!

John was foreman I guess you could say. He had been a navy pilot – aircraft carriers and all that. Maybe that's why the owner of the yard, Admiral Flick, picked him. John was an easy man to work with - a good joke he loved and always ready for a pint or a party – preferring both!

Familiarity breeds contempt? Not with the likes of John Duncan it doesn't. Many's a night we'd spend together round the flat Howard and I now rented or at 'The Crown' in Emsworth. I often wondered what he ended up doing – or just where he ended up full stop – as I did with the other lads I got to know!

The apartment Howard and I had – No 8 Osprey Quay – was owned by a Mr and Mrs Kite, the rent was 15 pounds a week – two in advance! It sat on stilts in a small complex of such places 5 minutes' walk from work. We had some good storms that year, one blowing force 10 – it shook her too – as did a couple of party's we had there.

Will Charlton – then aged 67 looking more like 50, we got to know at the pub – he owned a 23' Ocean Baby called 'Hunters Maid'. Needing some frames replaced in the stern section – Howard and I steamed some round for him in the flat using a cardboard carpet roll and steam from a kettle! Will would have dinner with us on occasions – and make 'em too while Howard and I worked late at the yard.

During this period of work, the strain taken off my immediate money problems, the problem of 'Jylland' persisted. Howard and I for financial reasons could not stay where the action was being played out in Essex. Hardly a day would go by though without a phone call made by us – and the odd train journey to Billericay to keep our finger on the pulse of events.

The plight of 'Jylland' was in had to be taken seriously, it was obvious she couldn't stay in Nassau, she needed dry-docking and us there to do it, if Denmark was too far – where Martinique? We couldn't let people know of her condition, nor a survey done – not till we had her on the 'ways' to do what was necessary first.

On the 23rd we found out just where she was too – in The Turks and Cacaos islands with a leak and needing some money - $1,200 for a pump. Billy had moved her from Nassau in an attempt to reach St Lucia – then on to Martinique for dry-docking!

Something had to be done and Howard first tried Dennis – then Graham, stressing the urgency of the situation on the 23rd and again on the 24th. On the 25th I spoke with Dennis, who in turn had spoken with brothers John and Henry for some assistance.

Dennis had obviously forgotten he had signed the ownership of 'Jylland' over to Wills name – and quoted from my log "----I gave Dennis a call – he's probably borrowing the money from John and Henry for Billy – he still persists with - "They're lending the money to me, and I've had to ask them to lend me the money!" I continued - Howard tried to call John Rich today; he was at lunch – try again tomorrow. I don't see why the hell we have to call when they went to see him yesterday – surely they explained all that was going on?" Unquote.

Without $1200 – she wasn't going anywhere and frustrated by the non-action and the seeming lack of seriousness of the position – Howard and I got the evening train to London and on to Essex on Friday 28th.

We also booked a call to Will in St Lucia – explaining the latest talks, while he gave us the position out there. Could two of us get out there and help with the dry-docking? It would be pretty hard for Howard and I money wise – not to mention boat contract wise too We learnt from him that day – 'Jylland' was booked to go on the ways Monday 7th November – also Bill had experienced some hard sailing to the Turks – took him 11 days! The thrill of actually leaving that flat, un-interesting, shit-hole of corruption could have only been dampened by a bloody leak.

18 months of wasted time and effort, and to leave there without enough being made to buy neither provisions nor a decent pump too!

I felt rather bad about all this – there was Bill Curry with our schooner needing provisions and parts – and here we were miles from the difficulty and the worries! Who could blame him if he walked away from it all – but not Bill – he wasn't like that, and knowing that, made it worse for me!

On Sunday 30th October, Dennis came round to Langham Crescent to talk about who could go to Martinique. Brian came while he was there and said he would go if it was alright by his wife – it was, so he could go – so could Geoff if the fares could be raised.

There came the news quote "--- Had news from the West Indies via Will to Geoff then on to Frankie, Bill has taken 'Jylland' to Puerto Rico – probably San Juan – he's having trouble with one of the con-rods – a white metal bearing no doubt, so it looks like she'll go on dry-dock there ----". What the problem turned out to be was the generator had thrown a con-rod through the block – not as we first thought, and with some relief, the main engine! This we found out in a telex from Will on the 5th November. Will also would like Howard to go out with both Geoff and Brian - - with $9,000! Where the bloody hell was that coming from?

Howard's wife Sue had been with us for a week with Rachael and Lee – half term break from school. They left for Cornwall that Monday. Howard and I had spent a long time away from our families through the past years – myself longer than he. I note here in my log a passage quote "--- Helen started play school today. I do miss my family and the thing is, if one spends too much time away from them, you get used to living alone, that's what I'm frightened of---!"

Tuesday the 8th came and still nothing. Yet from Will on the 9th November came a telex from Puerto Rico now, saying he might make 'other arrangements' if decisions can't be made that end.

Another telex arrived from Will on the 10th wanting Howard to be at Castlemain to receive a phone call from him at 14.00hrs. Howard couldn't make it – not in time! It turned out Bill Curry had left Puerto Rico for the States and home for the birth of his child – other than that Bill would have stayed.

Sat the 12th of November would see Howard and myself heading back again to Essex this time with Keith and Frankie by car.
I had only slept a couple of hours that night – for two weeks now it had been blowing hard – one gale after another charging up the channel. Friday night a storm 10 blew, the old flat felt like it was about to take off! Every blast seemed to wake me! I was happy to sit in the car that morning – maybe a little shut eye on the way.

Sister Peggy was home from the States visiting – so it was to see her and hopefully see John Rich at the same time. We arrived there at 13.00hrs and not only was Peg there but also my Auntie Alma – cousin Angie and her husband. I hadn't seen my Aunt for some years, nor heard the voice my Dads brother Victor fled from – cringing from the orders to show himself. The voice that was her downfall would again put her foot in it!

She let slip in John's company how concerned they've all been about not getting their share of Uncle Fred's Will. The grabbing made John rather sick – me too! As the eldest son of our father's eldest brother – John had every right to contest all – and felt like getting a solicitor involved to stir things up, but instead let them get on with it! The sad thing was what they were after was not what I would now have wished for – photos – papers – that would have been cast aside in the hunt for any cash!

There was only one way of us getting to see John Rich – which was visit him at home! We knew where that was - Noak Hill!! During our days of favour, he had giving his address – so the morning of the 13th being a Sunday, he may have wished he'd kept it from us!

He was very surprised to see us at his door. Confronting him there and then about the finance needed out in Puerto Rico – he agreed it must be done! He had asked Graham and Dennis to come in to see him Monday morning – whether his word on help could be trusted – we doubted it – but we knew where he lived, and another knock on his door he could expect if things didn't happen. We saw Dennis after and asked him to get things moving – plus get a letter off from the bank as a reference for Geoff's U.S visa.

We would spend some hours with my dear sister before we left for Emsworth on Sunday. I felt very sad waving to her as the old Morris turned out of John's driveway. Who knew when I might see her again?

We would have to drop Howard off at Charing Cross station before heading for home. Sue had called again that morning saying the headache had returned bad – so he would have to go home for a few days – "One thing after another!" I said that day! Sue suffered badly from migraines – bad ones that knocked her out for days on end. So we'd be without him on the Stag for a few days - it got complicated working out money.

On the 15th Frankie had said Howard had called her saying he might be back tomorrow the 16th – also Will had said he'd like Howard and I out there. Couldn't afford it – nor afford to leave the situation in Essex as it stood.

Howard did return the next day – that being Wed 16th – arrive 19.30, cold and hungry. I'd made enough for two, but he was too late and I'd eaten too much! We called Dennis and Geoff had got his visa okay – Howard also told me about the 'other arrangement' Will had in mind. It would seem Mike Atkinson was interested in putting up some money for a share of 'Jylland's chartering earnings. Mike knew just how much that could mount to by her time in St Lucia. As yet no decision was made – but I assumed it was for working out of St Lucia. Will also said if he hears nothing soon – he would give Mike the okay! I note I said on hearing this – "Pity it wasn't two years ago"

Speaking to Dennis on the 17th over the phone – a rather strange thing was said! Dennis said that Graham had thought it might be an idea if he (Graham) purchased 'Jylland' – then he could raise enough to pay off the creditors – it seemed strange!

There was something going on here – and Dennis thought that he and John Rich had had a little 'chat'. How could he raise money to buy the schooner – yet nothing to pay off his pressing creditors that were dragging us in to the mess? Howard called Graham that evening – telling him the consequences of he and John Rich messing up any plans we had! Graham asked Howard to call back later – he did but the phone was off the hook!

'Oh what a wicked web we weave when we first try to deceive!' Looking back over these logs, the thread slowly pulls apart that tangle of lies and deception.

It also turned out that Henry thought it not a good idea that Howard had a go at Graham – I didn't agree – the little bastard had to be reminded of his failing to keep his side of the bargain concerning Panama. I rang Dennis after – he didn't seem all that happy – all on his shoulders again – or so he thought!

The following day Howard again speaks with Henry, who seems to be getting involved in this on-going saga! He thinks we should get together for a friendly chat! Howard agrees!

On that day – the 19th November I note that Frankie sent Geoff 130 pounds – 100 from Keith for the lead he owed us for when we poured 'Chinkara's' keel – and 30 from me – it going towards his flight to Puerto Rico – leaving Monday.
Henry again wanted a word with Howard, who called to find out Henry and Dennis had been to see John Rich – could we go up there for a chat over certain issues.

We were at Henry's around 13.00 hrs and with Dennis there – we went through monies outstanding owed by Graham for his failing to honour the Panama expedition – and that still outstanding on the work done at his house at Danbury. It would seem that Henry had taken the role of mediator in all this – he was going to see John Rich in the morning – before Graham and Dennis went in. Henry wanted to see him to present our case first. Our meeting with Henry had opened up his eyes to a few points not understood – and points Dennis couldn't tell him – because he never listens! Howard and I were back at 22.15 hrs. meeting Keith and Frankie at 'The old house at home' before driving back to Emsworth.

Henry didn't go to see John Rich as he said he was on the 28th – but spoke instead with the man over the phone. Another phone call to Henry on the 29th by us – and from it came the response that Graham will bear no responsibilities whatsoever! Henry still thinks that saying something to Graham didn't help – again I disagreed!

I needed a break – so did Howard from all this shoving and pushing – so for 4 days I went to Scilly, Howard and I being dropped at Fratton station by John Duncan on Wed 30th. I always did spend less time with my family than Howard – waiting for the boat or Helicopter always put me back a day. I note in my logbook that on the 31st while in Penzance – I purchased a few bottles of the necessary to help the drinks cupboard out! For less than 20 pounds – I got two bottles of Martini – one Sherry – one Whisky – one Gin and one Brandy – we've never had it so good eh?

I might have got away to Scilly – but not the phone calls – Dennis rang me that evening on Scilly saying Henry might be able to help by raising some money – also Bill Curry would be going back to Puerto Rico next week – would like me there! A difficult thing to do, work wise I had unfinished commitments.

It was lovely waking up with my family round me as I did on the 2nd – I was a world away from all hassle and the frustrations of the mainland. Sue and I took a walk in to town despite a good wind blowing cold. I would meet up with Tony Armstrong on our way – did some shopping and stopped in to see Mrs Tippet for a moment, delivering the loaf of bread she asked for. Our next-door neighbour, alone and likely to be blown down by the gale blowing – needed friends this time of the year more than ever. One reason of coming back to Scilly – just for that brief period was to put up the polythene in the windows. Wedged in the reveals with wooden battens, they were Scilly's answer for double-glazing.

Gales were hard that year, and the old sliding sash windows howled like a dog. The bodged job worked, cutting some of the noise and keeping in most of the heat from the small fire. Cutting enough wood till I returned in a couple of weeks, was necessary – and by the time draft flaps were fitted and all seemed secure round the house – the days had flown and again I had to leave, which came on the 5th - a Monday for the long haul back to Emsworth.

Leaving on the 09.45 helicopter – a train to Exeter – change to the Salisbury one – then Fratton – then Havant trains – made it an all-day affair. Living on Scilly, not only did I get to see my family less – but paid the extra price to do so – a much bigger price!

Howard had already arrived – he had left Cornwall Sunday. We had spoken over the phone Sunday morning regarding this and any news he might have had – nothing was sure about Puerto Rico yet – Dennis had said he'd call me about the need for anyone to go there! – He hadn't!

Bang went his claim about keeping in touch! "If you say you're going to ring someone – ring them!" the quote he used on many an occasion – but of course that was when he was awaiting news!
The 6th of December was a Tuesday and it was back to work. No 044 still needed a day's work to complete before 048 could be rolled in to position. By 18.00 hrs. all was finished and by 20.00hrs the new hull was in place ready for the morning. We called Dennis for any news that day. He informed us he wouldn't know if he or Henry had achieved much till tomorrow – he said Graham still won't help or do what he was supposed to do. My log reads "----I feel that had

Howard and I stayed alongside Graham, things would have been okay – but we couldn't afford it!"

The 7th came and if nothing else proved a point I had only written down the day before. We had worked hard that day quote "----- felt very tired but we had to go out to ring Henry! He was out when Howard first rang. We found out later that he'd been at a meeting with Graham. He said that after their talk, Graham was willing to help, so we'll just have to wait and see. Graham said something that I'd said weeks and weeks ago – "When David and Howard were here, I knew what was going on and we could get things done!" un quote. We couldn't – nor could we watch his every devious sidestepping action he'd try to make!

Both Dennis and he played the game of blame – a tennis match of insults. All were partly responsible for the plight 'Jylland' was in – from Panama to Nassau little or no attention had been given to detail. Nor much thought in to the consequences if things went wrong. The words of Syd to that of Claus – to trusting the words of a brother or a brother and a friend. Words alone had got us in to a right mess - arguing wouldn't get us out of it.   Howard and I had spent a long time with Graham since our return from Nassau – a year of keeping heads cool – unfortunately we couldn't afford to stay with it any longer.

Dennis said he was going out to Puerto Rico this coming Sunday and would like Howard to go along he said nothing about neither where his airfare was coming from – nor how Sue and the children were expected to get by without him! To get some answers to some very important questions – Howard would call Henry on the 10th ^{of} December that being a Saturday. Henry was out said Lyn – 'Gone fishing!!' Such a sign one meets on the front door of a home – it means what it says or ---- they can't be bothered with visitors! Henry had gone fishing – yet it was on reflection, very apt I might add, for all that went on before and after concerning us! The right hand not telling the left hand what it needs not know! Dennis left for Puerto Rico on the 11th – the how and who was paying for him there, needed an answer – we were un-able to get that, not for some years to come too!

We would hear not a word – nor have one phone call on the 'Jylland' question for the rest of that year. No news is good news they say – but the silence to me meant only a lull in the storm. The 'Gone Fishing!' quotes surely means more to me now than it did then!

My last entry in '77 starts, quote –"After all that writing we are now to the last page and the last day of the year! What a funny old one it has been sometimes full of great promise, but mostly full of greater disappointments. We again did our best to pull through what was a bad move, and we still are struggling.

'Jylland's' in San Juan waiting for dry-docking – we are still not sure of our future with her. I would love to be with her, to see it through, but my family needs money – yet I'm ready!"

Chapter 42: January to February '78

Little did I realize, nor could have dreamed of in my wildest imaginations what 1978 held in store for me – who does? The weather was so clear that if the horizon had not been in the way, one could have seen America – such came from a quote in my diary that day! Sue and I had taken a walk round the Garrison after breakfast and the air was as clear as a bell. Bishop Rock Lighthouse sat where the sea and sky met seeming so much closer than its 8 miles. I would be leaving the next morning back to Emsworth and it would be another wrench leaving again! I knew the job in the Boatyard wouldn't last forever and what to do after was in my thoughts.

Howard had called later that evening saying he would meet me at the Heliport in Penzance! At least I wouldn't have to catch the train to St Austell. So on the 2nd January at 10.35 I was again on the move. First it was back to his place – a quick lunch then crammed in with Keith – Frankie – Grimble (the dog) we got underway for Emsworth arriving at 19.00 hrs full of the thoughts of those I'd left behind!

The clearness of the weather I had seen in Scilly – the still grey milky sea was a sure sign of bad weather to come. The night of the 2nd force 9 to 10 was shaking the hell out of our lodgings on stilts! Woke us up a few times too! It had been an extra windy winter so far.

Work is the best medicine to relieve the pain of anxiety and the worries of what tomorrows might bring, so in to it we went the next day with a will! The 'Stag' we were on we hoped to complete by Thurs and move on to another!

John Duncan was moving in to sales – and his performance at the coming Boat Show in Earls Court gave us the impression, his job relied upon it! Work is all about being round people you like, and John was an amiable likeable fellow – we hoped he would do well there – if he went, life in the yard would lose something to brighten up your day.

As Saturdays and Sundays were just days to Howard and me, we wished to push on and work through them – or call it a day when deciding to 'Let's go home!' Keith was really not too happy about it – even though Howard and I both agreed the three ways split would not be affected! It would have been hard for him lying there knowing we were working though! So instead of working on Saturday 7th – Howard, Will Charlton and I decided to take a run in to Chichester by bus – well we would have got the bus too had not 'Scouse' in the firms Wagon, stopped and given us a lift.

It gave Howard and I a chance to walk round that nice town – browse in bookshops while Will looked for a jacket – plus a riveting set for fastening some new frames we'd bent for 'Hunters Maid' his little 'Ocean Baby' a 23 foot double-ender he had intentions of heading for Australia in.

Will was 67 years old then, but looked 47! Returning with a sweater (not Jacket) the fastening set and Southey's 'Life of Nelson' for me, we spent the afternoon riveting some frames – and the evening talking to John Duncan over a pint in 'The Crown' about him not selling any 'Stags' as yet!

Doug and Margaret Havers, I was informed in a card from them sent to Castlemain, had brought their Baltic 'Our Svanen' to England for some fitting out before heading in to the wide blue yonder. She was now in Poole harbour, close to us – so Howard and I were sure to go down and see them.

It was Sunday the 7th of January when we made the hour and half drive there – and in the company of Anne Hyams who had stopped in that morning to visit with us. She was living now in Lyme Regis along the coast from us having moved down from Essex.

The first time I met her was when she was 15 – it was wow! If anyone owned, let alone wore a shorter mini-skirt – I'd like to have seen it! The knickers were impossible to hide – and the joy in men's eyes just as impossible to hide! 'Little Annie' was great fun and seeing her with her legs wrapped round a horse – one just longed to be Trigger! She was married now and like so many that had too much fun before it – marriage wasn't as much as it was made out to be!
Pleased to see us, though I had the feeling Margaret wanted to know more about who the young lady was with us, and why? She and Doug showed us over the Baltic preparing herself for the coming passage across the Atlantic. To me her shape was spoilt by the deck-housing structures built for the comforts of life! We spent an hour or so and departed for home with Margaret asking us back one day for lunch – which really was never to our liken nor habit – thus it is easy to leave if the company gets boring!

Monday 9th arrived and while I finished off the odds and ends to 048 – plumbing etc.! Keith and Howard started on 049. It would be Tuesday 10th before Howard and I would eventually hear from

Henry and anything concerning the 'Jylland'. Things had definitely gone quiet after all the great expectations.

The call put through to him as requested before 19.00hrs got the news - Dennis wasn't back from Puerto Rico yet – and Pat was in desperate need for money – could we help? How, was going to be difficult – we still owed sister Mary for telephone calls to St Lucia – just paid for electricity bill here – rent was due on the flat and can we help?

It just so happens here that my log proves that Fri 13th can be lucky for some – while unlucky for others – Quote! "They gave us two cheques to change 112 pounds odd. Sent 39 for our rent which takes us to the 23rd – also put 40 of it in our account in Scilly – dropped Mary a quick line and put in 10 towards telephone bill – sent Pat 20 – 11 from me 9 from Howard!"

Why nine from Howard, not Ten, I haven't a clue but can say – after the money we were making – he always seemed in difficulties to make ends meet! The next time I sent Pat 20 pounds – I had to send the lot – and the rest of the phone bill owed! I wrote on the 28th of that month – quote! "Howard did some ringing around for a car. Sue needs one. I lent him 60 pounds till next week – he owes me 40 from a few weeks back but that can wait, he's had a lot to pay out in the last few months – all this work we've had and he's back to square one!"

By the end of the month – Keith Howard and I were coming to the end of 049 – we were also coming to end of our working relationship in the boat building business! In such tight quarters you can't but get in each other's way – and it can stretch friendship to beyond the limit. By the 2nd of February '78 we completed the finishing touches and collected our cheques for 233 pounds each!

The finishing touches nearly finished our relationship with Keith too! You see Howard had gone home – spent 3 days away having a vasectomy operation! He wanted from Howard 87 pounds – split between he and I for the time off! 'Being business wise is an expression used by tight people' so I wrote at that time – All for one and one for all eh? Keith felt rather awkward when I didn't want anything to do with it!

On Fri 3rd February, our time had come to an end at Emsworth. The worst thing about moving around like I have done through the years is the friends you make! Good friends too that you think you'll see again – hope to see again but sadly is the case, you never do!! John Duncan – Will Charlton living aboard 'Hunters Maid' that spent time in our flat – bending frames – cooking dinner for the three of us – taking a bath – and coming in when the weather was cold – and it was cold too at times that windy year!

Young Mark? – a nice lad that helped us on one boat – Bob Sutcliffe! All good fellows!

I would be back on Scilly on Monday 6th after spending Sunday night in Redruth with Bill and Shirley Harvey, Sue's brother and his wife. My thoughts on staying put on Scilly were given a boost when Sue told me Graham and Penny Browning wanted some Dormer windows put in to 'Wingletang'.

The only problem I saw right then for such a job - was the weather – it had been a year of gales – heavy rain and to top it off – on the 12th February Scillonians awoke to find for the first time in many years – snow! It was a sight I won't forget – all the islands covered making it look wonderfully strange for a day! Of course Frank Gibson was out fast taking photos for his collection before it was gone! Devon and Cornwall at the same time got the brunt of it – 20 foot drifts so we heard!
It would not be until the 1st of March that a chance could be taken to start the job. Graham rang me to say "What about it?" for I had left the decision in his hands whether or not to risk it! Luck was with me (and Trevessa the guesthouse) for I had it watertight
in two days, that was achieved and all completed by the 13th. As for the Dormers to 'Wingletang' – they would have to wait due to the

time wasted waiting for the weather – and the preparations for the arrival of the holiday period! But I had other work in hand to keep me going!

John Bourdeaux had now pursued his interest in the Pottery business and to carry out such had got himself an old stone barn close to Old Town. Needing shelves for his works of art and the necessary product to pay the bills he asked me to build what he required! Thus for some weeks – it kept the very amiable John and me busy and happy!

Does fate play a bigger role in life than we ever imagine it can? The roads that we take in life already lay down before us.

I was quite content in Scilly just pottering around doing the odd job here and there – and, I might add, charging people far less for a job than others would have done! As I read and look back over events – there was nothing to suggest that a vast change in my life was waiting and for what a meeting with Dr Davies might have done! Sue had made an appointment for me to go see him about a vasectomy, for the thought of her being on the pill was bothering us! Howard had been 'done' one might say – hoping it would stop those horrible headaches she had – it didn't! On the 16th of March '78 both Sue and I were supposed to convince him I wanted it done! I note on that day – quote "—the only thing was, I hadn't convinced myself – I don't know why, it just doesn't seem right some way!" We cancelled the appointment for that night to talk about it! I went to see him eventually on the 31st – Quote: " – went to see Dr Davies about having the op' – had a good chat, he felt the same way as I did about it, the reason he said he hadn't had it done. It is not an operation that makes you feel better – and could do the opposite – have another chat about it!" Sue and I did – and I didn't – she said I took after my Mum – I said - that can't be bad!

Two boys – one 26 years old – and one 24, would not be walking around today if I had been more convinced it was the right thing to do!

The 'Jylland' in the meantime, after one delay and another, and little information reaching us, had left dry-dock – and had reached St Martin on the 16th March! It was pretty obvious Will had come to some agreement with Mike Atkinson about some sort of charter work out of that Island – but to what agreement and what sort of work I had yet to hear!

As for Dennis, he had wondered if Pat would like to go out there! Having just moved in to a place in School Road she was not about to give that up – and the last thing we wanted was he being there in charge of the running of things! He, having forgotten the 'Jylland' had been signed over in to Wills charge – meant little to him! Had there not been so many roads open to me during that period of March '78 – I might have still been in Scilly. On the 14th March Sue and I had spoken about the possibilities of us returning to the West Indies. Will seemed to be getting plenty of building work and had asked if Howard and I were interested! I had spoken to Howard on the subject – but there was no way Susan was taking 'her' children back – she hated it there!

I was getting a few calls from Brother Henry during March – one on Thurs 23rd which informed me Dennis had arrived home on Sunday 19th.

It was pretty obvious Henry was getting deeper and deeper involved in 'Jylland' - which I first thought was concern for our interests – but it turned much later it was more to do with his concerns over the money he had been paying Pat whilst Dennis was away!

Obviously after three days of grilling Dennis as to the facts of the situation out there – he calls me concerned about the 'sensitive' position. He was concerned as to Will's 'shrewdness' as to the wording of the contract – I told him on the 28th, he had not to worry about that!

On the 29th another call from Henry stated that he had heard from Will who seemed upset that I was not going out there. I had to write to Will the next day– tell him of Howard's position – and that of my own! With Dennis home – Geoff also wishing for a break – that would leave Bill holding the Fort again! An idea was thought, that if I went to St Martin to assist Bill – and Howard to get involved with Will in St Lucia – it might be the solution!

Will had been working on work permits for us out there and I had not given up the idea. Air fares to St Lucia were not cheap – one solution that came to mind was, I had been given a letter from Margaret Havers saying they were leaving in two weeks' time for their trip across the Atlantic – I could certainly join them, but that would not go down too well with Sue due to how long I'd take to get there!

On the 8th April – Will having spoken to Howard, having just got back from St Martin said quote: "as I thought, I'm wanted in St Martin – and Howard will be going to St Lucia – Will is getting Howards ticket – Henry will pay for mine to St Martin!" On the 9th, the next day, Howard calls me saying he's spoken with Henry who spoke about the wisdom of him going to St Lucia! I told Howard to make it clear with Will his intentions!

With this entire going on – I would hear from Richard Price saying there was a job going on the oilrig in Norway if I wanted it! It was make your mind up time! On the 12th Howard called – he had told Will that Sue would not be going! This meant for Will, one thing – Howard's time in St Lucia would not be long term – and he could leave at a moment's notice or when it took his fancy – as he and I had experienced! By the 13th of April I had worked myself in to a corner and a position I could not avoid! So on the 16th April 1978 I quote: "Writing this Monday morning on the Penzance to London train, very sad!! - Gave Howard a call in the evening, he said he might come up with me tomorrow to see Henry! (He didn't) Gave Wim a game of Table Tennis – our last for a while! Very sad night with my family – I hope it's all worthwhile!"

Earlier on the 13th of Feb, having said to Helen a large smack was in store if she didn't stop scribbling in her books, she looked at me and said "It's about time you left again wasn't it?"

Little did I know then, that on the 16th of April 1978, I would be leaving Scilly again – and the outcome of this move, after events that I thought I was able to control - be for good!!!

Chapter 43: April 16th '78

I would write on the 17th April "The way I feel now, I don't blame Howard for not going – but someone has to and that fool is me!"

Leaving had been a wrench that got worse each time and without my brother's company on the train to Billericay to take my mind off things – I sat and wondered why, and just what was I leading myself in to?

My flight out to St Lucia was booked for the 20th but before that I sat chatting with Dennis and Henry – ever the business man and concerned that I should check all was in order contract wise with the deal Will had entered in to before I went on to St Martin and join the schooner. In retrospect it would have been far better had he gone himself on such an errant – he would have seen the situation first hand that in the long run might have saved himself much agony in the months to come.

It was about a 10hr flight with a stop in Antigua first, and being daylight all the way – I slept little!

I had not seen Will and Sharman since Nassau, though tired; we sat chatting over what has been going on since those times. Will and Roland had started a building company and construction of their first place was underway already – the reason why Howard was asked to go there. As for my reason – that would have to wait till the next day and we were alone to talk!

There is a surprise waiting round every corner for those not expecting them – if they come from a quarter where least expected. Henry's reason for talking some 'sense' in to Howard not going to St Lucia was for his own reason – he wished Howard to go and help him in Essex for his business was on the up and up! I would get from my conversation with Will the next day a little piece of unexpected news too that one could be seen as to another reason – Will wanted me there to assist him in his business!

I quote on the 21st :" One piece of news that didn't go down too well – I will not be paid for my time on 'Jylland' when I go there – also what Will was hoping was, I should go there for a few weeks to 'please' the boys – then in the meantime – get me a work permit here!" -- If it didn't strike home then, it certainly did now – I'd been misled – misguided and was in a corner!!

The very reason for my coming here to watch over the business in St Martin would have been unnecessary had Will done so! Knowing the reason for one of us to be there – he had not covered it in his agreement with Mike and Co – and like that reason Henry gave such 'free wise' words to Howard – such an oversight could be said as to have me firmly by the Balls!

The idea I had in my mind, of Sue and the children joining me if things turned out right in St Martin, was now a different kettle of fish. Such thoughts I put to Will on the 24th – for I was in some confusion. I would have to wait and see now if working in St Lucia was the right decision – would I be working with Will or for him?

As for Bill and Geoff expecting me to be with them – how will that go down! I knew Geoff wanted to get home for a spell – and Bill, that had already been 'lumbered' one might say with our 'business' when left with 'Jylland' in Nassau – what will he think? The train of my thoughts had come off the rails slightly! All would have to be put on hold till I saw those in St Martin.

I left for there on the 26th on Liat on what I believed was an hour away. Just one stop – Antigua and -------forget it! Someone somewhere failed to tell me this flight only went as far as this – the flight to St Martin didn't leave till the next day! Thus for a day I paced restlessly with too much going on in my mind in one pissed off state!

'Jylland' was out on a charter when I arrived in Marigot – at least one thing seemed positive for a change. She was working, and in a place under a certain French civilized society where the heads of State saw little gain in back handers as small as we could offer!

It was always nice to be back aboard and sit down with my old mates for a chat over things. Boat things rather than building things. The last few days of concerns evaporated in a moment. I hadn't recognized Geoff from the back, he was wearing a hat to keep the sun off – and his hair on (what was left of it) you see – baldness was attacking him on all fronts!

The small Jetty was hidden from view by a hill from where I sat and I was quiet surprised to see her there as I walked the road that wound round its northern side. Geoff had been in the dingy washing something off the schooners side, sick probably – "ello Dave – when j'ew get 'ere?" He said with the usual grin of seeing an old mate!

I had never met Dave Marchant; he had made the trip down with Bill from Nassau to Puerto Rico and stayed aboard! David was likeable from the start. Stocky build, good handshake, big wide feet from wearing no shoes, blond hair and with enough of it for both he and Geoff! David was English – out of Florida and had been working in Nassau lobster diving. Something he said he was good at till he had to do it day in day out for a living!

As I look back on those times we had aboard 'Jylland' – the things I missed most were those times together. All good mates in the same boat (to use a pun) trusting one another implicitly and their ability to get by no matter what!

'Jylland' was not a Ted Turner racer with nothing to do but trim expensive Hood sails, washed down with salt spray, close hauled and talk tactics in the saloon at night with a cold one! Sailing was just a part of the action – keeping her afloat – mending useless sails – mast making – Prop building and making a broken anchors work – it was a mixture of all and everything – and I loved it!

To run the shore side of the charter business, Mike Atkinson had installed his wife Maddie. She like Mike was from Yorkshire – and you know what they say about them –"you can tell a Yorkshire man – but not very much!' Mike knew her from his hometown - Sheffield – and this would be the first time I would meet her!

She was living on the boat when I arrived but moved off that day to a flat ashore! Life aboard a boat does not suit most people – especially those that like to shower as long as they want and when they choose to do so. Clothes become damp – and washing your small bits for all to see can be embarrassing.

I would meet her in the coming days and though I found her a nice enough girl – I could only judge her capable for the position by how many she was attracting out for day sailing trips!

Timing is so important in any business - you could say we had two left feet when it came to that! Plus some bloody hard luck! "Jylland's late arrival from Puerto Rico in March meant we'd missed the best part of the season for in April it tapers off dramatically!

It would be hard for Maddie – hard for the boat and crew – and hard on those that had put some money in to her! In the next few weeks the passenger list for day sailing was pretty slim – so slim it seemed at times not worth the effort! The 28th, the day after my arrival we only took out 4 – 29th – 8 – Tues 2nd May 6 aboard – the 3rd – only 2 people. And so it went on - it was upsetting in a way – for the trip, especially to Sandy Island off the northern coast of Anguilla was a lovely spot – perfect for a sail down channel – a beat to windward and anchor for lunch!

The island itself reminded me of those we had visited in The San Blas – not a soul around – white sand and just a few trees. Those few we did take – loved it!

'It never rains but it pours' goes the saying – 'Bad luck comes in three's' is another little gem. Sat May the 6th – I write: 'What a day – with 10 passengers aboard we did our run up the coast (Grande Cass) Geoff and I took some of yesterday's passengers ashore – they came down to take some pictures and say farewell! (These we had taken to Sandy Island) As we caught up with 'Jylland' we saw her mizzen down (he and I in the whaler) ripped at the leach. On dropping our Port anchor, the stock broke so we dragged her flat for a hundred yards.

I swam off to find the bits – Dave came with the whaler so we could haul them up! Then the outboard sheared a pin! Billy started the main engine without opening the oil vales – blew a hole in the reservoir - then went to go astern at the dock – no astern – had to go about and drop our main anchor! Had fun and games getting the passengers ashore!!" For us you see – ever day was an adventure!

I had never met Maurice Widowson – he was one of the fellows Mike had got interested in the business of investing in – a sure bet! Mike had seen what we were capable of earning from his time as skipper aboard in St Lucia – Maurice was one who saw dollars floating before his eyes and like the rest of his group – bar one other than Mike - knew nothing of boats!

Maurice was in to screen-printing – T-shirts – Wraps – scarf's etc! Had one business in St Lucia – one in St Kitts. I thought Maurice was nice enough fellow. I met him for the first time the day after our 'lucky' one on the 6th.

He was obviously from the 'slim' tribe of peoples – those who all have the same features that bother you, for you are sure to have met him elsewhere in your life – but just can't remember!!! They can eat like a horse too and never put on an ounce of weight – that bothers the fat tribe very much!

Another 'involved' in this 'wait and see' before we commit ourselves' project was a fellow called Chris Dallow. Chris – married to Sue – was a teacher in St Lucia by week – sailor at weekends!

He was from the stocky tribe people - those that mostly grow black beards! He had packed in his teaching – and gone in with Maurice and now living in St Kitts – he was also about to pack in his marriage so it seemed – for when he came to visit his investment in St Martin it was in company with another, other than his wife Sue!

Chris was okay – quiet easy going – very unlike the other two involved – which I would later meet – and dislike immediately!

The Sandy Island trips, though a favourite for the passengers was a long haul for little reward. What really was needed was a quick sail – walk and swim – eat lunch and an easy sail back!

Such an area was 'Rendezvous Bay' directly across the channel from Marigot. Permission was granted and by the end of May – it became our usual run, the best thing about it too – mostly all done without ever starting the engine – I loved that! The old Iron lung needed a good overhaul – and a much needed rest.

In the handling of all craft at sea – one needs to swing the compass on occasions. Headings – one must take in to account Variation plus Deviation of the compass on courses set – all sailors know that – but only those that have worked in the Caribbean and have hired Black crews know there is another to take in to consideration – and that is - Negrovation?

Even to utter such in this 'correct' world is thought racial! Most Caribbean islanders – unlike African American – call themselves by whatever Island they were born in. Most believe that their Island produces the best people – whether cricketers or Sailors! Working out of Marigot in St Martin – and running to Anguilla – we hired three from Anguilla – in charge of these - Johnny, Elbert and Dolphous was Jerry from Dominica!

Now Jerry was not just older than the others – he was also more ready to carry out his duty with a certain eagerness and a seeming amount of knowledge of having been at sea. So saying he was made Bosun. In this capacity – respect was afforded him yet resented by a difference of opinion as to who were the better people!

Channels of water between islands were not lines on maps, and through the years, each island became its own nation within itself – and if you like, tribal! Many times one had to step in and put down some dissent shown to Jerry.

Dolphous – being the eldest of the three likely mutineers, was always the leader in the 'backchat' department! This made Jerry very 'Vexed'! He, Dolphous, reminded me of a young 'Fats Domino'.
A joke a minute and a smile that showed a gold 'chip' implanted in one his front teeth.

In many a situation – concerns over 'Jylland's' condition – passengers to pay enough wages – let alone food! Their banter above you on deck – that no care in the world attitude – had me smiling and kept me utterly amused! You daren't show it of course and had to shout – "Dolphous – a man talking can't have his mind on the job – pipe down!" said only after the fun of the topic was through!

Bill Curry, in a mad surge of compassion – and one if he succeeded could change the very course of their lives – decided to teach them navigation! A wonderful idea and to be given below decks to his pupils round the dining room table for a certain amount of moments each day! – he would even provide pencils and paper!

Elbert was around 14 years of age – Johnny 16 – Fats Domino 20 – and Jerry around 26! As it was assumed Jerry knew most that was required by his position alone – he could sit in if he so desired!

Bill – gone home for a spell - living me in charge! I decided to test the boys on their progress so far!

With passengers gone ashore in 'Rendezvous Bay' and the schooner ready for our sail back – the boys were down below in the galley having their lunch – me with 'em!

"Okay lads – now let's hear how much you've remembered from what Cap't Bill taught ya'?" All looked at me over larger than totally necessary sandwiches of French bread, confused just as to what that might be – "Navigation lads – navigation!"

Eye's looked at one another as if to say, what's he on about! "Right – which one of you lot can tell me how many inches there are in a foot? – And Jerry don't tell 'em!"

Mouths full of breakfast – lunch and the coming evenings dinner, they waited for the bright and eldest to respond – "Well – surely one of you know? - - - Anyone?" Maybe one of them did – but they weren't saying. "Right tell 'em Jerry?" Jerry having time to think and realizing a guess was better than looking as dumb as the Anguillians said "Ten cap't!" ---- "Right said I – Now! If there are ten in a foot – how many then are in a yard? – and Jerry, as yet won't help you here!"

I looked at Dolphous given him a nod - swallowing something that most people would be happy to cut in to smaller pieces he coughed up with - "Two!" there was no way he was going to look a total dunce – or to be outdone by a bloody Dominican. "Anyone else?" Nothing ----- "Jerry ----?" "Six!" came the immediate response. "Right!" my reply being taken as the correct response – rather than 'right, next question!'

"Okay – let's say if there are six feet in a yard – how many yards are in a fathom then?" I'm certain for Jerry – the word fathom meant something – something his last answer 'six' and the Dolphous answer of 'two' was significant in some way. Jerry – added the two together sat dying to give the answer – and did once 'Many, many boss' came from Bills class!

"Now – I said – You can understand why Jerry is Bosun – and you are not!" For some days after that – Jerry was treated with a little more respect!

Jerry lived not too far from the schooner in Marigot. An area of ram shackled dwellings that lay to the east of town – so close together – take one away and the whole lot would collapse. Jerry – like most of the inhabitants – drank in the local bar there – as I did one night at an invitation to join him! In the light of day you might ever wonder you did – but in the darkness – lit by a few candles – you don't see the old boards dried out by the trades and seasoned enough to make some good furniture.

There is the smell of the ever present charcoal – chicken, the favourite dish of the islanders being cooked outside. How Jerry found his place to sleep after too many beers among that encampment – I never knew.
Away from 'The Whiteman's World' you walk in to a different society entirely. St Martin was a Free Port – and a nest of illegalities was the way of life!

Sailing up the coast – Bill and David Marchant working on the slipping clutch below, me above watching the sails and Jerry at the helm. He starts singing a song – it was one he had written the night before whilst under the influence! He was singing it to Dolphous and the boys and having some trouble remembering what came easy and with such beauty only a few hours before.

"DA-da – da-da-da-da - daaaa – I sat there, with my baby – da – da – da – daaaa – down by the -------"River?"cut in Dolphous getting in to it and with a word Jerry seemed to looking for in the sky. "No – No! Dolphous it was not river – let me think man! Da-da da-da-da-da-daaaa. I sat there, with my baby – da-da-da-daaaa - down by the --------!!!!!!"   Dolphous stood waiting, hands and body moving with the music – top lip over bottom and head rolling side to side ---- he just couldn't wait any longer for Jerry – it was his song too now – "SEA!" he inserted -- "Dolphous" – said the abrupt music maker – this is MY song – You let de words come man – you make me vexed!!!!!"

Oblivious to the wind – sails and heading – another attempt to find last night's catchy phrase was attempted – it would have to wait till after the bar shut and the Marijuana was rolled I was afraid – for with "Jerry – watch your heading!" – he stopped his music and put the helm up!

That was another of their carefree traits – heading! Setting a close-hauled course for Marigot – 'Jylland' creeping along slowly. Bill had gone off in the whaler with David – to take a few shots of her under sail. "Keep her head up!" had been his last order. Un-aware of his intentions – I lay back in my bunk before the anchorage was reached.

What brought me on deck was a slight heel and a look up the mainsail hoops from below. Not loose, they gripped the mast firm – we were making good headway indeed! Had the wind changed I thought – odd for the time of season! Expecting to see Bill at the helm or David – I was met with four Black faces all smiling broadly – one of them at that helm! Looking forward – I was met with the sight of a part of St Martin rare to be seen by 'Jylland's' bowsprit – land dead ahead!

"Where is the skipper – and put her helm down now!!" I called out. Far behind us – and in an obvious chase to catch up was Billy and David. With the bit between her teeth and nearly on a reach – something they would never have done! Other questions than navigation were asked of them when we got home! If Bill had one fault – it was to believe everyone had common sense!!

Chapter 44: June too soon

So the saying goes when referring to Hurricanes in the Caribbean. Something would come out of that month that would knock me over far stronger than any wind – and I was not ready for such!!

The last day of May '78 - the confirmation of a charter had been made. $ 2,000.00 a week – paid weekly in advance. First stop St Croix – then on to St Thomas – maybe Puerto Rico after. Cargo was clothes!! Owners of a Boutique in Marigot wanted to sell their product in the American Islands. Desperate for work – and unsure if I would be making the trip – the thought of this strange cargo didn't come to mind till some days later!

Brother Will arrived at the end of May and on the last day – spent most of the day talking to the ones wishing to charter 'Jylland' – The decision on my going would depend on a work permit in St Lucia – a call to Sharman on the 1st of June made it for me – it wasn't through yet so I was aboard. That day, five lorry loads came aboard – boxes and boxes of what we could only guess was clothing!! It was late when they finished and with the last aboard – saying farewell to Will – we set sail at 20.30 for St Croix!

With a course mainly due west – and having bent on the square sail some days before – we run under that – mainsail and mizzen wing and wing at times. It was Geoff and I that stood watch together – the 03.00 – 06.00 spell. It was an uneventful passage as 'Jylland' slipped along at 4/5 knots. St Croix was in haze ten miles off and at

16.30 on the 2nd – we dropped anchor unable to get alongside. I say here – "The passengers are a strange bunch – they strike a funny cord!"

The four – two men and two women – French – were not very talkative! The usual thing – on such a unique old sailing boat – would be to stroll round the deck on such a night – come back aft and talk to those on watch – as it was – and after David (Chef for the charter) had done with cooking dinner – they stayed in their cabins!
What made me think these were not your ordinary 'Honest John' shop owners – was their determination to keep to themselves – it just wasn't normal. It was as if orders had been laid down – "Ask no questions – can't tell lies!" We moved alongside the following morning – Sat the 3rd. Customs had been cleared and the okay by port officials to do so was granted. I thought, as we were carrying cargo – just maybe someone might have wanted to check it – they didn't! and why?

It was obvious they were getting 'high' on something. Sat afternoon – as if celebrating a success – our guests were in very 'High' spirits. The smaller fellow of the two, a little higher than the others – for up he went to the hounds of the mainmast and dived in to the Harbour! - rather too good as well for many people. The whole set up was pretty obvious something was in those boxes worth more than clothes – the more you thought about it – the more you tried to not think about the consequences of being caught in some sort of drugs run! But I am certain that's what it was!
We had word from them they would like to leave Monday evening – to make St Thomas at first light! Some of their cargo was moved ashore that afternoon – again I thought it rather odd – for where was the customs – duty to be collected?

We left St Croix at 20.45 – motor sailing rather longer than necessary – for we made St Thomas before light at 04.30 – moving in to the harbour and dropping anchor at 06.00hrs.

We had trouble with the customs here – they gave us hassle about not clearing when leaving St Croix. Both Bill and I thought, as it was the same territory – it wasn't necessary! Well it was, they said – "Now that's settled and we know who's in charge -- How many tons of cargo are you carrying – and how much did you put ashore in St Croix? – it is 65cents a ton you know – and it must be paid!!!" Seeing at the most – we were carrying only 2 tons - - $1.30 seemed to me a lot to make a fuss about when inside some of those boxes – could be the real prize. After all the ranting and raving about protocol – did one official bother to have a peek – no!

Whatever they were selling – was selling well – by Wed the 7th – they were asking us about Panama instead of San Juan. We certainly were desperate for money – and the 3 weeks at $2000.00 a week looked tempting – but the request to run to Panama was just too obvious to me of what they really were about. Panama – the centre of Cocaine distribution front was laughable. Ignorance will not save you from the law and apart from that – did we not leave that place in '75 under trying circumstances. Getting back from there might take a bit longer than our last passage!

With the thought of the charter business back in St Martin on our minds a little sooner than expected. It was thought we could employ a cook. David – more the engineer than employed in that department – was only too happy to rid himself of it! Putting the word out we were looking for someone – two girls came forward.

Just a slight ripple across the water I had not noticed!

Cheryl Summers and Anita Bowman had been working as teachers in Puerto Rico. Cheryl thought it a good idea during the school break to go see the islands. Anita, with an old school reunion about to happen – wished to return to Ohio – being talked in to the alternative – both girls found themselves being told of the position on board this schooner by a taxi driver while they were in St Thomas.

Cheryl, the great opportunist taker was all for it – seeing yet another free ride south! Anita – not so forthcoming – but got herself painted with the same brush!

While working on our broken anchor – fixing it with a wooden stock this time. Bill spoke with both girls who had applied. Much to their surprise – not only was a free trip on offer – but wages too! Just one problem though – the position was only for one – that's unless they wished to split it! Fate plays games with us! Had my work permit come through – I would not have been there. Had Anita been more determined about her reunion – nor would she! We have been married now nearly 29 of the 32 years since we first met!
Love what at first sight – a face – a figure – a smile – a laugh – a one-night stand. I had enough of those through my life to know. My record, as a devoted, – faithful husband had been torn to shreds long ago – but the thought of actually breaking away from Sue – was totally beyond my thoughts!

There was nothing about her at first to suggest that she would make my life change! She was just one of two girls that had come aboard like so many before – and of course like so many would soon be gone!

It did not happen!! What did, came in the coming months – and years! The face became more beautiful – the figure so warm – the smile enchanting – the laugh so needed – and the one night, too unbearable to think it would end!

There was little both she and I could do about it – for the suffering would be too painful – we did try! Maybe I should have been stronger – but I would have been broken in two forever!

Both girls rose early on the 10th of June – having moved their things aboard the night before. Bed was early for them for they didn't want to miss a thing of their first day aboard, and first aboard a large old sailing schooner sailing out of St Thomas.

It was 06.15 when we sprung her off the dock under sail – quietly without the engine to disturb the peaceful at sleep ashore, we moved out of the harbour. The mornings – the most beautiful time of the day – especially in the Caribbean. Everything so bright as the sun displayed its colours. White sailing craft dotted across a blue sea bordered by the purest yellow sand. Greenery shining from the night's rain and the gaily-painted homes and shops bringing life to it all! For me right then and there – I knew only one thing – we were bound for St Martin and the wind soon heading us once out of the harbour was the least of my worries. Both Bill and Geoff had been talking of going home for a spell. Will had been trying to sort out a work permit for me in St Lucia. So who will take care of 'Jylland'?

Chapter 45: June 12th '78

One days sailing downwind can take 4 to claw back in an old gaff-rigger. Without a good wind to keep her head up – leeway kills you. Bill, Geoff and I remember such a slog on our return from Panama. The first day we only made 25 miles of easting. Keeping her moving in a head wind was a case of experience in ship handling.

The two girls made 8 crew – Bill, Geoff, David and I - Dolphous and Jerry the others. Elbert and Johnny had been laid off till we returned. We met with some heavy squalls on the afternoon of the 11th – and here, due to the condition of our sails – we couldn't take full advantage of them – it was a sad case of close haul her through them with the engine running. Even then – we had to reef the fore mainsail – the throat stretching to the point of bursting. What a badly cut lot we had to put up with. When such wind struck – it was attention and steady work with the helm. The usual 'cocky' attitude of Dolphous I noticed suddenly became subdued during such times Both he and Jerry were rather different people when out of sight of land – now with Dog Island fine off the Port Bow – that being 10.30 on the 12th. They were full of beans now, and arguing what land it was.

Had it not been for a good wind veering easterly, we might not have reached Marigot till the 13th – as it was we dropped anchor at 16.45. I had been working on the wooden stock since we had left – and ready now – in she went. I noted then we had taking a lot of water during the good pounding – it would slow down we knew – or taken care of from diving on her hull – a thing that in the coming months would become a daily procedure!

Few were the occasions one could lay back and watch her go – and in the direction you were heading. With the easterly wind – Bill and I lay in the netting just watching her come at us – her 100 tons punching the Caribbean away! It was times such as that one forgot everything wrong in the world and with 'Jylland' especially. As if launched from some underwater pad, flying fish flew out ahead of us – catching the good wind to dive back in some great distance in to those blue warm waters!

Geoff had sent his passport to Martinique to get a U.S visa before we had gone to St Croix – needed if flying back to England through that country. Without a passport, going ashore in both places, St Croix and St Thomas was not permitted.

It also went too for Jerry! Getting 'bored' with it out here before we left – the confinement to the boat for the past week made him more than ever determined to get home for a spell. Bill also deserved a break, so it looked more like I shall be needed here rather than going to St Lucia work permit or no work permit.

Passport through – Geoff would leave on the 15th. There was no point in pressing him to stay! He would have been unbearable to put up with. What Geoff was in dire need of was, in his words, "A good clear out!!!" Put in a tenderer phrase - one might say "In desperate need of a young girls arms sweating profusely in the love making mode!" Girls were as hard to come by as passengers were in this June month. Hotels were pretty empty and he was pretty full of desire.

For Bill and me, the next few days were on sail maintenance – trying to make a silk purse out of a sow's ear one might say. For Dave it was the electrics – blown lights from too much water coming through the decks when she was working in the blow!
Being such a quiet period and the hurricane months soon upon us – there was thought of laying her up for a period. Skeleton crew of Dave Marchant and Jerry aboard – Bill could go home, – with me to St Lucia. The costs were worked out against what it takes to keep her in commission. It was $1200.00 against $250.00 – such we put to Will in a call on the 16th. He was of the same opinion – and would put the idea forward to those concerned. Chris Dallow – we were told – would be there tomorrow – we could talk to him about it also! Not only did we see Chris on the 17th – but also with him was Mike Atkinson – a surprise! As far as I heard – Mike was $6,000.00 light on his share payment to the company – here was us scraping a living – always in need – eating beans on toast and fishing for our dinner – and suddenly we see Maddie – Chris and Mike seated down at the 'Creperie' eating a fine dinner!

It suddenly brought back memories of 'The Wicky Up' - the Club sandwiches before Millie had dinner ready! Mike was broke then too! Still there was nothing I could say, this was something Will would have to sort out!

Speaking with both on the subject of laying her up, it was thought that July could be worthwhile! As for Bill going home for a spell, – Mike said he could come and replace him, – but would like me here also! Life was becoming a bit confusing – there was little chance of me earning as much as I could with Will in St Lucia, – yet one of us should be here to watch over things.

Mike, from past experiences, was not one to spend time aboard – after dinner in St Lucia he was dressed and gone, sometimes not back till the next day. Whatever was the case, Bill needed to get home and on 21 June after much head scratching and searching for his passport, I ran him over to the airport by dingy to catch his flight home to Laurie at last! Also Jerry left on the 23rd for Dominica for two weeks at home. So with the all secured and 'Jylland's' big bower down we would sit quiet for two weeks before the 'worthwhile' July came.

If things had gone well – Sue and the children were to come out to St Lucia – though she hated having to leave her Mom. I missed them all – but I was having second thoughts on the wisdom of such a move. We had done that before! I had yet to see if the business there could support us – and as far as 'Jylland' was concerned – this was not as it was in St Lucia.

Jylland was having a hard time of it – sails – engine – and hull were in desperate need of 'Proper' attention. We were coming apart at the seams – literally – yet right then and there, none of us knew to what extent! Coming out here did not seem a good idea right now! I wrote on the 20th June: "Really mixed up at the moment on my feelings about things!!!!!"

The breeze that caused the ripple over the waters in St Thomas was beginning to rise!

Chapter 46: A Good Catch

David Marchant's big wide flat feet stuck out from beneath very clean and terribly white sheets! His thick mop of curly blond hair lay back on a pillow to match.

Above him the ceiling fan cut through the sticky evening air but did little to improve matters. "How are you feeling?" I asked. "Apart from being bloody hot – okay!" he replied. It came as some relief too for earlier his condition was rather worrying! Complaining of a pain in his side as he got in to the whaler – we returned to the schooner rather than look for some dinner in the shape of Lobster. Within moments on deck – he was in agony. So here he was – a couple of days off in hospital!

Like most tropical hospitals, it was built on a high point to catch any passing breeze for the bedridden – let alone those working there. Large window openings had just shutters to close out the bad weather – no glass to fly as missiles in a Hurricane finishing off those in the bed rather than under it! Run by Nuns, it was spick and span - very quiet and orderly.

It was either Gallstones – or Kidney stones that had been the diagnosis. David had been in to the calcium tablets lately – something perfect for the making of Kidney stones. If it was those – a good flushing out with water was the cure – as much as you can take too. Time alone would tell – and a good pee! At $35.00 a day for room and board – I hoped he would be peeing sooner than later. The $275.00 bill was a greater pain when he got out some days later. As it turned out, it was Kidney stones, and he could have suffered on the boat rather than lying bored to tears in bed!

To substitute our food – the searching for Lobster and Conch was not only fun – but also at times essential. What money we had wasn't really enough to keep us other than in a state we were becoming accustomed – broke yet eating Lobster salad after marinated Conch hors d'oeuvre day after day. We ate like Princes yet lived like Paupers. Strange though it may sound - it was a wonderful change when Jackie – David's French girlfriend cooked us Rabbit stew one night.

I'm not sure just when 'Paula' came in, for like many craft their comings and goings are not a matter of real importance unless they strike you by their odd appearance – and in some cases – beauty! 'Paula' came in size! At 78' she was then the largest Cat in the world – so the owner Paul Hedermann told us!

Paul was a Canadian and worked in the film industry – underwater sets etc! Invited over to see her 'Largeness' – for such a craft is all beam, we were told she could sail at 28 knots – which we couldn't doubt! She was leaving the next day for St Barts for a couple of days – Would we like to go? The thought of seeing her go would have been fun – but leaving 'Jylland' was not the thing to do.

People like Paul, their bilges as dry as a Mummies Tomb, would have found it odd to hear us say – "We have this leak you see!"So instead, the next day we watched her take the slight breeze and move rapidly across the harbour.

I sent Paul across a little present one day. A girl we'd met in St Thomas came over to St Martin for a visit – making the crossing in a local freighter. Sitting on "Jylland's" deck in the afternoon sun she decided on a swim – would we mind? With "Go ahead!" off comes everything apart from a pair of knickers. Now this girl was a big girl (the size drawn by artists on seaside naughty postcards – her breasts included) standing there unabashed before us all and ready to do battle with the waves.

She had a pretty face and upon seeing just that in the water – who would not say 'Well – come aboard then!!" With that in mind and she quite at home afloat now, I suggested to her 'Why not swim over to see our friend – Paul is his name!"

Anxious to see his response – we watched by binoculars as she slid through the water with perfect ease towards her prey. We saw Paul come aft – and very soon after, started hauling her aboard like some Eskimo landing a good catch. A catch I could say – but wouldn't – well why not! – a much bigger meal than he ever imagined! She went over that stern alive and kicking bollock naked now – her knickers gone in a fight to get at her tormenter.

Who ate who that afternoon is but a guess – but both seemed happy when they came back to collect her clothes later that day!

Chapter 47: July stand by

Mike would eventually turn up on the 8th July. Cheryl from the states arrived on the 11th – and with the crew back, we were ready for work again on the 13th.

I note here that Caroline Hartman came aboard – she had got married since we last met her in Nassau, and was with her husband Chris (Sutch) on their honeymoon. 'Sweet Caroline' – nearly 40 years ago it has been since those days. I wonder where you are now! She was in a bit of a fix – could I lend her $20.00. She had forgotten the airport tax! Several weeks went by and several questions arose when I collected the mail, to be answered with – "She'll write when she's ready and pay me back when she has it – and who cares any way!!" Dear girl did write – and those who were convinced it was the last I'd hear from her – I went on deck and waved 'two' twenty dollar bills under their doubting noses. I sent Caroline back one saying; I do believe one is all I lent you!

With 16 aboard (the most paying passengers since I'd been here) the usual sail to Rendezvous Bay went well except for the mizzen blowing out again. With 'Bastille Day' following, work was brought to a halt, – and I just wondered how many realized what the holiday meant – still I could work on the mizzen and put some coasters on the boarding ladder. We were moored stern to 'Mediterranean style' and our boarding ladder was lacking some rollers.

Saturday 15th we had 4 aboard – Sunday the 16th the same. Thurs 20th – ditto! Sat 22nd with 16 aboard, and so it went on! Only once did we hit anything likely to get us out of the mess we were in – and it did rather show Mike could do a better job at selling 'Jylland' than his wife. He had spent that Saturday with a group from Venezuela and got us 45 for a day sail – 47 with two Americans for Sunday 23rd.

A far cry from our 130 per trip in St Lucia – but! But indeed, it was back down to 4 again for the 27th - and thus it was the end of July and we were just keeping our heads above water – literally!

Though Mike's stay with us had shown what you can do if you had got the right person for the job – it was still not the right time of the year. The thought about wages was a constant worry – but not so much as the worry about 'Jylland' – she was taking water and the need to pump her out was becoming a bloody frustrating affair. Still, July had its laughs too.

I was getting rather tired of keeping telling the crew about losing buckets! Though inexpensive ($2.00) they failed to remember about 'dipping' it when underway. Coming up to the anchorage at Rendezvous – Johnny not only failed to remember – but failed to recall I told them – the next person that loses one, pays for it!

John – eager to get on with washing down the decks, let fly just as we rounded her up in Anguilla. There was no way he could hide the fact – not with Dolphous around laughing at the broken splice that once held a bucket! Once anchored, and with the passengers ashore for their walk, swim or do as you please – the usual quietness that descended over the schooner was broken by three black West Indians telling one black West Indian 'Where it at!'

I had said to Johnny "You owe me $2.00 but, if you go get it - or whoever gets it, the money will be in their wages taken from yours!" Having come to rest, and drifting back on the anchor, the bucket could be seen not more than two fathoms beneath us!

Whether Johnny had seen the movie 'Jaws' or not I didn't ask but he was not going in there come hell or high water – but Dolphous was!! Donned in mask, snorkel, and flippers he had walked down the boarding ladder talking big, though difficult to understand due to the snorkel in his mouth. Getting him afloat first was done in the usual quiet manner – three back seated non-drivers screaming advice to the first timer on where to drive the stolen car! Now here he is afloat and paddling aft with the rising excitement of the same three telling him 'Where it at!'

For me it was fun to watch, yet I wondered just how long a South Sea Islander would have taken to retrieve such a thing. There were these fellows – all born in the most idyllic conditions for such sport – and yet when out of their depth, so uncomfortable! "Dolphous – Dolphous!" came the cry from our Bosun in that echo Caribbean way – "Look – look, it there it there!" Again Dolphous took another dive, but yet again he failed to come up trumps. Maybe it had something to do with him not trying hard enough – not enough weight on him – for though he flipped himself down – he just couldn't seem to get his legs beneath the water.

He was six feet short of the bottom every time! There was another deciding factor – Dolphous, each time he surfaced, was bewildered as to how far he had moved from the boat – he couldn't figure it out – he moved himself accordingly.

Mike, disturbed from a short nap, came on deck to find out what all the noise was about. Watching, and as amused as I – took a dive off the side hidden from Dolphous - going underwater to the bucket, he came up alongside him slowly with it over his head. The laughter that accompanied such from the three fellows, was in the best of humour – not in any way to embarrass Dolphous – who might still have been there today looking! Mike gave him the money for the effort!

Smoking below decks was never allowed. That went for all and everyone. Memories of just what a cigarette can do were still strong with us after the Cadaques fire.

Seven people had come aboard for the afternoon sail – it had been cancelled due to the lack of people! Someone had forgotten to inform us of this seven out of 'Los Alamos'. Invited aboard, and told of the morning sailing to Anguilla, they would come back for that. "By the way," said Cheryl "we don't allow smoking below decks!"

People on stage or on the screen are never the same close up! "I think that's David Bowie!" said Dave Marchant as he passed my cabin – and so saying went off for a closer look!

They did turn up for the sail the following day, and as usual, the run over to Rendezvous went well. One doesn't know the thrill of sailing in a large schooner till you've tried it! The mystery of the wind and the sails – what halyard does what – is all-fascinating. For us, each block had been roved one at a time – so it was obvious – each Halyard had its proper place at the belaying rail too. If anyone had noticed – one would have seen sets – learn one and you know the lot. For us it was routine – a day like any other day – but for the likes of the Bowie group – it was all fun! So much so – they chartered us for Monday 31st – the last day of that July, 34 years ago now.

David Bowie turned out to be a nice fellow. Chatting more this time than last – we never saw him again – though he wanted our address, for he would have loved a longer sail in her! David never knew our problems – nor we to that extent.

One thing I note at the end of the same month was I had a Miss Connie Hjelmerg from San Juan come aboard – it was something to do about our bill to the shipyard there! "Why hadn't Frank Singleton heard from any of us yet?" such news was new to me!
Was there an un-paid bill outstanding? We would find out to our cost later for such an oversight.

Chapter 48: August get ready

It began wet and windy – a tropical depression running through the area. At such times living aboard was difficult – leaking decks adding to the leaking hull. We would not get out till the 4th and with 20 aboard and made the run to Anguilla in choppy seas – six of which were sick.

On the 7th, Mike started to moan about the cost of things – he didn't think it was down to them – them being on whom ever shoulders lays the greater burden – to pay for maintenance. That didn't seem to bother him in the least when the greater burden was on our shoulders in St Lucia. When things get tight – start moaning! I thought all this had been already sorted out in the contract – it seems it wasn't!

With Hurricane 'Cora' forming on 9th August at 13.9N 48 West – the need to move in to 'Simpson Bay' might just have to happen. Low on water – low on diesel – and with brake pawls off the windlass – things were not right for such a move. Mike had been informed about the fuel situation – but seemed to be hanging it out. Later in the day I got a report that 'Cora' had gone slightly south at 13.2 N 52 West. Picked up speed from 10 knots to 20 – wind speed 80 knots. It was a tropical depression by the 10th and so we went out with 9 aboard. Johnny and Elbert failed to show – the work was difficult manually – but easier mentally! I decided to lay them off till Billy got back – that would be on the 12th.

Before that brother Will and Sharman turned up on the 11th. We needed to talk about my working out of St Lucia – and the situation here. They didn't stay aboard – booked in at 'Le Pirate' instead. I figured out the building project was doing okay – that or Sharman's boutiques were flourishing!

With 27 aboard for the next day's sail – having Will aboard to help with the sails – life was a little easier. Made easier by Bill being there to meet us when we returned!

With Bill back aboard now, it was easier for me to go to St Lucia. Will had got the difficulty of the work permit sorted out, but there was a bigger difficulty coming over my horizon, one I had hoped would never happen – could never happen.

I figured out, the break away from the Schooner, where it was impossible not to get attached to Anita, would do me good – the problem was, the closer it got to the day of my leaving, I was beginning to miss her already. When I left there on Wednesday 16th August, my thoughts were all jumbled – and what was I going to do about it?

Wednesday 16th of August started off on the wrong foot anyway! Up at 05.30 – said goodbye to someone I might never see again and headed with Will and Sharman to the airport. The weather was very wet and windy – but in the end we got off.

My worry's – present and future – could have ended then and there. Diverted to Barbados due to the bad weather, the warning light came on. Asked to assist passengers from the wreck, my brother and I were re-seated next to the emergency door. "So, what's the problem?" we asked – "The undercarriage wasn't locking in! – we might have to land on our belly!" was the reply. It is strange, and I said so to my brother "Rather a bit of an anti-climax eh?" after a long low approach we came to a perfect touchdown. "Exactly what I thought!" he replied. Having to await a plane was another – and we didn't get to St Lucia till 20.30 – a 15hr day for what could have been just 2hrs.

Chapter 49: September Remember

If the saying be true that it is easy to be wise after the event – then I must be the wisest man I know! Whether I am clever enough to write of that which made me 'Wise' - I doubt it – but I must try while my head is still clear and my body shows no signs yet of failing me.

The Mike Atkinson's of this world are spread among us like so many other characters. They settle among the poor and the rich and can be at ease in either. They go to the parties and mix with those you would find difficult to talk with – yet as was the case in St Lucia and Panama - came back 'Home' to 'Jylland' with his tail between his legs, falling among the litter unashamed.

"Good day – good day, the General said as he waved to his men on the way to the line!

E's a cheery old chap says Harry to Jack, as they marched to Arras with rife and pack! But he did for 'em both by his plan of attack, and we're cursing his staff for incompetent swine!" So wrote Sassoon, and so would one write of Mike!

In another time – in another period, he could have made that position – General, and but for the grace of God could I have been Harry before a bullet eased the pain of life!

Short arms and deep pockets was Mike's make-up! As he would drink others wine at the social gatherings – it would never had occurred to him the decent thing to do was to provide his own consumption as it was to commit himself to any deal until he saw the interest on the table far outweighed the initial investment. He would play the waiting game. While the boat – the crew – the whole operation suffered – Mike failed to play his role – pleading poverty while eating BLT's at the 'Wicky-up' and planning his future!

Mike had returned to St Lucia the day after us. His wife Maddie had been left there to do a job she was incapable of doing. She just wasn't cut out for it. The 2 and a 1/2% Will and I had said she was to be paid – had been raised to 5% by Mike just before he left there – this was news to us which we received on the 25th Aug. Bill would have to be informed about our not knowing of this change in policy. A change I believed was done to keep her on the job!

On the 26th – a Saturday. Will read me of the hassle he'd had with Mike and Co – page after page of his unreliability concerning 'Jylland's' time before going on to dry-dock in Puerto Rico. It was a sorry tale of one with the begging bowl and the other with nothing to put in it but other people's money in the end. Given time and money – both of which were not afforded us – 'Jylland' could have made it

work – but no, those induced in to the investment wanted 'Action' – 'Action' as Bill Curry and I would hear from a couple of those 'Wide Boy' clowns backing the Schooner.
I could take Chris Dallow – I liked Maurice Widowson – I could handle Mike Atkinson – but the two that turned up and wanted to talk with Bill and I one night at their hotel, wanting to know about 'Action' – and what we intended to do about it – they could kiss my arse!

$1200 a week plus 10% of gross had been the deal to hire 'Jylland'– rising to $1500 starting 1st November with 15% of gross. With an earning capacity of over $20,000 a week – it had not been a bad deal – but it would have to be worked at – given a chance – not pounced upon when things didn't go quite as expected – and those expectations were coming from Mike's mouth not ours!

By the 1st of September, the company was $15,570.00 (and counting) behind on her lease payments, and Mike was still hedging his bets. Maurice Widowson had given us a cheque for $700.00 – the bouncing kind – the kind that gives you enough time to be on the plane North to St Kitts and out of harm's way. The cheque from the 'other book' – the book that hasn't got, and never had anything in it anyway! "Sorry – it was a mistake" he'll say if and when you next see him "This one will do the trick!" - if you accept that rather than going to the bank with him – you deserve to be caught!

We actually found out that Maurice had gone to England not St Kitts– and wouldn't be back for a bollocking for a month. With Mike pleading poverty – yet talking about going to the States to get his Pilot's license – it seemed this little set-up would last as long as an American Treaty with the Indians.

I would stay with Will and Sharman while in St Lucia. They had rented a place on Cap Estate with a great view of both The Atlantic and the Caribbean – the problem for me was the place being too bloody far from the action! Will had contracts set up with his father-in-law Roland to complete some homes – yet come the end of the day; it was too far from the beach and a swim! Will, never much for some light entertainment, was content to sit with his wife after the day's work – have a couple of drinks before dinner - while I took a book to bed!

After all the activity on 'Jylland' – and after a couple of weeks of this routine, it was becoming unbearable.

Quote from my log 29th August '78 - "Been in St Lucia now 12 long days – long and lonely. What makes it so bad are the evenings after work – nothing to do! I long to go to bed just to get rid of another day – terrible!"

On the 15th of September I'd fly back to St Martin – I just needed a break and time to think!

Chapter 50: September, I said, Remember

I would leave St Lucia on the 15th of September – the flight taking just 40 minutes, a lot different than the 15hrs it had taken to get here.

I wasn't surprised to be met by Bob Sutcliffe either. Bill had called some days before saying he and his brother Roger had turned up – was it alright if they stayed aboard?

Bob was all smiles as we ran back to the schooner in the Whaler. Of course he didn't realize what Howard and I said was true – that we actually did own a boat – and if we did? – Not as big as this. He and his elder brother had decided to stop in on their 'walkabout' round the area. He was wondering if they could stay for a spell too! That would depend on Bill I said, but I would talk with him! It was great being back on board again – though things hadn't changed much – we were still just making ends meet. We went out in the evening with just 10 aboard. September remember? Not the right month of the year for tourists.

It was 5 days till we took out another charter – and that was only 8! Things were so tight it was down to getting the dinner with the spear again – and I was getting more Lobster than we were tourists.

If the water coming in the stern had been fresh – we would not have had to go to the Desalinization plant so often. To look over that area we had decided to run up the coast to 'Grande Case' after loading our tanks. The water there being clearer at this time of the year, the searching of the leak in the stern could be done – plus we wished to check out the position of submerged rocks at the entrance - just off 'Harry Point'.

If we were to use this area at any time – fixing them was important! They were found – and some of the leak stemmed. It was decided to spend the night there – for a Cinema was showing a 'James Bond movie – 'The Spy Who Loved Me' – Roger Moore's portrayal of Bond was amusing!

To watch a group of people playing on a beach laughing and joking – totally oblivious to life outside that circle of friends, one can feel a sort of envy! I have passed through the Island airports and watched the 'Caribbean Tanned' couple on their way back to wherever, and felt a slight tinge of such still – as I have envied the freedom of those holiday workers on Scilly recently – for I have been there and I know what it's like to be free! Being 'caged' by a society that have never experienced such a thing, we were called 'irresponsible' – 'Beach bums' – 'Lay-abouts' – all manner of names by those caught in the net too early in life, and have too much to lose now to get out. You are 'made' to be responsible – it is never your desire!

Chapter 51: Shylah Boyd

Francis Whyatt (nee Grannis) wrote under the name of Shylah Boyd. I first met her when passing behind 'Deliverance' one afternoon – Ian Murray was spotted entertaining someone on the after deck. I took the invitation to come aboard not out of nosiness – for it was something I did from time to time for a chat! Ian was English and skipper of this lovely two-masted schooner.

Francis was renting the house close to small quiet beach area where we used to go sometimes for a game of Volleyball – or just to swim. Her husband, somewhat older than her, was back in Washington on business, leaving her – alone in the big home.

Saturday the 23rd of Sept, we had a little get together on board 'Jylland' – the crew of 'Ilander' – Ian etc. – bringing their own dishes. Francis came also – she brought for me her book to read – 'American Made'. It was a tale of a young 14 year olds experience! Whether being raped was one of them, or the fantasy of the experience – is hard to tell – but it came across as one sordid tale, written as if she knew what she was talking about.

Sunday came, and Cheryl wished to 'Bomb' the boat – not blow it up, but to kill the ever nuisance Cockroach! They were our 'Rats' aboard and with so many places to hide 'Bombing' them was the only course you could take.

As it would take several hours – and with all doors and skylights shut! – We decided to go ashore at 'Bay Rouge'- play some volleyball to get away from the schooner while this delousing went on.

I guess from a distance to Francis Whyatt, those on the beach looked as happy as anyone could be – and in a way she envied them, for really they were not much older than herself – given a couple of months, she too could have a tan like they – not covered up in this silly but necessary beach dress!
She sat and watched, feeling rather out of place as those close to the water's edge, racing in to retrieve the volleyball – and felt relieved when they all followed her up to her home overlooking 'Bay Rouge' – a typical Caribbean hideaway to hideaway some ones cash. Isolated, a pathway lead up to a much sort after spot that looked across the sound to Anguilla. Francis was here to write another book

– if as good as the last, it was a sure bet to be on the best sellers list – every book is!

Chapter 52: Saba

Taking a brief spell off work and our minds off matters concerning the schooner – we decided to take a run over to St Barts – that pleasant and unique little island still in French hands.

So late on Saturday night (23.00 hr.) on the 30th September, we left the anchorage – hoping the wind would turn favourable for us. It didn't, so instead we turned our heading towards Saba arriving at 14.00hrs.

There was a large buoy situated on its leeward side for the convenience of larger vessels – such as the Dutch navy who visit this island on occasions in a tour of their possessions in these parts. We naturally took advantage of it and were thankful to do so due to the swell encountered around this inactive volcano. The deep water north – south and east, makes for some strange wave patterns on the western side which is shallow by comparison, and during the afternoon and evening we rolled heavily at times.

We left Saba on Monday afternoon with still the hope of making St Barts, but it was still doubtful – confirmed by still being in the Saba channel at 06.00 hrs the following morning and making leeway back from whence we came. At around 09.00 hrs the usual sea breeze came upon us and raised the spirit of forward movement at last, but as usual the wind was not in our favour, so we had no choice but to head for home where we arrived at 20.00hrs. Though we had failed to get to St Barts twice, the trip had been a pleasant one.

Chapter 53: October all over

I would have to leave yet again for St Lucia on Friday 6th October but I had by then made my mind up that my position was with the 'Jylland' and that it was total madness to have Sue and my children out there in a situation that wasn't clear by any means.

First I had been duped in to believing I was needed in St Martin, then got shackled in the building program due to Howard's refusal to go. It was bread and butter with the occasional Lobster thrown in aboard 'Jylland' – with Will it was just bread and water and locked up for the night till my release the next day.

Will had ideas for me that were not mine, wages for me that never seemed mine and ideas to employ me in his company not mine. What was mine now was the problem floating (just) in St Martin – if Will believed he could let Bill 'handle' that while I help Will build a nest egg in St Lucia, with just the occasional hand-outs, then he must have thought I was Brian and he was Henry!!

Will, one must remember, had been given control of 'Jylland', been there when the deal involving Mike and Co had been struck. Had wisdom been the mover, not a wife, he should have taken control of things in St Martin first. Sharman should have been doing Maddie's work as the rep – as she had done in St Lucia and was bloody good at it too – and the need for Howard and I would have been unnecessary!

In retrospect and why we never went back to St Lucia to take up where we had left off, I'll never know. Time was against us and each month matters were not improving – promises never being fulfilled by a conglomerate of 'Action' men who wanted results yesterday, and as owner of 'our boat' I should leave all the worries to Bill – never!

Come what may, it was our responsibility! All for one, eh? I was slowly beginning to see the light, but not just yet was I able to turn the spotlight on whom!

I would be back in St Martin by the 20th to find the 'Diligence', an old Brixham trawler built in 1894, she sat alongside the dock in Marigot. Like us, she had a leak, and like us, she was a long way from someone's capable hands.

The skipper came across for a chat and all we could do was take a look at her hull from underwater – a thing we had become pretty accustomed to. You hope you can help and feel pretty sad when your expectations of success leave you frustrated with failure. I'm certain we could have done better but it takes time to isolate the area, pump her dry and listen!

'Diligence' was soon to be on her way, and we had our own concerns to worry about. One was passengers, two was wages and three was keeping the water out of her.

None of us realized to what extent the problems were and none of us had a clue why they were getting worse by the day. Frustrated by the lack of finding anything externally wrong with the hull, a hull that seamed twice her size beneath the water, something 'Sinister' was happening of which we were totally unaware.

Hours spent searching methodically revealed nothing that could warrant what was coming in to her. All we could do was suck her dry and listen – nothing! There was no mad rush of water to say, "There it is!" and get in the water, patch in hand! It was obvious she was leaking in many places and only another dry-docking would provide the clues and the solution.

Maybe Mike Atkinson, in his stay with us, had been worried about the extent of her condition – he never said – but during my stopover in St Lucia, I'd learnt he had sold his share in the partnership to others – or rather, backed out of the deal – leaving others to pay up what he owed!

George Noon and Brendan McShane arrived with Maurice Widowson on one of his visits in November - they were two ex-pats living in St Lucia. From the outset they came across as not those I'd wished to be involved with. These were the 'Action' men, those Bill and I went to talk to one evening at a small hotel. They had with them a girl, a pretty Mulatto that I thought could have chosen better company. Action man with action woman! 'Mullet Bay' was one of the hotels on the island that wished to see our schedule for the coming season and Maddie had brought down Caroline Whathey, the tour director to meet with us on the 24th October.

That hotel had around 1,800 guests staying there by November 12th, and in the coming weeks we were only averaging 8 a week from them – someone wasn't doing their job!!

'Ilander' was taking out 20 – while we stood idle or carried half what she had aboard. Less than half our size with twice as many, we felt as if Maddie was working for them while we paid her wages. Such was confirmed when the skipper of 'Perky' Jimmy told me on the 2nd December – Maddie had offered passengers to them for 10%. I confronted her on the same day – it was all becoming very difficult We were getting pretty low on everything aboard – down to $10.00 by the 30th October, whether we could last out till the season started up around mid to late December was touch and go. One good day saw several bleak ones.

Hiding the fact of our financial position was getting difficult too. It would have been disastrous for us to let those ashore know our plight – what would have been the point to all the advertising if you may not be here? It was a case of put on a brave face and try to smile – bloody difficult with an empty stomach!! Had seafood not surrounded us we would have perished long ago.

There are many people not knowing the concerns of 'Boating', old wooden boating especially, that would come to see us while in St Martin. Many would be envious of our position too, surrounded by sun, sea and sand, and in Paradise. But to those living there, not on a long weekend or on a two-week holiday, one sees it so differently.

They come and then go taking with them the beauty of the place, while you struggle to survive. It is rather like visiting another home, where beautiful blue water flows to flush mere toilets, not a speck of dust to be seen, and cutlery sparkles on exceptionally clean tableware – it makes one envious of how others live that makes some dissatisfied with their own surroundings.

Eating Lobster and Conch most days is unheard of and the thought of sleeping on deck at night with a light warm tropical breeze – heaven! It was – and had I been owner of 'Deliverance', built in 1956, a 70' two masted gaff rigged topsail schooner with its 'Wipe me down with a paper towel bilge' and with an engine that worked - I'd have noticed Paradise rather more than I did.

Anita's sister Sandra and family would come to see us over the thanksgiving weekend – Billy Ross and family! Debbie, another of Anita's friends from Ohio came for two weeks, all not knowing that life is not always as it seems.

Sandra lived with her husband Phil in Puerto Rico. They had two daughters, Raquel and Lorelei – too young at the time to be aboard an old sailing ship and, having been born in the tropics it would have had little effect on them. Sandra herself was a sweet warm thing – and in the coming years Phil would make the great mistake of not recognizing that quality. That marriage didn't last, for within two years of our meeting, it was over. Sandra was, and had been, nothing but a crutch for Phil to lean upon – till he found he could stand alone.

The main reason for me being here was to give Bill a break – and on the 5th of December that time had come. My first chance at taking command had arrived.

For Bill the long trip home to Seattle was for a purpose – not only to see his wife Laurie and children, but also to check out the interest of the Northwest Seaports who had shown some interest in using 'Jylland' for educational purposes – trips in around Puget Sound for youngsters at school there. It was something that had always been both our choices – a break from scratching a living dealing with those we had nothing in common with. It was a place where she could get the attention she needed too. I kept my fingers crossed for his success.

There is a great difference from being in charge of a vessel to that for being owner – or just being aboard as crew. The backseat driver is now at the helm, and the concerns you had before increase two fold. The decisions, the responsibilities, the welfare and safety of the ship and her crew are all down to you. You just hope you make the right ones.

Handling her alone makes one more aware than you would think. You become alive to all that happens aboard the ship from day one. I had always given Bill credit as to who was in charge – as I had to Mike. Bills time aboard as skipper since Nassau was worthy of respect, and his ability to handle her was without question. What lay ahead for me, I did not know, but whatever, it was would be an experience.

Ian William Murray was skipper of 'Deliverance'. He had worked for the owner Harvey Howarte for some years and ready to meet him when called upon to play his role as captain, butler and loyal friend. Harvey used her on and off through the year, coming down with friends for a couple of weeks through the year. Other than that, Ian Murray kept his eye on her till that time was called upon. Ian was a tall man in his 50's when I knew him in St Martin – English, with a Roger Moore "Good Morning Miss Moneypenny?" voice. There was no need to look to see whom it was coming alongside in 'Deliverance's' lovely little sailing dingy.

Ian was an army man and in Suez when the Americans' told us and the French "Out!" – it was yet another insult that the French never forgot and America would pay dearly for in the future when in the need of an ally. It was also the end of Anthony Eden's reign as Prime minister at the time over the humiliation.

It was on one of our runs to Anguilla that I met Tony Heath. He had come along with Ian for the run across to Rendezvous Bay. We had only 8 passengers and while they were ashore on that rather deserted island beach – walking the shoreline and wondering what the hell they were doing living in Chicago – we sat aboard and chatted.

Tony was in his late 50's and ran a small plane out of the Turk and Caicos Islands running general cargo for Puerto Rico, St Thomas etc. He had brought his plane to St Martin for engine repairs and had got chatting to Ian in Town. Ian, always the gentleman and inquisitive about the accent, offered his countryman a berth aboard 'Deliverance' till his engine was fixed. For Ian, alone on the boat, Tony's company and conversation was interesting and made a change from watching the harbour activities.

Tony had been a Pilot for B.E.A. before it became British Airways, took early retirement and did what he always wanted to do – buy a plane and run around under the sunny skies of the Caribbean. He had also been a Pilot during the war. When the Red Caps knocked on his door his Mum said - "Tony? – He's already enlisted." Lying about his age just to be able to fly. Got shot down over North Africa in a night fighter! "This one's had it!" said the soldier turning him over with his foot. "I'm not!" tried to say our Tony, unable to speak.

 I would see a lot of him in the coming weeks – more than I'd bargained for – and more than Tony had expected too, yet the mystery surrounded him, and his intelligent conversations would be missed when he had gone. Like many of those you meet in the Caribbean, one is never sure of who they are, what they are, or if their business is just a front to some undercover operations.

We, as I've said before (I think?) were always caught up in the minds of people as – Not Real! St Martin was a hive of illegal activity from human cargo to drugs, a real 'Freeport' without customs nor controls on who went in or out with what.

From distinguished residents and businessmen like Roger from the store of M&S – we were always under suspicion as working for the U.S and British drug enforcement organization. Other wise – why were we not bothering about passengers? The truth was/is, always met with an "Oh ye---a???"

Going stern to the small dock in Marigot during the winter months can be uncomfortable. If a norther comes in, the movement can put too much strain on your lines – something can give. It was therefore, best to lie at anchor. Passengers were light and could be collected by dingy. So could those wishing to go ashore – or to be picked up.

Just a whistle and Bob's your uncle! Thus saying, David Marchant and I returned from Phillipsburg and I gave the whistle and Bob Sutcliffe came to collect us. We watched him coming, picking up speed to put the Whaler on a plane. She could move with just one aboard and young Bob could handle her pretty well. Now outboards are fixed to the stern by threw bolts – bolts that attach firmly the engine to a wooden plate fixed permanently to the stern. If one just relies on the screw bolts of the engine alone – any tight turn can put so much torque on boat and engine – the engine can come adrift!

Bob had just recently heard his best friend back in England, Kevin, had been killed in a car crash – I knew Kevin from our days at Emsworth, he was a nice lad too. It had upset Bob, so much so he would leave us for home shortly after, so I guess his mind was elsewhere as he came in rather speedily towards us. Bob had recently been working on the engine and was a good mechanic. Like everything else aboard, the outboard was in constant need of attention – impeller or sheer pin – always something seemed in need of repairs.

His intension was to turn her at speed and come to a halt starboard side to, with no way on her, as he throttled down. Bob was young, and like all youngsters loved the speed bit. Many times he had done the same thing in a real show of boat handling ability. Only this time the engine went on as the boat did the 180 degree turn – much lighter in the water now. The throttle had been snatched from his hand like some mysterious monster from the deep, and his wide eyes looked rather bewildered at the shock.

I had watched from the shore and kept mine focused on the spot where the engine had sunk – the quicker it was out the better and as that area was shallow. A leap over the side with the painter and bingo! It is very easy to lose your bearings, and even in shallow clear water, a 35Hp outboard is hard to spot.

The boys found it as I shouted from the shore 'There!' We returned rather slower to 'Jylland' – paddling! But he soon had it fired up once aboard – and this time with her through bolts secured.

Chapter 54: To the rescue

There was another occasion of an engine under water – but this time attached to a boat! Not ours just yet – but that of someone doing another a favour.

Sheryl Sommers had taken the temporary position as 'Jylland's' rep while Maddie had taken a break to go see Mike in St Lucia. Now Sheryl was a bustling go-getting Jewish girl from Cleveland Ohio and the job of liaison officer was right up her street for she had the chat that sold you something before you knew you couldn't do without it – and getting people to do things for you they would otherwise not, as was the case of getting a black fellow to give her a lift out to the schooner one day!!

Sheryl could whistle as loud as any man, it was the way for those that could to hail the boat and get the dingy to pick them up. What surprised us was just how many on board couldn't – both she and I were the only ones! I guess it's something one learns from an early age like riding a bike.

Big black dirty fingers shoved in mouths trying to blow their teeth away was quite hilarious to watch. Puffed out red faces giving up with, "Ah fuck it! I have to shout louder that's all!!" We had tried teaching old dogs new tricks, and failed!

We heard her notes coming from the shore but she would have to wait awhile for David Marchant was working on the outboard. Unbeknown to us though her whistling had stopped another in his tracks and he was about to be the Sir Galahad! He saw standing on the dock a white girl – a pretty white girl at that – and whistling at him!

The sound the approaching boat and a quick look saw Sheryl in the bow of this small craft. All's well you thought and concentrated on the job at hand – working on the mizzen mast with Bill Curry.

"You guys! – Hey you guys!!" said a voice below us.

"Strange," you thought, "coming from the starboard side too – why not the boarding ladder?" But not enough to stop you from what you were doing! Just the fellow had decided to drop her off there and she needed someone to take her bow line!
"YOU GUYS – HEY YOU GUYS!!" the louder shouts made me look over the side! There was our Sheryl in the water, a mouthful of tickets and a black guy mounting her.

Panic written all over his face the poor sod couldn't swim! But what happen to his boat? I threw them a line which Sir Galahad came up like a trapeze artiste, using Sheryl's head as a launching pad to safety. Free of him she swam to the boarding ladder!

The poor fellow was in a state of distress, not for what he'd just gone through, but what will happen to him when he returns to his Captain without the dingy and engine!

What had happened was pretty obvious. Rounding up under 'Jylland's' stern and us going backwards on the chain, we flipped him over! It was just a matter of waiting till she went back again and there below us lay his dingy in the clear water. "There she blows!" and David was down on it in a flash with a line. It was only a light aluminium craft and easy to haul to the surface. Once on the ships davits – water out – a couple of shots of WD40 and, to our friend's utter disbelief and gratitude, the seagull fired up!

The last I saw of him was a big smiling face and a hand waving us goodbye, flat out for home and a Captain of one of those island freighters wondering where the fuck he'd been. Our friend wouldn't mind the bollocking – it was better than the certain death he'd have gotten without it!

Chapter 55: A bit of trouble

The end of '78 was drawing to a close and as if to end it with a bang, on the 27th we had one. The fork that drove our prop from forward to astern, broke, just as we were going to get water from the desalinization plant. This large cast iron piece that had worked for 30 odd years – driving the shaft backwards and forwards, backwards and forwards countless times – had given up the ghost.

We had an evening cruise booked too, and with two decent days ahead of us, passenger wise, despair could have set in – but it would have had little effect on one tortured by the mischievous acts that seemed to bedevilled us. David Marchant worked hard to get it off and to someone capable of welding cast iron. With the wind playing tricks on us, it was go that evening with 15 aboard without an engine.

David was at the dock to meet us when we returned with the piece welded, but it would have to wait till the morning to see if Richardson's Machine Shop could do what they said they could.

They couldn't!! – For when David and I fitted it early the next morning, one bit of pressure and the weld gave! There was nothing we could do but cancel the morning trip and get it back to the shop pronto with instructions to do as requested first time round – that was to pin it, then weld! I had another bit to remind me of rushing that morning – a crushed toe.

The 29th of December is my birthday. I was hoping for a nice day, but I write in my log 'Not a very nice day – rain and with it a wind that blew from all directions – Engine still wouldn't give ahead – couldn't fix it before the 'La Samana' crowd came aboard'.

Those that ran this Hotel had booked us for a cruise to Anguilla and had invited friends – I guess there were about 40 with their children. I had told Maddie beforehand that I could do Rendezvous Bay if the wind was fair, with or without an engine, but either way they must be here ready to go at 10.00hrs.

Without power and the wind playing up and, worst of all, they were still not aboard at 11.00hrs – it was going to be touch and go if I'd be back in time for the evening cruise. I was ready to go when a man in woman's clothing, with the attitude of authority way and above her station, approached me! She had come aboard with the last boatload and marched up to me with "Okay – you can go now!" And thus giving her orders, turned to join her happy group.

Maybe my toe was giving pain!
"Just a minute?"
Maybe it was the bilges playing up again.
"I can go where?"

Maybe it was the frustration of being in charge of ship hanging on to dear life and not being able to do a thing about it
"Do you know what the time is?"
Maybe I took offence at her attitude
"It's Rendezvous Bay or nothing!"
Maybe I was tired of the whole bloody business
"I couldn't care less, madam, if the Queen of England was waiting to dub me as I walked ashore!"
Maybe I should have gone below for a minute and taken a deep breath.
"You aren't going anywhere – so get your lot together and get off!"
– and they went!
But not before the man in man's clothing asked me rather confused what was the problem. "Her" I replied. He looked Greek – South American or the like, and I found out was the true owner of 'La Samana'. His younger 'voice' in this affair and the running of things, having obviously got him by the balls.

Her demands of where I should be heading that day – further down the coast to where, as she pointed out, "People in high places will be waiting for us!" – as far as I was concerned right then, could be waiting a long time!

I felt bad for the kids – they couldn't have cared less where we'd gone – but being ordered like some peasant by a serf, a woman serf at that, was too much!!

The word soon got round that I had brought her down a peg or two - and in front of her friends too, wonderful they said. Miss, 'Do you know who you're talking to?' from 'La Samana' being put in her place – do tell all, I was asked. She was fuming okay, saying words like, "You'll never get a person from us again." I guess she was so mad she never heard Bob Curry say, as he helped her down the boarding ladder, "That's alright – we never had anyone from you in the first place!"
We got the trouble fixed and went out on the evening cruise with 12 aboard. But the bilges were at 1 1/2 hours – worrying!

On the 30th I had again to cancel the day cruise – I had no option, I had to find that leak. Bob Curry was the only one available to go search – David Marchant had a rotten cold and my toe was giving me hell, couldn't get a flipper on. Bob found one leak forward, but it wasn't the one. It was pump her out and listen – water could be heard coming in under the engine – and, toe or no toe, I went in without a flipper and found two good leaks. The bilges went from 1½ hrs. to 6 – and on the last day of the year we took out 16 to Anguilla!

A friend of Anita's, Debbie, had arrived on the 5th December, bringing with her some Bowman and Landes' Turkey. Ian and Tony joined us on New Year's Eve for dinner where the remnants of it went down with the last hours of '78. It had been an interesting year alright – I was dying to see what '79 held in store. It could surpass '78 – or could it?

Chapter 56: January 1st 1979

The start to the year had come with a Gale, for it was the season of Northeasters. It had torn from its mooring the little red sloop we had saved so many times – it now lay down wind close to the entrance of Simpson Bay. It's nice lines broken up by the pounded of the surf.

We had dragged some during those blows but hauling up and laying out of more chain had checked us. It would take a week to blow itself out. Our main Bower – the one that I'd purchased for 70 pounds with chain, and one that I knew would hold us in no matter what – did us proud at such times. With hardly any scope out, she never moved from where she lay!

The only problem was, getting her aboard. It took ages and had to be done in enough time for the days sail while you hung to the working anchor. Big Bertha we named her and Big Bertha came aboard dripping like some reluctant woman having just fallen over the side.

The 'season' was upon us now for once the New Year had been done with and Christmas was out the way – hotels looked forward to a boost in numbers. It would not be until the 4th we had any – 8 to be exact, but it was a start!

Come the 10th we had 10 for the evening cruise, 22 for the day sail to Anguilla on the 11th, 18 for the evening of the 12th and on the 13th, 16 to Anguilla again.

A week in which 66 paying passengers helped ease our problems. By the end of January the total was 168 passengers, with one private charter not included. A far cry from what we had in St Lucia.

But with as many problems as we had, just how long could it continue with a boat in desperate need of attention, let alone the 'staff' we had ashore that seemed more concerned with their appearance than to let us know how many to be prepared for the next day!

Roger Sutcliffe had left the schooner on the 1st of January – neither a word of thanks nor a word of goodbye from his lips. He left with a pocket full of address's too, all given in the course of time by 'Friendly' Americans we had aboard.

It would not be the last I should hear of him as he went from one to another, taking and leaving a trail of "Thanks for nothing!" from those whose door he knocked upon, by those that sent him! Leaving dirty socks with one, he would take another from another poor unsuspecting host.

Roger's idea of standing watch was to invent a gadget to do it for him. I saw him working away on his invention – a device that switched the bilge pump on without waking himself in the small hours. I let him finish it – a floating device. He even showed me how affective it was too. "So," I said, "while we're all asleep – you too, a gale starts to blow from the North – heavy swells – what gadget have you invented to wake you up before we're all aground?"

He was rather put out as he sat up in the early hours of his watch with his invention!

He is probably head of some department today, one that is pushing for cloning people – the working type clone, while he can lie in bed thinking of other ways to make life easier for the human race!

One thing I note from my logs of the period was that Geoff returned on the 6th January, and he fell in to place like a well-oiled block! I do believe words of his 'Coming' prompted the early departure of Mr Sutcliffe. Geoff was not one to tolerate their likes, and in a fine string of Ye Olde Anglo-Saxon wording, would have had Roger praying for his University dorm.

I would have another un-expected guest arrive too, and one that would be with us for a lot longer than I expected! Tony Heath. Ian Murray had indicated that he was taking 'Deliverance' to Antigua on the 12th January and wasn't sure when he'd be back. Would I mind if Tony spent a few days with us till his plane was fixed?

Always ready to assist those in need or trouble, one more mouth to feed was not too much to ask, so he came aboard. Tony was no trouble at all, but his stay turned in to a bit longer than I'd anticipate.

"When is he going to leave?" "What's the position with Tony?" "When are you going to ask him?" Came the questions at me as the time went on. "Listen," I would say, "When Tony's ready to tell me, he will, so leave it at that!"

It was not that he didn't pull his weight. Light framed and in his mid 50's, Tony did his bit. Not only that, he was good conversation, something I needed at times. Many a time, while at the helm, I'd see him talking to the passengers and they certainly enjoy him – why I'm certain they thought he was the skipper too, which took the burden off my shoulders, if not the mantle of authority, which I certainly didn't mind!

People like to talk with the skipper, and can ask some daft questions. It was rare to meet someone who knew a thing about boats, so whatever position Tony put himself in, was okay by me!

Chapter 57: The Hustle

People came and people went, it seemed only I that couldn't leave. First it was Sheryl's father that came to visit us on the 5th January, then David Marchant's father came, Anita's brother and wife on the 16th February, followed by her sister, Mom and Dad and two friends on the 9th of March. The company was nice and was a diversion to the everyday happenings on board.

Meeting the good, the bad and the ugly of life is what makes it all worth living. David's father for instance – a wheeler-dealer if there ever was one - and on land, a man to avoid!

Anita was thinking of selling the car, the one she had delivered from Puerto Rico. David's father came up with a suggestion – one that he'd obviously used when in the trade back in England – one once used to catch the greedy, and best left with those who are caught by it.
"Now," he says laying open his own character before us, "take the car to a dealer with the price in your mind of what you want for it, not what he'll give you. Say to him, you are thinking of selling it and ask him if he's interested. Of course if he is, but it won't match what you're thinking. Then you say, well put it on your lot for what I think it's worth to see if there are any takers. If he agrees – you're in!

Now for the sting. Give it a few days, then one of the crew go down there with his 'wife'. Just looking, you say, while giving the car more than one look over. The price on it will not be what Anita wanted, but will be what he expects to make on the deal. Ask him to start up the engine, look around inside, sit at the wheel and nod to the 'wife' with that look on your lips that's says - fine! Look at the price again and say – would you take any less! I can't, he'll say, I'm making nothing on it as is. Have another little chat with the 'wife' who might say so as he can hear – I like it!

Now you 'the husband' will say would he take a deposit on it – all I have on me is a $100.00 till Monday. He'll take it!!!!! Now later that day, and that day being a Friday, Anita goes back and asks – any luck? If not I'll take it back, as I think I've got an interested party. The man will say okay, I'll give you what you asked, with all the spiel about you're a hard bargainer you are. He'll pay you by cheque – but make sure the banks are open first and cash it before Monday. All you've lost is $100.00 while gaining $400.00."

Somewhere I have an old wallet. It has followed me around for years carrying bits and pieces of my life. I never carried one, but like some faithful dog, it's always turning up when so much else has gone.

Wrapped in a piece of tissue is a stone, a green stone, a stone that one could mistake for an Emerald – especially those doing a deal in which they believe favours them by several hundred bucks. Now David's Dad owed his son for a car I believe – or something, I can't quite recall. "Take these instead!" said his Dad, pushing across the table a small packet. .

Now any son in his right mind wouldn't sell such a present, it wouldn't be right, not from his father! It would be like smashing open the clear resin that held 'The Gold Medal' given by Prince Phillip to find out if it was pure gold or not!

Naaa! Wouldn't be right – not unless hunger set in – set in so bad just one little Emerald sold would buy you a meal set for a King, ready to share it with a round table full of hungry Knight's too it would! Well I wouldn't say David was that hungry, but he was definitely inquisitive, so much so he had them valued in Phillipsburg.

"Two Dollars – One Dollar – Three dollars!" said the little Indian Jeweller as each 'Gem' passed beneath the eyepiece.

"One for you – one for you – one for you!" said David, passing out to each of us on deck one night an 'Emerald' from his father's collection. "And the Meek shall inherit the Earth" or what's left of it, after the greedy bastards have had their fill! I felt terribly sorry for him, even though he laughed it off.

Chapter 58: More challenges

Sharman called me on the 29th January, a rather shaking voice. My brother Will had cut his fingers off! Using a planer, his mind must have not been on the job at hand, thus his left hand suffered. He was in hospital suffering from the shock mainly – and the pain mostly! Seattle was on his mind at the time I guess. Bill had been trying to sort out the contracts with Don Thaw on a deal to get her there, but negotiations were going too slow. She called again on the 30th in tears – the deal there was off! It was not a good day for me, and a worse piece of news to tell Will! As for 'Jylland' and her future? A bleak outlook. Wrapped up in thoughts of what to do about it, we sailed in to February! February was no different than January – the same problems existed.

Quote: "1st February 1979. Variable winds with calms. Swell running. Sunny and hot! Not a good day. Cancelled because of swell and lack of people. Maddie came at 08.45, late again. Said we had only 8 booked. 27 turned up, stupid woman lost us $800.00. If I'd known that, swell or no swell I'd have gone!" End of Quote!

The problem we had to encounter was a lack of communication between the ship and our girl ashore. We depended on her to inform us of how many we had for the next day to allow time for the girls to do their shopping and prepare the lunch.

Had she bothered to rise at the right time, enough time for us to get food and to prepare the schooner for sailing, it might have been easier, but to turn up when she did – 45 minutes beforehand – and still get the numbers wrong, was totally frustrating. She was just like the Yorkshire man – 'you can tell 'em – but not very much!' Tight-fisted, tight-arsed and totally wrong for the job. Maddie was given it by Mike and the rest of the untrustworthy bastards to keep an eye on things! A lot of money could have been made, and she was employed to that end, rather than do the job we thought she was employed to do! If you can't trust one another, you stand little chance of getting anywhere.

The heavy swell was a sure sign that something was going through, and in the evening the wind came out of the North which required 'Big Bertha' to be dropped with 10 fathoms of chain. It was the swells more than the wind that night and we rolled pretty well throughout it, and on till the 6th when they finally went down.

Mad with Maddie and her supercilious ways, I'd asked David Marchant to pop in to see the tour reps about passenger lists. He'd had his Triumph motor bike sent down from the States by then, and with his blond long hair blowing in the wind, did the tours of the Hotels.

Most girls liked David and, as most tour reps were girls, he found them easier to deal with. It resulted in 22 for an evening cruise on the 7th and 18 to Anguilla on the 8th. 10 for another evening cruise on the 9th and 23 to Anguilla on the 10th. From now on, Maddie would only get 10% of what she sent us.

One thing became clear during the swells, 'Jylland's' bilge time increased from 4 hours to 9. The ground being churned up had done the job that Dilbury used on her when she arrived back from Denmark. I small problem of water running could be heard in the locked waters at Heybridge Basin. Dilbury saunters off to his place of work and returns with a sack of sawdust. Close to the hull and above where water was running – he lets some drop to gradually sink. It did seem to me then and there, that out problem was not just one or two, but many small leaks. Ones that, to the naked eye were impossible to stem! The inflow increased as we sailed and we were soon back to our usual chore of pumping to keep our feet above water.

Our running time to Rendezvous Bay was usually 2/3 hours, depending on the wind. One had to keep her close hauled all the way with the wind heading N.E. It was a different run home though, usually achieved in 1hr, and very much under reduced sail - the state of them being another cross to bear! The times we had to have them down to mend with Evo-Stick was nearly an everyday chore.

Passengers had increased as February drew on; 42 for the 22nd and 72 for the 23rd to Angiulla plus 16 for the evening one – a good day for once but short of what we did each day back in St Lucia. Getting back there was important, but the risks involved had to be taken in to consideration! In total, the month of February saw us take out 230 passengers, something we had achieved at our 'Home' base, one could say, in three days.

Such thoughts played on my mind at times. The crazy idea of Panama, the stupidity of going to Nassau,. Now here I was in charge of a sinking boat in St Martin, a suit of sails you couldn't fly in anything other than a breeze and a Boston whaler falling to pieces with a Dickie over-worked outboard!

If and when I decided to make a run for it, our luck would have to change for once. I spoke to the crew about it in March with our only alternatives. Which in the end, there were none. It was St Lucia or bust trying.

Month after month of such strain got at me at times, I quote from my logs on 25th February: 'Find myself getting short with people now a days. Tension maybe – Feel like an old moaner at times.'

March came in like a Lion. 30 for the first day to Anguilla, but could it last? No! Slowly and surely things got worse; on the 2nd we had 12 for the evening cruise, on the 8th 20 to Anguilla again, the 10th saw just 8 for the day's sail to Rendezvous, the 15th 8 to the same place. By the 22nd we had taken only 134 passengers.

I gave Will a call on the 20th of my concerns and hopeful intentions. Much to my surprise he said Dennis had arrived to help him after his loss of his fingers, but of things on my mind, the question that needed an answer, was to make sure we were insured to make the passage down.

He said he'd call me on the Saturday, being the 24th, the day being my Williams birthday. It came with my thoughts of just how many I had missed too – of not only his, but my dear Helens.

From my logs I quote: "Had the expected call from Will in the evening. After talking with him I've made the decision to leave here as soon as possible – probably within the week. Have some work to do on the bottom – pick up moorings etc! Will did say there might be some film work coming our way.

The people we met in St Thomas last June who took our particulars and photos of 'Jylland' got in touch with him. They said they would like her for at least six weeks commencing mid-May to June. Grenadines and Antigua - $7,000 a week – be nice – but I'm being optimistic!"

So it was, after a struggle to survive there, another struggle lay ahead of us – in getting 'Jylland' to St Lucia. First it was get her bottom scrubbed of weed, for I wanted speed on this passage, and I couldn't rely on the engine. I got the weather report on the 2nd of April, which said N.E to Easterlies, and I made the decision to leave here on the 3rd – the next day!

It is always sad to say goodbyes to the nice people I'd met here. Ian Murray on 'Deliverance', the Petite family Roger, Robiar. Paul on

'Pualu', Fritz and Jeanne and the boys, Jerry, Dolphous, Jimmy, all would be remembered – but we must be off and so we did!

Chapter 59: April '79

It was only 280 miles to St Lucia, a run that would take us a couple of days if all went well. The wind, if it lasted, was blowing Easterly and strong, so as soon as we got the last of our supplies aboard we hastened to make the most of it. On the 3rd of April 1979 at 12.45 we weighed anchor and set sail for St Lucia, with the wind East to N.E 4-6.

The decision to do so had been a difficult one – but my choices were few. It was a simple case of 'sink or swim'! The state of 'Jylland's' hull had concerned me and the frustrations of searching for her leaks had proved pointless. We were losing the battle daily. Four hours on the time they took to fill was the best we could achieve, and a final check on her hull before we left, found nothing! It was pretty certain, once at sea, that time would diminish to zero. It was now down to a 3 and a half horsepower Briggs and Stratton to do the work or we'd be in the boats – and that pump wasn't up to much!

Scrubbing her hull made a difference and we slipped along making around 7 knots I note.

I had hoped to make a heading for Antigua, going to Windward of Eustatius, St Kitts Nevis etc. – making for The Saints – but it would have been a slower passage having to keep her head up, so I decided to let her run between Saba and Eustatius on a course of 175 magnetic and she loved it with a bone in her teeth.

By 19.00hrs we were in the channel and I altered the course to 155 Mag. By 05.00 on the 4th, it saw us abeam of Montserrat. The wind had blown hard all night but I couldn't afford to reduce sail, I could be wishing for it later.

The problem foreseen about our bilges, happened! Not long in to the passage, water was coming in fast – the bilge pump was on most of the time, taken 7 minutes to fill and 20 minutes to pump dry. So it continued in to the night. Due to that, I had to change the watches from 2 on 6 off to 3 on 3 off – 4 to a watch. As it was, I hardly slept and lay awake with my thoughts.

The log read on the 4th: 'Wind East to N.E 3-5 cloud 3/8. Hard night on the Briggs, she's been pumping now continuously with just the odd break when the Genny went on – if she packed up we'd be in desperate trouble!! Had a slow passage past Guadeloupe

Met some really sloppy seas at the end (Channel!) 'Jylland rolling like a pig. Winds picked up once in the channel – Had to have the main down to stick a patch on the head. One of the lashing eyes pulled out and it tore.

Fixed our position at noon as 15 - 58.6' N. 62 – 3' W. Course 155 M. Only got one glimpse of Dominica – couldn't even get a sight off her. By 23.00hrs my estimated position put us 23 miles N.W Martinique – A good clear night! Shot Polaris which gave my Latitude as 15 19.5' N at 19.15 hrs. – having run 39.1 miles in 7 hours – just over 5 knots!'

Log on the 5th reads: 'Wind ENE 4/5 cloud 3/8. Passed Martinique during the day – only saw the southern tip 20 miles to the east. Found another thing to jeopardize our journey. The frame on the steering gear broke – the four legs fixing it to the deck were completely rusted away. Briggs is still the only thing keeping us afloat, if she packs up 'Jylland' would sink as the Genny pump can't keep pace with the flow – seams probably open here and there. Can't get much sleep – too many things on my mind. Fixed Lat 14 33.8 N at 05.30. Due West of Fort du France.

13.30 sighted The Pitons of St Lucia 18.00hrs. Fixed position 14 miles due west of Soufriere. Put in a quick good tack to get some Northing at 18.45. 21.20hrs. Castries harbour light abeam 090 M.

Bilges taking 7 minutes to fill 20 to pump out – a lot of water. 23.00 hrs. tried putting in another tack – with the steering gear in such bad shape I couldn't give it too much helm so jibed instead – What happened? Fore main clew tore out – an already poor sail is now totally useless. Continued under Main – Mizzen and headsails – went about again during the early hours of the 6th.'

It had taken us just over two days to make the trip. Not bad for an old girl under sail alone – that which we had.

I had decided against taking her in that night and would wait till first light. A lot of changes had taken place in Castries – dredging of channels and earth works, plus I wasn't sure of my engine – much in need of an overhaul.

Log that day reads: '6th April Wind East 3/4, Cloud 2/8 Went about at 07.00hrs on course 185 M. Castries Harbour 10 miles S.E – Speed 2/3 knots. Had engine started 09.30 hrs. – clutch slipping and missing on one cylinder – anything else? On entering the Harbour one would think you were somewhere else with all the alterations going on – good job I didn't try bringing her in last-night – thrown me right off. Dropped anchor none too soon at 10.20 hrs.'

We had left there 3 years ago with a leak – and had come back with a bigger one! For the want of a phone call and some honesty, 3 years had taken its toll on her. I sat there listening to the pumping of water from her hull and thought of the times we laid against Ganters Wharf dry and in fine shape for the next day's sail.

3 years of being broke, yet not broken. If only, I thought, if only! I was tired out – and I was angry, not really for myself, but to think of what might have been.

There is a fine line between success and failure – so fine, luck plays more of a role than those who have made it are prepared to admit. Just how many times had we had it in our hands to be snatched from us unexpectedly. Too many of us had their hands on the ball and not one of us was watching the 'game' I'm afraid. It was as much our fault as Dennis's as to the position we were in.

Had we not seen his actions from childhood? Had we, of all people, not experienced the mystery of his attachment to others than his brothers? Each and every time he came back to us, we failed to see the reason. It would take me a lifetime to figure him out, and I still don't know the motives behind his thoughts today other than self – nor does he I would guess!

His brothers held the only medicine chest for what ailed him – once patched up and running, he was soon back to his old ways while we sat and waited for the inevitable fall! In business he was a disaster, making decisions alone that affected us all, as in this very fiasco.
I found myself frustrated – why? I heard he was here, and on the pretence to give Will a hand after his accident. I should have given him 'Jylland' then and there and said you get on with it – I've had enough! But I didn't – couldn't. He was as incapable of handling her as he was irresponsible for his actions. He'd have had Mike Atkinson aboard in no time, on a grand a week and a percentage of the take without thought for where that take was coming from.

All that day we had been in and out of the water trying to find leaks. With the amount coming in, surely it wouldn't be hard to find one, but nothing of any significance was found. The only thing we did find was on the inside – stones – stones blocking the limber holes. The concrete placed in plastic bags had torn and low and behold had washed clear of cement. Had just one got in it would have smashed the impeller and bingo, no Briggs and very probably no 'Jylland'.
This 'Lean Mix' had been put in her back in '74 when alongside Ganters. About 16 tons to give her something amidships. It looked like the bags had either broken when placed or deteriorated. I'd have to get in there in the next couple of days and remove what I could otherwise we'd never be able to pump her dry. At the moment we had to pump her every hour.

I hadn't been unable to tell Will when we had left, and he just waited anxiously for us to call. I rang him from the 'Wicky-up' and he, Dennis and, of all people, Dia Neale came down later that evening. He, Mary and son 'Sailor' were here with the boat they'd put together in England 'Ty-Bach' - Emsworth area to be exact. Why anyone would call a boy 'Sailor' I'll never know – "Hello Sailor!" just a couple of times would be enough to start a fight or make a boy change his name!

It was pretty obvious 'Jylland' would have to stay where she was and until I could get the steering gear fixed , I couldn't move to Rodney Bay where we intended to lay up till decisions could be made at what to do next. That was taken off on the 8th and delivered to the workshop.

Always the opportunist, Dia Neale was to make a run to St Barts on the 9th. The customs in St Lucia were on strike, and Dia saw an opening to make a little on running some contraband. This short stocky laugh-a-minute Welshman was built in the John Hancock mode. "What's yours is mine and what's mine my own!" The idea of him joining Will and Roland in the building up on Cap sounded good at the time, till the time came for Dia to leave (and while Will was away) to take what he thought was his due – the kitty!

I would eventually leave in the early hours of the 11th of April for Rodney – the wind being light at that time of the morning. It was a slow progress up the coast without much ahead I was getting from the prop – any more force could break the fork piece. The 4/5-mile run would take us 2 hours.

Bob Curry and Geoff set off in the dingy to sound the Lagoon out while I waited outside. 10/12 feet was what they reported, so I took her in to rest close to the roadway – and 1 mile from Wills house on Cap Estate.

I note here: "On the 13th Of April whilst sitting at Wills house chatting over things concerning the schooner, Dennis happened to look out the door and noticed to the south an odd looking cloud forming. It grew fast, upwards and outwards like some giant explosion without the bang!"

It was the Volcano on the northern end of St Vincent erupting. She had been on the move for the last couple of days and those that didn't heed it are moaning and groaning now and running for their lives!

Roland's brother Ivor had a plantation close by and worked right up to its rim, and all feared for him and his workers. The last time it went off was in 1902 and 2,000 people perished. I heard they evacuated 9,000 in the next couple of days. It continued blowing for several days after, the next big bang on the 17th.

A note here from my Log reads: "St Vincent blew again yesterday – biggest yet – heard their Prime Minister on the radio talking to the locals. The expert Volcanologists have said it could blow again within 10 hours. His speech was very reassuring quote - "The Volcano can do one of three things – stay as it is – go down slowly – or get worse!" Such a clever speech covered him all aspects! He should have added 'You can do one of three things – stay where you are – go back to your homes - or join me in Martinique – But remember this – wherever you are my Police are watching you!!!!"

With 'Jylland' safely inside the Lagoon it was time for a wash and brush up – the repainting of the hull etc! For those abroad, some would be leaving, while some would stay. Tony Heath had got his plane at last fixed and would be leaving for St Martin.
He had arranged an evening out (much to our surprise) ordering Taxi's to take the crew to 'Rain'. He rose towards the end and made a speech in which he thanked all for their hospitality - then handed me an envelope, which contained a cheque for $1,000. I was humbled. It was sad to see him leave and though one thinks you will meet up again somewhere – you never do! I often think of him, even after so many years, and wonder what became of him!

David and Jackie would head up to Antigua for race week – hoping to spend some time with Ian Murray aboard 'Deliverance' while Helen went to Grenada to join a boat for a week or so. On the 22nd Anita would also leave, to Puerto Rico to join her sister, then on to her younger sister's wedding in Washington. With Geoff and Bob Curry left to take care of things, I would at last be free to go home and visit my waiting family! So on the 23rd April I left – left with a heavy heart too.

Chapter 60: April/May '79

I remember nothing of the flight back to England that day, only our stopover in Gander while outside men in great heaps of fur hurried to fill her with fuel. Little did I notice of Luton airport, other than I got stopped yet again for having the very likely face of a man up to no good! The bloody fools couldn't pick out Osama Bin Laden from Rabbi Blue in a 'Name that Muslim' show.

I had returned yet again with little other than my belongings and a future of which was uncertain. My mind drifted upon the last few days aboard and if anything was certain, it was to do with the relationship I'd had with Anita. On saying goodbye to her only a day before, the thought of never seeing her again only struck me the moment she was gone!

Women had come and women had gone in my life (nothing at which I am proud to boast I might add) and my marriage had survived – but this was different. Her character, her loyalty, her personality had shone through all the hardships without question. I remembered her sitting on the taffrail – a red head scarf tying up her long hair as we brought 'Jylland' up from Castries – and I looked and I wondered then – is this it? Is this how it must end? Or must I end something to make a new beginning?

The thoughts of such sadness it would bring – the tears of a broken heart – broken hearts, would never leave me I knew, and with all to think about I sat alone with my thoughts of home – my dearest children.

As I reflect on those times years after, the pain I caused, I know I can never be forgiven! Even though time heals the wounds, scars are left that never go away. They lay hidden beneath a cloak of deception upon youth, and are revealed to you when it becomes necessary to remind you of your own failings.

I'm afraid life is very much like the old sop that has turned to temperance and delivers speech after speech about the evils of drink – people remind him of it, but will not give him the benefit that he knows what he is talking about! Such goes for all that have experienced life at first hand – people will believe the word written, rather than listen to the story told.

Every man, every woman is born different, and that difference changes the older you get. Some grow together some grow apart – it is part of growing up! What seemed right at the time cannot always be, for if one wishes to hang on to his identity, that which made him appealing in the first place, unless he does, he bends to the stronger of the two, and is never the man he was – and never the man he could be!

Two strong willed people can live happily together – yet once married, fight like cats and Dogs for dominance of the other partner. Why are the jeans you always wore no longer acceptable to her – you must change, not only in to 'Proper' clothes now, but change the person who wears them!

In many cases today, women are the dominant partners – by their 'Liberation' they have been elevated to being the breadwinner – but the price to pay has yet to be evaluated for such foolhardiness. Two masters in a house are like two determined women in a kitchen cooking different meals at the same time – impossible!

Marriage is but a word. Middle English or Old French meaning, a union between two people who have become man and wife. It was a word where each person knew his or her place. Man provided – women prepared. It was a custom of the past – yet today its only meaning is to make people responsible for their actions. Laws passed in modern times to create incentives for people to get married – or stay together longer than they otherwise would. It is nothing but bribery, for what do they really care about family life, other than what it's costing the State to keep them? They are prepared to quote God in all this, but have left him out of all else.

Did a women, one who lived her life being beaten by a bully, or a man tormented by an Old Hag, know any difference! Maybe they thought they were lucky, one to have a wife the other not be beaten to death, for who talked about such things in public? Marriage is grand they would say, yet just how many experienced another man or another woman to be able to compare theirs with!

It was a coach to Kings Cross and from there I caught the underground and train to Billericay from Liverpool St. Fare was then one pound 54 pence single I note. I would spend the night with my brother John, his wife Jean and a very much ailing son Howard.

The dear boy's health had deteriorated so much since I last saw him. From my logs I note: 'John and Jean's poor boy Howard isn't too good. His condition has taken a turn for the worse. The long winter hasn't helped. I can't see him lasting much longer poor Boy – John and Jean have such a hard time – constant tending!'

The morning of the 25th of April, the next day, I note: 'Awoke early 05.30, Howard poor boy calling Dad! Dad! How can life be so sad? Poor John and Jean have put on age more than anyone – the Zombie style of life they spend looking after their fated Son! Please God he should be taken now – rather than all three!'

Howard had got to the stage where he couldn't move his legs, and my brother and his wife had to tend his every calling. I stood above his bed and watched a 21-year-old boy, one that should be in the prime of his life struggling for another day. Unable to move a limb now, the inevitable was about to reach its sad conclusion. Muscular Dystrophy of all diseases puts upon parents a terrible burden, yet in a sense, shows how much they will endure.

This bright intelligent boy – for that is what he was – was destined never to show his capabilities. As I stood there, I seemed to be grabbed by a spirit of despair. It sat on the bed, on the chair, walked round the kitchen and cried silently in every room in the house. The years of torment and anguish had consumed all by the helpless situation that was finally about to end. When I said goodbye to that dear boy, I knew it would be the last time I'd see him, and I was sad so terribly sad!

As I sat on the train to London, the thought of Howard's position made my own far clearer.

What was the point to life if it wasn't worth living? Not being with the one person you know you're destined to be with? Who cares what others may think, you are not living with them. You must do what you must do regardless of the pain – for no pain could ever be as bad, last so long, as I had seen and felt! Clear in my head for the first time in weeks, I caught the train to Penzance.

Oh yes! The price of the ticket was exorbitant – 31 pounds 70 pence! An increase of 10 pounds from last year! The saying at the time was - British Rail are getting there! There, I would assume meant in to your wallet!!!!!!

The next two weeks for me would be the hardest I'd ever experience in my stupid life.

Sue had met me in Penzance, arriving on the 09.15 flight from Scilly. The idea was to spend a day and a night together before heading home the next day. It was lovely seeing her, always was, for Sue was and always will be special to me.

For 13 years she had stuck by me through thick and thin, mostly thin – very thin indeed – especially with two children in your arms waiting for some relief from a hubby out looking for some thick stuff to walk on! The last thing I wanted to do was hurt her, and though I had the opportunity to talk there and then, it would have destroyed the moment and the people completely. So putting away my thoughts, we spent the day shopping in Penzance and taking the bus to St Ives.

It was a cold day as I remember, but the flowers were out to warm the eyes if nothing else. We sat that evening facing one another across the table at 'The Admiral Benbow' for dinner before retiring to 'The George' in Chapel street. I knew Sue thought I had changed, but she didn't say. I guess she thought I'd get over what was bothering me, and she never asked for fear of just what it could entail.

If she wasn't sure then, the realization would soon dawn on her that night, for that which we had before, had gone! It was the final realization that whatever it was that had kept us together through the years had left, that words never need be said. Words would just lead to other words in an emotional outburst – followed by tears – then threats for all that's gone wrong! Sue knew, but hoped all was not lost – not yet!

Seeing Helen jump across the wall from next door was as emotional as seeing my son arrive in a hurry on his bike from school. Both unaware, and both too young to realize or understand why a father was about to leave them yet again – only this time for a different reason.

To say the next two weeks was the most difficult period of my life would be an understatement. It was as heart-breaking for me as it was for Sue. The intuition of women is nothing new – and Nora, dear Nora, knew – and like any mother would be when the hurt involves her daughter, shunned me with the silence, which was worse than any words. I had to be gone – and the sooner the better!

Word reached me on the 6th of May that young Howard had died on the 5th. Henry, over the phone had said he would let me know when the funeral would be – which turned out to be on 11th. I would try and be there. It did seem at the time, God had answered my prayers!

It is terribly difficult for a man to write about his failings – they creep up on you in good enough time! The emotions that came about during the next months would play heavy on me, and to talk about them still hurts today. I did not wish to play the Bastard, but I played the Bastards role. Time would prove, if it were afforded me, that it was only a temporary role, and in the coming years I would do all I could to make the bed I made for myself as comfortable as I could for my children.

So on May 10th I left Scilly for what I believed would be my final time.

Chapter 61: May '79

I would spend the night at Howard's – Sue dropping us off to catch the early train to London the next morning. Everything was late that day – including us for the funeral on the 11th May.

We went to John and Jean's where friends and family had gathered instead of visiting the grave. It was a sombre moment, yet one thing I noticed – both John and Jean looked suddenly younger! The first night's sleep in years for both had achieved the transformation, though the sadness was apparent, both looked relieved it was over with, having done all as parents they could!

We visited Howard's grave later that day, and the emotion as I placed the two Roses I'd brought from Scilly, their petals ready to drop, was too much. Both Howard and I shed tears!

I would spend a couple of days with John and Jean before leaving for St Lucia on the 15th via New York. It had been 20 years since I last set foot there and how different things had become.

Immigrants no longer came by boat – the plane now was their transport to the land of 'OZ'. Search as I may for the large Irish American that open the small hatch in the door and said "Whatdoyouwant?" – but to no avail. He had obviously retired by now, that or dead! Whatever the case, he would be missed – missed for his utter rudeness and inability to understand the meaning of the word 'Politeness'.

I needed to see Anita before returning – and remembered her sister's wedding to be held in Washington D.C. on the 19th of May. So that's where I made for!

As I sit here – some 23 years after that meeting in Washington, I have often wonder what she would have done had I not shown up! Who she would have married – where she would have ended up? There is no doubt about the love we had and have for each, but what is love? If it is missing someone so much it hurts, if it brings to a halt to all the cheating, the total trust between you, then I guess I can have a fair shot at the answer. But love for someone is only part of a relationship – the biggest part without doubt – but there must be happiness too!

Happy ones do not have to worry about paying the bills – happy that the car will make it to the shops and back – a happiness that only money relieves! That I believe is the cause of so many worries, and the reason of too many failed marriages. It is also the answer to love for some women whose desire is money!

It has been my misfortune, some might say, to never crave for fame nor for fortune – in fact the talk of money I find repulsive. It is the cause of all trouble and apart from Religion – the reason for all wars! I have believed in the 'Provider', and when needed he has not let me down – well not yet anyway! Though I must admit, I have sailed a bit close to the wind on too many occasions.

Money sorts out your true friends and if anyone had a truer friend in Anita through the years, it is I. I also had friends waiting for me in St Lucia, and like the forces wife who knew she played second fiddle to the Army – I had to be gone!

1979 would be a year of Hurricanes – the first to form was 'Anna' – the earliest to arrive in a 100 years too! On June 21st a tropical depression had formed 400 miles East of the Windwards. Early on the 22nd it hadn't changed, only its position, now it was 275 miles, moving W.N.W 10 M.P.H. It wouldn't be until 22.00hrs that it was to be the first reported Hurricane of the season - now it was bearing down on us 110 miles due East with wind speeds at 55 knots – but in 110 miles that could all change, I knew. I also knew I was not in the best position to receive it!

It was rather late in the day to move back in to the Lagoon from whence I came, so I prepared to meet it outside hoping she would move North or at best – not increase in strength. Since my return to 'Jylland' on the 11th June, the problem of the bilges had gone from bad to worse. Trying to stem flows and the searching for them was difficult in the Lagoon with a visibility of two feet, so I had to move her outside to clear water which I did on the 18th.

Raising anchor had been fun and games, the mud inside held on to our anchors like a hungry Lion to its kill. Mushrooms are made for such ground and the only way to get them up and down was to 'Suck' them out - a link at a time with our old windlass. It would take us all morning and at 12.30, four and a half later with our Fisherman shackled back on, we were at anchor outside in the Bay on the 18th June. Now we could get at the Hull – but first it was how to handle that Hurricane?

I was awake early on the 23rd and waited anxiously for a weather report, or the expected wind! Visibility was poor and the rain just fell in torrents! For two hours the Atlantic dropped into the Caribbean, millions of tons that, but for a degree or so warmer, would have powered up the generator of all generators! And we didn't catch a drop! The centre had passed us, being 80 miles to the West by 08.00hrs and though it rained all day, it had passed - we had been lucky!

The constant attention to the Hull, all the patches nailed on in an attempt to stop the leaks, was rather soul destroying, especially when for all the effort, the time gained was relatively slight, from two and half hours – to three and a half hours. We would have to wait until dry-docking to find the problem. But when would that happen?

June was fast becoming July and still no news of any financial support from England. William had made a trip home to find the necessary funds to provide the dry-docking fees – the response we awaited. As for the crew and myself, we had been too long without wages and too long relying on hand outs from Will and Sharman to buy food! I felt I was fast becoming the one to be avoided – rather like the beggar on 5th Avenue who sees his only hope turn and walk down 4th.

It wouldn't be till the 3rd of July some news reached us of any respite to the constant worry! In my log I note the following: "Will came down for me – we went back to Roland's and waited on the call from Henry. The money we wanted for dry-docking has been cut from 20,000 to 13,000 pounds. This is due (he said) to Graham not being able to assure the bank of the contract to work in Spain yet – he wants another day to work on it which he was given! So if that comes off we'll get the rest. The 13,000 has been guaranteed by Henry!"

One may ask what had Graham to do with it – and why on Earth had Henry got himself involved! Graham, one must remember, had reneged on his part in the Panama contract, a contract that the bank was fully aware of I might add – it looked like pressure had been brought to bear on him for his shortfall of 20,000. His answer was rather like the Nassau answer from where I stood. "There's this guy I've met who'll give us more work than you can handle – only this time he lives in Spain!"

I was pretty certain my brother knew what he was doing, and sure of the consequences of his guarantees! Something the Bank couldn't make Graham give with his money now in Germany – hidden! Surely my brother would not be so foolish?

Far from the questions that needed answers, I had enough of my own worries to fill my head than concern myself with where, and from whom, the money was coming from.

My Log reads on 5th July: "Saw Will in the afternoon. Henry it seems doesn't want to send the money till the last moment (I can see why now!) he will do so when he knows the dry-docking date. This penny pinching is beyond me. Henry doesn't want it making money in Wills account, and him having to pay interest on the loan. I could understand that if we were talking many months – but money is needed now! How do they think I'm getting to Grenada? To Martinique, and how shall I pay for supplies that I need to get now – Timber, Oakum, Trenails, bottom paint, wedges, through fastenings, etc,etc! Maybe he thinks they can be picked off the shelf. For all the hard work that's to be done – stripping her out – not to mention getting her there – all done for nothing? Right now I'm sick of the whole bloody thing – if only there was an honourable way to get out from under this burden – but I'm stuck with it to the end – stuck as surely as Brier Rabbit to the Tar Baby! ----------Then, when I get so down on it all, I might come back to 'Jylland' at night quietly laying to her anchors looking the true little ship she is and say to myself – if I, your Captain, leaves – who'll hold the rest here? Then you'll surely die. I did more than any to instigate your buying and though it's not my fault you're here, I'll do my best to get you out – but the fight is hard – and I have no 'Arms' – Roll on tomorrow!" End of quote!

Will had asked Henry to make a visit to St Lucia – to see for himself the situation regarding the deal in St Martin, but he never did. In fact Henry had never sailed on 'Jylland' – never got involved other than financially!

All boats make but a hole in the sea in to which people throw their money the bigger the boat, the bigger the money. As many that made their fortunes from such, there are countless numbers that were financially ruined!

I would learn years later that Howard had warned Henry about getting involved – but he failed to listen to wise words – or had he other intentions on his mind, such as ownership?

John Compton had been in power since their Independence from Britain and for many years had held the reins of government with steady hands. I had met him on occasion, but we never spoke, that was left to Will and Sharman who saw him and his wife Janice more than I. That closeness led to a rumour – a rumour that involved the 'Jylland'. 1979 was another election year and Labour's quest for power had switched tac-tics. Having lost election after election, they had at last watched what Ol' Whitey does in such a situation. If you throw enough dirt – some is bound to stick! One piece of news to reach me in this run up for the prize was that the opposing party had fingered us, saying we had been chartered by Compton's government to bring in 'Arms' to put down any rebellion in a touch and go race.

By the 9th July, whether such rumours had any sway with the people didn't matter, but I'm certain all the promises from such hypocrites did, for Labour had won – much to their own surprise! It was a day of celebrations, wild ones for a people who really didn't care either way as long as there was a party after!

A party, I might add, that David Marchant nearly missed. Taking a Pee off the boarding ladder in the small hours he had a dizzy spell, tried grabbing a shroud, missed and fell. Before hitting the water, he hit the Boston Whaler, touching the bottom he wondered what the hell had happened. Pulled aboard by Tony Heath who heard the splash, he sat bruised, shaken and lucky that Tony had returned after I'd had gone to England. His plane was not as ready as first thought!

The coming months and the coming of Labour's promises, proved to the mob that voted for them, promises made must be kept! The 'New' St Lucia shall be a place where all are free to do as they please! The rapist can rape – and he did – the murderer can murder – and he did – and the robbers can rob – and they certainly did!

My brother Will and Sharman were held up at gunpoint outside a Pizza Parlour in Castries with demands for money (what else) but got Pizza instead - in the face. Will grabbed the $13.00 he'd given them as they fled empty handed.

Some fellows marched in to 'The Malabar' Hotel, demanding all the guests to get out; this is now our Island they said! Labour had told these fools, Hotels would become old people's homes, but only if they got in power! Promises made to fools, yet forgot to mention about certain rules, like who owns them?

With the certainty of funds to fix the schooner, my next task was to call those who would be needed. Bob Curry had gone home while I was in England – a phone call to him on the 10th of July saw him in a custody battle over his children – he would make it if he could, and such went for Bill his brother. Bill back in Nassau after delivering a 'Crate' (in his words) to that area – he couldn't make it through till the 29th, had to give two weeks' notice.

But what I did learn from him was that David and Jackie would be leaving us for Nassau – something Bill was aware of and long before I was informed of David's intentions.

When you think you know someone – think again! We tend to judge people by our own character, by what we know about ourselves in a given situation, if and when you are lucky enough to be given them!

David I had known for getting on two years and I thought I knew him – but I didn't! I honestly thought I could trust David – trust him enough to let me know his thoughts – but I was wrong! I had kept nothing back from the crew and all knew our position. In trust of such, I trusted all in return.

A cable from Bill Curry on the 3rd of July saying he'd call us on Saturday – but to tell David his ticket will be ready soon! It left me wondering! On the 7th July, a Saturday, true to form Bill called and, after our chat, confirmed with David a job was waiting for him in Nassau. What was plain to me now was, David had been writing to Bill asking about a job, and either out of embarrassment or a let's wait and see attitude – didn't inform me!

The two weeks' notice Bill had to give was never afforded me – why? Thus both David and Jackie left on the 12th for I had nothing to hold them – no two weeks wages – no prospects but a hard dry-docking and little but hope for the future.

It was a heavy blow and I realized an important factor about life – loyalty for some comes in a packet!

I guess, looking back on it 34 years after the event – I expected too much of people! David was only deciding his future before informing me, a certainty before leaving an uncertainty. A good meal every night before going to bed, no more diving on the hull for nothing! And wages too! It is self-interest, self-survival, that is more important than honour to your friends, your shipmates, and to trust your friends to understand your position - can you? It is not the pain of them departing, more the pain of being let down when they are gone that hurts.

The day before David left 'Bob' arrived – not the Curry Bob but a Hurricane Bob. This one hit the Gulf – dumping a lot of Caribbean shit on America this time, while America was dumping its shit elsewhere – Skylab!

India was in panic that the Space station might hit them, while engineers tried to ease all fears saying the Ocean is much bigger than the Earth – meanwhile it hits western Australia!

The day David and Jackie left – I would too! Not for Nassau, but for Martinique. Dia Neale had offered to take me in 'Ty-Bach' to see the manager of the dry-dock to make arrangements for 'Jylland' – an offer I took due to the lack of funds to fly there!

We would leave at 17.45 leaving Geoff and Tony aboard. It was an easy passage and we dropped anchor at Grand Anse D'arlet at 23.00hrs to spend the night, before entering Fort-du-France the next morning to clear Customs! It was strange for me to be aboard a small craft, not having to worry about watching the bilge, to be able to sleep all night in peace for a change – but I realized it wasn't to be the same for Geoff and Tony, being a man light.

Sleep for them would be a broken one. The time to pump her when I left was still around 3 to 4 hours. Had it not been for Tony's company aboard while I was in England – Geoff would have gone insane! Tony had got his money okay – but as yet no plane! He'd often say to Geoff, "Let's go for a beer?" and off they'd pop to the Holiday Inn – always on Tony too, which was not to Geoff's liking, nor fault. Not tonight though, they wouldn't have time to get one down before pumping time was due!

It was up early on the 13th and after a quick cuppa, hauled the anchor aboard and made for Fort-du-France. Cleared Customs and sorted out my arrangements; Bottom paint, Ballast, Caulkers and dry-docking for the 6th August, all in the morning. Not wanting to push Dia to return that day we would leave the next! So we motored across the bay to Joinville, an area of hotels and beaches where we spent that afternoon and evening.

By the time we had downed another cuppa , we were underway around 06.30 on a lovely morning that turned in to a lovely day. The sail back with a nice breeze was a tonic. We arrived at Rodney Bay at 13.00 to find Geoff leaning over the rail, glad to see us back! Just one problem, someone had stolen our gas tank from the whaler.

With the 6th of August in mind – one month away, it was a date to fix my mind upon rather than the continuous diving on the hull. The bilges were staying about 3 hours, and try as I may, I couldn't improve upon it! I hadn't heard from Bob Curry as to whether he could make it for the dry-docking but Bill sent a cable on the 16th of July saying he couldn't get down till the 14th August – can we wait on him? We could but could 'Jylland'? Not to mention changing the date.

The third storm of the season came on the 17th – 'Claudette' was situated 60 miles due east of Barbuda moving N.N.W and, being no threat to us, we continue preparing 'Jylland' for a complete overhaul. But on that day, it was again in the water searching for leaks! Log reads that day: "Pumped a couple of bottles up and yet again spent some time in the water – the bilge problem is not allowing me time to do some stripping down. I really need a hand. It's the mental strain as much as anything. I found a couple of holes and patched some suspect areas – and to my surprise got an extra 15 minutes!" End of quote. 15 minutes doesn't sound much, but satisfying after spending hours and getting nowhere. I was still baffled as to how and where it was getting in, for outward signs said the hull was in pretty good shape – little did I know. Wisdom comes from experience!

Henry called on the 17th, wanted us to wait for Bill and said that Howard would be out on the first available flight to help out – some good news! We continued, Tony, Geoff and I with the task at hand! That task of stripping her out involved those cement bags that were disintegrating. To get at them, and do a proper job, was to strip her down inside completely. A big change round to the interior was considered necessary afterwards, for the main concern was outside not in!

On the 18th July 1979 John Compton's party held a meeting in town. This was to thank those that had voted for them. We had got reports there was some shooting going on too! A couple of things I'd heard on the radio were that the new government was setting up a committee to look in to the 'misuse' of funds by the Compton party. A ploy used to gain support – the old point the finger game while they misuse their own! Also, ex-pats will not be welcome (Mugabe tactics) and with all the other Islands involved, set up a joint agriculture program.

Talk was of more schools and free hospitals! It all was just talk, and it all came to nothing! Only fools believe such talk, and a fool is always a fool, and the educated fool, the biggest fool of them all. It is not only illiterate people that are taken in by bullshit – offer anything for free and people will take it! The only thing free in this world (for now!) is the air we breathe!

I had a nice surprise on the 19th of July. Fritz and Jeannine came in on 'Dragonessa'. We had become friendly with them in St Martin and their presence made a nice change to our conversation round the table at night. 'Dragonessa' was a pretty new vessel that both had crewed over from Europe. Fritz was now in charge and Jeannine (with new baby) stayed on as the only crew.

How Fritz got the money to own this 50 footer, who knew or cared, let alone ask! We are all novices when it comes to the sea, for the sea is the only master. I would fear being with those who think otherwise. If I was in my 10th year of learning, Fritz was definitely in his first and he knew it. Sailing the Caribbean is a good place to get your grades – no tides of any great range and trades blowing from the right quarter most of the time and it allows you to get the feel of your vessel before venturing out in to the Atlantic.

Fritz had one problem, he always anchored outside me in St Martin. Outside and slightly upwind of us! He believed that where 'Jylland' anchored, he was safe. This made it difficult for us to clear him at times. Cranking in our anchor, by the time it was up we were abreast of him. Without an engine (for it was down at the time) passing him was a case of wind direction – for it could be fickle at times, as it wound itself round the old hill fort that once guarded this bay.

Once having made up your mind, it is best to stick with your plans! Before breaking free the anchor, the mizzen was set, main and fore sail hoisted but their pecks left un-canted. The staysail was up and ready and headsails lay prepared to be hoisted. To bring her off on the port tack - our working anchor being on the port side - could make life difficult if a good wind caught you and you started to drag.

The helm lashed hard to starboard would drive her round in such a situation. Backing the staysail and mizzen when her head was up, it was a matter of getting the anchor up and leave. Having dragged a little further than usual, the decision to pass him ahead or go past his stern had been made before the anchor had been broken out. I would go past his stern! Or would I?

It looked very much like we could go past his bow once underway. Sails now pulling, 'Jylland' dug in pretty fast. While catting the anchor took at least two men, inner and outer Jibs would we hoisted at the same time, while the peaks were raised on fore and main! A 'what to do?' situation arose for I was now closing in on him fast – fast enough to cut him in half!

Made fast amidships till raised, the mainsails were doing their job, drawing her to windward! I had to think fast – unlashing the helm I threw it hard to port and lashed it, then rushed to the mainsheet and let it fly, as I'd done with the mizzen. Fritz had been watching us get underway – he usually did – and as I passed his stern, close enough for a stretched out handshake I might add, he shouted something I didn't quite hear. I was probably thinking of the consequences of my bobstay sawing through him. I could just see him hanging on the end of it, leaving in my wake Jeannine holding the baby, where moments before she was happy cooking breakfast!

"I've only been wrong once in my life, that's when I thought I was wrong, but was right!" For just one brief moment I believed I could pass him ahead! I asked him many times to give me room to manoeuvre, but I guess he liked the view from outside us – passing sometimes to windward, sometimes behind him. After this close encounter he did, but only once I told him just how close he was to a view he wouldn't forget!

Getting her underway without an engine, our working anchor should have been the starboard one, but changing 'Big Bertha' over was not thought necessary. When leaving Rendezvous Bay this worked in our favour. I should have let her drag further before breaking out the anchor, but seamanship is all about having another chance to learn!

On a return from an evening cruise, when the wind was very light, to gain the anchorage I used to get one of the boys to give us a push with the whaler. In the calm waters with 'Jylland' moving slowly ahead, a slight nudge was all that was necessary to keep her moving. Creeping slowly up to the position, sails luffing and doing nothing but hang there, Fritz was amazed of her sailing abilities, not seeing the whaler under the stern. "It's those Vikings for you Fritz," I said, "they knew more about building boats than they let on!"

Chapter 62: July '79

It was on the 24th of July that Tony learnt his plane was ready at last and would be leaving us on Friday. Tony Heath had been a good companion and had kept the conversation going when times got one down. It would leave just Geoff and I now to take care of 'Jylland' – less to feed on a ship without money or food!

We had figured the need of timber for her hull to be around 300 feet – but where to get 12"x 3" and in long lengths was the problem. All St Lucia had to offer was 12" x 1 ½" so I called Phil Ark, Anita's brother-in-law in Puerto Rico, on the 26th to see if he could find something. By 31st he had what was required which would be sent to Martinique on the 6th of August, to arrive on the 8th - cost $415.00.

Things were hotting up in St Lucia about this time. The elected Labour party had made certain promises to people they couldn't keep and, not only that, had arranged a 'Little coup' if things didn't turn out the way they had.

Before the elections they had armed the Rasters, we heard, and now wanted those arms back! Hard to believe, for Rastafarians are a peaceful bunch in all, but rumours were rife in those days. The local Police had been dis-armed for reasons of their support to Compton's U.W.P (United Workers Party) and to halt a supposed counter move against the now Labour Party.

The police were as disrespected as any at the time, despised even, and at a very low ebb – one of their own had been shot a few nights ago. As I'd predicted it would, for fear of their own existence and that the arms given may be turned on those who had obviously lied, they - the Labour Party - had rearmed the Police with the request of "Go get 'em boys!!!"

They were seen patrolling the streets of Castries now with 'Machine Guns', which of course brought with it a little more respect! It was still rather dangerous in town – Will and Dia had a knife pulled on them when someone tried to steal their Mini-Moke. When shopping, your car best be never left unattended.

For the safety of his boat, Dia pulled 'Ty Bach' alongside when he left her during the day and we put aboard the shotgun and rifle, just in case things got out of hand.

What with trying to organize dry-docking, the materials for it and the preparation inside, diving on the hull were still a part of everyday life. They speeded up for no apparent cause and searching a dirtier hull became a frustrating headache.

For both Geoff and I, sleep was a two-hour sifts at times – we needed help! That wouldn't happen till the 6th of August when Howard and Dennis arrived. On the 8th, and unexpectedly, Bill Curry arrived – "Good old Bill!" says my log at the time.

By the 9th I wrote "Things are coming together slowly". I also note on the same day, "Dennis has hired a 'Suzuki' jeep while here for running around – money once so very scarce – will go fast if carelessly used!" Howard had moved aboard the day after his arrival, but not Dennis!

So his excuse to do the 'running around' was more for his enjoyment than for the boats. Things didn't change - nor would it whenever it came to such things - and for the sake of an argument, yet again he was allow the freedom of his choosing!

Anita and Helen had returned on the 30th July. Anita's presence had brought a great relief, mentally and physically. We hadn't seen one another since the 8th of June, and for a man whose eyes were once upon every girl – I had found it difficult to concentrate on one without seeing the other.

One night, all gone ashore, we sat under a gibbous moon – across the water drifted the music from the Yacht Club and that of the Holiday Inn. The music was 'Just When I needed You Most' – and right then and there, what I needed most had arrived. I knew then, whatever would be the outcome, nothing would part us!

I had been able to concentrate on scrubbing the hull now Bill and Howard had arrived, and it was on the 10th August when I completed this and I found what I believed to be the problem that had kept Geoff and I awake for so many nights. Under one patch, put on without any backing, water flowed in at a good pace – but it still failed to slow. It wasn't until I had put on my third bottle of the day that I found yet another – another patch that leaked so badly I had to replace it with a much bigger one. In one moment, the bilges went from 2 ½ hours to 5 and the thought at the time was it would be simple to put right!

"Bill arrived on the late Eastern flight – had every confidence he would not let me down!!" Such I wrote on the 13th August. Both of the Curry boys, Bill and Bob, were not the sort to turn away when faced with a challenge, whatever that challenge may be! Both Bill and I, similar in our ideas for what 'Jylland' was all about, clung to that position in an idealistic fashion. Both of us hated this charter business – to us it was prostitution for the sake of cash alone!

We wanted her in a position to be admired for what she was, by people who knew and understood about wooden boats – not ridden just for the thrill of the quick ride by holidaymakers not knowing a ship from a schooner, or a Barque from a Brig.

The very reason both answered the calling was for the 'Jylland's' sake, nothing else. A man could never wish for such companions, and only at times such as this – through all the stress and the strains – could anyone say they have met such people.

Millions of people nowadays, sit behind desks punching away at life on computers, never knowing the mind behind the face of he or she opposite. They go home to their mortgages and hardly speak to wives, let alone know her! Who can when the stress and the strains pulls you apart rather than together. You can tell more about a man by working with him for a week, than you can by talking to him for a year! In that sense, I worked with two great fellows whose actions spoke louder than words!

The money eventually arrived on the 15th August. Word came by telegram saying it had been sent on the 19th July to New York. Nearly a month to inform us of its arrival in Will's account there! With all the last bits and pieces brought aboard, and bits taken ashore, we would leave for Martinique at 01.00 hrs on the 19th August – none too soon!

Chapter 63: Dry-dock Martinique

As if knowing our problem, the weather stayed fair for her crossing to Martinique. The slight Easterly breeze throughout that night was kind to her. With what sails we could hoist, we made slow progress – averaging just 3 ½ knots. It would take a couple of good blasts of air to start up the engine, and though ahead was hard to achieve due to the fork problem, the old girl sounded just find. We dropped anchor at Fort-de-France at 10.30 on the 19th of August 1979 – the day before we were due to enter the dry-dock – the day I had waited for so long had nearly arrived.

The 20th came and with it an early start. Both Bill and Dennis took a run to see if all was okay to enter the dock and, being so, we raised anchor and at 07.30 started our slow approach… till…Nothing! Our progress was halted soon after putting her ahead – the fork had broken! Hastily we cut wedges and with them I dived in to the engine room and drove them home – this gave us less ahead than before, but we were moving. In such a position I stayed while Bill eased her in alongside, very slowly, for we had no astern. Making fast with lines ashore, we had arrived!

We would be just one of four boats on the ways. One, a fishing boat about our size but steel built, and two smaller sailing craft, one being 'Dragonessa', the reason for Fritz coming to St Lucia.

It would be a long slow progress in getting them set up in position before pumping out the dock could begin. As 'Jylland' settled, Bill and I put on tanks and slipped wedges under her keel. 4½" amidships to nothing as she slowly went down on the way.

Her hogging from the Barbados mistake had increased to 12" – ballasting and refastening we hoped would hold her. We had made up treenails in St Lucia, Greenheart and Pitch pine, which were to hold the new planking and do the job of refastening.

Such had been used since ships were first built but because of the time it took to make them, drive and wedge had dismissed this from shipbuilding.. It is far quicker to drive in a boat nail, yet nails are less superior and in time, cause a blemish called, naturally, 'Nail Rot' – wood is a living thing, and wood does not reject a fastening of the same nature!

It is difficult now to write about those times – the feeling of relief to be on the ways, of no more worries about pumping every moment of the day and night, and though we wouldn't be totally dry in the dock till the 21st it was, none the less, a great feeling to be there at last!

There was so much to do and, though we would be on for two weeks, so little time to achieve all we had planned. Our main concern was the hull, then how to hold her from hogging so badly. It was thought a whale built inside her was the answer, yet the cost to build such had to be considered. I was in charge of the finances – an unenviable job to say the least. Will had given me $2,950 when in St Lucia, changing $1,000 dollars in to Francs, of which $2,000 went on supplies. After other small bits and pieces that needed paying for, I was left with $930.00. Such a large boat – and such a deep Hole! Lucky I was to have Jeanine with me to translate, for all spoke French except I. It would have been handy to have had Will with us to do such running around, but he couldn't make it, and a note in my Log says: "If we all didn't – 'Jylland' would be at the bottom now!" Thursday 23rd August, quote from Log: "A day of ups and downs. Funny how you can mentally defeat yourself if you allow the vastness of work get on top of you. One must be able to brush it aside when it's only you that has to do it!

It started this day with Bill's help taking the rudder off to enable us to take out the engine shaft (this I'd like to take out for good!) Had to slam in wedges to start her moving – holding it with the Mizzen sheet. Got stopped by Dennis who asked me "Come look at this?" He had started ripping off the Planking. His depressed state brought me down. Worm! ...on the inside!! Scalloped out between each frame, a type of gribble had eaten her nearly through in places.

Thought it best to stop all engine room work because the money might be needed on the hull! Would not have been so bad if the first one taken off looked like the last of the day, for by then they looked healthier.

We reckon now we'll need about 400' – if only it wasn't such a rush!

I went to see about our timber at G.C.M – what a pain – spent the whole afternoon messing around with customs just because I didn't have an invoice. All week I've been unable to do anything constructive – felt very frustrated. But I'm up again – evening now, another day tomorrow!" End of quote. So at last the truth had come about as to why we failed to find anything on the outside!

If Thursday had been a blow, Friday would knock me down. The timber, once extracted from customs after paying them 500 francs for not having an invoice, turned out to be totally useless!! 12" x 3", 252 feet long - useless!

Pine – a pile of shit one couldn't get rid of, had been sent us from Puerto Rico. So bad was it, that one wouldn't use it to walk upon – drive over it yes – but never safe enough to use. Had Frank Singleton purposely sent this load of crap? Payback time? Was it the boats fault to do such a thing?

$1,000 down the drain too. We had gambled on that men wouldn't do such a thing, not to a boat, and had lost! Such was that loss, she now sat with her bare frames and us without a stick to apply to them! The bill that seemed outstanding at the shipyard – which I knew nothing of – paid us back okay! Without time to think, both Dennis and Bill rushed off to try and locate something while the others quietly cleaned off the frames ready for what they might achieve. I went to bed that night very tired!

The sand blasting of her topsides that began on the 22nd was followed by water blasting her underwater area on the 23rd. That was when the true extent of our problems were revealed. The high water pressure was not only blasting off all growth, but also knocking holes through seams one could pass their hand through.

Had we been able to see beneath her inside ceiling we would have seen the problem. It was then, and only then, did we understand why boats that sailed in these waters on a regular basis, tarred their insides thoroughly.

My brother Will arrived on the 24th August, that being a Friday – he and Dia Neale had sailed over for the weekend for a little look-see. Though Wills fingers were still a problem, his assistance at such a time was sorely missed. Eight of us had our work cut out – Bob, Bill, Geoff, Howard, Dennis and Tim Verdant (one of the fellows that worked with Will) made up the men's team – while Anita, Helen and Sonny (later) pulled for the women.

We would add one more member to the men's side – Brooks! Brooks Frazier arrived on the evening of the 24th on an invite from Bill, who was quite surprised to see him as we were!

He had sailed over from Amsterdam with Bill on the 'Crate' and tales of the Caribbean and old ships had fascinated this geologist so much, he just had to come see for himself. Had he seen what he was up against beforehand, he might have gone to ground one might say! But Brooksie turned his hand in without asking why first, and became one of us – just like Tim. Tim Verdant, the only West Indian we had aboard. Tim had sat quietly alone for the first few days, till he realized he was part of a team – and was treated no different than anyone aboard! We had no time to think of differences, to concentrate on a man's colour – Tim worked as hard as any, so was treated him like any. Tim would always appreciate his time with us – and appreciate all who made him feel at home!

Another thing was sailing towards us too at that time – a rather large Hurricane!

Will and Dia left on Sunday, and reports reached us on the Monday that Hurricane 'David' had formed.

Mon 27th August 1979, I write: "Heard today the first big one of the year has formed. This one being my namesake, and it's situated due East of Barbados near 12 degrees North. Wind strength 110 mph plus, with a good chance of an increase.

If she does – or rather he does decide Martinique is the place to strike, it will be certainly catch us with our pants down. The water has only to rise six feet and it'll be in on us like Niagara Falls! Tomorrow we shall have to see its position and track and take what action is necessary. Strike yard – topmasts and clear the decks – guy lines ashore. Living aboard might be impossible if she gets close – but where to go could be a problem also!" End of quote.

Saturday and Sunday had been hard work. Dennis had been lucky in finding some timber and arranged for 400' to be delivered. If anyone could, he would. Searching for a needle in a haystack or the Holy Grail – if it was there, he'd find it! To help hold her shape – trunnelling had begun. These were placed at 2' centres on her topsides, being an inch in diameter, and wedged. Greenheart above the waterline, Pitch Pine beneath was decided due to Greenhearts lack of absorption of water.

The firm we had hired to do the caulking – Grants – had also started and seemed to be moving well, ripping out old stuff and replacing with the new bale we had brought over from St Lucia. We were on our way, but for that Hurricane!

I write on Tuesday 28th August: "A day I'll always remember – the Day we sunk 'Jylland'. Sunk her for her own safety. The weather report this morning gave 'David' an even better chance of hitting Martinique – and with a bit more wind in his lungs than yesterday.

The centre was situated just East of Barbados 12.7 North with sustained winds of over 150 M.P.H. A Low of 932 – said to be the worst storm of the century.

Her West by North drift looks like it will hit St Lucia or us. We asked the management here what they intend to do – having got the answer after lunch that they might have to flood the dock – we had to get off all that was moveable and stow it in one of their sheds.

Obviously we didn't need this Hurricane, for all work came to a halt – decks cleared and personal gear ashore into a hotel, somewhere safe!

This we found by ringing someone we knew in the American Embassy. Given the name of the Hotel 'Victoria' – high above the town and made of concrete – how strong we have yet to find out! It is now 23.00 hrs. – I'm in the Hotel surrounded by electrical tools and all our bags. Terlin (the dock manager) decided to flood at 22.00hrs!" End of quote! We had left her snugged down on the ways – made fast by her throat halyards.

It was not until the 31st that work could commence. The Hurricane had moved to the North and west of us, leaving us with a force 9 yet delivering Dominica a most terrible blow. Enough to cause it to be classed a disaster area. 200 boats were lost in the Northern area of Martinique – Eric Taberly lost 15 so we heard.

They had started pumping out the dock on the Thursday, leaving behind it the mess as imagined – such a mess that we would have to be housed in the shed we had put our bits in. Under such diverse conditions we lived and, but for the right companions, the sufferings would have been too much.

Filthy toilets, sleeping on floors and cooking with bottle gas – not to mention thieves who preyed on us while asleep! It was all very trying, yet we kept at it! Had I the time to think, or had just a touch of foresight, I should have realized it was all for nothing, but I was not the only one blinded to the cause – and that cause was an old wooden boat! Such loyalty by my companions made it very clear to me that they were the type that would see all safely in the lifeboats, then found it was too late to save themselves! Such were my friends!

In the rush to catch up on 'business as usual', the dry-dock had informed us they would like us to move by Thursday 6th September – just five days away – a "fuck you" attitude!
I noted on the 31st August: "Jylland is having a fine job done on the caulking – it's a pleasure to watch craftsmen!" By the time we moved forward on the 6th September – our caulkers never returned. Either pissed off for the second time by the flooding or that they had found work elsewhere – no one said! Boxes, irons and mallets had left, and with them the men whose steady rhythm was a joy to watch.

I understood the reason, but not the sudden abandoning of ethics. One flooding was enough, two was too much, caulk marks had vanished, oakum had swollen from seams and tainted by dirty water, but it wasn't our fault!! It left us in the shit – and left yet another job to do!

By that time all the new planking was on but caulking wasn't completed. In less than 5 days Dennis had not only got the boards, but also had cut them and had them on too.

Coming behind him we fastened them with trunnels – their holding power second to none! The caulkers were doing a fine job, but the rush to move them on a bit was as frustrating for them as us! When the locks were flooded, but for the sake of a couple of days, we would have had them all completed.

We had decided to place some cokes in her scarves and upper boarding inside. This was in an attempt to stop the slide of her ceiling planking. With pumps aboard and our hearts in our mouths we waited! My log then reads: 5th September, "With the flooding tomorrow, it's been one mad rush to get her ready, All the seams that are caulked, must be painted at least, to keep some of the water out. Wooden ships now have to take second place to steel, for they can be up and down in no time. Every ones waiting on us, but we'll hang it out as long as possible. By late evening, we still had caulking to do, what doesn't get done will have to wait till the morning. One problem here is supplies, Pitch for seams etc!"

The 6th September: "Up early 06.00hrs to get last of seams caulked. Brought pumps aboard in case of problems! At 09.15hrs dock was starting to fill, Took a long time to get the others moved out! We moved forward and in position first, by the time all the messing around went on, it was certain we wouldn't be down on the ways till morning - very slow here!" Didn't get down till 17.00hrs on the 7th, but for some reason they stopped pumping at 18.00hrs before the dock was dry, and in the evening were totally switched off, not even keeping pace with the in-flow. Electrical problem someone said.

It would not be till Saturday the 8th September before we were settled once more upon the ways – or so we believed – yet another surprise lay in store for us before work could commence. I write on that day: "This dry-docking is one I'll always remember. 'Jylland' and ourselves are taking a real battering. This morning at 07.30 when I checked the bilges I could hardly believe my eyes. The water was above the Cooker – 6 feet must have come back in the dock during the night. Either their pumps were blocked or turned off! Most of the electrical tools are below water – my wallet – money – Passports and guns all in the safe. The Oakum Tim got to allow us to work over the weekend – ruined!"

The pumps had failed – an electrical fault and a manning fault – no watchman as such to report on the problem! Though to bring a lighter note to our troubles, the watchman they had brought a smile to our faces at a time most needed. This elderly fellow employed as a night watchman was seen roaming the place at times when it was totally un-necessary; at the close of our work period, washing up time, that time when thieves are all asleep or getting ready for the nights work. You just heard a whistle, then another, then following the whistle out of the evening air came our night watchman!

He was not as dark as some. and at one time or another his mother had come across a Frenchman doing up his trousers that, on seeing her thought, "Well, why not?" The result stood before us whistle in hand!

It had brought to a halt two younger fellows on their way to the shower who tried to ask him what the problem was! He spoke to them in short and long blasts, pointing with his one free hand for them to come to heel! Rather bewildered by it all, they first looked at us, then at this obviously authoritative person blowing his whistle. Having found out their intentions, due to the towels and soap in their hands, he whistled one long blast to say all's okay. He wished to show us he was on the ball, if not on the Rum after lights out!

That shower by the way was for the use of crewmembers that were unable to use their own due to obvious reasons. We found it at times left in such a state that one wonders why people didn't use the toilets – till one looked at the toilet! Left in the middle of the shower pan was one huge dollop, still steaming – the smell of which I'll leave to your imagination!

Monday 10th, Bill found out they wanted to flood again on Thursday, 3 days to put right what damage the last sinking did. Oh! Yes, and could we then also leave, for they are fully booked! Telling him the only way we were leaving was by plane, he gave us another 8 days.

Wednesday 12th of September shows what we were up against, My logs reads: "A day of pushing ahead trying to get 'Jylland's' hull ready for tomorrows flooding. Spent all day caulking with Bill, Howard and an old local boy. Bit of a rush still, we always seem to have the problem! Seams caulked and not pitched, are being sprayed by the painter, making it difficult to see what's been done and what hasn't. The seams soaked by the last flooding will have to be pulled - swollen and soaked that pitch won't adhere!!!!"

At 12.30 with the dock virtually full we moved aside and let those ahead of us out. All made of steel and all painted up for another season – with them went Fritz and 'Dragonessa'. We moved ahead, behind us was positioned a French Naval vessel (the obvious reason for the rush for us to move) – a tug towing a dredger barge that had been sunk in the storm was next – a local fishing boat and two sloops.

By the time all were in, it was pretty obvious the dock would not be pumped dry – so for us it was bilge watches again! Pumping out with a large electric one borrowed from the dock! What was coming in was slight, but came from un-caulked seams in the madness of it all!

One thing we did notice was the strain the Cokes were taking. Upon rising these 3" square Oak blocks had tried to shear across the grain – forward and after ones the most noticeable. We decided to make them 6" by 3" now! Though we had not had time to finish what was intended, she rose far prettier than before, her lines holding!

Jylland in dry dock Martinique, August 1979
Her hull is being refastened with treenails to alleviate the hog

Some work ahead of us boys!!

Being prepared for hurricane David - me lowering the top mast

Chapter 64: September -79

David Simmons was to be the insurance agent that had been employed by Bayle-Martin and Faye to assess the damage. Living the life of Reilly in Antigua, he and Bill Fowler had teamed up to become 'their men on the spot' one might say.

He didn't arrive till the 13th of September, two weeks later, it had been a busy and profitable business this hurricane! On a tour with my brother Howard, a rough assessment of $50.000,00 was considered – and he would inform our company that funds should be sent immediately! The next day, before he left for Antigua, the price was settled on $52,000.00.

Much to our concern, least to our surprise, we would learn that part of that sum was sent to Antigua with the wording from Ray Alston, quote: "The money is not, I repeat, not to be made available to F.D.Hamber!"

Mr Alston told Dennis, on calling him in London and confronting on such, that he meant no malice, but was directed by the underwriters as to their requirements! He added, "We were very fortunate how quickly they responded to our plight!" Not as quickly as they stuck our fees in their banks for ten years one might presume!!
I note on that day I said: "This gives us the task of wheedling it out of their hands!" Those in Antigua, and some wheedling it took too!

There were three things we couldn't remove at the time of the Hurricane. The main engine, of course, the generator and the ships radio, it being the large sailor type!

With all there was to think about when making a claim, there is always much you will miss which is obvious after the event. Diesel tanks, water tanks, batteries, water damaged caulking, seams swollen – etc.!

The first thing to get on with was the main engine, cleaned down and running. It was suggested by Mr Simmons on his initial visit that we should get outside help – stripped down for a complete overhaul. Taking Simmons on his word here, Bill had gone ahead and hired someone.

As I had been left in charge of funds, I insisted on a price first. The two fellows came up with 8,000 Francs. Deciding our money would soon be gone at that rate, we had to do it ourselves! The fellows left with 300 Francs for their trouble! The radio and generator would be supplied from Antigua. Not knowing who would supply it and when that would appear, we concentrated on other projects – for time was moving on, and we were moving know where.

What I never understood was, why come up with a settlement figure if that settlement was left to the likes of Mr Simmons to settle on our behalf. It was I that had insisted on a price to overhaul the engine, so what was I doing negotiating two days after he left and I found it exorbitant!

We were in a bad enough position as it was, extortion was on the lips and ideas of all in such situations. As yet, we had received nothing from our insurers – and here we were being asked to get the main engine completely overhauled without first asking for a price? Ludicrous – it was a ripping off process of underwriters by all concerned except those it was intended for!

Sometimes luck comes your way, you meet it in a form where least expected too! 'Jylland' needed ballast, not the concrete kind – something small enough to handle but heavy enough to go between the floor space. The last of the slimy bags had been taken ashore stinking from the diesel after the flooding and what to replace it had to be found!

We had asked about it before leaving for Martinique and had been told there was a large consignment of it here, gathered from the old sugar Mills – all ready and waiting to be shipped to Chicago.

It was obvious the two fellows near this large heap of iron were French, but without Jeanine to interpret it might be difficult in making us understood. Dennis as usual, decided to have a go!

"Excuse me!" he said, at the two who were in some discussion.

"This metal – whose is it?"

"Bon!" replied the older fellow looking up.

"This metal", continued my brother pointing at the large heap, "whose is it?"

The older fellow shrugged his shoulders – clearly not understanding the English.

Deciding upon speaking more clearly and far slower as we do in such situations, Dennis was certain he had their attention now.

"T-h-i-s m-e-t-a-l. W-h-o-s-e i-s i-t?" and grabbing a piece held it up for them to look at.

"La we monsieur, champ blur!!!!" the man replied, again with that shrug of the shoulders and that look of a right unhelpful bastard!

"Leave it!" said Howard "Wait till we find someone who can translate!"

"Naa!" said Dennis, and he continued till even he gave in.

We started to walk away when the older fellow shouted at us something not quite understood. He walked up to us – put his mouth close to Dennis's ear and said "What do you want you c- - t!" in the very same accent as my brother.

What could one do but laugh – laugh out loud too. He had got us – just like we might have got him on another day. It is the humour that is so hard to understand by all but the British!

Dave (and I can't think of his last name) was here on a contract for Thomas Ward, scraping all the sugar mills and workshops, and in the coming days would help us to Ballast 'Jylland' – men, iron the lot. I never did find out was it French he spoke that day – then how would I know?

One of the smaller craft that had followed us to the Dock was called 'Cilin' – a pretty little craft too. All heard the loud crack – and looking, saw her mast had broken in two! She been positioned not on the ways but alongside the lower tier – the chock under her 'nose' had not been fixed properly – slipping, she fell on it.

We all felt so sorry for the owner – for we knew the feeling of the incompetence that surrounded us. Where the hell was he going to get a new mast from in the Caribbean? Insurance might pay for that, but not for the aggravation – the messing up of his plans – our plans! One bad worker in a group of good taints the whole bunch – who can you trust but your own!

As you can't judge a book by its cover – nor can you by the clothes a man wears! Professional people – from Doctors and Lawyers to Generals, they need the uniform to hide the idiot from the idiot who believes in all they say. Question any and you are doomed!

Chapter 65: Bill the Badger

Bill worked for Simmonds, or with Simmonds I wasn't quite sure. Bill Fowler had decided some time in his life to keep his mouth firmly shut! He came down soon after David Simmons had left to do a structural survey of 'Jylland' – our underwriters requested it after the damage done. What was strange to me, no quote was given for this work which we had to pay for out of the Insurance claim. The seaworthiness certificate later required by our insurers before the trip to Grenada, and something I knew nothing of until after the sinking, should have been done at the same time, or after we were ready for leaving the dock. Not left for over 8 months before a request was made!

With flat cap and awl he scratched and poked like a 'Badger' for a day. The scratching of timber was replaced by the scratching of pen as he made notes – notes that were not for our eyes, not yet, but those who place their bets on us – the underwriters!

Bill Fowler had a character perfect to match that of his accomplice, Simmonds. He could be anything in the professions that require a man to be aloof in his own knowledge and thought that he knows all, knows best, and knows how to read. He won't compromise, won't argue, won't listen to any other than his superiors, or those whose books better his opinion.

There is not a book written on common sense, so he lacks it through reading too much. The saying 'Education is for those that read books, while the rest must learn common sense!' fitted him to a tee! Of course one can say, by the sinking. Mr Fowlers report proved his point on certain issues. But it was not 'Slight softening of deck beam ends' or any of the points he brought up in that report. It was through lack of urgency, lack of his partners willingness to depart with our money, lack of peoples help to get her back quickly on dry dock, lack of care by those who were responsible for not looking upon her as an old lady who needed help, they were really to blame for her going!

Bill the Badger said not a word, not a dickey bird! I wondered just how much he knew, how many old schooners he'd surveyed. I wished to ask him but he said nothing. Words might just show his capabilities I thought! Bill would obviously scratch another note, one to his own company, when he got back to Antigua. 'For work carried out to the Schooner 'Jylland'… followed by a load of other scratching which ended with the bill from Bill - paid by us from the money sent them by our underwriters. We never saw that bill either. Somehow in some way, it all seemed wrong!

Chapter 66: At Last

We were supposed to leave the dock on the 24th September, but the word came it would be the next day instead. It gave us time to go over all the spots missed by the spraying from 'Camic'- the company employed for the job to sand blast and paint the hull. Complaints to Mr Oger the manager of a rough piece of workmanship only brought us 10 gallons of 'Hempels' and a paintbrush – plus the usual shrug of the shoulders!

So it would not be until the 25th September, two months, that we had done all we could and were ready to leave the dry-dock. We were certainly not ready to leave for St Lucia, but at least we could get out of that place. Howard and Geoff were still working on the Main engine – waiting for the pump and injectors – until we had those we weren't going anywhere. We also were not going anywhere until we had some money to pay bills. The request of $14,000.00 we had asked for on the 20th had come to nothing, and on the day of our leaving this bloody hole – still nothing. So much for Ray Alston and his 'quick response'!

I wrote that day quote! "A slow day. Waited all morning and most of the afternoon to get out of the dock – mostly due to the barge taking their time – tugs in and out towing. 'Jylland' came off the ways with the lines in her – the same as when we first got her. If they stay – it will be a big achievement!" End of quote! In an attempt to remove the hogging we had removed the large water tanks from forward – weighing 4 tons when full – anchor lockers had been moved further aft. Refastening and with iron ballast – approximately 40 tons amidships – she looked well! I just hoped she'd hold. We all felt rather tired yet elated in a sense to get out of that place. Though we would lay alongside the area, we would at least be afloat.

David Simmons arrived on the 27th. The first thing he did, being in charge of our money, was buy us a Honda generator – a temporary substitute for the promised Onan he had in 'mind' for us. He squared away all dry-docking bills and left us with $10,000 in traveller's cheques, in which we had one hell of a job changing - there being a run on the dollar at the time. 3.98 against 4.10 some days before. We lost 700F on that deal when the dry-dock took them, giving us the going rate!

There was just one bright spot – we caught the thief! He had struck a few times, mostly when the boys were asleep dead-beat from the hard hot work! First he got Bob for 1400F on the 11th September. Next, on the 21st September he decided to rifle the after cabin and stole Helens handbag with the shopping money and over $400 from Bill.

It would seem the Curry boys were being picked on. I had decided that a few bottles fastened together by thread and set on upper concrete steps leading to their sleeping quarters, might just catch him.

Thurs 27th September, quote – "My bottle trick worked – last night the accomplice of our thief was caught after the bottles went crashing down and awoke the boys. The one bolted and got away jumping across the wall, but his friend stayed behind hiding in the shower! Bob and Geoff caught him. The dock manager was called and the police – whether he will lead them to the bright boy we shall see – the police here seem not too careless! Bill saw a file on him the next day at the station, it was an inch thick – so why was he not in Guadeloupe? Just maybe they all shared in the pickings - Any bets?

The first bill to be presented was for the hull timber 14,000F on the 19th September. On the 29th Camic's presented theirs for 17,000F

After some haggling over the price, we got the inside flooring for 10,240F. Our money was draining away too fast and the need to leave here was becoming a necessity due to the cost of things.

Two of the 'Windjammer' boats had entered the dock behind us, 'Flying Cloud' and 'Barefoot Rogue'. The restrictions in Martinique dry-dock are pretty clear when it comes to pumping your shit in to the dock once upon the ways. Shit in this instance being engine oil. Policing of such actions is left to the very same people who were so 'very' concerned about thieving! "If it doesn't concern me, why should it concern you?" type of attitude.

Well it did concern us! We had been painting our topsides and noticed one morning we were floating in oil! It had been pumped from the docks mixed with the ever-flowing water and held against the wharf by the strong wind. Lapping it up our sides leaving a mess, un-paintable and stinking! 'Barefoot Rogue' was the culprit and two Captains met my brother that day - pissed off with life, pissed off with the world and pissed off with 'f--king Wankers' They sent us round detergent!

The strain of the weeks was getting on top of us. People were anxious to be gone – get home – get anywhere but here! Howard had got the Iron Lung going, started first go and a job well done for a fraction of the price given! We had managed to get the props from Denmark at last, and with them on he, most of all, was longing to be underway! Memories of our trip back from Panama came to me at times – his unbearable attitude that descends upon all was infectious, and the frustrations of it all were hard to bear!

On the 8th October I wrote: "Dennis and Bill had words this morning, about our leaving here. People seem to think Bill wants to stay here indefinitely – doing jobs that aren't necessary – which isn't so! The flooring, which both he and Dennis are pushing on with, is very important. How can we live aboard without one? We can't just rush off to St Lucia – for when we are there it will be harder – at least here we have power and water. Howard I'm afraid is the nigger in the wood pile – always on about getting to St Lucia and letting everyone see his feelings. To him (I'm sorry to say) those who have to live aboard after he's gone – he cares little about. He said he was booking a flight out of here – just talk maybe – but what a shame – a shame not to finish what we have started!"

He didn't leave – his bark was worse than his bite!

The 1,500 pounds Henry had sent was in the bank on the 5th October, and gave me 13,397F. It was soon gone, as the continuous flow of those we owed money to never seemed to stop! What, with David Simmons saying we should leave for St Lucia as soon as possible, didn't help. "Things are so much cheaper there!" were his words. But I knew as soon as we reached there, my help would be gone! I had to get as much done here as possible. We had to be ready to work when we reached St Lucia, not be left with things to do.

Though we had the small Honda generator, when were we to get the Onan? The radio? The necessary equipment to make life aboard liveable, let alone back to normal? To make matters worse, by the 9th of October I was having to borrow money off the crew - $400.00 to get food.

By the 10th I write, quote: "Decided to leave Brooks finishing off the painting while I got on with the rigging. Set up the main shrouds – put both the mizzen and fore topmasts back up – have just a little more to do on the fore – masthead lamp, then I can get on with getting the sails back on her. A few more hours tomorrow will see the flooring completed below – Tim made up a temporary counter. Sometime tomorrow all our gear can be moved aboard. Should leave here Saturday morning with any luck!" End of quote.

Mike Atkinson showed on the 9th October – he used to show on occasions throughout the docking, to look at our progress and to tell of his own. Mike's interest was always self, yet I sensed a sort of envy in him of wishing he was aboard, back helping out. I said on that day: "Mike showed again – just for a minute –said he is getting a job as skipper aboard a large tug – 1500 H.P engine – right up his street!" He must have meant 15,000H.P for 1500 would not have been large! The job didn't happen, for the simple reason, it wasn't Mike!

Reading my logs of that period I have come across Dave's name at last. David Stonehouse who, behind the exterior of roughness, lay a heart of gold. I have also noted the names of others from Thomas Ward, Roger Wilson one of the directors of the scrap dealership. Mike, Roger and Liz his wife – and there was of course Joe, Joe the American scrap dealer who was there watching it being loaded aboard - then by ship to Chicago.

We had them over for our first meal aboard on the 12th October, thanking them all for their help, which responded in an invite the next day to lunch at their canteen, and a look over the ship carrying the scrap! We would pop down to the local bar on our last night there – a beer and a final farewell to all – we were leaving the next day, at last!

Sun 14th October we left for St Lucia. The two weeks turning in to nearly 3 months. I write that day, quote: "An early start – 05.45 By the time all was ready it wasn't till 07.20 before we left. Started the engine to make sure all was okay there – but shut it down before we left. Sailed off the dock with not very much wind – but enough for the old girl to clear the channel markers.

It's been one hard slog this dry-docking and cost a lot of money – leaving now with just a few Franc's – borrowed from Bill, Anita and Geoff – but we made it and all still together!
One could not have been surprised if 'tops' had blown under the strain of two sinkings – one Hurricane and all the very hard work – but it shows our metal by slogging on!

With the wind about force 3 E.S.E, 'Jylland' made slow progress to windward – you could feel the difference the extra ballast made.

With it she needs all her sails to compensate – but again she handles well!

6 miles off Pigeon Island we started the Iron Lung – for under sail alone we wouldn't make the anchorage before dark - navigation lights not up to being relied upon. Had to stop it once (engine) – clutch adjustment. - still didn't get till 19.30 hrs. – A 12 hr. passage we have done in 3 & half. Bilges stayed good most of the way, but we opened a seam – starboard, amidships. Bill took a dive, but it was too dark to see – it shall have to wait till tomorrow. So Briggs and watches will break our long awaited peaceful night!!" End of quote!

Life is full of surprises, more so for those living aboard an old sailing boat than for those ashore. You get used to them afloat, for they come at you on a regular basis – but I never expected the surprise that lay in store for me the next day!

Chapter 67: The Aftermath

Monday 15th October 1979 my log writes: "Another heart breaking blow I viewed this morning. Up early and over the side to caulk the leak – a seam that had been missed (as suspected!) to be met with a hull that looked like it was ready for dry-docking – not having just come off! All the seams that had been cold-tarred hadn't held – the anti-fouling looking as if it had been burnt off – flaking everywhere. The Hessian Bill did along the keel has rippled with two area's completely missing – enough to make you want to cry – what to do now!"

What we should have done then, and what we could have done was to have told our insurers at the time of her sinking the impossible position the Hurricane had put us in, and until she was put right to our satisfaction, she would stay where she was! We might as well have all gone home by what we had achieved.

We had been forced by circumstances to do things we would not have done otherwise! Cold Tar with thickening agent because Pitch was unavailable – seams uncaulked due to the rush – soaked Oakum saturated with Diesel – and paint peeling like some old distempered ceiling leaving areas bare!

I often wonder how I put up with it, one blow after another, and when you think there is some respite – bang! – you are hit by a bigger blow.

Something had to be done about it, and fast, for I knew Howard, Dennis and Bill would be off home as soon as possible - within the week probably!

Getting ply on all bare areas and checking seams for any un-caulked areas had to be done while still anchored outside – sorting out what to do after would have to wait another day. So with 6 sheets of 8'x 4' - 3/16" ply cut in to 5" strips and anti-fouled, we tried to cover every exposed area.

We would move inside the Lagoon having done the best we could on the 22nd October – and Dennis and Howard left for home the very same day.

Quote: "Dennis and Howard stopped by to wave their farewells from the bank. Words drifting across the water of "See you soon Dave – Take care!" left me rather sad. They, I know didn't like leaving me again - to face what! Their hearts were just as heavy as mine. They went to Stevens (Yachts) to say their farewells to the rest of the crew who had left for holiday Inn to take a shower.

David Simmons was called – not there, left a message for him to call back. Will found out the money was here in St Lucia for him – arrived last week. There should be no reason for him not to come immediately!!" End of quote.

Why Howard and Dennis left before calling Simmons – before the money had arrived was beyond me – I can only assume now it was due to the once weekly flights – and Howard's impatience to be gone.

David Simmons arrived on the 23rd, and we dropped him at the Malabar hotel. On the 24th we went through the finances!

Quote: "David Simmons came down about 08.30. He came aboard for a look at what we'd done. Gave a few suggestions about employing local labour to do the scraping and painting. "Put a sign up on the road" – (this was a suggestion based on cheapness – not competence) was his answer!

Without going in to too much detail on prices – for his and Howard's claims clashed along the way. We got as much of the 20,000 pounds as possible – 13,860 – he took out for the generator and surveying report!!" End of quote.

The generator we had not seen yet, or approved of, but I glanced at Bill The Badgers report and, as expected, it was something I could have told him.

6,140 pounds stopped by Simmons and we were never told just how much went for what - the same man who told us "Put a sign in the road!" If only Howard had held back two days in his eagerness to be gone, he could have argued with Mr Simmons over who said what. As it was, we had to accept his (the paymasters) words. At least I was now able to pay the crew all their wages, the wages they had patiently waited for!

That same day I heard both Will and Sharman were to leave for the States to visit my sisters in California – two weeks! Bill would also be leaving at the same time and at 06.54 on the 25th, the three left by taxi for the airport!

So with Geoff, Bob, Brooks, Helen and Anita, I was left with 'Jylland' - incapable of working and in need of another dry-docking, yet the hope was still alive we would get her out of here, one way or the other!

Bill was to see some fellow while home who sounded enthusiastic about moving her up there. Laurie (Bills wife) had rung while we were in Martinique about such, so his journey home was something to hold on to – but how long could we hold on was the question?

The bilges were still okay – 10 hours and holding – but the pumping system was in a bad shape. The Briggs was forever playing up – I write on the 28th: "The Briggs isn't working too well – taking 2 hours to pump out – lucky for us though the bilges are lasting. Around 10 hrs – otherwise it could be a problem – must do something about it tomorrow!"

A new pump in St Lucia costs over $3,000 e.c (Eastern Caribbean) something beyond our meagre supply – but something we should have insisted upon from our insurers – and something they should have insisted on us having!

It became a bloody pain having to keep messing with it. Every time I asked someone to get us parts for it – Puerto Rico mainly – they kept bring us parts for a 3 H.P, not 3 and a half – stripped down rings didn't fit, with "Oh no!" from Geoff in frustration.

The 29th October quote: "A frustrating morning with Geoff trying to get the Briggs running properly. So much time is wasted on this thing. Found out a couple of things – the new spark plug wasn't any good – then the air filter needed cleaning. Got it running satisfactory but still wouldn't prime – ended up having to take the deck fitting off that I put on the other day – it now primes okay and is running better – also not as long, it pumps out in 15 minutes!"

Though the new generator had been in St Lucia since 11th November, we didn't find out till the 7th December – it wasn't addressed to us!! Upon its arrival at the Schooner I noticed it didn't have with it an Aqua-lift, and couldn't run without it! David Simmons was told and would send one down – more waiting.

Something else arrived on the 7th December too – My cousin Chris and girlfriend Edna! They had rented an apartment close by for a month, and in the coming weeks the laughs we had together were a lift to ones spirits.

'The Lion's Den' - where we shot pool for 25 cents a game – 'Greenvue' and dear old Bessie's place for a Guinness and to 'Lily's' restaurant where 8 of us ate and drank Sour-sop, Tamarind and all those wonderful fresh fruits from tropical trees and all for $136,00 EC ($50 U.S), all in Gros Islet and all but for some finery for others – great places for us! We had been accepted by that time – not as tourists, but as people wanting to eat very cheaply and have a beer for a quarter the price in the Holiday Inn.

Anita and Helen had broken the Ice – they used to take the Schooners washing to the public washbasins in town, right along the beachfront. First they were looked upon as whites taking the piss, till the locals found out it wasn't so! Tim was from Gros Islet and many a nice person lived there too – it was just a case of they thought all whites are rich – they were wrong!

In that month with my cousin and Edna, it was a time never forgotten due to the unique experience, the worries of the daily chore washed away with a Guinness. A good laugh round a pool table held straight by beer mats and an eye on part of a building that was built without a level. Chris longed for my position – would have exchanged his for mine in a moment.

Living on Toronto Island, across from the City from where he worked, he was gathering good money – but very little in memories other than when he came to visit us. 'Blood On The Jylland' was written by a vivid imagination – held to the desk by 'Golden Handcuffs' he let his mind enter the world he would have loved to be part of. The story went something like this – He and Edna on a holiday to St Lucia were met by his cousin (Me) at the airport. Asked to help out on a fourth-coming charter due to being shorthanded as cook and deckhand they agreed! A group of Germans had hired us for a month and through it the plot thickened – they were after a U-Boat sunk in the Bahamas during the last part of the war. Purposely of course and full of Gold (what else) from Jewish teeth!

Not only did he see me as blond giant in it, but also I was able to swim faster than Mark Spitz ever dreamed. He'd have me over the side, tackle a shark over a steak and swim to catch up 'Jylland' - doing 22 knots by the way!

He sent me down a draft, which I read to the crew, for all were involved like the Argonauts! A farmer's wife in Idaho having never seen the sea might just swallow the unbelievable to us! What happened to that draft? Like many of my possessions – lost, but they lie in my head never forgotten. Whatever happened to my dear cousin? Lost but never forgotten.

When at last he was released from his handcuffs in the 1990s after doing his time, he purchased a trailer and headed west. The Mounties phoned my sister in California (her address was with him) asking did she know him? They found his body in a trailer park – been dead about two weeks – cause, Brain tumour! He left it too late! real from the unreal world in which we live. Chained to the treadmill of life we create a better one for the few, while delivering ourselves to the knackers yard. So many envied our life style – to smell that fresh air of freedom, much like the Galley slave free of his chains at last.

People gather possessions out of boredom, a home full of what they can't afford to divert the mind from, the everyday existence. They watch on T.V things they would love to be doing, but wouldn't sell the bloody thing to do it! If they were happy with their lot – they wouldn't be waiting for the day to leave it for the Caribbean and a wonderful vacation! Who hasn't come home after and said 'Back to the grind!' – felt rather fidgety about being home – all except those that say 'It's nice to go away, but so much nicer to be home!' – Usually sung by women who love the stable life and feet nailed to the kitchen floor.

Though it seemed an ideal existence, what Chris saw was not a bed of roses for us right then. Though 'Jylland' was coming together topside, the most important part of her was worrying. The Bilges were 36 hrs or more in November – down to 12hrs on December 8th – and down to a little under 6hrs by the 15th - and the thoughts were again to go out in to the Bay.

Quote: "Saturday December 15th. With the bilges now down to a little under 6hrs The Briggs decided it wouldn't start – in fact it had seized! With the water lapping the keelson it was to the deck pump – this wasn't throwing out like it should. We were putting more in to her than pumping out trying to prime it! Why – can't get the right leather – pump leather that should be soaked in oiled wasn't available! Geoff went to Wills to rouse him from his bed – while away I let the Briggs cool – took a wrench to it freeing the piston. It stopped on us due to lack of oil – using more than usual. By the time Will and Geoff arrived with one of Roland's pumps – our old friend had nearly done its duty! – One must take it all as a joke and in his stride otherwise I might cry! All that work on dry-dock, now back to this. I suppose now I must take her outside and spend time underwater! (Deciding first to investigate before moving).

One good leak we heard was low down on the portside just aft of the engine – I could not rest till it was looked at (the water beneath her hull was not more than 3 feet, that made searching even more difficult, let alone fixing it. Mud, several feet deep here, threw it in to your face making murky waters now impossible; it was hard to see a thing. One tried working upside down – very uncomfortable!) So I got my gear on and viewed it through these very murky waters – difficult to find, but I did and patched it – also a small one near the waterline!" End of quote. We were back where we were – for I had achieved little!"

The last days of December were approaching – 1980 was just round the corner! The battle over settlement of our claim was in England, still unsettled! It was now in the hands of Henry, Bob Abraham's for underwriters, and David Simmons in Antigua. Confusion reigned. David had failed to send his figures on the settlement to England as requested (that I heard on the 27th). Will pressured him in to saying what that figure was, and got one which said something around $60,000.00.

Henry, instead of coming to see the problem, delivered Will some abuse saying we should have sent bills to Mr Simmons, not knowing Mr Simmons doesn't want them. If such a sum was settled upon it would limit what we could do. Martinique had so far said nothing about getting us back on dry-dock. Hempel had promised to send a rep to look at why the paint was peeling …and from Bill, no news from the North West, and as for wages, the money has been exhausted. We were meeting the New Year broke! I guess the last day's entry sums it up!

Quote: "And now the last day of 1979 is upon us. A lot has happened too – as this log portrays. I just wonder how many words are contained in it, and whether in years to come it will be worth reading? The last world event to happen was 25,000 Russian troops are moving in to 'Help' (a nice word for invading) Afghanistan. The old Bear is still on the prowl – chewing up small countries. To feed its war machine – the 80's will have to be the taming of him if the West is to survive. America (Jimmy Carter) has told him – in Bear talk – to go back to his woods and stop being a naughty baby Bear. That same strong voice he used on Iran telling them to release the hostages – they're still there!! I'm just afraid Daddies voices carries little authority "For being bad children you can only have two sweets tonight instead of the usual three before going to bed – that's if you come home tonight!"

The last evening of the last day of '79 we would spend with Chris and Edna at their apartment, joined by all the crew and Bob MacLean. Bob was a crop sprayer – Canadian and married to a Jamaican with one young daughter, all three were staying in the apartment next door.

We sat round listening to his tales of this most dangerous profession, from the Philippians to St Lucia, where he was employed at the time spraying bananas. Never were these pilots told of overhead cables laid by the electricity companies in faraway places, it was a case of find out for yourself! Some of his friends did, and returned home in a box. Swooping down in to a valley to deliver the goods one day – he came roaring up and over the top on which stood a school. The black youngsters had fun throwing stones at him,. He complained to the teacher which had little effect, so holding back his spraying, he waited, and there they were, about to throw stones, he dumped a load right of top of them! Action speaks louder than words. It did the trick!

Spraying Potatoes in Canada, a farmer complained to his company that they were spraying too high. Still too high he reported, the last run of the day his wheels took the tops off the crops, the man complained they were now flying too low! You can't please everyone!

The night was topped off by a dip in the swimming pool – not by me; I'd had my fill of swimming under the boat. It was Bob and Brooks that made us laugh! Bob Curry at 6'4" took on Brooks Frazier at 5'10" in a 'See who throws who in first' competition.
Before the rules had been laid down and properly accessed, Bob with his back to the pool got just a slight push from the Scotsman, which saw the Irishman's large frame unable to go backwards without being dumped! "Foul!" shouted we. "Bastard!" shouted Bob, and hauling himself from the pool attempted to chase the foul round the pool. It was a laugh not only enjoyed by all, but also by those caught up in the chase.

To top it off, while we boarded the dingy to take us back to the schooner, Bob (thinking Brooks had forgotten) attempted to dump him, but was met by the perfect block – a straight arm that caught Bob so unawares, he went back and landed in 4' of the Lagoon.
"Foul!" we shouted. "Bastard!" said Bob, and tried getting Brooks as he hung on to the thwarts – and me!

It's not the clothes that make the woman – it's the man she's married to!

Chapter 68: Has any one seen a Ghost around?

I was convinced for many years the Jylland had an extra hand aboard. Certain happenings that couldn't be explained did so to people not primed for that 'Feeling', or knew what they saw!

An example of what I mean! Nancy, an American girl making the trip back with us from Panama, asked us round the dinner table one night - "Has anyone ever experienced anything strange aboard before?" This was not the core of the conversation then, but we soon made it so and asked her why, what had she encountered!

Hers was a story not to be ridiculed, for some, by then, had experiences of their own! Nancy had been taken on to help in the Galley - that hot hole of a spot most men steer clear of except when its 'Grub-up!' time. Having finished her task till morning, dinner over with and those not on watch gone to their bunks - a walk on deck for some fresh air was luxury!

We were on passage back from Panama with a light breeze just heeling us slightly. Coming over the weather rail, bright and clear shone a full autumn moon. For a moment she lay back on the hatch combings bathing in its beauty, breathing deeply the clear sea air. She could so easily have been alone, for little sound came from those back aft, just the sound of the wind disturbing rigging and testing the masts met her ears.

Wondering whether to take the chances of this weather continuing till morning and sleep on deck, she rose before the choice was made for her by tiredness. It was not the months for settled weather, rain squalls had before washed her and bedding below decks, then passed laughing as she stood drenched in her cabin.

Not wanting to leave before each memory of the scene was recorded, she walked across the deck to gaze at the sea being swept aside, her reflection cast on the water by the moon. Noticing another shadow join hers, she turned to speak but who it was had left as silently as they had come. Puzzled by the silence she returned her gaze to the water. It was then she was hit with the tingling sensation and cold fright, for in the water, only much closer to her now, stood the reflection of a man! Petrified she stood, frozen on the spot, not daring to move, nor look again to where she now knew there stood something she didn't believe in! Instead she turned and ran below, not looking back!!!

I had slept many a night alone on-board, Yes! I'd have a .38 under my pillow at times, but that was for he with a Machete in his hand, not for something I felt that, if there is such a thing as a friendly ghost, we had aboard with us.

Only once did I see real fear from its being. Bill Curry, who was and is a fearless fellow, came out of the after cabin one night sweating. Something back there had made him wake in the night, it petrified him so much he couldn't return for days. Nightmare? No! he said. What then? He couldn't say. Bill, who might have been sceptical about such things before, certainly wasn't after!

Geoff Terry would see things too. Now here is a fellow who, if he sees something and meets someone who insists he didn't, wasn't there, or has no good explanation other than his own opinion, sparks will fly! Many poo-poo ideas or suggestions they haven't thought of themselves. They were the same type who had the power to stretch people on the rack years ago for expressing free open-minded opinion!

Who know of such things, who can speak with any authority on unnatural events? I know I have seen things I can't explain, nor would I be fool enough to try, and certainly never would I dismiss them as total rubbish! Whether or not Guardian Angels do exist, or the phenomena that scares us be real, it is for us all one day to find out.

What is premonition that forewarns us of a pending disaster? Where do the thoughts come from that become a wonderful idea or invention? Is it just someone whispering in your ear when asleep, just like the mouse in 'Dumbo'. That when we awake we believe it's our idea in the first place? While others not question anything but praise your genius!

Once in Panama, in the early hours of sleep, my wife Sue awoke me, afraid there'd been an accident outside. We lived at the time in an old bus close to the camp-site, not far from the road that ran to Portobello from Colon. It was a road with plenty of twists and turns with a surface of crushed rock. Not the perfect road covering to take corners fast.

She insisted I get up and look outside, so slipping something on my feet I went to find what had bothered her. Nothing was there just the still air and the usual sound of the forests, "I heard a bus go over the edge! People screaming!" she said, when asked what brought this on.

It was about 05.30 then, William and Helen were still fast asleep in the only hours of comfort in that hot area. I got back in to bed and tried to catch them up, but Sue had difficulty still troubled by something!

It was lunchtime before I found out what she had heard. The Guardia hadn't arrived that morning for some reason, so we left for the reef without them for the mornings dive. What held them up was an accident! A bus had gone over the edge on a bad bend - many people on their way to work hurt. What time did this happen?

Between 05.00hrs and 05.30hrs! Strange – weird – odd? Certainly when it happened over ten miles from us!

People, who have had strange things happen like this, usually don't like to talk about it. Certainly not in the company of intellectuals, or in a world ready to name them 'Cranks' or 'Weirdo's', for to recognize phenomena in a person it is better to do so when they're dead, that they can't then upset proceedings of the short-sighted. If you happen to have even greater powers, you're likely to be nailed to a cross!

Two weeks before making the trip to Grenada, I woke one morning after having a dream. Sitting having a cup of coffee with the crew, I related it to them, due to it being so real. It was all to do with me sailing 'Jylland' on a final passage, to an area where ships are buried. It was a sad dream, and I was full of emotion as I steered her towards a graveyard of water from which masts of others stuck out from the surface.

I found a spot for her to rest but, before departing I went round gathering some of her belaying pins, the ones with the brass heads. To each of the crew I gave one, as thanks for their support and loyalty, for it was all I had to give, and a part of me! Having told it, like all dreams it was soon forgotten.

Chapter 69: Waiting – Waiting –Waiting!!

The beginning of 1980 was the beginning of a frustrating year. Money to feed the crew was hard to come by, let alone pay them for the work they were doing! Half wages they were on now, and that couldn't be paid.

On the 4th of January Will had spoken with Abraham's from the insurers in London about the situation, who said he'd telexed Simmonds telling him to advance the money we'd asked for. A call to Simmonds later found him most un-helpful - he hadn't heard any such thing from London, but would call there and ring back.

That would take a day, then with some reluctance called to say he would send down something over a $1.000 he had left. Didn't say how much over that amount it was, nor, if it was ours why he hadn't sent it before! The game he was up to was plain, it was better in his bank then ours.

He still hadn't sent it when Will later called him on the 9th, but by the 10th $4.200 E.C arrived. Paying some wages I could now do, but not all that I owed for the work done. 'Jylland' was now looking good above the water, but what was going on below bothered me. Where was that rep from Hempels who was supposed to come? Everyone seemed to be dragging their heels!

By the 16th, Simmonds had been told by insures to come down to reassess damage. Brokers for some reason don't want to go to arbitration!

All this was getting to me, o n the 13th of January my log reads: "Trying to lift myself out of these slight depressing times. The heavy burden of 'Jylland' on my shoulders is hard to bear. The state of the Bilges this morning didn't help. After spending time on a leak aft yesterday and stemming its flow to give us 5.30hrs before pumping is needed, I received from the watch this morning they are back to just 3hrs. So it's the task of pumping her dry and listening!

Nothing can go on while this is done for total silence is needed. Heard one large flow high on the port bow, donned my gear and stemmed another small area lacking oakum! Back to 5 hrs. again! Lot of places where Cold-tar has turned 'Muddy', not enough Resin added to mixture, not the right stuff, should have been pitch with a little tallow. It will surely wash out in any seaway!"

We would all take turns looking for leaks, especially when the water was clear. But the time spent doing this gets little done on deck!

Simmonds was supposed to arrive on the 22nd, but failed to show. Came on the 23rd instead. Will and I spent the day haggling over labour costs with him. This continued the next day in the company of his friend in business, Bill Fowler. I was fed-up with the whole shabby affair and told them, take the Schooner to Antigua, do the work themselves and bring it back if they think they can do it for less than us! With that and what we thought a fair final sum as a settlement, the meeting was over!

On the 26th Jan, The bilges were back to 4 hrs, Log reads: "I got the boys to prepare to dive on the hull. I was un-able to through sun burns on my lips, and salt water hard to bear. Asked Bob and Brooks so one wouldn't give up so easily. Brooks found the one giving us trouble, under the engine room area which, by its mass, made it hard to hear. Two good things came out of that bit of success - the bilges went for four to seven hours, and I've got two more divers!" In fact they were 8 hrs by the next day!

Brooks Frazier was an American that joined us in dry-dock, He'd worked with Bill sometime before and, through that connection, came down to spend some time with us. He was an easy fellow to get on with, and given a task put all in to it. For the next few months, having found out the principals of diving, he'd be in and out of that water like an eager beagle searching for leaks, which was a great help. Both Bob and Geoff could dive, but with Geoff more concerned about not drowning, then looking for holes, it wasn't fair to ask him. Plus he didn't like getting in the murky waters too much.

February 1st, Will had again been in touch with Simmonds, Log states: "Saw Will in the afternoon. Told me after getting in touch with Simmonds yet again, the money had been sent to St Lucia by our insurers. He intends to make arrangements to have this transferred to Wills account. I owe $2.000.00 U.S in wages, Might have to stop these - what happens after that, who knows!"

February 5th, from my log: "Slowly the days go ticking by. Soon our chances for leaving the Caribbean will be numbered! The bilges have gone from 12hrs to 7½. Another slight leak in the stern. Seem to fix one then spring another. This was easy to see and had Brooksie in the water plugging it, Helps to have another diver and he makes little fuss about going in, in fact he likes it I believe! Will came, brought the Aqua-lift, (Not bad, only had to wait two months for it!) money should be available in a few days!"

6th February saw us run out of paint for engine room, and no money to buy any! And the 7th gave yet another leak port side to take bilges to 7 hrs. Found the problem, area un-chaulked, and covered by hasty patch, Back to 12hrs. On the 9th of February Will and I spoke about finances. Log reads: "I'm pushed for money again. It looks like I'll have to stop wages as from the 8th. We just haven't got it. Don't know what the reaction will be - if some decide to leave. I can't blame them, just makes a hard task harder!" As to what happened to the money that was supposedly sent by insurers, so stated by Simmonds, can only have been lies!

I intended to wait a few days before telling the crew of the problem, just in case things might change! But it was plain they weren't and on the 13th I told them the news after a chat with Will. He'd had lengthy phone call with brother Henry, who by now was running that side of the Atlantic. Howard, being in Cornwall, I just wasn't sure what his share to proceedings were, and wouldn't be surprised if he'd washed his hands of the whole affair.

Henry was asked to come out here if it would help, but declined. Things seemed to have come to a halt and the outlook bleak! If Henry couldn't come here then maybe it might be best if Will went there, so he made arrangements to go on the following Monday.

On Saturday 16th February, with the Hempels rep still not showing, it was plain to us we'd better get someone outside as an independent witness to take a sample of paint, and see our problem first hand.

The only one we knew there was John Kessel, and some sort of

Lloyds agent in St Lucia. He arrived that morning and with a little gentle persuasion I got him in the water with snorkel and flippers to take a sample and view the hull. His Australian response was what we already knew, "Bloody mess Dave, she needs to get on dry-dock now!" I met him again on the Sunday to answer a few questions like; How many times were we wet before paint was applied? And, why was it so long before we complained? I told him we'd complained immediately, and the rest he required. With Will leaving on Tuesday now, he wanted these samples with him, and John's assessment!

I guess the crew now would await the outcome of Wills trip to England before deciding their future. Bob had made inquiries about flights, what little he had he might need it. But for the others, Brooks, Geoff, Helen and Anita, waiting like I was, is what they would do before looking in to things!

I started getting another problem about now. While Will was in England immigration department wanted to know about us. I went in to see them the next day. It didn't seem anything to worry about.

Will was back by the 26th February. Things to report was, all moving slowly, and a lot of talk going on of litigation against Lloyds bank and their Mr John Rich for fraudulent actions! As for our situation, it was in the hands of the Gods! A lot of help to me. Got a cheque off Will to clear my books up.

March saw us going round her topsides, caulking and filling, ready for some paint. Hanging on the hook for so long had dried her out, and some caulking needed paying home, and some just above the water line - thin plywood tingles to cover all till they could be attended properly on dry-docking - whenever that came!

The month of February, between taking care of her slow restoration through lack of funds for materials, I'd managed to make her a topsail yard cut from a large pole dragged by a land rover from a beach on the windward side. 30 feet in length is what I needed and it was well over that. We pulled her back, floated her out, and through the weeks I cut it down with axe and sweat to make a pole one man could carry, which before, four would hurt their backs trying. Rigging it aloft, I made up the necessary blocks from our sheave store, and lastly a fife rail below for her lines.

Another project and something 'Jylland' lacked, was a sailing dinghy. So when we saw this old girl which hadn't seen the water for many a year, we gave $300 E.C for it and spent some time bringing it to sail!

She was a heavy old thing 17 feet in length with a beam around 4'x6". Stem post had suffered from someone trying to pull her ashore by it. We took it to Will and Sharman's house on Cap. To keep our minds busy, and off other problems, we went about restoring it. There's plenty of White Cedar on St Lucia and Roland got us part of a fallen tree. From that a new stem and stern post was cut, plus replacement frames. I extended two of these, one port and one starboard, to take the shrouds for the mast.. With a couple of planks replaced, new capping and rubbing rails, new fore deck and Samson post, caulked and painted, we had her in the water within a month, which was good, seeing the time we spent on it!

Made a mast, sails from 'Jylland's' old set, and even a pair of oars. With 5 cwt. of sand in bags as ballast she sailed well, and 'Jylland' had another tender!

The paint sample we'd taken, had been analysed and on March 12th my log reads: "Had a talk with Will, Henry called yesterday, Hemple's (the manufactures of the paint) said 'Camic' used the wrong paint!!!! Not down to the Insurers" which indicated, it was left to us to take our own action against them!

Us, in St Lucia with just enough money to feed ourselves stood a great chance of success against a company who'd already shown, by not replying to our Telex, what they were made of! The translation from French to English would have read something like "Go Stuff Yourselves!"

Nothing but a wreck when we got it! But after a couple of weeks-we had it! – A trim little craft says I

Rob, Dave and Brooks at Cap Estate, circa 1978-80

Rob, Dave and Brooks at Cap Estate, circa 1978-80

With the ever deepening hole we found ourselves in and with no settlement in sight, so no funds to make plans for a dry-docking, we made it known that if the right buyer came along, she would have to go. Of course, with the state of her hull worsening by the week, we knew she wouldn't realize a good price, if one at all!

Several interested parties came, from aircraft Pilots needing to make a few more bucks chartering her to people wanting to carry cargo. Liverpool Maritime Museum in England, were at one time interested, but nothing more was heard from them, nor those who came to us for a look round. If she was to go, I just hoped it was to the people with the money and heart in the right place - like a Museum!

On the 14th March the bilges were running at 15 hrs. or more, and it seemed then we were finding underwater and caulking that which had been missed on dry-dock with some success! With the bilges becoming less of a problem, like everything else, another would arise to take its place, and again money was now the pressing obstacle!

Jobs couldn't be finished for lack of it to buy supplies, wages had stopped, and what little I had was being eaten up, literally. By March 20th the total funds aboard were $1.500 U.S, Will having given me $1.000 U.S the day before. As it owed me personally just over this, the only one to be eating if I didn't use it for the schooner, would be me.

Friday March the 21st, log reads: "Will had a call from Henry - Banks are not willing to advance money in lieu of settlement from Insurers for re-dry-docking! Also underwriters want us to sign a paper saying, once we've agreed to a settlement, that we won't press them about bottom damage!" We were in a barrel, and the bastards knew it! On the 25th we heard that the claim had been settled at $80.000 U.S, But nothing on whether the conditions they wanted were met!

Immigration people were giving us problems again. On the 27th

March they came to the Schooner to see our condition, brought with them a mechanic to verify our position. We were un-able to move even if asked to, for at the time the fork that changed the propeller pitch was out of her needing some attention. An extension by them was granted sometime after, they couldn't do less. Again the Briggs was playing up, spares were impossible to get for a 3 hp, plenty around for a 3½ though!

By the end of March, it was money problems mixed with Briggs. Log reads: "Spoke With Will on the subject of money. Always enough to turn me off for the rest of the day! I've just about had my lot with this, not sure how much longer I can go on! Up till midnight trying to get Briggs sorted out, left it exhausted till the morning, just lucky bilges are holding up!"

I know the conditions for me, as hard as they were to make ends meet, were no easier for Will. He was having to borrow from Sharman, whose shop in 'Carib Blue' was probably borrowing from the bank. It was a Peter to pay Paul situation I hated. And made worse by my having to raise the subject on every occasion!

April was upon us and the news that the money from the settlement was going through. It was only now we could make arrangements for dry-docking again, but where?

Will and I had spoken before this. Martinique was the closest and hence the safest, but we would need 14 dry days to do what was needed - denied us by the Hurricane. I doubted they would take us, having had no response from them and the hassle of our last visit. Our other alternative was Grenada, sure to be dry if their traveling slipway was big enough to haul us out!

Both would have to be checked out, Will called Grenada on the 2nd to find out they couldn't take us until May 21st. Worried over wage bills and the long wait till then, Martinique was called on the 3rd, but we couldn't get them due to communication problem with phones!

The choices we had was between those we knew and those we

didn't. The nightmare of our last visit was fresh in our minds, but it couldn't repeat itself, not unless Hurricanes started 3 months early, also we could do our own work, whereas in Grenada, it was done by the yard and we knew what a rip off that could be!! It seemed, though I dreaded the thought, Fort-du-France was about to see us again!

The extension to our stay from immigration came on the 5th April - that was very helpful, for it gave us till the 7th to leave. In the engineer's opinion, the clutch fork was a minor problem. Roland went to see them for he spoke their language. We asked him to tell them to send their engineer to us; we would leave when he fixed it. Roland returned with the date now standing at May 21st!

On the 10th April in anticipation of a quick return to dry-dock, Bill Curry came back to join us. With the 11th and nothing from Martinique, Grenada had to be told we'd take the spot now set for the 23rd May.

The trip we took with Bessie Julie on the 6th April to Millet left me with a case of a severe need to visit the toilet at steady intervals. That would plague me for a week! On the 14th April, Log reads: "Heard a leak on the port bow, another un-caulked area, Should have money within the week, Said we'd have about $14.000 U.S to do the Grenada dry-docking, don't think it will be enough to do all we need to do!"

on the 17th of April I found myself again having to ask for money from Will for food. I got $500.00 E.C the next day, which would last us about a week. That same day, the 18th, I got a Telex from a Don Crowe. Seems he is a friend of Doug and Margaret Havers, the people we knew who owned a Baltic 'Our Svanen'. Doug and he are coming down to look over some Baltics on the 24th - St Croix - St Thomas. Wanted me to help in some way, could I call him! I did that on the 19th, Log reads: "Called Don Crowe, he wanted to know if I could meet him and Doug in St Thomas to look over a couple of boats there. One being the 'Topaz' another being the 'Unicorn', William Smiths lovely little Brig, its going for $250.000 U.S - cheap if you're rich!, Told Don it was impossible to get away, Why? I didn't have the money for the air fare, was the reason, he would have paid it I'm sure, and I wouldn't have minded the break, but I wasn't going to ask him!"

The 'Unicorn' on which Smith lavished a fortune ($750.000 U.S) would end up in the hands of Bob Elliot, later replacing his 'Rum-Runner'. It goes to show what a business we gave him, and one he was desperate to hang on to at all costs. 'Jylland's' presence in St Lucia was always going to be of a threat to him. I often wondered if he was behind the hassle we were getting from immigration officials. In '74 we were certain of this. His wife Sonja, a St Lucian, was related to someone high up in the opposition to John Compton's government,

With 'Jylland' taking most of the work, leaving him with very little passengers, a phone call to the authorities from an angry wife sent down to us the white uniformed brigade wishing to speak to the captain on matters of some importance! "What were we doing working! Why have we no work permits! We must stop this practice forthwith!" etc!

It was strange, this never happened when Bob and Sonja were earning money for old rope as 'Jylland's' agents! Bob is a person that gets others to do his dirty work I believe, for there is not the man in him to do otherwise. Poor old Sonja would find out in time what she married, having had the prettiest days of her life, and served her purpose, he dumped her! I would say right now, that she is not the happiest woman on the Island!

By the 22nd April we are again broke, but Roland dropped us down some on the 23rd. Bill was sorting out our Diesel tanks, which hadn't been cleaned after the sinking, and generally organizing the engine room, making the usual thorough job!

On the 24th April Logs reads: "Still no money from England! It will be a big problem if some doesn't arrive shortly. Will and Sharman are having to supply our needs and its making life difficult for them.

Problems! Problems! Going through the cash aboard I haven't enough to give each $20.00 e.c for a weekend beer!"

By the 26th April things were pretty bad money wise. There was none aboard, just a promise to all that it was on its way. Though wages had been stopped early February, April had brought the news we were to go to dry-dock, so it was employment again. That which was owed to me looked certain to be lost in keeping my promise to the crew of theirs.

Things were getting hot for Will and I, and to let off steam at someone, anyone, all we had was each other. It didn't, or couldn't achieve anything other than to get it off your frustrated chest!

The Log reads on the Sunday 27th April: " Half the crew took the sailing boat round to Pelican rock while I waited with Anita for Will and Sharman to arrive! Not here by 10.30 so went to meet the others taking the whaler. Boys were already there at anchor, so tied off their stern. Spent some time searching for lobster, got some and a red snapper! It was just as well we got something to eat for there was nothing on board except a tin of ham that when opened, was as rotten as a pair! We were also lucky in those friends we'd made in Millet, as they dropped us by fruit whenever they were passing, and thankful we were for that too, but Bananas alone was not enough.

I had to call Don Crowe again, he'd left a message with Roland which I responded to. He said he'd purchased the 'Topaz' but, while making final arrangements the crew took it to sea, he thinks on a drug run. I believe it might have been a case of the owner owing wages, and them using it to get them home to the States. He asked me to keep my eye open!

A call to Henry on the 29th advised he should have the money any day and would send it off immediately! I just hoped the desperate words of our position were not lost on the wind!

May had come now, but still nothing from England. Will had been in bed running a temperature, which he passed on to Sharman. Bill had worked on the electrics below and the rest of the crew, in preparation for sailing, were mending her sails, which were in a poor state, and rigging the running rigging. The fore main was thought useless, so instead we rigged wire to take a large headsail as a staysail in its place. Roland sent us down $140.00 E.C, which petrol and oil for outboard and Briggs took up.

On the 4th May my log reads: "No money to eat, so went to bed early! Had Roland to our rescue the next day, and $125 E.C the following day from Will. Again he'd rung Henry in England to be told a familiar tale. "The underwriters have released the money to the brokers, expecting it any day!"

The 7th of May I awoke from a dream of some warning, and the sad consequences of that filled my exhausted body with any enthusiasm for the day. I had dreamed of water coming in faster than we could keep pace with, yet continued till we could get her in to shallow water, a graveyard for old ships, and where was that resting place - Porthcressa Bay on Scilly where all this idea started from!!!

That day I had one of our main fuel tanks ashore, and up to Wills. Not a small thing (nor in fact a clean thing) two men needed to carry it. Bill in his organizing of the engine room thought, while it possible, we should check them over, re-paint and replace before bedding home the generator. I was passed the point of arguing against it, other than a gut feeling it could all be a waste of time and energy, of which I had little of. Even asking Will had he heard anything from England now was as much a strain as asking for money, both which I had to do, and both met with the answer from a man as pissed off with it as I was, but with a slight difference I was living aboard and the only one of the brothers going to make the trip to Grenada.

By May the 8th at last we heard from England, Log reads: "Will came down in the evening! Henry had spoken to Roland, The money was in his hands and he had transferred it on to us!

May the 10th being a Saturday, Will brought us down a little money to get a beer with, Billy got the generator running, but needed diesel, which you can't buy without money.

Monday 12th May, the long struggle to make ends meet had got to the point where it was now touch and go whether we would get away from here in time. We couldn't check out the main engine or the genny, through lack of fuel, nor any of the equipment that thing ran.

It wouldn't be until the 15th of May that we received some money, $7.930 U.S. With what Will has left from the same amount sent to New York, it would give us around 10 - not $14.000 we first visualized! One big problem we had right then was the bottom paint we needed in Grenada hadn't arrived yet from Barbados where it was ordered 4 weeks ago, someone might have to go and get it.

With money and some supplies aboard, it was the 18th before the main engine was fired up and running, and had Bob Curry hitching up the radio with 3 days to our planned departure date 21st. That day Geoff and I was checking seams above the waterline forward, caulking, cementing and tingles where needed. The starboard side was in the worst condition. The long months of being at anchor, the drying winds and hot afternoon sun on that area, had dried her out till there were places rope was needed as caulking, not oakum! It was all becoming a shit or bust situation in the rush now with the money available but not the time to do all.

Two Pilots working for the local airline 'Liat', Tam Goodman and Phil Byrne, had become good friends. Tam was an American, who's Mom and Dad had a house on Cap. He and his then girlfriend Josset (French) had gone on our trip to Millet that Sunday. Phil was an English fellow that from an early age wanted to do nothing but fly planes.

Both these fellows did many things for us, getting supplies for us in Martinique not available in St Lucia. Phil had got us rope needed for running rigging only days before we left, driving up with the customs man who needed to see it delivered aboard. Phil had asked could he make the trip with us to Grenada, having never been aboard a sailing boat before.

Little did he know his first would be something he'd never forget, and something he was lucky to walk away from! We intended to get outside in the clear waters in plenty of time to check over the bottom, but the slowness of getting our mooring aboard, not getting ahead or astern properly, and having to shut her down and re-adjust the fork on the variable pitch, made it not till the 20th at 10.00 hrs. To get to Grenada on the 23rd we must leave no later than the 21st.

For me the whole day of the 20th was one of complete lack of energy. I'd woken after a rough night in which I'd hardly slept. Five minutes work and I was knackered for an hour. My log reads that day Tuesday 20th April: "It must have been something I ate, or drunk for I really had a rough night. Slept below and it was hot, lack of it made me completely useless. Didn't get out of the lagoon till gone 10.00hrs, Bill and Geoff working away on the ahead and astern gear. Once outside I had to lay down, the anchor work exhausting me. Fixed up the main-boom for lifting aboard the sailing boat, took me far too long! The state I was in the obvious became obscure, and in the end all a complete waste of time for once it was aboard, we took it off to leave in the Lagoon, it being too big to carry in comfort! Brooks has been checking the Hull over, bilges running about 8hrs! Phil came aboard late!"

Wed the 21st had been another day of rushing around for last bits, Bill had gone in to Castries to get some light fittings and timber, and on his return I went up to see Will, the bottom paint hadn't arrived from Barbados but Phil had said he could get it to us by plane when it did.

I also took up some bits of Anita's and my personal items that we wouldn't need till we returned. Below decks at sea I'd seen many a decent dress ruined, even a guitar fall to pieces, as it did on our return from Panama.

In reference to this sentence, the insurance company, and solicitors for the bank, would have much to chew over, suggesting skulduggery, that it could by this statement in my logs, which I made available to them, that we might have in some way known she was to sink, and in few words without actually accusing us, we might have been the cause of it!!

Now the next day there is no entry in my log until Thursday 22nd, but it reads such: "Sitting at the chart table now and its 03.30hrs of the 22nd, Only slept one hour last night, It's very hard work trying to get a sinking ship anywhere, We are at the moment just keeping pace with it (the water) if one pump fails, we're in the boats and I've never felt more anxious than I did in the early hours of this morning!"

"Jylland" at anchor in Rodney Bay St Lucia – just before her last trip to Grenada

Bill would be Skipper, for the reason of greater experience, and a ticket! But on all decisions we spoke, each giving the other credit for a brain! Bill and I, if we had one thing in common more than anything else, it was the love of old sailing boats. We both envied those that lived in the period when they were in their prime and angered by those that couldn't appreciate such vessels as 'Jylland', to keep them afloat for others to admire and sail in.

Frustrated by lack of the right materials and the lack of care from those who'd burn her if her fastenings would make a profit; Bill did more than any could do to fight for her survival.

It wouldn't have mattered who of us was in charge to make the decision to leave at 15.00hrs - that was made by a clock, and nothing to do with who was the Captain! Mentally my mind was clear, though my physical strength had been drained by the past months. Raising the anchor was a chore, the pawls not wishing to grab the drum to turn home the chain; it was as if she was reluctant to leave, knowing in some way the fate that lay in store!

Cursing a task that was once simple to us the mizzen and staysail flogged as impatient to get on with it as we. Then at last with it up and down, her old head swung for the open sea not resisting us as we hauled it in short and catted it up for the last time!

Eyes would be on us for sure, as holiday makers sat sipping a Rum-punch at the hotel, some would envy the life of those aboard, "Lucky buggers!" they could well say. Oh! to feel the freedom from the rat-race that holds them to man's shore, for soon they must return from this Paradise to the stage and the role they chose to play. Children might say "The Pirate Ship is leaving - look!" and point at us from the shore and make a wish upon a star, that one day...! For many though, we would be just be part of a picture that has been paid for, what the brochure said it was, for who could contemplate a sea without such things, why it would be like painting a Cornish fishing village without the fishing boats, or sitting in the woods without the sounds of birds! No! It could never be!

Whatever the picture we made from the shore was, for those in it, a different story, it would be one of fighting to hold on to that picture for others to see and, just maybe, be a part of one day!

Slipping along, being on a soldiers wind the mainsail was raised. We knew well, that come sundown this off shore breeze could leave us, so we needed to drive her in these flat seas as long as they held. Our old sails though were in no cut or condition, even in a breeze such as this, within a half hour the power-house, our main, tore at the throat and had to be dropped. Always the cut at this point had been wrong, and lashed too tight it went. Repaired with contact cement and spare cloth, it was up again in an hour, to tear again, but this time at the peak, again she was down and up with fingers crossed this time!

By 19.50hrs we had the Pitons abeam, making 4½ knots over the ground. We wished to get across the Channel in the lee of St Vincent before the morning sea could be picked up on the usual strong breeze. 'Jylland' was in no condition to take on any sort of seaway that can come through these channels as she has done on many an occasion. Nice and easy was the word with pumps ready! Any water coming in to her must be kept down, for work that had been done on dry-dock, the re-fastening, the re-planking had left waste chippings of wood in her between her ceiling, ready to make its way back to the pumps! I had seen through the years, from wheat to fire debris, how this rubbish can block your strum-box in minutes, making a large pump useless!

It was always the practice, that those coming to the end of their watch, pass on to those coming on, a dry bilge! Checking throughout your turn, however un-necessary it might seem, constantly the state of its condition! With me, I had the man that when it came to checking bilges, did so with the regularity of a man looking out the window for the postman, bringing with him the news of a big pools win! Geoff! Maybe this cautious attitude came from the fact he was no great swimmer, but one could be sure, that while he was on watch, you and all aboard would soon know if there was a problem.

The watches were set, Bob, Brooks and Phil, Myself, Geoff and

Anita, then Bill and Helen! We had 5 means of pumping her out. The old deck pump close to the main mast, Briggs and Stratton set up on deck, the one rigged to the Onan generator, one running off the main engine and, as a last resort, the compressor used for pumping up air tanks, rigged to pump water instead.

Before we'd left, bilges had been about 8 hrs, twice what they were when we brought it down from St Martin in April last year. But for the Briggs running without fault, we'd have lost her then, two days it was in constant use, bilges were filling in 7 minutes and taking 20 to empty! But the slight difference then was, she'd been working and I knew her condition to certain extent, seams above the water line had been kept wet by our daily sailing trips, and although she was in desperate need of attention below, I wasn't as concerned about her seams as on this trip!

It wasn't long after leaving Gros Islet Bay that she needed to be pumped, nothing to worry about, just something to keep an eye on. Running down the lee of St Lucia that evening there was no real cause for alarm. Bill and Helen came on watch from 22.00hrs till midnight, and with a dry bilge they settled down to a peaceful couple of hours, taking in the quietness of it all after the long slog, for ahead of them lay another hard one!

Water in great quantities was entering her hull, and as she sat deeper to them, more entered through un-detected areas, Picking up wood and waste a mixture was afloat, a mixture so potent it can kill you as sure as a deadly poison!

Now there is nothing quite so frightening as looking in a bilge and seeing water!! I'm not talking about a few gallons here. I'm talking big stuff, stuff if you had the nerve and desire, to swim in! Deep enough to raise Hippo's or basking shark - for that's what met Helens eyes when her torch decided it was time to go below and check!

It was only natural to think we're sinking, because we were, but before we abandon ship in to a dark sea you fight to save your best chance of survival. So that's what we tried doing for nearly 24hrs. Those who thought they were in for an easy watch, and those who thought they could rest now, would spend one hell of a night thinking of what a bad boy they'd been, and promising never to be a rotten little bastard ever again, while I'm certain dear old Phil wished he'd brought along an airplane.

Shaken from my slumber by worried hands and the sound of the genny starting. I went on deck to see Bill and hear the position. The problem I'd felt under my feet already, before I went on deck. The water was rippling through that lower deck we'd laid but hadn't caulked after Martinique. While Briggs was got ready, and deck pump primed, I went to the safe below, took our money, passports and personal items - plus the hand guns!

Putting these in a bag, I told Anita, it would be best to grab her things, and put them on the deck, for if sleep comes to any this night, that's where it will happen, giving her the things from the safe to take care of I returned to the task ahead!

By experience, and revolutions, the Jabsco with its rubber impeller, is far superior rigged up to a Briggs engine then to the generator. But two running in harmony it can shift water of vast quantity, but that's if you have clear water not hindered by rubbish. Strum-boxes that block give little chance for machines to work at their full potential, running dry for too long, they can burn out and, used without a box, a piece of debris can smash one of the blades if not the whole impeller. At $40.00 U.S a shot, we didn't have any spares other than old worn ones.

The initial rush from both Jabsco's gave us hope that we'd beat this inflow, but would the faithful old Briggs last, for that was our big gun. Geoff and I had spent days through the months before, frustrated through lack of parts, and parts sent and brought being of the wrong type, stripping old ones for spares, grinding in valves, and willing to swap two new sets $3^1/_2$ hp piston rings for an old 3 hp set to anyone willing to barter. A new one there was beyond us, $3000.00 E.C, $1500.00 U.S, €400.00 didn't matter how you saw it, it was just too much.

The slowing down of water from these pumps was not something to jump for joy at, but more with concern, for we knew the sign, and it wasn't an empty bilge one! One of us at least would have to stay down below keeping strum-boxes clear at all times - a bucket at his side for rubbish grabbed by hands This task, head down in stinking water, is not one to ask of those likely to die of seasickness, and it is a place those who thought they didn't suffer from such things, will soon find out the truth to their claim.

To stop the impellers burning out, someone would have to pull them out of gear, disengage them, then with an okay! Give them another blast till again they slow, repeating again and again the process, while another dumps the debris over the side! Trying to catch this illusive crap, is like trying to grab a handful of minnows in a fast flowing stream, hands try to keep back or grab bits stuck to its sides. Up and down, side to side you go as you try to shake off the mess, and all the time you hear an engine running free without the load you want by your efforts to give it!

Between manning the deck pump, which wasn't bothered by this rubbish, just throwing it on the deck, all spent time at this fruitless task! Because of it, we were just keeping pace throughout a most tiring night. Till we got it down, the main engine couldn't be started, for its spinning flywheel would cover the generator with so much spray, it could well blow out our electrics.

With the day light came the look on faces of exhaustion, the deck pump had been going constantly, each man relieving his friend with a sudden rush of energy that drained quicker each time he flew at the handle.

I will always remember seeing the ashen face of Phil coming below to change my bucket. I was at the time sitting; my feet down the galley bilge trap door, trying in vain to clear pipes.

It was a bright sunny morning on deck, the perfect Caribbean weather. I knew out there flying fish would be leaping to escape something wishing it for breakfast, and carried by the morning trades it would plunge far from its pursuer in to the blue water, white capped by the breeze. But for our problem, we would all be aft drinking morning coffee, happy to be alive, and Phil wishing he'd done this years ago!

Water at the time was washing inside her, the slight roll of the ocean making it look even worse than it was. One minute the hole was brimming to overflow, then to a heel from a sea, vanish like some great surging tide, up it went behind her ceiling to hit the covering board and burst inboard like snarling teeth from the salt-tray gaps. Running now on the inside it washed round me, that not entering the hole, rushing past we up the port side in a mighty whoosh!

Trying to hold himself on to what he could grab, with a look of some despair, I felt sorry for him! "Don't worry Phil!" I said, trying to make fun of the situation - "We used to do this sort of thing regularly for American passengers, give em a real taste of what it's like at sea!" You have to make fun at times like this - it is the tonic that kills the disease that makes you give up,

The generator had been running constantly since it was started at midnight, between that and the Briggs, which was beginning to play up; our position had not got any easier. We had for some hours now kept pace, but started to lose when the Briggs stopped, and another Jabsco was hitched to it. By afternoon and still no sighting of land, Bill and I had a chat about our position.

It was pretty well certain we wouldn't last another night, Bill had tried calling for assistance on the radio, but for some reason, was only getting static back. My earlier fears, that we had received a second-hand radio from Simmonds, were answered!

In such desperate situations, where the responsibility for others' lives is upon your shoulders, all suggestions are considered. Bill, knowing the radio now could not be relied upon to call for assistance, suggested sending for help. Someone, Geoff maybe, in the Boston Whaler, making for Bequia or one of the Islands in the northern chain of the Grenadines.

With no land in sight, and knowing the whaler made hard going of any sea, especially with one man aboard, we would find ourselves with another worry on our hands. While they could find themselves in bigger danger than they stood now, I had seen that worry before in Spain. Bill, I knew would have gone himself, by his suggestion, his bravery in such an action was beyond question, but for me, I wouldn't ask someone to do anything I wouldn't have done myself, for whatever reason, and thought it best we stick together. Not only did we need every man aboard to help pump, but they would be taking our only sure hope of jumping in to anything if she did go!

The two 8 man life rafts were in their cases, and though serviced in Martinique 8 months ago, not a thing I liked to rely upon. I was thinking right then of the sailing boat we'd left behind, wishing after all we'd made room, however awkward it might have been. Fading light was against pursuing the issue!

Just before light gave way to darkness land was sighted to the S.E, reckoned to be Union Island, distance about 20 miles! Our position down below was deteriorating rapidly, making some easting was essential, and the only way to do that was with the engine. The decision to send out distress signals in the hope we were being heard was made, and left Bob at the radio doing that while another decision was come to, and that was dispense with the strum-boxes!

Guarding the generator the best we could from the spray, we started her up. Though awash with water she ran, gaining us miles to windward, bringing to view more Islands, running south. How long she would run before water entered the clutch was guess work, For 15 hrs the deck pump had been manned continuously and was the first to fail, the bolt connecting its handle wore through the plunger shaft, as if giving notice to the others it was time to quit!

One after another they failed in rapid succession. So much water was aboard her now, that the clutch, though running completely submerged for some time, started to slip, the powerful engine driving nothing but the large flywheel throwing masses of water over all and everything, and would have continued doing so for many more hours if that was asked of it. Shutting it down before the water would knock out the genny was the only option. The Onan was for now still clear of the water and right then pumping a losing battle.

Brooks had been aloft some time keeping a lookout towards land. The broken deck pump beyond repair, he could rest his body now, but not his eyes and mind as they searched with a longing to see some sign of life towards that distant shore!

Personal belongings had been brought on deck sometime before, each going through his pile to take only the essential if we should suddenly have to abandon her. Two feet of water now covered the lower deck, washing inside her in great surges picking up things not fixed down, timber needed for dry-docking floated with hatch covers and odd bedding. Anita, seeing a photo album pass, ran down among the flotsam to grab it -- "I couldn't stand to see it just floating there!" she said emerging with many memories clutched to her chest.

The two life rafts in their plastic containers were un-lashed, making sure the pull cords were securely fastened, and the whaler got ready, for it was certain, unless help arrived soon, we would be in them!

The Generator that had been running constantly for 17hrs was now awash with water, fear that someone could be hurt by the current it was producing, kept people out of the water near it. There was no panic aboard, no fear reflected in people's faces, it was as if all knew in some way they would survive, that or they were just too drained by the hours of battle to think.

For myself, flashes of the past years came to me, the happy times, the time I was sitting in the netting under the bowsprits with my brother Will, the old girl with a bone in her teeth on a return from Martinique! Showing to us then what she could do in a good breeze! Heybridge Basin, Cuxhaven, Spain, Panama and Nassau, all soon to vanish beneath me, gone forever! I wished my brothers could have been with me, not that they could have done any more I'm sure, just be there at the end is what I would have liked!

The sea had beaten me at last, my exhausted body and mind nearly finished. It was in this realization of defeat, a feeling of relief came over me too, that all the struggles in the last years would not continue, that I was being told in some way it was the end of the story.

When Brooks shouted lights had been seen to the S.E, I was as sure they were for us, as it was they could do nothing for 'Jylland'! Then, for the first time since I was woken at midnight, silence, one wash of water putting out the Genny like a match in a rain-barrel. It was as if 'Jylland' had also given up then, sitting stubborn and heavy on the sea refusing to budge, having resisted all our efforts by us to get her to safety, her sails doing nothing but keep her comfortable till it was time to say goodbye!

With no running, or spreader lights to guide those to us on that dark night and the flares that worked, spent, port and starboard lights of two boats could be clearly seen heading in some direction towards our blackness. "Shine a light upon the sails!" said a voice in my ear, "Remember what you read!" it said, and from somewhere came to my hand the torch to show the way.

The first to reach us was 'Macoa II' with two English fellows aboard, Jan Cox and John Bevan. They and many others had heard our call, and realized at once the radio problem. Their boat was around 40', which could save us but not 'Jylland', but coming up behind them was the Island ferry out of Grenada, the 'Seimstrand', she might have a pump aboard.

Dropping all sail we heaved-to under mizzen and fore staysail till he arrived. Taking the whaler Bill and Geoff went across to speak with its Captain Frank Oliver, returning with 2" pump and two of his crew members to man it! Plus an offer to tow us to Grenada for $400 E.C an hour. For a moment 1 thought, maybe, just maybe there was a chance, that the certainty of the outcome I knew awaited us an hour before, would not happen!

With the pump running and throwing water out as one should, and if we'd been able to afford such, would not have needed theirs. The next thing was to get all aboard the 'Seimstrand' not needed for the tow when it happened. Watching the water in her hold as crew and belongings were transferred, gave me the impression it was receding. When the towline was brought to us, it would have to be very slow ahead indeed before she was safe though.

Bob would be aboard the ferry to watch the line and signals from our torch, with a radio. It was important to keep it slow and an eye on us. With the staysail stowed, and Whaler trailing astern, Bill, Geoff and I stayed aboard, leaving the two black crew members manning their pump!

It was a large hawser sent to us from the 'Seimstrand', 8" braided nylon. Made fast to the Samson post it took up the strain, the powerful engines of the iron ferry hauling it out of the sea, wringing the water along its length till it was lost in the darkness, leading for the mass of lights ahead. The water in her had certainly not risen since their petrol pump had been at work, all I had to determine that, was the companionway steps, counting from the top one down, or through the engine room hatch, taking a mark on the flywheel just showing at times in a surge.

Now being aboard any boat for years, one can estimate pretty well by just a glance at the sea what speed you think you're making. Within 15 minutes of putting her ahead Frank Oliver was moving 'Jylland' faster through the water than she'd been for many a year. 8 knots we guessed. I moved fast for the companionway to check the condition in her, and noticed in her movements a roll I didn't like; she was picking up the sea through her freeing ports amidships! We were sinking fast!

Water in the engine room had risen to her valve covers, 2' or more from our first inspection. Those manning the pumps wished to get off - and fast! Shutting down their engine making haste in wishing to depart with it. Bills and my fear now was of being towed under and whether those aboard the ferry would react fast enough in cutting or slipping the tow before the 'Seimstrand' had a fish on the end of a line bigger than they could handle!

Not taking the chance they would, I ran forward to cut us off while Bill made signals to stop! Cutting such a large line with so many braids, even under such strain, is not quick work for just a knife. Stuck under the slat-work, forward of the sampson post, was also not the best place to be if she did suddenly go. Before my job was complete though, a slackness came indicating the pulling had ceased. So did my cutting, made harder by the loose line. Now it was faster to take out the turns instead!

Going aft, with the certainty she was about to go, something made me stop, I had something to do, the belaying pins without lines made to them I grabbed, and with this armful, worthless in value, went aft!

The whaler had been loaded by then with its men and pump, and hanging close astern of us by Geoff's hand, they sat white eyed wishing to be gone. Bill and I could do no more now, the race was run, it was over for us now and we knew it. "Let's go!" was all we said, and as a man we left her for the last time!

The next hours, and the next few days even would have me in a daze. Exhaustion set in and some cuts to feet and face festered from being run down. We abandoned her at 21.30hrs and, once aboard 'Seimstrand', caught snippets of the conversation between its Captain and someone asking him over the radio, was it possible to get some men aboard her for obvious salvage rights. Frank wouldn't have to wait too long before replying, for at 21.45hrs on Thursday 22nd May she went, pitching on her starboard bow not to recover. The last bell ringer she would ever make, for it rang aft in the kick forward as she plunged bow first below the waves, the Union Jack still hoisted from the peak of her mizzen, and the last to leave the scene!

The loss of the 'Jylland' on that passage to Grenada brought to an end a 12 year chapter in my life. All we could do to save her was done, but it seemed the ghost in her gave up and wished to rest, being weary of the long struggle like us!

The 'Seimstrand' circled the area among the flotsam, its searchlight scanning the waters, One of the two life rafts had made it, bobbing up and was hauled aboard, the mass of jackets we'd got on deck from below to show our position if we'd gone in a rush, now covered the water like a sign of some real disaster and heavy loss of life!

My heart was heavy, for among them was those of my children, whose lives were mixed with the debris of it all. The paint-locker Bill had built, right down to its brass hinges, sat like some deadman's chest, white against the dark sea. Frank didn't bother to pick much up, he was saddened by the scene as anyone I believe, for as those who live on the sea realize, it could just as easterly be them. Just more a memento of one or two jackets that was all, leaving the now scattered bits to the Ocean's currents and the winds to drive them West to shores we didn't see.

While Frank took us to Union Inland as a last request, and us sitting below waiting for the 15 mile trip to the S.E to come to an end. I handed to all, my thanks for all they'd done, as if some medal for all they had tried to do. For it was all I had left from something dear to me, and the only gift I had — Just a brass topped belaying pin!

It was Helen that looked at me strangely, to then remind me of my dream, but right then I was too tired, too numb to think of what I'd said some weeks before. But now? If whatever joined the ship in Cuxhaven, did so to watch over us, he had done so before departing.

The reason for going to Union, was that Phil Byrne knew some people there, and also might be able to get us back to St Lucia by air. We said our thanks to Frank Oliver around midnight, and he left rather late for where he was bound, Carriacou, which lay larger and further on the same course. We cleared Customs late, and slept a short night as guests aboard the 'Shiney Penny' shutting our eyes to catch up the sleeping mind for the first time in over 24 tiring hours.

The writing of this episode, the going over of that time, is as tiring as it was then, for it brings back so vividly the difficulty of our fight. The lost battle that leaves only memories as some reward for your endeavours, yet with a clear conscience you did all, if not more than you were asked!

Phil's holiday was much shorter than he'd expected, and flying a plane again sooner than he'd thought, a phone call to St Lucia Airways had an Islander coming to pick us up that afternoon of Friday 23rd. So, until then we spent a quiet day oblivious to the beauty of our surroundings, walking the beaches so many come to admire on a dream tour of this perfection. I was too punch-drunk to consider the past, the present or the future, just sit with un-seeing eyes at an Azure sky upon a turquoise shallow sea. I don't remember much of thanking people for putting us up, but I would have, before cramming ourselves and bits in to the plane.

Phil had said we were a bit heavy, as he joined his friend who flew down for us, but he'd get us off, just take her the whole length of the runway if he had to. Right then I really wasn't concerned if we'd make it or not for, after the night before, I was convinced now that what will be will be, that the future you so desperately plan for does not belong to you to have, but for others to give, that the only thing for sure we know is the past and that of this very moment in time!

Will and Roland met us at the airport, a phone call to meet 'A' crew off the schooner had been made ahead of our landing at Vigie. But when 'THE' crew landed, shock, dismay, followed later by Sharman's tears!

It would take another 6 years before her bones could be laid to rest, claim and counter claim, accusations of foul deeds or that of incompetence wove the desired web of litigation from the Vultures making a meal of this tragedy. It would take the court of law, like it always does, to point out the cheats and liars, to bring honesty to the honourable, to make the crook pay his debt! But the crook here did not pay, they never do, they leave the company to pick up the tab, the investor, shareholder and Lloyds Bank customer.

My log reads on the 25th May, referring to who or what was responsible for the loss of 'Jylland': "Bill came round and we made out a report on the passage of 'Jylland'. Many questions I'm sure will be asked as to whose fault it was! Had we had this, had we had that, are all too easy answers to console one's self with - but the one thing we did need more than anything, was money. It all came too late! Had it arrived two weeks earlier, it would have allowed us to leave the lagoon in enough time to do some sea trials. Her head hadn't been wet since September, and the un-caulked seams would have become apparent in a couple of good sails, I'm sure. No one would have thought so many could have been missed! Those that were, we thought we had found! ...but of course we hadn't!

So comes to an end a story of much of my life up to the age of 38. It has been easier to live it than to write about it, yet for some odd reason I had to tell my story – tell of all those I had met, the good and the bad. I would like to think I have been fair, yet I'm sure some will feel hard done by in my assessment of them. I have been very lucky to have known some that to write a reference for would be too difficult!

I can only say; I have some people I can call friends, and any man who can count them on one hand is lucky. I think I could count them on two.

Before closing, there are some I'd like to thank on behalf of the 'Jylland', that brave little schooner we took, not knowing the consciences of what did incur. It includes all in this story – each and every one of them – for without them it would not have been worth a mention.

Last and certainly not least, my 'good old brother-in-law Ken Hill – for his patience in scanning, copying and putting on to disc most, if not all I have written!

David Robert Hamber.

Epilogue

We'll send you a Solicitor

Such a sentence conjures up in the mind that help is on the way, a man who knows a thing or two, a Knight in shining armour, ready to assist you in your time of need. We would have to wait several weeks/years before such a coming.

I would spend 3 weeks in St Lucia after the sinking for one thing or another. The money from the safe for dry-docking I'd given Anita when she left for the safety of the ferry. It could be used to get people home now and pay the wages owing.

I write on the 27th May '79: "Felt very, very tired today, just don't feel able to do a thing - but then, there isn't anything to do! Feel rather strange sitting around like this. My mind is in a bit of a whirl at what to do from here!"

But the next day things would liven up somewhat, a call to Henry from Will informed him that Henry wasn't sure if she'd been insured for the passage, whether or not Mr Stanton from Lloyds Bank had passed on the message to Brokers of her leaving for Grenada and therefore to make sure she was covered.

On the 23th of May (so I was told) when Dennis and Henry went to see them at the Billericay branch, the white and worried Mr Stanton told them, having called the insurers on the morning of the 21st, he found the line busy, and would call back - but forgot!! Now having done so, the Brokers informed him, before she left for Grenada, they would like a seaworthiness certificate! Unfortunately old boy, the balls in your court they said!

So, the shit had hit the fan, and large lumps of it were landing on all that side of the Atlantic. It was time for all our 'Betters' and those who have chosen the role of 'Rat' on stage to do their 'Peter' denial bit! The Pin-striped Brigade, infamous for never having won any medals in the Honesty, integrity and sincerity fields, were passing the buck. It was the "each man for himself" time, Head for the Hills, wipe all fingerprints clean in a Mum's the word stance.

Meanwhile, just in case, index linked pensions were calculated, early retirement schemes totalled up and false medical records gathered.

The man called in to find the naughty boy, the one disrupting the class, causing all to stay behind after school for not owning up in the first place, was somewhere else in the country at the time, with his learned head stuck in a book looking for a precedence to justify the sentence he was about to deliver to another, all confessing Toad!

"Nope!" he says, "Nope!" - going over the books where page one was started at Runnymede. "Nowhere does it say I can set an example in this case. An example that will make others think twice before wasting my time and that of others. Nowhere does it say, that all the suffering he laid on others by his silence can I consider. Nor can I punish those who made him what he is, and advised him what to do!"

News came from England that a solicitor was willing to come out and take statements from us, and thus Roger Green arrived. We'd been asked beforehand to see John Kessel, the reason? To get an opinion whether he thought 'Jylland' was at the time seaworthy to make the passage to Grenada. Rather a strange request for, by her sinking, it was obvious she wasn't.

John was a Lloyds surveyor and knowing us the way he did, he knew we'd not have risked lives if we'd known her true condition, and one, only a dry-docking could determine. John wrote out what he could on the fact of characters involved, to have committed himself to a statement for what he was not qualified, and one that would have made a mockery of his opinion, was not what we wanted to commit himself to. His report was a glowing tribute to those aboard, of their qualities and sense. In his opinion, none would have made such a passage unless they were certain it could not be completed! I had him over the side in the murky waters of the lagoon to check the seam compound – which he took and sent off for some research to be done.

Tues 10th June I write: "Spent the day with Roger (Barry) Green. Geoff and I had made some form of statement, which will have to be gone over! We must not harp on too much about Seams, 'The checking of!' - 'I thought the seams!' - 'In my opinion the seams!' etc! etc! It will look too contrived. In my logs I hardly mention them, which goes to show surely my concern. To me their 'Time!' alone was sufficient!"

By time here I mean bilge, 8 hrs. when we left, and that I thought enough. Anyway, what options did we have, two only, make certain she was covered then take her out and sink her, or get her to Grenada and try and save her! If we'd done the former, there is little doubt our dishonesty would have been rewarded from those who thought this could well have been the case, but surely were baffled why we hadn't confirmed the cover beforehand!

Roland was renting a place on Cap at the time, a most lovely view out and across the Caribbean. Down the coast from this high perch, a tropical Island lay before you. The sun, as usual shining bright and warm, and through the open doors and shutters, blew the trade winds of a temperature God intended man to live in. Bougainvillea's bloomed in profusion, and covered the trellis, while among them darted and hovered a hummingbird, burning up the fuel their nectar provided, Coconut and Palms, Lime and orange trees grew in this well water garden, and the green of their leaves, a picture of health!

"Uhmmmm!" murmured Roger, who was staying as a guest here till our business was done. Statements and paper work lay on the table before him, scribbles of large handwriting coming to an abrupt end where pen had dropped, yet he stared out of the window as if in deep thought to an answer I'd given, his hand slowly stroking his bearded chin. "Yeeeess!" he murmured, as if any moment, what he was employed to do would come to him in a flash of brilliance.

Roger was not a tall man, but had a friendly face sitting upon a body that lack of exercise had made round. Six months on 'Jylland', I thought, and he'd have a figure a wife couldn't wait to see at night, and his tailor shaking his head in disbelief! "Uhmmmm!" he repeated, then, as if he'd found what troubled him, turned mind and chair round to face the pen and paper.

Tearing off the page of un-intelligible writing, it followed a previous sheet in to the bin! "So in your opinion, the seams were in great shape?" Boy, we had got a good one, a right little Perry Mason who was letting me think about it, then came back trying to catch me out.

This was the second day running we'd talked about seams and though I'd stressed the point over and over again, by her situation of being afloat, it was impossible to assess for certain her condition. Again we had returned to the subject and yet again I repeated the answer, but in doing so, gave a picture of the procedure on dry-dock in Martinique. A rough lesson on caulking, anti-fouling, and the life story as seen through the eyes of a Teredo, at which Roger took notes that to me looked very much like his last ones.

Dropping pen at the end of a Latin phrase meaning 'wonderful view', he this time rose to stretch his legs, to wander the room and balcony, looking for, I thought, some inspiration.

What I didn't know then was, what really had him thinking, was not the sinking of 'Jylland', but that of the Sun upon the waters of The Lesser Antilles. The Uhmmms and Yes's were that which many make when they first come here, not answers to my problems at all. I would learn through the years, much to my cost, that Roger knew as much about boats and the sea, as I about where electricity comes from and how to harness a thunderbolt of lightning. That was not Rogers fault, nor ours to a certain extent, for without funds to employ the right man for the job, we entered the Derby with a horse supplied by the legal aid system, one who's fed on inferior oats, has not the right sire - whose usual job is pulling milk carts!

Roger was easy to make laugh, no fool, and for the next six years would be laughing all the way to the bank, representing us in our claim against the 'Lloyds' and Bayle Martin and Faye - the brokers for the underwriters.

Tangled webs take a long time to unravel. Mixed in this fibber, spun by the spidery John Rich (an obvious descendant to the notorious Richard Rich of Tudor England) emerged tasty morsels, un-disposed of in his greed for bigger game! Transference of client's money to different accounts without permission to 'balance' the books!! Derogatory remarks in memos to head office concerning us, and replies that sounded like orders from Don Corleone!

At the high court in Dunston House, London, it was easy for us to stand before the 'wigs' to be grilled about our behaviour in this affair. To tell the truth, the whole truth, and nothing but the truth was pretty simple, one just said it as it was!!

For five days the banks, well paid, learned gentlemen, tried to pull us apart, to make a meal of innuendo and the, out of water fish!! But they were left frustrated by each witness. This though, was not the case, when we could relax, to watch the banks representatives give their version of events!

First to be called, to swear before God not to lie, was the receiver of the request to make the call to London, to inform the brokers that cover was needed to move the schooner to Grenada for dry-docking! Dick Stanton was the under manager, the man with a 'Fuzzy' memory, the born liar! When this type take the stand, on oath, it doesn't take a very bright person to see his word can't be trusted. He fudged the issues raised, making a right mess of the answers. The fool was obviously ill at ease with his conscience.

This piece of shit, that comes from the arse of 'The Black Horse' company, his maker, was not prepared to perjure himself entirely, for his masters had not been able to convince him wholly, he'd never meet-the real one! He left the stand in some discomfort, an embarrassment to all there, especially his legal advisors.

When it came to the next villain to take the stand, I found the look upon John Rich's face one of satisfaction!! This puzzled me for the moment but all became clear once he'd been allowed to 'Talk'. Dick Stanton's presentation in the witness box that of the meek innocent dog's body had turned the spotlight on him as the culprit!!

The look that I found odd was the look of a man dying for a crap having found a toilet! He had a case of verbal diarrhoea!!! All it took to flush him out was one question, and the man didn't stop talking!! It was his clear objective to make up for all he'd done wrong in his life, to make peace with the Lord!! No-one was going to blame him for it all!!

His appearance in the courtroom that afternoon was a big surprise to us. 'Never' we were told, would his boss of bosses allow him to spill the beans! Evidence had been submitted to Judge Webster, in the form of a 'Doctors Report' saying Mr Rich couldn't take the stand due to a 'Heart' condition and was attending a hospital bed in Brentwood. Judge Webster's reply to the ploy was, "He's not the only one this case is giving heart-trouble! Tell your Mr Rich to be here or we will bring the court to Mr Rich in Brentwood!"

If I regret one thing, it would be not to hear John Rich's full 'confession'. A meeting had been called for between our 'wigs and frocks' and theirs at the end of the day's session. It was plain that the uncomfortable position the bank was being placed, could not continue. Come Monday morning Mr. Rich would deny us, and the packed courtroom, a performance worthy of a stuck Pig!!!

Our Q.C, Mr Mawry, and Barrister, Mr Jeffery Littman of quote "We can't go around acting like the Lone Ranger ya know!!" fame, were both so overjoyed with 'Their' success, and the thought of a 'tick' beside their name for such a Coup. They gently persuaded us (with threats of a life of total misery if we continued our action) with legal jargon that had us confused. Legal aid etc! etc!! – court costs etc etc! – If the judge judges less than the offer on the table etc! etc! Lloyds Bank paid costs in this loss - Estimated at £400,000. They could have saved £300,000 if they'd have admitted in the first place it was their mistake!! But that's not how the system works, liars out to cause mischief for others are never punished – in the meantime who paid for all that costing? Those who bank with these people, not those who manage their funds!

Who got the money!! "Jylland" was insured for £100,000, all we could afford at the time. Not what she was worth! My brothers and I got £25,000. Less than the Lawyers, but then, that's to be expected, they did all the work right?

The deflated look upon Rogers face, and somewhat bitter reference towards the un-fair system, I can see now was more of a relief it was done with. Pages he thought relevant to the case, had been discarded by Judge Webster as irrelevant – he had warned both parties – his mind had already been made up as who was responsible, and suggested a settlement or else he would.

We had that Big Black Stallion by the balls, but our grip was relaxed by a sedative of legal manoeuvring! Each time I see that horse rise in a T-V commercial, it represents to me yet another client which had him by the lower parts, yet fails to make him whinny!

We had breached the walls of this fine institute that poured scorn and accusation upon us from its ramparts. 6 years of hard work to bring them to the sword we would endure to clear our name and see justice done, but in our planning we had forgotten, nor had been informed by our aides, that we would not be allowed to win the case or share in the spoils of victory! That was theirs, along with the glory.

The persuasive tac-tics of our treacherous 'Allies' saw us capitulate with our opponent on the floor. Threats we had no time to check on, that the legal aid afforded us to fight this case, would have to be paid by us if we continued the action - and lost, that even if we won, and the judge awarded us less than the offer on the table, we should also pay. This had us in the turmoil expected! The Bastards had us in a trap, and they sprung it!

What Rogers share of the Booty was can only be estimated, but it was more than I got, more than our total settlement. If I asked him he'd probably be too embarrassed to tell. But outside the courtroom, the ashen look upon his face after speaking with our legal counsel was a sign it must have been a considerable offer to pay his 'Before legal aid' fee.

Legal aid is a farce! The poor, without any disposable income, have been led to believe by Government that all its citizens deserve a fair trial. When indeed its real purpose is to hand out bread and butter money to those of their own breed. For they are themselves all lawyers who see the need to nourish and hold the purse strings to an army that maintains their power.

The large coffer, built with tax payer's money, is nothing but a vast watering hole by which the Legal Lions gather beside for an easy meal. For far too many, this has become an Oasis of plenty, never to dry up even in the hottest conditions, thus never far from its source do they roam.

Fattened to the state of opulence they feed upon a human herd, driven to their wells in a false belief that some sanctuary of fairness awaits them, that they will find solace from harassment while they sip the sweet waters of justice! Cornered in this well laid trap of deception, they fall prey to a bunch of hypocrites that gorge themselves in a frenzy of financial greed oblivious in the madness of gain!

Our 'Betters' should know better! That the fat of the land on which they feed is provided by the poor, and it is with their tolerance they do so, unhindered. But History has proven so many times that, when pushed too far, the heads that roll are those grown to obese proportions in their gluttony that dulls sense and reason!

Since our first meeting with Roger back in 1980, I have seen his company go from strength to strength, for even in hard times they don't seem to suffer, nor taste the hard medicine dished out to the rest as they handle broken business, broken homes and broken hearts.

Roger has managed, by the misfortunes of others, to build as they crumble, to acquire a larger more prestigious property in the High Street, yet still not have to sell his old one.

When the property market was booming, he got on that bandwagon while the harvest was ripe with a development Co. For what reason? To make a living? To do his bit for the country by filling a position un-occupied that he may supply the need to its citizens? Or was it the greed to carry off more than his share of the cake! More than he needs, or can eat.

As money can never fill the stomach of an ambitious man, its only other purpose is to make them more attractable, to make up for all they lack without it in a hope they can buy the character they so wished to be. Like the child that wishes to own the ultimate toy to gain his friends, so does the man desire money to keep them! Such friends and such men chase one another up a ladder with no top while those content with life laugh at their foolish antics.

Money has been the destroyer of morals, as in a materialistic world possession of wealth is the power that 'stills' the altruistic tongue. The greedy no longer feel un-comfortable in Church even, but sit now in the front without embarrassment, for they own the best Pews and the conscience of the man of God before them!

One can't blame Roger for this, from making a bob or two, but can a road-sweeper drop tools for a law book when the wind has changed. No! There is a 'Law' that says so too! But not one for the lawyers that can steal his broom when the 'Pennies from Heaven' fall upon the poor! 'Roger Green and Co' and many such reputable firms of Solicitors can't be blamed for taking advantage - who can, are those bastards that allow him the whip-hand!

www.ingramcontent.com/pod-product-compliance
Lightning Source LLC
Chambersburg PA
CBHW020321170426
43200CB00006B/232